STORAGE AND COMPUTATION IN THE LANGUAGE FACULTY

STUDIES IN THEORETICAL PSYCHOLINGUISTICS

VOLUME 30

The titles published in this series are listed at the end of this volume.

STORAGE AND COMPUTATION IN THE LANGUAGE FACULTY

edited by

SIEB NOOTEBOOM
Utrecht Institute of Linguistics OTS, Utrecht University, The Netherlands

FRED WEERMAN
University of Amsterdam, The Netherlands

and

FRANK WIJNEN
Utrecht Institute of Linguistics OTS, Utrecht University, The Netherlands

KLUWER ACADEMIC PUBLISHERS
DORDRECHT / BOSTON / LONDON

A C.I.P. Catalogue record for this book is available from the Library of Congress.

ISBN 1-4020-0526-1

Published by Kluwer Academic Publishers,
P.O. Box 17, 3300 AA Dordrecht, The Netherlands.

Sold and distributed in North, Central and South America
by Kluwer Academic Publishers,
101 Philip Drive, Norwell, MA 02061, U.S.A.

In all other countries, sold and distributed
by Kluwer Academic Publishers,
P.O. Box 322, 3300 AH Dordrecht, The Netherlands.

Printed on acid-free paper

Printed in the Netherlands.

Contents

Contributing authors

Peter Ackema <P.Ackema@let.uu.nl>
Utrecht Institute of Linguistics OTS (UiL OTS), Utrecht University, The Netherlands.

Nicholas Asher <nasher@mail.la.utexas.edu>
Department of Philosophy, The University of Texas at Austin, U.S.A.

Harald Baayen <Baayen@mpi.nl>
Interfaculty Research Unit for Language and Speech, University of Nijmegen, The Netherlands.

Geert Booij <Booijg@let.vu.nl>
Faculteit der Letteren, Vrije Universiteit Amsterdam, The Netherlands.

Harald Clahsen <harald@essex.ac.uk>
Department of Linguistics, University of Essex, U.K.

Ray Jackendoff <jackendoff@binah.cc.brandeis.edu>
Department of Psychology, Brandeis University, USA.

Nivja de Jong <nivja.dejong@mpi.nl>
Interfaculty Research Unit for Language and Speech, University of Nijmegen, The Netherlands.

Edith Kaan <Kaan@duke.edu>
Center for Cognitive Neuroscience, Duke University, U.S.A.

Andrea Krott <andrea.krott@mpi.nl>
Interfaculty Research Unit for Language and Speech, University of Nijmegen, the Netherlands.

Pieter Muysken <P.Muysken@let.kun.nl>
Department of Linguistics, University of Nijmegen, The Netherlands.

Ad Neeleman <ad@ling.ucl.ac.uk>
Department of Linguistics, University College London, U.K.

Sieb Nooteboom <Sieb.Nooteboom@let.uu.nl>
Utrecht Institute of Linguistics OTS (UiL OTS), Utrecht University, The Netherlands.

Steven Pinker <Steve@psyche.mit.edu>
Department of Brain and Cognitive Sciences, Massachusetts Institute of Technology (MIT), Cambridge, U.S.A.

Ardi Roelofs <ardi.roelofs@mpi.nl>
Max Planck Institute for Psycholinguistics, Nijmegen, The Netherlands.

Tessa Say <tessa_say@hotmail.com>
Department of Linguistics, University of Essex, U.K.

Rob Schreuder <Rob.Schreuder@mpi.nl>
Interfaculty Research Unit for Language and Speech, University of Nijmegen, The Netherlands.

Laurie Stowe <L.A.Stowe@let.rug.nl>
Department of Linguistics, University of Groningen, The Netherlands.

Fred Weerman <Fred.Weerman@hum.uva.nl>
Dutch Department, University of Amsterdam, The Netherlands.

Frank Wijnen <Frank.Wijnen@let.uu.nl>
Utrecht Institute of Linguistics OTS (UiL OTS), Utrecht University, The Netherlands.

Preface

Every now and again I receive a lengthy manuscript from a kind of theoretician known to psychiatrists as the "triangle people" - kooks who have independently discovered that everything in the universe comes in threes (solid, liquid, gas; protons, neutrons, electrons; the Father, the Son, the Holy Ghost; Moe, Larry, Curly; and so on). At the risk of sounding like a triangle person, let me explain why I think that the topic of this volume — storage and computation in the language faculty — though having just two sides rather than three, is the key to understanding every interesting issue in the study of language.

I will begin with the fundamental scientific problem in linguistics: explaining the vast expressive power of language. What is the trick behind our ability to fill each others' heads with so many different ideas? I submit there is not one trick but two, and they have been emphasized by different thinkers throughout the history of linguistics.

There is the arbitrary sound-meaning pairing underlying the word, emphasized by Locke, de Saussure, and Austin; it allows us to communicate tens of thousands of ideas by exploiting the capacious faculty of human memory — that is, storage. And there is the infinite use of finite media, emphasized by the Cartesian linguists, Humboldt, and Chomsky, which allows us to combine words into an unlimited number of sentences in which the meaning of the sentence can be inferred from the meanings of the words and the way they are arranged — that is, computation.

I am fond of the storage–computation distinction for a more parochial reason, too: it has made sense of my own area of research, the psychology of irregular inflection (as in *take–took* and *foot–feet*). Linguists and language learners have long wondered why irregularity should exist at all. Why should languages have a feature whose only purpose is to torment foreign language learners, complicate linguistic theories, and set traps for children to produce errors like *taked* and *foots*? The answer, I argue, is that the human language faculty consists of a component for storage and a component for computation, and they can often do the same kind of work in the language system as a whole. *Feet* is stored; *hands* may be computed by concatenating the stem *hand* with the suffix *-s* (though sometimes the product of a computation may be stored as well).

The idea that the language faculty consists of these two systems means that they can compete for the franchise to express a linguistic distinction. Many examples of historical change can be understood as a series of battles in that struggle. Anything computed by one person may be simply stored by another person, and at various points in history, one listener may have memorized a product of computation (such as the umlauted *o* in the Old English plural of *foot*) as an unanalyzed chunk, which was then free to mutate and drift as it was passed from memory to memory down the centuries. Conversely, the storage/computation fight can explain how a word can pass in the other direction, from irregular to regular. Storage depends on human memory, a fallible system that is apt to forget low-frequency words. When a generation of Middle English speakers could not remember that *chid* is the past of *chide*, they defaulted to the computation system, converting the word to *chided* for their generation and all subsequent ones.

We tend to call a phenomenon "irregular" when it belongs to inflectional morphology, but the same thing can happen in every other component of language. Idioms, collocations, and verb-particle combinations can be seen as chunks of syntax that are stored in memory rather than computed by compositional syntax and semantics. Productive "Level 2" derivation and not-so-productive "Level 1" derivation in theories of level-ordered morphology and lexical phonology may represent the same distinction: Level 2 is computed, Level 1 stored. We see the distinction in phonology in the difference between *obscene–obscenity* and *obese–obesity*, and everyone knows about it in orthography, where, as the poem says, "A *moth* is not a *moth* in *mother*, Nor *both* in *bother*, *broth* in *brother*."

The major theoretical approaches to language can be distinguished by how they partition storage and computation. Classic Bloomfieldian structural linguistics, and classic Chomskyan and Hallean generative linguistics, try to squeeze every drop of redundancy out of linguistic constructions and retain only the dessicated residue in the storage component. The full forms are reconstituted by interacting rules, constraints, and other symbolic combinatorial operations. The theory most diametrically opposed to this tradition, neural networks or connectionism, does the opposite: it pretends that the computational component does not exist, and tries to account for linguistic productivity by beefing up the storage component so that it no longer merely stores and retrieves items verbatim but can generalize by analogy to similar items.

In my view the most promising approach to language, deriving from Mark Aronoff, Joan Bresnan, Edwin Williams, Rochelle Lieber, Ray Jackendoff, and others, makes full use of both storage and computation. Some linguistic regularities really are computed on-line by symbolic operations, others are patterns of redundancies stored in the lexicon. The storage mechanism need not be like a computer memory with a list of addresses; it may have some of the properties of connectionist pattern associators, superimposing similar items and thereby strengthening their overlapping features. And the computational component need not be a set of rules; it may be a general mechanism of unifying structures that contain variables. This strikes me as an optimal partition, allowing one to avoid overly baroque formulations of the computational system typical of some grammatical theories, without pretending that our magnificent capacity to combine words does not exist. This synthetic theory is worked out in complementary ways in my own *Words and Rules* (1999), and in Jackendoff's *The Architecture of the Language Faculty* (1997).

Child language acquisition, too, can be understood in terms of an interplay between storage and computation. In many areas of development, children appear to memorize a large set of forms (words, chunks of phrases, verbs and their argument structures) and only later analyze them into pieces that may be productively recombined. The textbook example is the so-called "U-shaped" development of the past tense in English, in which children may produce unmarked verbs and correct irregular past tense forms like *broke* for months before producing their first error like *breaked*. In my books *Language Learnability and Language Development* (1994) and *Learnability and Cognition: The Acquisition of Argument Structure* (1989), I tried to account for many phenomena of language development in these terms, and in our 1992 monograph *Overregularization in Language Acquisition*, Gary Marcus, Michael Ullman, and I were able to confirm statistically that it is a real phenomenon.

Finally, the differences between storage and computation may shed light on the evolution of language — both its adaptive engineering design and its phylogenetic history. Imagine a language with no computation, only storage. The use and acquisition of language would be a snap, because we could just store and retrieve chunks of sound. But we would be restricted to blurting out single words, or at best clichés for familiar situations, and would have no way of sharing new combinations of ideas about novel thoughts or events. Now imagine a language with a minimum of storage, such as the "perfect languages" of 17th-century John Wilkins and other enlightenment thinkers. Every vowel or consonant in a word would pick out a semantic feature of its referent, exhaustively specifying every conceivable object in the universe. The problem here is that we would have to engage in full-blown computation in figuring out what every lexical item meant, in effect playing a game of Twenty Questions as we worked our way through the vowels and consonants of each word. I submit that language is like many other biological systems that combine two mechanisms with different costs and benefits, like the fast-twitch and slow-twitch fibers making up our muscles. We have lexical storage for common and simple entities, which we can quickly look up whole, and we have computational operations for novel combinations of entities, which we can assemble and parse on-line.

And even the neural substrate and evolutionary origin of these mechanisms may not be utterly obscure. On the basis of a series of experiments that presented several kinds of neurological patients with regular and irregular forms to inflect, Ullman and I have suggested that the storage component of language is concentrated in the declarative memory system of the brain, comprising the temporal and parietal lobes and structures that connect with it, primarily the hippocampus. The computational component may be concentrated in the procedural memory system, comprising the basal ganglia and the frontal lobe areas that form circuits with it. Both systems are phylogenetically very old, suggesting that the storage/computation distinction may be deeply rooted indeed, having appeared literally hundreds of millions of years ago.

These are some of the reasons I think the distinction between storage and computation runs through the study of language and is indispensable to understanding its many manifestations. The volume you are holding contains the ideas and data of many ingenious scholars, including other triangle people like me, who feel that the distinction is worth exploring.

STEVEN PINKER

Acknowledgment

This book is an offshoot of the *Utrecht Congress on Storage and Computation in the Language Faculty*, which was organised to celebrate the tenth anniversary of the Utrecht Institute of Linguistics OTS at Utrecht University, October 1998.

The congress succeeded in attracting linguists of quite diverse persuasions and with highly varied interests, and it appeared to inspire lively and constructive discussions among them. Apparently, the theme of the congress had struck a chord that resonated in many, even unsuspected corners of linguistic science. It seemed a good idea, therefore, to make some of the most pertinent concepts, hypotheses, and new empirical evidence presented at the congress available to a larger audience. We asked several of our invited speakers to contribute a chapter to this volume, and invited some others, who had not presented, to supply material that would contribute to a comprehensive overview of the issue.

We are grateful to all contributors to this volume for their enthousiastic cooperation. Most of them willingly rewrote their chapters often more than once in order to improve consistency and readability. We are also grateful for the most helpful comments made by three anonymous reviewers and the editors of the Studies in Theoretical Psycholinguistics series. A number of our authors made critical comments on an earlier version of the introductory chapter, enabling us to improve the text considerably. The Utrecht Institute of Linguistics OTS has been generous in providing necessary support throughout the preparation of this volume, and particularly when the final version of the text had to be made camera-ready. For this we would especially like to thank Anne-Marie Mineur. If this volume will form a positive contribution to the on-going discussion on the relative parts storage and computation play in the human language faculty, this has been made possible by all those mentioned above. Of course, all errors in the volume remain the full responsibility of the editors.

SIEB NOOTEBOOM, FRED WEERMAN AND FRANK WIJNEN

STORAGE AND COMPUTATION IN THE LANGUAGE FACULTY

Chapter 1

MINIMISING OR MAXIMISING STORAGE? AN INTRODUCTION

Sieb Nooteboom,
Fred Weerman,
and Frank Wijnen

1. Why this volume?

"The lexicon is really an appendix of the grammar, a list of basic irregularities". These words, written a long time ago by Leonard Bloomfield (Bloomfield, 1933, p. 274), have set the stage for focusing linguistic and psycholinguistic research on the compositional nature of linguistic objects, a view that has culminated, from the mid-fifties until today, in generative linguistics as proposed and elaborated by Noam Chomsky (Chomsky, 1957; 1965). This attention for the computational nature of language over many decades of linguistic investigation has proven to be tremendously fruitful. Without it, our insight in the nature of human language would be much smaller than it is. Inevitably, the continually high level of attention for computational rules has led to some neglect of the possibility of massive storage not only of irregular but also of regular linguistic objects. The idea for this volume was inspired by the observation that a growing number of linguists and psycholinguists are dissatisfied with the traditional Bloomfieldian idea that the lexicon is a list of irregularities, and all other linguistic objects are computed by rules. So the question appeared to be: if Bloomfield's view was wrong, or at least not the full truth, what then is stored in the lexicon, and what is computed by rule?

2. Why storage and computation?

When we asked a number of linguists and psycholinguists to write a chapter for this volume, reflecting on their own attempts to deal with the issue of storage and computation in the language faculty, we soon discovered that our original question can be approached in very different

S. Nooteboom et al. (eds.), Storage and Computation in the Language Faculty, 1–19.

ways. It can be applied to rather disparate aspects of the language faculty, and attempts to answer it may lead to widely different views of how the language faculty is organised and how it goes about doing its job. By way of introduction, we will briefly discuss those issues that in our perception are most relevant to what the reader will find in the different chapters of this book. Let us begin with the notions storage and computation themselves. Why would there be a need for this opposition in accounting for the human language faculty? As an analogy, one may think of the human capacity to calculate ("calculate", of course, is just another word for "compute"). The primitives of calculation are numbers. Calculation or computation is applying rules to these numbers. We need computation because there may be good reasons to want to know how much, for example, is 638 x 823, and the outcome cannot be found in a lexicon. This is similar to the need for computation in linguistics. Without computation we cannot account for our prolific capacity to generate new words, new phrases, new sentences, new interpretations, and new discourses.

Although we can imagine there is only one primitive number, the number one, and all others are derived by addition, subtraction, multiplication, division, raising to a higher power, root extraction etc., we know this is not how it works. In primary school we have learned the tables of multiplication by heart, and few of us have to do any computation to know how much is 7 times 9. So there are some real questions: Which simple and less simple "calculations" are stored, together with their outcomes, which outcomes have to be computed, and what are the strategies in doing these computations? Of course the answers to these questions may differ for different individuals, but it is of interest that it has been convincingly shown that so-called "calculating prodigies", the kind of people who tell you within a few seconds how much is 638 x 823 without using a pocket calculator, do not differ from us normal mortals in their capacity to do mental computation. What they differ in is in their memory for numbers and for outcomes of calculations. They have at their disposal a vast lexicon of outcomes of calculations plus a limited number of algebraic tricks for reducing complex numerical questions to simpler or more familiar ones (Dehaene, 1997). Their minds maximise storage and minimise computation. Of course, all 'normal' people are prodigies in using language. That is part of what makes us human. Is it possible that our minds also maximise storage and minimise computation in constructing words, phrases, sentences, and discourses?

Whereas linguists generally account for creativity in the language faculty by combinatorial rules and variables, connectionists believe that the creative aspect of language can be wholly accounted for by pattern association. Unfortunately, our attempt to include at least one chapter in this volume representing the connectionist view, has failed. Yet it may be worthwhile to discuss briefly the opposition between the rule-based approach and the neural-network or connectionist approach. It is not difficult to see why connectionists prefer pattern association to rules. They are inspired by theories about the functioning of neurons and networks of neurons, and they implement their theories of language in computational models of such neural networks (Elman, 1993; Elman et al., 1996; Fodor and Pylyshyn, 1988). Now neural networks are very good at pattern association, but it is not easy to see how abstract rules using variables could be implemented in such networks. The problem is that rules can be and are applied to objects that are widely different in all respects except in the single, possibly minute, feature that makes the rule applicable. It is a bit of a problem for connectionists that humans behave as if they use rules with variables, and currently a number of attempts are being made to bend neural networks every which way to simulate rule-like behaviour without using rules. It would seem that some 30 years of work in this domain has not yet produced a solution to this problem. Nonetheless, progress has been made, in the sense that it has become clear that the classic models — multilayer networks trained by backpropagation or similar supervisory techniques — which were once introduced as the answer to most if not all problems in cognitive science, are principally incapable of learning generalized operations on variables (Marcus, 1998). This is, however, certainly not the end of an episode. As Ray Jackendoff (this volume) and others note, other classes of models still hold the promise of successfully implementing rule- and variable-governed cognitive capacities, including language. Most likely, further developments along these lines will put the storage–computation issue in a different light.

The connectionist challenge did have a considerable impact because most of us are convinced that rules and variables are psychologically real. How, otherwise, could we learn to do simple and precise calculation, how could we learn to play chess or checkers, how could we learn to do formal logic, consisting of rule-governed operations on abstract symbols that have no preset associations with reality? Furthermore, there are good reasons why we have this capacity for applying rules. Steven Pinker, in his recent book "Words and rules" (Pinker, 1999), convincingly argues that in order to make optimal sense of the world around us, we need both "family resemblances" between objects, and rule-governed "good categories" that allow us to make valid predictions about aspects of objects that are not readily observable. The reason is that the world is structured that way. An animal that looks very much like a dog, may well be a dog, but an animal that does not at all look like an eagle, may still be a bird. Sometimes it is advantageous to go for resemblances, sometimes it is advantageous to generalise from single features.

Note that rules with variables may well be older than language. It seems most likely, however, that the use of combinatorial relationships within sets of symbols, most easily described in terms of rules and variables, as in language or calculation or chess, is typically human (Deacon, 1997). Nonhumans primarily work with "family resemblances". Again, the world of numbers can serve as an analogy. We humans can do precise calculation. Seven times 9 is not 62, but 63. Other animals like rats can be shown to estimate numbers, but they do not do precise calculation. Their number sense works in an analogue way, the number of things or events being represented as some value on a continuous scale. On such a scale 1 and 2 may be very different, but 5 and 6 very much the same (Dehaene, 1997). Pattern association does the trick. Digital computation, where 62 definitely is not the same as 63, where a rose is a rose is a rose, and where the plural of "wug" is "wugs" and never anything else, is a very late invention in evolution. Apparently, brains had to become very complex before they were able to work with even very simple combinatorial systems. No wonder that connectionists have such a hard time simulating this. Nature also took its time to evolve combinatorial symbol systems, and, as far as we know, did this only once. It should not surprise us, then, if humans do not rely on computation alone whenever they can avoid it. The brain has a massive capacity for storage, and it is reasonable to assume that processing of all kinds is supported by stored information whenever possible.

In his 1999 book, Steven Pinker cites extensive psycholinguistic evidence for the 'psychological reality' (to use the old-fashioned term) of both computation and storage-based processes in language. From his overview, the conclusion seems inevitable that the use of regular verb morphology (in English, but in principle in all human languages) rests on a rule-and-variable based computational mechanism, whereas irregular verb forms are, basically, stored. Many of the chapters in this volume provide corroboration for the 'dual mechanism' hypothesis, and, more importantly, extend it beyond the domain of verbal morphology. It is argued, and to our minds convincingly, that computation *and* storage (as defined by Pinker) are intrinsically involved in such diverse areas as syntax, phonology, and second language acquisition, and the strong implication is that it is no longer useful to think of the language faculty as being exclusively associated with either computation *or* storage.

3. Setting the stage

Jackendoff's opening chapter sets the stage for exploring the question of whether the human language faculty maximises computation or maximises storage by sketching a linguistic theory that would certainly allow the latter view. He observes that we cannot equate lexical units with words. We produce many words that are not lexical units and there are many lexical units both below and above word level. The latter include, of course, idioms, but also certain types of constructions in which all words are exchangeable for others, such as English resultative constructions exemplified by "Mary watered the tulips flat". This suggests that grammatical constructions, not containing a single individual word, are stored in the lexicon. In line with adherents of "Construction Grammar" Jackendoff then tentatively reduces his account of the creative aspect of language to a single rule: UNIFY PIECES, all pieces being stored in a common format that permits unification, and all necessary variables being specified in the lexical items and not in the rule.

This suggestion by Jackendoff not only sets the stage for discussing what is in the lexicon, but also for discussing the nature of computation. At one end of the spectrum we find complex rules containing many variables, at the other end of the spectrum we are asked to believe that there are no rules containing variables at all. The reader may note that, in Jackendoff's account, many phenomena that are traditionally used as arguments for computation by rule are explained by stored structures plus a very simple operation of free combination.

4. Accessing regular and irregular word forms

As soon as we have acknowledged the possibility that the lexicon is not only a list of exceptions, but can also contain regular constructions, we are faced with the possibility that retrieval from storage and computing by rule do not exclude each other. Is it possible that, when we need a particular linguistic object during processing, we simultaneously attempt to retrieve this object from storage and compute this object by rule? This sounds very inefficient, but the reader should note that the capacity of the human brain is such that efficiency in the sense of involving as few neuronal structures as possible is not called for. Current theories of how the brain might go about doing its many jobs emphasize the enormous redundancy in neuronal processes (Edelman, 1992; Gazzaniga, 1992; Calvin, 1996; Damasio, 1999). If we interpret efficiency in terms of speed of processing, the brain may be wise to follow more routes simultaneously and see which is fastest. Moreover, it is not inconceivable that accessing stored items and computing these very same items simultaneously, may reinforce each other, making processing more reliable and faster. In some cases it is even very likely that we retrieve and compute in parallel. Think of idiomatic expressions like: "Bill took Janet to task". In comprehension we do not know in advance whether we are dealing with an idiom, so we have to follow the route of compositional construction in this case until the very end. The message might turn out to be "Bill took Janet to the ball". But we are wise to simultaneously access the idiomatic construction "take to task", so that as soon as we have heard "task" we do not have to go back and repair our earlier construction. In production, we retrieve the idiomatic construction from the lexicon, but still have to do some computation to fill in its empty places. But what about more prototypical building blocks of sentences, such as word forms?

Here we find that not all our authors agree. Harald Baayen, Robert Schreuder, Nivja de Jong and Andrea Krott, by looking at frequency effects of surface full forms and of their constituting morphemes on processing times, cleverly demonstrate that apparently regular full forms are simultaneously both retrieved from the lexicon and computed by rule. This supports the "parallel dual route model" proposed in earlier publications by Baayen and his collaborators. It also shows that the mental lexicon can no longer be seen as basically a list of exceptions. Regular computable forms are massively stored. One may speculate with these authors that, where retrieval of the full form will often be faster than the parsing route, the outcome of the direct route may serve as a pointer to the interpretation arrived at via the parsing route.

Tessa Say and Harald Clahsen, in their chapter on word formation in Italian, strongly claim that in on-line processing regular verb forms are computed by rule, and irregular verb forms retrieved from storage. Their psycholinguistic experiments nicely reveal what the default verb category in Italian is, and how the choice between different categories can be influenced by phonological similarity. Their psycholinguistic evidence for rule application leans heavily on nonsense words, which of course leaves open the possibility that frequent regular full forms of real words are retrieved from the lexicon. However, Say and Clahsen support their claim by a study in which they measure electrical activity in the brain (Event Related Potentials or ERPs), showing that overapplication of regular verb morphology to irregular verbs gives rise to a considerably stronger "early negativity" effect than incorrectly applying irregular verb morphology to regular verbs. This difference is explained by their claim that regular forms are computed by rule whereas irregular forms are retrieved from the lexicon.

5. Changing the rules

In English we find that in closed syllables the duration of the vowel is considerably longer before voiced obstruents than before unvoiced obstruents. The vowel in "bad" takes more time than the vowel in "bat". This difference is in the same direction as one would predict as a universal and physiologically conditioned side-effect of the production of voiced and unvoiced obstruents (Slis and Cohen, 1969a; 1969b). The difference in English is, however, much bigger than in other languages, and much too big to be explained by automatic effects of the articulatory mechanism. It seems that speakers of English have noticed the slight difference between vowels preceding voiced and unvoiced obstruents, and at some point have taken to the habit of exaggerating this difference. The result is that the perceptual distinction between syllable-final voiced and unvoiced obstruents is largely carried by vowel duration. Other characteristics have become less relevant, and we may predict that in a few generations the syllable-final contrast between voiced and unvoiced obstruents will have been replaced by a contrast between long and short vowels. We observe a phonological change in action.

This sketch of the sequence of events constituting a particular phonological change heavily leans on the supposition that minor subphonemic phonetic details are part of what is stored in the lexicon. Only what is there can be exaggerated. In the same vein, Geert Booij argues in his chapter "The balance between storage and computation in phonology" that phonological changes in Dutch suggest that the predictable output of phonological rules is massively stored in the mental lexicon. Whereas in the traditional generative analysis change is merely caused by the imperfect learning of the next generation that has to acquire the language on the basis of outputs of the older generation, Booij sketches an account in which language change is also an effect of the adult language user who is able to analyze the phonetic forms which are accessible in his memory. That language users do have access to minor phonetic details in their mental representations of word forms, was shown by one of us a long time ago in experiments in which subjects had to adjust durations of vowels in synthetised words so as to make these words sound well. In doing so, these subjects reproduced minor acoustic-phonetic details of temporal patterning (Nooteboom, 1973). With respect to the relation between underlying form and phonetic form, Booij suggests that it is not the phonetic form that is computed by the speaker, but rather the underlying form — and apparently this is only necessary in particular situations. Again we see evidence that our brain does not behave according to the adage "What can be computed should not be stored".

Obviously, if there ever was a single first language, it has blossomed into thousands of different languages. It is not uncommon that language users regularly use more than one language, and in communities where this happens, one may frequently encounter cases of code-switching, i.e. switching from one language to another and back again in midsentence. Interestingly, within such communities patterns of code-switching may change over time. Such changes do not appear to be governed by changes in one of the shared languages, but rather are controlled by changes in the conventions in the code-switching community. If so, obviously these conventions do not automatically follow from similarities and differences between the two grammars concerned, but have to be learned as if these code-switchers have their own little third grammar. As it happens, and as in the case of pidgins, apparently the "learners" of code-switching conventions are often adults. Pieter Muysken, in his chapter on "Computation and storage in language-contact", argues that changes in code-switching behaviour are possible because code-switching does not only involve computation by rule but also storage of particular patterns or structures. Such patterns are stored and transmitted within the community and thereby may undergo change. But, Muysken seems to suggest, because transmission occurs within a community of adults, the changes may lead to structures that are never encountered in normal natural languages, because they are in conflict with language universals. An example in point is formed by the verb-plus-verb compounds in Sarnami Hindustani-Dutch code-switching, where the head + complement relations do not seem to be constrained by a universal principle such as the Unlike Category Condition (Hoekstra, 1984). It would be interesting to see what would happen if very young children started to learn these anomalous adult structures. We would probably see another case in which changing the rules is mediated by stored templates, for which the children then would compute more acceptable underlying structures.

6. Pronouncing words

Speaking is many things, but it certainly is also retrieving words from the lexicon, and deriving and executing articulatory patterns for these words. We are so good at this skill that it is hard to imagine that the mental processes involved are highly complex and intricate. One way of forcing oneself to make this realisation, is to implement a computational model of speech production in such a way that the model accounts for as many empirical facts and experimental data as possible. This is precisely what Ardi Roelofs has done, and what he describes in his chapter on "Storage and computation in spoken word production". For many readers it may be interesting to see how many questions have to be answered during such an enterprise, often questions one might not have thought of without the aid of computational modeling.

Are concepts driving word selection computed on-line from conceptual primitives, or are they rather stored as lexical concepts? Roelofs suggest the latter. Primitive features are connected with the "chunks" that form lexical concepts, but they do not drive lemma selection.

Are word forms stored in the lexicon as sequences of syllable nodes, each node defining its onset, nucleus and coda positions? Roelofs argues they are not. Syllable positions have to be computed on the basis of morphological structure and context, in order to account for /d/ being syllable final in "evade", but syllable initial in "evading" and "evade it".

Are motor programs for articulating syllables computed on-line or retrieved from a syllabary containing packages of articulatory scores? In line with earlier work by Levelt (1989; 1992), it is argued that motor programs for infrequent syllables may be computed and motor programs for frequent syllables may be retrieved from a syllabary.

All these and other choices are implemented in the WEAVER++ computational model, which is then used to test predictions on the relative speed with which certain production tasks are carried out. It is fascinating to see how detailed predictions about timing, for example as related to semantic chunking, or frequency of morphemes, or frequency of motor programs for syllables, are corroborated by the data.

7. Working memory and computation

So far we have limited the notion of storage to putting things into some permanent data base, where these things can be accessed without being deleted. But obviously, in language processing, in production as well as comprehension, we need temporary copies of these permanent things, and hold these copies for some limited time in some buffer memory. The reason is that, for example, in comprehension incoming information often has to be connected with later information before syntactic structure can be resolved. In a sentence like: "the yacht that I like most Harry sailed to Norway", it takes some time before it is clear that "the yacht" ends up as an object instead of a subject. All the time the listener must keep "the yacht" and its unresolved syntactic function in working memory. Meanwhile "the yacht" has also to be connected with "that I like". Note that the speaker of the sentence had a similar problem. Although he may have decided early on that the yacht is an object, he still has to keep in mind, i.e. in working memory, that he has done so, in order not to get lost in his own sentence. These are processing problems, assigned to the parser, which by many linguists, notably those who like to keep competence and performance separate in their theorizing, is distinguished from the grammar.

For a long time it seemed only natural that linguists focused on competence, and left the study of performance to psychologists. However, imagine that certain types of construction do not occur in languages, not because the grammar of these languages does not allow them, but rather because the parser cannot deal with such structures. In such a situation linguists would be well advised not to ignore the study of the parser. This is precisely the main point of the chapter by Peter Ackema and Ad Neeleman. They observe that there is an asymmetry of head movement. For example, in constructions like "determiner – numeral – adjective – noun", there is no problem with head movement of the noun to the left, but in constructions like "noun – adjective – numeral – determiner", head movement of the noun to the right is impossible. Any attempt to explain such asymmetries by the grammar comes into conflict with the assumption that grammars are basically symmetrical — an assumption for which Ackema and Neeleman give independent support. Ackema and Neeleman propose leaving grammars symmetrical, and to explain the observed phenomena by limitations of the parser. They convincingly argue that rightward movement has to place a "trace" as placeholder in a partially analyzed string, whereas leftward movement allows the trace to be placed at the time of analysis. The parser, however, is unable to adapt already stored information. This makes rightward movement, although grammatical, highly infelicitous from a processing point of view. What seems to be happening is that the very limited buffer of the parser forces the listener to make decisions before the relevant information is available. This virtually excludes some grammatical structures from actually being used. The severe limitations of working memory, containing active items, of course contrast sharply with the nearly unlimited capacity for permanent storage of inactive or dispositional items we discussed earlier.

We have already seen that during processing of language, two things are going on in working memory. One is the temporary storage of things (words, syntactic trees, traces), the other is the computation necessary for building, for example, syntactic tree and interpretations. As the things in temporary storage are the building blocks for such computation, one might think that there is a particular part of the brain serving as working memory, where things are stored and where computation is going on. This is not how it works. During processing very different neuronal structures are active and apparently work together in good harmony to produce the phenomena we refer to as "working memory" and "computation". Given that there are several techniques for measuring brain activity, it does not seem to be too far-fetched to ask which part(s) of the brain is/are most involved in storing things and which in syntactic and/or semantic computation. This is the main question asked by Edith Kaan and Laurie Stowe in their chapter on "Storage and computation in sentence processing". They discuss relevant evidence obtained with three different techniques for measuring brain activity. Two of these techniques, Positron Emission Tomography (PET) and functional Magnetic Resonance Imaging (fMRI), basically measure blood flow in different parts of the brain. These techniques give fairly reliable information on localization of brain activity, but do not fare well in showing timing of brain activity. A third technique, measuring Event-Related Potentials (ERP), gives relatively precise information on timing but not on place.

The evidence Kaan and Stowe discuss suggests that temporary storage and computation are supported by different neuronal structures, storage mainly involving Broca's area, and computation Wernicke's area. It is also shown that distinct temporal patterns of brain activity as measured with ERP are associated with storage and computation, storage being associated with a slow negative wave, computational difficulty with a negativity after some 400 ms for semantic integration and a positivity after some 600 ms for syntactic integration. These are fascinating findings, the more so because this line of research is only beginning. Techniques and combinations of techniques for measuring brain activity are currently being developed, and the number of researchers getting access to such techniques is rapidly increasing. In the years to come our insight in the relation between the human language faculty and activity of neuronal structures in the brain will doubtlessly expand.

8. Computing and storing aspects of discourse

As we have seen, it is plausible that language users massively store irregular and regular patterns, not only on the level of phonetic detail, but also (mor)phonological alternations, lexical concepts, morphological structures, and even syntax and semantics. What happens if we go beyond the level of the sentence? We now enter the field of discourse linguistics. Do humans retain whole discourses in memory, as they do with proverbs and idioms? Well, of course they can. Most of us have a stock of stories and anecdotes that vary relatively little when repeated. And unfortunately other people may get to know these stories and anecdotes, and get bored by the repetition. But this is not what the discussion on storage and computation in discourse is about. This discussion focuses on the patterns and rules or strategies invoked in the interpretation of "a discourse", i.e. a story or an anecdote that the listener has not heard before.

As discussed by Nicholas Asher in his chapter on "Computation and storage in discourse interpretation", in the past some researchers have suggested that discourse interpretation heavily leans on stored data structures with empty places to be filled in. Asher himself argues that this approach cannot account for the dynamic changes in context caused by the meaning of a sentence or phrase. Discourse interpretation can be seen as building a discourse structure, where discourse structure is understood not as syntactic structure but as logical form, mainly because coherence of discourse is basically a matter of content. The dynamics involved can best be captured by rules aiming for resolving ambiguities. The discussion focuses mainly on the strategies for timing the resolution of ambiguities: Does one resolve an ambiguity locally and as soon as possible, running the risk of making the wrong decision, or does one wait and see whether more information comes in, until one is forced to take a decision, running the risk of getting lost in a forest of open possible structures? Asher argues for a middle way, according to which ambiguities are resolved locally when possible, but can, if necessary, remain open. Ambiguity resolution operates under a constraint called "Maximise Coherence", and is supposed to draw on a vast amount of stored knowledge, particularly on how people interact, and the typical ways in which situations unfold, but the proper role of this stored information can best be figured out by making a realistic computational model of discourse interpretation.

9. Concluding

We hope that this volume will show that the topic of storage and computation is a felicitous one in its power to provoke interesting ideas and discussions on the organisation and functioning of the language faculty. From the preceding overview, the reader will have gathered that most of the contributors to this book are dissatisfied with the premise that there exists a clear, categorical and unmistakable boundary between what is computed, and what is taken from long-term storage, one way or another. All of the contributions to this volume, we think, show in various ways the limitation of this axiom, and point to alternative vistas. The shared assumption is that a reconsideration and a (renewed) empirical exploration of the boundary between storage and computation in the human language faculty will help to move linguistic science ahead.

This stance goes hand in hand with a tendency to bridge the gap between theoretical linguistics — the study of grammar — and psycholinguistics (in a broad sense) — the study of language processing. Jackendoff, a long-time advocate of the "continuity of the neurosciences", considers this to be a desirable development. We agree with him, and we hope and expect that this volume may have a positive impact on this development. At the same time we realise that, despite the efforts of a great many students of language through the ages, we are only at the beginning of coming to grips with the architecture and functioning of the language faculty, as seen from the perspective of the different disciplines involved. Perhaps it is still too early to try to re-integrate competence and performance. In this concluding section of our preview, we will try to anticipate on what may happen, as suggested by the studies assembled in this book.

Let us first consider, once again, the lexicon. In the Bloomfieldian conception, as our opening quotation clearly indicates, it is a repository of the unpredictable. Nothing is more unpredictable in language than the association between lexical forms and meanings. Jackendoff shows that the 'arbitrariness' in language extends into the realm of what is traditionally considered to be syntax. Every language possesses a vast array of expressions that are structured according to standard syntax, but that, at the same time, defy a strictly computational account of their meaning. In providing the arguments for a new view of the boundary between grammar and lexicon, Jackendoff's anchor point remains with the unpredictable connection between meaning and form (the tripartite structure, as he calls it). Say and Clahsen and Baayen et al. go beyond this and investigate the possibility that also structures are stored that have a predictable, computable, meaning. We already noted that they reach different conclusions. Say and Clahsen argue that irregular forms are stored, whereas regular forms are computed (as Bloomfield would probably have it). Baayen et al., by contrast, argue that evidence for storage can no longer be an argument in the decision on whether a form is regular or irregular; even regular ones are stored.

There are a number of interrelated questions that come up here. First, is 'being stored' equivalent to 'being in the lexicon'? Secondly, what, in fact, is the lexicon? Is the mental lexicon in psycholinguistic theorizing the same as the linguist's lexicon? And thirdly, how should linguists respond to psycholinguistic claims with regard to storage, either inside or outside the mental lexicon? With regard to the last question, let us assume that it is the linguist's job to account for linguistic structures and the relations between them, and that it is the job of the psycholinguist to study how these structures are produced and perceived. Obviously then, the psycholinguist must pay close attention to linguistics, in order to learn more about the structures that are produced and perceived. But can the linguist safely ignore psycholinguistic evidence?

People store immense amounts of information of all kinds and in various formats. The assumption in psycholinguistics is that part of the long-term store in which all of this is kept is reserved for specifically linguistic knowledge, and this part is called the mental lexicon. As an initial theory of what is in the mental lexicon, we can take Bloomfield's (linguistic) axiom that it contains only information that cannot be computed by the rules of grammar. Now we find evidence for storage of regular, computable structures, as Baayen and his co-workers did. This must mean that, somewhere in the cognitive system, a representation has been formed, which, under certain processing conditions, may be substituted for a mental computation. The question is whether this representation is or is not a part of the mental lexicon. If we were able to decide that it is in the lexicon, obviously the strong Bloomfieldian hypothesis would be refuted. More generally, the answer to the question whether this representation is in the lexicon, i.e., the specifically linguistic repository, may have consequences for the way the evidence bears on linguistic theorizing.

Can we make a distinction between the mental lexicon and the remainder of long-term memory? In some cases it would seem rather clearcut. A list of, say, the persons we know that have a predilection for a particular word, may very well be stored in our long-term memory, but it would most likely not be part of the mental lexicon, by any criterion. In many other cases it is less easy to decide. A visual representation of a prototypical tree (i.e., a mental image) would not be considered by many linguists to be part of the lexicon entry of *tree*. Others, notably Jackendoff, think it is. In the same vein, is a stored representation of the shape of the mouth in pronouncing the sound [b] part of the lexicon? And what about the "access representations" Baayen et al. speak of, and their counterparts for language production (cf. the chapter by Roelofs)? These would seem to be more or less abstract representations of linguistic structures, coded in correspondence to the physical characteristics of the input and output modalities. Are they in the mental lexicon, or should we consider them to be in the domain of perception or motor control? It would seem that deciding what (levels of) representations are to be considered part of the mental lexicon is not a matter that can be easily solved.

How does this bear on the relation between 'performance' and 'competence', and particularly the role of the performance notion 'storage' in linguistic hypotheses? As we see it, there are two ways of handling this state of affairs. The first is to formulate (principled) criteria with regard to what levels of representation are and are not part of the lexicon. If storage of a computable structure can be shown to be within the bounds of the lexicon, it is the responsibility of linguistic theory. If, on the other hand, the evidence points to storage in a different compartment of long term memory, linguistic theory is free to ignore it. The examples above suggest, however, that it may be very difficult, perhaps even impossible to find valid and uncontroversial criteria. The alternative approach is to eschew principled claims as to the boundary between lexicon and non-lexicon, and just incorporate any psycholinguistic evidence that may be helpful in explaining a set of linguistic facts. It would seem that the latter approach implies giving up the conception of a distinct, specifically linguistic lexicon, and this may in fact lead to abandoning the modular perspective on the language faculty, which over the years has proved to be highly productive.

Needless to say, adopting the more conservative strategy does not necessarily imply that one is committed to the claim that the mental lexicon is similar to the Bloomfieldian lexicon. As the chapters by Booij and Muysken show, employing a notion like storage, including storage of predictable information, in hypotheses on language structure, change and acquisition may be fruitful. One may feel, however, that it would go too far to make all matters that belong to the realm of processing in production or perception of speech the responsibility of linguistic theory. Linguists should only take those kinds of information into account that bear on the structure of language. Of course, which kinds of information do and which don't is an open question.

The dissolution of the competence-performance distinction takes a slightly different form in the case of the contrast between computation and (short term) storage in grammar and sentence processing. Traditional approaches to parsing, starting with the work by Mitch Marcus and his students (e.g. Marcus, 1980), have considered temporary storage (buffering) and computation (unification or rewriting) as complementary operations, supported by different devices (a stack and a symbol reader). Psycholinguistic approaches to parsing have kept the distinction, but at the same time, in a number of cases (e.g. Just and Carpenter, 1992; Gibson, 1998), discarded the independence between them. Resource limitations in the human sentence processing system set limits to what can be stored and/or computed. This might suggest that storage and computation are in fact subserved by the same neural substrates. Kaan and Stowe, however, argue against this, which, it would seem, corroborates the 'old' parsology. At the same time, it calls for a new hypothesis on the resource-limited trade-offs between computation and storage. This, in itself, is exciting work, and will undoubtedly be pivotal in the further development of ideas in psycholinguistics and cognitive neuroscience.

When we look upon it from the perspective of understanding the human language faculty, an even more exciting move is made when insights in human parsing from psycholinguistics are brought to bear on systematic structural phenomena in human language. This is what Ackema and Neeleman do. They start from reasonable, relatively well documented and well understood characteristics of the human parser — in particular with regard to the storage of intermediate parse results — combine this with an independently motivated model of the grammar, and are thus capable of accounting for widely observed asymmetries in head movement.

It would seem that the rapprochement between grammar and processing, competence and performance studies, creates a number of potential pitfalls. Over the last five decades or so, much of the considerable progress that has been made in linguistics is due to rigorous idealisation and formalisation. Inspired by Noam Chomsky, many linguists have tried to ignore phenomena that appear to be beyond their grasp and have striven for maximal precision and generality with regard to what have been considered the tractable questions about the language faculty. This, in fact, is how the competence–performance distinction came into existence. A possible worst-case scenario for linguistics is that ill-understood and imprecisely defined processing concepts are going to be used indiscriminately, and without bounds. This will not advance our understanding of the language faculty.

An alternative, more optimistic scenario is that performance notions, such as 'storage' (or 'processing cost', 'automaticity', etc.) will gain in clarity as a result of the advancement of cognitive neuroscience. Furthermore, linguists will succeed in remaining rigorous and disciplined in their theorizing, and hence will only allow well-understood processing phenomena to enter into their hypotheses. The result of this will be a gradual and cautious incorporation of insights from psycholinguistics into linguistic theorizing, the result being a gradual extension of both empirical coverage and conceptual richness. It is our conviction that the studies in this volume foreshadow the latter scenario. Each of them illustrates the development by which an axiomatic approach to the distinction between storage and computation is replaced by an approach based on evidence from psycholinguistic and neurolinguistic studies. There is a growing body of relatively uncontroversial evidence on what language users can and do store. As a consequence, 'storage' has become a valid component in explanatory linguistic hypotheses, with the potential of generating new predictions for processing. Thus, to our minds, we are witnessing progress.

Where do we go from here? We have seen that storage and computation do not always exclude each other in achieving the same end. We have also seen that there is evidence that some aspects of language, such as syllabification, are always computed. So there is every reason to ask which further aspects of language are always computed, and which can be stored and retrieved. For example, are accent patterns in stock phrases sometimes fossilized, or are they always computed anew? Superficial observations suggest that accent patterns can be more or less fixed. In many stock phrases accent patterns cannot be changed without such phrases changing into new expressions with regular compositional meaning. But this may have to be explained by the fixed interpretation of these stock phrases. Similarly, one may ask whether speech melodies can belong to lexical information. These questions and many similar ones are still to be answered.

For the immediate future, one of the most fascinating areas of language studies may well be neurolinguistics. This seems to have the potential to show us when and where retrieval from inactive or dispositional storage is going on, when and where computation is going on, and when and where these are combined. Admittedly, measurements of brain activity are still rather gross, but this will undoubtedly improve over time. We have seen already that temporary storage and computation can be pulled apart. Other studies in the past have shown that retrieval of different categories of words involves different neuronal structures (Damasio et al., 1996). Future refinement of such studies may well make it possible to answer a range of other questions. One of these questions stems immediately from the topic of this volume. There are quite convincing ideas about how objects with all their properties can be represented neurally as so-called dispositional structures. Lexical items are a special class of object. Although most details still escape us, it can be imagined how lexical items are held in store by neuronal structures. But language seems to depend crucially on abstract symbols and their rule-governed combinations. What form do symbols and combinatorial rules have in the brain, and how do these arise? We hope to live and see the answer.

References

Bloomfield, L. (1933). *Language*. London: George Allen & Unwin Ltd. 7th printing 1962.

Calvin, W. H. (1996). *How brains think; Evolving intelligence, then and now.* New York: Basic Books.

Chomsky, N. (1957). *Syntactic structures.* The Hague: Mouton.

Chomsky, N. (1965). *Aspects of the theory of syntax.* Cambridge MA: MIT Press.

Damasio, A. (1999). *The feeling of what happens; Body and emotion in the making of consciousness.* New York: Harcourt Brace & Company.

Damasio, H., Grabowski, T., Tranel, D., Hichwa, R., and Damasio, A. (1996). A neural basis for lexical retrieval. *Nature*, 380:499–505.

Deacon, T. (1997). *The symbolic species.* London: Allen Lane, the Penguin Press.

Dehaene, S. (1997). *The number sense.* London: Penguin Books.

Edelman, G. (1992). *Bright air, brilliant fire; On the matter of the mind.* London: Penguin Books.

Elman, J. (1993). Learning and development in neural networks: the importance of starting small. *Cognition*, 48:71–99.

Elman, J., Bates, E., Johnson, M., Karmiloff-Smith, A., Parisi, D., and Plunkett, K. (1996). *Rethinking innateness. A connectionist perspective on development.* Cambridge, MA: MIT Press.

Fodor, J. and Pylyshyn, Z. (1988). Connectionism and cognitive architecture: A critical analysis. In Pinker, S. and Mehler, J., editors, *Connections and symbols. (Cognition Special Issue)*, pages 3–71. Cambridge, MA: MIT Press/Bradford Books.

Gazzaniga, M. (1992). *Nature's mind; The biological roots of thinking, emotions, sexuality, language and thinking.* London: Penguin Books.

Gibson, E. (1998). Linguistic complexity. Locality of syntactic dependencies. *Cognition*, 68:1–76.

Hoekstra, T. (1984). *Transitivity; Grammatical relations in government-binding theory.* PhD thesis, Rijksuniversiteit Leiden.

Just, M. and Carpenter, P. (1992). A capacity theory of comprehension: Individual differences in working memory. *Psychological Review*, 99:122–149.

Levelt, W. (1989). *Speaking; From intention to articulation.* Cambridge, Ma: MIT Press.

Levelt, W. (1992). Accessing words in speech production: Stages, processes and representations. *Cognition*, 42:1–22.

Marcus, G. (1998). Rethinking eliminative connectionism. *Cognitive Psychology*, 37:243–282.

Marcus, M. (1980). *A theory of syntactic recognition for natural language.* MIT Press Series in Artificial Intelligence. Cambridge, MA: MIT Press.

Nooteboom, S. (1973). The perceptual reality of some prosodic durations. *Journal of Phonetics*, 1:25–54.

Pinker, S. (1999). *Words and rules.* London: Weidenfeld & Nicholson.

Slis, I. and Cohen, A. (1969a). On the complex regulating the voiced-voiceless distinction I. *Language and Speech*, 12:80–102.

Slis, I. and Cohen, A. (1969b). On the complex regulating the voiced-voiceless distinction II. *Language and Speech*, 12:137–155.

I

SETTING THE STAGE

Chapter 2

WHAT'S IN THE LEXICON?

Ray Jackendoff

Abstract What aspects of an utterance must be stored in long-term memory, and what aspects can be constructed on-line in working memory? This question has not played a significant role in linguistic theory, and indeed it would seem to be a question of performance rather than competence. However, if taken seriously, it leads to some radical conclusions about the organization of the grammar. In particular, the lexicon — the store of memorized elements — contains not only words but regular affixes and stems, plus phrasal units such as idioms and constructions. One consequence is a much less rigid divide than usual between lexical items and rules of grammar. The resulting architecture in part resembles the approaches of HPSG, Construction Grammar, and other non-Chomskyan versions of generative grammar. It offers the possibility of a better rapprochement between linguistic theory and psycholinguistic studies on language processing than has been possible in more traditional Chomskyan architectures.

Keywords: Lexicon, grammar, idioms, grammatical constructions, linguistic theory, psycholinguistic studies.

1. Introduction to the architecture

Chomsky's *Aspects of the Theory of Syntax* (Chomsky, 1965) set a program for linguistic theory that has essentially defined the field for 35 years. Over that time much has changed in our conception of rules of grammar and how they interact. However, certain more basic claims and assumptions of the theory have remained unchanged. During the past few years I have been engaged in a re-evaluation of this program, asking what has changed and why, what has not changed and why not, and, of the parts that have remained intact, which are worth preserving and which are in retrospect probably mistaken in light of subsequent research in linguistics, psychology, and neuroscience (Jackendoff, 1997a;

S. Nooteboom et al. (eds.), Storage and Computation in the Language Faculty, 23–58.

2001). The present paper explores some issues within this re-evaluation, in particular addressing the question of storage versus computation that is the topic of this volume. It is useful to begin with a brief outline of the larger picture.

Three foundational observations lie at the heart of all generative linguistics since *Aspects*. The first is that the object of investigation is language as encoded in the human mind/brain, rather than language as an abstract object or as a cultural artifact. This stance is essentially agreed upon by everyone working on language within cognitive science. The second observation, a point driven home in Chomsky's earlier *Syntactic Structures* (Chomsky, 1957), is that human language permits the encoding of an unlimited number of messages of potentially unlimited complexity, based on combinatorial principles (or *rules of grammar*) applying to a finite stock of discrete elements. Chomsky proposes that the central issue for theoretical linguistics is the characterization of these combinatorial principles, in a way compatible with their instantiation in the mind. This proposal is taken for granted in most of the linguistics community, but in much of cognitive science and neuroscience it either does not play a central role or is even disputed, as we shall see presently.

The third observation, which has led to the most controversy, is that the rules of grammar differ from one human language to the next, and therefore that adults must have acquired these different principles as children, on the basis of the language in their environment. Moreover, the principles cannot be acquired by instruction from those who already speak the language, since speakers have no awareness of the principles — they have only intuitions regarding grammaticality and appropriateness of sentences. Therefore, children must be constructing the principles on their own, largely unconsciously. Chomsky claims that the nature of grammatical principles is such that they cannot be acquired unaided by a general-purpose information processing device; rather, children must come to the task of language acquisition with some inherent preconception of what language is supposed to be like. Following the terminology of linguists of the Cartesian tradition, he calls this unlearned preconception *Universal Grammar*. He proposes that a higher goal for linguistic theory is to characterize Universal Grammar, which he sees as the basis of the human language capacity.

The idea that there is a specialized human language capacity has provoked widespread dissent over the years (e.g. Edelman, 1992; Elman et al., 1996; Deacon, 1997). Many linguists and psycholinguists dispute it as well (e.g. Lakoff, 1987). I agree that we should reject a cartoonish view of Universal Grammar as a "box" in the mind totally isolated in form and function from other mental capacities — a view that Chomsky sometimes seems to be proposing (e.g. Chomsky, 1995). But I believe there is merit in regarding the language capacity as a specialization built on top of other cognitive capacities in the primate repertoire, different in content but not in overall character from other cognitive specializations. One can then ask exactly what new must be added to preexisting capacities (beyond more memory) in order for a primate to learn human language; it seems reasonable to hypothesize that the additions are nonzero, given the complexity of language. One finds strains of this way of posing the issue in *Aspects*, but it is not the way the issue has been framed in the collective consciousness of the field.

These three foundational observations and the issues they raise are in my opinion absolutely essential to linguistic theory — as important now as they were in 1965. *Aspects* instantiated them in the theory by means of a basic assumption about the form of the grammar that seemed reasonable at the time and that has driven research ever since, but which I think on reflection has proven to be mistaken. This assumption concerns the way in which the grammar realizes the "discrete infinity" of language. In *Aspects* the creative or generative power of language is invested in the syntactic component, specifically the principles that combine lexical items into phrase-structure (the *base* component). By contrast, the phonological and semantic components of language are taken to be "interpretive," that is, their structure is taken to arise by means of a derivation from syntactic structure. Moreover, lexical items (words) are taken to be inserted in their entirety into syntactic structures; their phonological and semantic aspects are carried over into phonological and semantic structures respectively through the process of "interpretation."

Perhaps because this "syntactocentric" architecture was so successful in promoting lively research on linguistic structure, it was not noticed that by 1980 or so evidence against it had begun to accumulate. A revolution in phonology during the middle 1970s (e.g. Goldsmith, 1976; Liberman and Prince, 1977) led to a view of phonological structure in which many of its properties are autonomous of syntactic structure. It is built not out of units derivable from syntactic structure by "bracket erasure" and "re-adjustment" (Chomsky and Halle, 1968), but out of a collection of independent "tiers" such as segmental and syllabic structure, metrical structure, and intonational structure, connected by "association lines." In other words, the unlimited class of phonological structures of a language is the product of an autonomous generative phonological component — perhaps not as elaborately recursive as syntax, but autonomous and generative nevertheless. This view of phonological structure rapidly came to be universally accepted by phonologists, but few in either syntax or phonology seem to have noticed how it challenges the syntactocentric architecture.

Similarly in semantics. At the time of *Aspects*, virtually nothing was known about the formulation of semantics in generative grammar (only the rudimentary and much-attacked work of Katz and Fodor, 1963 and Katz and Postal, 1964). But in the following fifteen years, at least three different traditions of semantics were developing: the formal semantics of Montague and his school (Partee, 1975; 1976), the Cognitive Grammar of Langacker, 1987; Lakoff, 1987, and their school, and my own Conceptual Semantics (Jackendoff, 1978; 1983; Pinker, 1989). Despite the mutual incompatibility of these traditions, they concur in viewing semantics as a combinatorial system of considerable complexity and subtlety — and one *not* strictly derivable from syntactic structure. Thus semantics too is properly viewed as an autonomous generative component, not as a derivative of syntactic generativity.

However, three autonomous generative components cannot simply operate independently of each other. A sentence is after all a correlation between sound and meaning, mediated by syntactic structure. Rather, as a matter of "conceptual necessity" (to use the term of Chomsky, 1995), the grammar also must contain *interface* rules that determine how the three structures correspond to each other or that place the three structures "in registration" (or that "bind" them in the neuroscience sense). The resulting skeletal architecture of the grammar is shown in Figure 2.1; this is a bare minimum. (In particular, a further interface directly between phonology and semantics would be a promising addition, in order to account for the well-known topic/focus effects that are based on stress and intonation without any additional syntactic marking.)

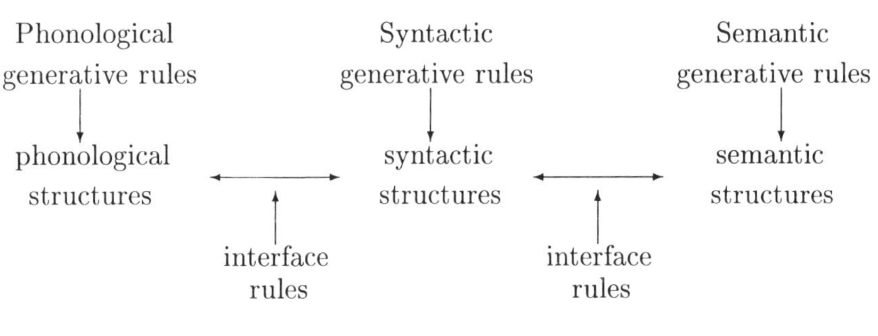

Figure 2.1. The skeletal architecture of the grammar.

The structure of a sentence can thus be segregated into independent substructures, each of which contains only information proper to one of the components of the grammar. (2.1) is the structure of the phrase *the cat* (phonological and syntactic structures in standard notation; semantic notation in the formalization of Jackendoff, 1983—readers should feel free to substitute their own favored semantic notation).

(2.1)

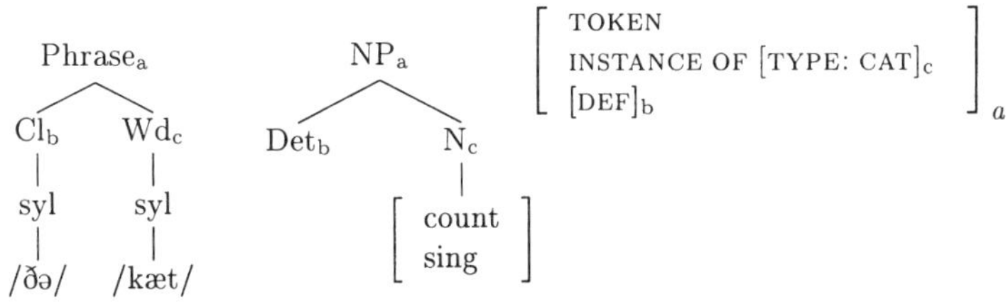

In (2.1) the subscripts indicate how the parts of the structures correspond: the entire phonological phrase corresponds to the entire NP and the entire semantic constituent; the Clitic corresponds to the Determiner in syntax and the definiteness feature in semantics; the Word corresponds to the N in syntax and the type-constituent in semantics. This treatment contrasts with the traditional notation for this phrase, shown in (2.2), which on one hand mixes phonological and syntactic information — *the* and *cat* are after all phonological information — and which on the other hand fails to show all the phonological and semantic structure.

(2.2)

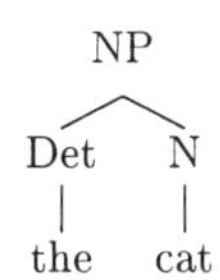

What is the structure of a word in this architecture? As in every theory, a word is a bundle of phonological, syntactic, and semantic features. However, in the present theory, it is impossible to insert a word in its entirety into any of the three tree structures, because that would mix types of information. Rather, a word is distributed across the three structures, and provides part of the linkage between them. For instance, *cat* looks like this:

(2.3)

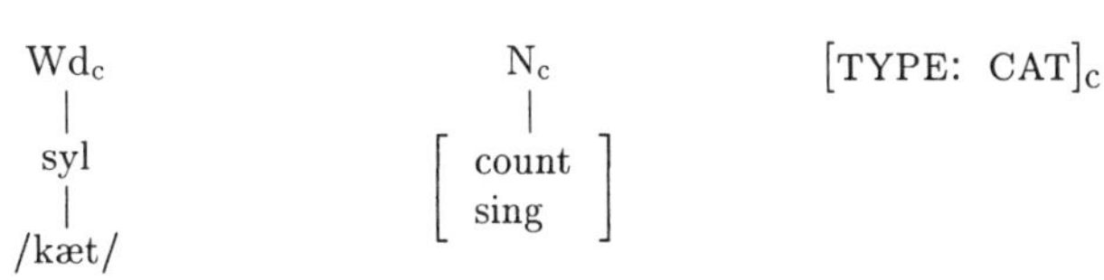

Thus a word is a stored association of three kinds of structures, plus a subscript that links them. In other words, the lexicon is not a component that inputs to the syntactic component, but rather a part of the interface components: it helps establish the relation among phonology, syntax, and semantics.

It is worth mentioning at this point that there are "defective" words that lack one of the three structures. The most interesting are words like *ouch* and *hello*, which have phonology and semantics, but no syntactic structure: they serve as independent single-word utterances. They can appear in combination only in contexts such as direct quotes, which permit any possibility at all, even nonsense words and utterances in a different language (*"Ouch/Fendle/la plume de ma tante," she exclaimed*). There are also words that have syntactic and phonological structure but no meaning, for instance the *do* of *do*-support (*She* ***didn't*** *leave*) and expletive *it* (***It*** *seems that she's smart*). And, in some versions of syntactic theory, there are words that have syntactic structure and meaning but no phonological structure: the so-called empty categories such as trace and PRO. Finally, nonsense syllables can be regarded as phonological constituents with no syntactic *or* semantic structure. These classes of "defective" words will play a role in what follows here.

The tripartite parallel generative architecture sketched in Figure 2.1 is a sort of generalization of several alternative frameworks in contemporary generative grammar. As already mentioned, much work in phonology presumes that within phonological structure are a number of independent subcomponents or "tiers," such as segmental structure, metrical structure, and intonational structure. The principles that connect these tiers with association lines are interface components in the present sense; the association lines are a notational variant of the subscripts employed in (2.1). Lexical-Functional Grammar (LFG: Bresnan, 1982b, Dalrymple et al., 1995) proposes two independent subcomponents of syntax, constituent structure and functional structure; these too are independent generative components whose structures are linked by interface principles. Head-Driven Phrase Structure Grammar (HPSG: Pollard and Sag, 1994) segments its constituents into three major independent bundles of features (phonological, syntactic, and semantic) connected by indices. Role and Reference Grammar (Van Valin and LaPolla, 1997) has two independent components of syntactic structure (morphological structure and phrase-structure) cross-linked with each other and with two independent components of semantic structure (thematic structure and focus structure). Autolexical Syntax (Sadock, 1991) has two independent syntactic trees (morphological and phrasal), both linked to the phonological structure. In other words, Figure 2.1 is altogether within the ambit of these frameworks, but is not a version of the usual Chomskyan framework; and these other frameworks can be viewed as more detailed componential decompositions of certain parts of the tripartite architecture.

The reader is referred to Jackendoff, 1997a for a detailed exposition of the architecture sketched in Figure 2.1 and the arguments for it. We now turn to an issue which played only a minor part in Jackendoff, 1997a, and which to my knowledge has played no significant role in any other generative theories. I have now begun to think it is absolutely essential in working out the instantiation of language in the mind.

2. The question

The issue I have in mind is the topic of this book:

What aspects of an utterance must be stored in long-term memory, and what aspects can be constructed on-line in working memory?

The modalities in the two parts of this question are important. Consider two stereotypical examples. The word *dog* must be stored in longterm memory: there is no way to construct it on-line from smaller parts. By contrast, the reader probably understands the utterance *My dog just threw up on your carpet* by constructing it on-line from its constituent words, making use of the rules of English grammar to do so. But since I have memorized this sentence, having used it as an example in many talks, it is present in *my* longterm memory. In fact any utterance can be memorized, all the way from little clichés to the words of *Take Me Out to the Ballgame* to the entire text of the *Iliad*. Thus we cannot predict in advance that any particular part of an utterance *must* be constructed on-line by a given speaker, we can predict only that speakers *can* construct some part on-line on demand if it hasn't already been memorized.

One might be moved to wonder whether the possible memorization of the *Iliad* is relevant to the question at all. It might be that words are one thing for the brain (e.g. use one kind of memory), and long passages of text are something else (e.g. use another kind of memory). I would reply by pointing out, first, that such long passages are made up of linguistic information — they are linked phonological, syntactic, and semantic structures that (at least mostly) conform to rules of grammar. Therefore they invoke the language faculty in their production and comprehension. Like individual words, there is no other faculty that they necessarily invoke. Second, there is no principled dividing line between little clichés such as *happy birthday* and *signed, sealed, and delivered*, larger units such as *the bigger they are, the harder they fall*, still larger units such as song lyrics, and monsters such as the *Iliad*. The main difference is that the units we call clichés will tend to be in everyone's longterm memory, but linguistic examples, poems, song lyrics, and epics are likely to be only known by some small proportion of speakers. In any event, in terms of the question at hand, the longer passages *can* be constructed on-line (say when hearing them for the first time) but need not be.

The doubt whether long texts are stored as linguistic information likely arises thanks to a widespread stereotype in linguistic theory (as well as in the popular conception of language): that the memorized units of language are *words*. In fact, the terms *word* and *lexical item* are often used virtually interchangeably. The term *lexicon* is introduced in *Aspects* roughly to mean the repository of all the words the speaker knows. Chomsky, following Bloomfield, 1933, points out correctly that the lexicon must contain all the exceptional, nonpredictable features of words. He further stipulates, without much argument, that the lexicon contains *only* nonpredictable features, that is, that it contains no redundancy (it is not clear to me that this was Bloomfield's intention, however). Here, I believe, Chomsky deviates from psychological reality: there is no reason to believe that the brain stores information without redundancy. Moreover, as argued in Jackendoff, 1997a, chapters 5, 6, the assumption of nonredundancy leads to difficulties in linguistic description — generalizations that are difficult or impossible to capture properly.

Let us use the term *lexical item* exclusively to denote an item stored in the lexicon, i.e. in longterm memory. We then observe that the theory also contains quite a different notion of *word*. In phonology, a *phonological word* is a constituent such as those dominated by *Wd* in (2.1) and (2.3); it is a domain over which certain segmental and prosodic constraints are defined. In syntax, a roughly corresponding notion is that of an X^0 (or so-called *lexical*) category such as N, V, A, or P. Di Sciullo and Williams, 1987 point out the distinction between grammatical words and what are here called lexical items (they call them "listemes"), and declare from the outset (p. 1) that the theory of listemes is "of no interest to the grammarian." By contrast, I will take the theory of listemes quite seriously here: the question posed at the beginning of this section concerns precisely this theory. And we will see that it is indeed of considerable interest to the grammarian — as well as to those who study language processing, of course.

The argument to be pursued here is that, under the definition of lexical item as a unit stored in longterm memory,

- Lexical items may be bigger or smaller than grammatical words.
- Not all grammatical words are lexical items.
- More controversially, there are rather complex lexical items that contain no phonological material.

As a preview of the argument, let me just briefly mention the two basic problems with the stereotype of lexical items as words.

First, consider the situation in a language with massively productive morphology, say Turkish or Navajo. In such a language, a grammatical word consists of a stem plus all its inflections. Thus on one hand the number of grammatical words is too large to store in longterm memory; and on the other hand it is possible to construct most grammatical words on-line from units that *are* stored in longterm memory: the independent stems and affixes. These elements are smaller than grammatical words, and cannot be produced in isolation.

Second, consider the treatment of idioms such as *kick the bucket*. These are units larger than grammatical words – in this case, apparently a VP. And because it means something different than its constituent parts, it must be stored in longterm memory as a unit, in this case a lexical VP. As will be elaborated in section 4, there have been proposals to treat *kick the bucket* and the like as grammatical X^0s, and for this particular idiom such a treatment might be plausible. But it is far less plausible for idioms such as *the cat's got X's tongue* and *NP_i's got NP_j where pro_i want(s) pro_j*; these are full sentences and so it is hardly plausible to treat them as Vs. We thus must consider the possibility of lexically listed phrases of various sizes (as already hinted at in the beginning of this section).

We take these two cases in order.

3. Lexical items smaller than words

The fundamental principle behind generative syntax is that the combination of grammatical words into phrases is accomplished by productive rules of phrasal combination, i.e. "syntax." However, in many approaches to generative grammar (most notably HPSG among widespread theories but also earlier LFG (Bresnan, 1982b) and such work as Hale and Keyser, 1993), the combination of stems and affixes into grammatical words is taken to be accomplished "in the lexicon" by so-called *lexical rules*, "before" the words are "inserted" into syntactic trees. For example, the word *unfortunately* is composed in the lexicon by a lexical rule that converts adjectives into adverbs by adding *-ly* to them; the word *enjoyment* is composed in the lexicon by a lexical rule that converts verbs into nouns by adding *-ment* to them.

However, this treatment neglects an important distinction among word-building rules, between what I will call *productive* and *semiproductive* lexical rules. Let us look at these types in turn.

3.1. Productive morphology

Productive morphology is totally regular, except where blocked (or supplanted) by irregular forms. A prototypical case is the English present participle (*-ing*) form, which applies without exception to all the verbs of the language. The English past tense affix *-d* is similarly productive (given the predictable phonetic alternations between /-d/, /-t/, and /-əd/), except that it is supplanted in about 180 verbs by irregular forms. Productive morphology is not confined to inflectional morphology (i.e. affixes like agreement, tense, and case); it appears also in derivational morphology. For example, just about any English adjective can be converted into an adverb by adding *-ly*, aside from marked exceptions such as *good–well*, *fast–fast* and adjectives that already end in *-ly* such as *friendly*.

In patterns of productive morphology, speakers confronted with a new base form know exactly how to form the derived form and exactly what it means. This is the point, for instance, of the often-cited *wug* experiments of Berko, 1958: by the age of 6 or so children have mastered the regular plural ending of English and can apply it to nonsense words they have never heard before. Likewise, speakers often create and encounter new regular forms they have never encountered before, without noticing they are doing anything special. For instance, Dutch speakers constantly affix the productive diminutive suffix *-tje* to every noun in sight. This property of productive morphology is of particular interest in a heavily affixing language such as Turkish, in which word forms like (2.4) are not unusual:

(2.4) gel- emi- yebel- ir- im.
come- unable- possible- past- 1sg.
'I may be unable to come.'
Van Valin and LaPolla, 1997, p.44

çalış- tır- ıl- ma- malıy- mış.
work- cause- passive- neg- oblig- infer.
'Supposedly he ought not to be made to work.'

Spencer, 1991, p.189

It is of no consequence whether a speaker of Turkish has heard these particular forms before: they can be created and interpreted on the spot.

Now consider what it might mean for such forms to be created "in the lexicon." If "in the lexicon" means "stored in longterm memory," the implication is that speakers store all regular forms. On this hypothesis, when one hears a new noun stem like *wug*, one immediately adds not just *wug* but also *wugs* to one's longterm store. Similarly, Dutch speakers who learn a new noun also add to their longterm memory the diminutive form.

For a more striking case, there is a register of American English in which one can for emphasis insert an expletive into the interior of a word that has the appropriate stress pattern, creating such forms as *manu-fuckin-facture*, *ele-fuckin-mentary*, and so on (but not **ele-fuckin-phant*, because *elephant* has the wrong stress pattern) (McCarthy, 1982). Within the constraint of appropriate stress (roughly, that the main stress must be preceded by a secondary stress and preferably an unstressed syllable), this morphological process is perfectly productive. Thus the hypothesis that these forms are created "in the lexicon" implies that whenever one learns a new word of appropriate stress pattern, one also tucks away in memory the *-fuckin-* form as well!

These cases are at least technically possible. The case of massively affixing languages like Turkish is more problematic. Hankamer, 1989 observes that in such languages every verb has tens of thousands of possible forms, all constructed through productive morphology. If all these forms are created "in the lexicon," then the demands on longterm memory are multiplied by several orders of magnitude over a meagerly inflected language like English. When it comes to the capacity of longterm memory one is hard-pressed to say how much is implausible, but cases like Turkish do stretch the imagination.

In fact, the productivity of Turkish helps make clearer what is going on. The variety of possibilities available in a typical largish inflectional system is not unlike that in, say, the Determiner system of English. (2.5) illustrates, going from simple cases to rather complex ones. (Toward the end, contexts are added in italics to help make sense of the examples.)

(2.5) a/the/this/that/what/which/whichever/every/each/some house
these/those/such/some/which/what houses
both/all/enough houses
such a/many a house
{so/too/how} {tall/expensive/old/...} a house
{much/far} too {tall/expensive/old/...} a house
{nearly/almost/practically/not quite} every house
{nearly/almost/practically/not quite} {all/enough} houses
how much more expensive a house *did Bill buy*?
Bill bought 5 times as expensive a car *as I did*
you can get {more than/almost} 5 times as fast a computer *for cheaper*
...

No one would claim that when one learns a new noun, one adds to one's lexicon versions of that noun with all the dozens of possible determiner combinations. Rather, every theory assumes these are built "in the syntax", i.e. by principles of free combination putting together complex determiner structures and prefixing them to nouns, in accordance with syntactic and semantic restrictions on the individual parts.

The same approach seems altogether appropriate for productive morphology. Words can be composed by combining stems and affixes according to principles of free combination, in accordance with the phonological, syntactic, and semantic restrictions on the individual parts. For instance, English progressive *-ing* can be specified phonologically as a suffix, syntactically as something added to a verb to form a participle, and semantically as something that (roughly) operates on an event to form a process. A verb form like *cutting* then is the product of free combination of this suffix with the verb stem *cut.*

For our purposes, the important question is: What does it mean to say this free combination is the result of a "lexical rule" that takes place "in the lexicon"? Taking to heart the cases of expletive infixation and Turkish verb inflection, and bearing in mind the close parallel to the determiner system, it seems implausible that "in the lexicon" here means "stored in longterm memory." Rather, like the examples in (2.5), the outputs of productive lexical rules are more likely to be constructed online in working memory. (And like remembered phrases or song lyrics, they *can* be memorized and stored, but they need not be.) From what material stored in longterm memory are they constructed, then? Obviously, the individual stems and affixes. In other words, "lexical rule" here means "principle of free combination whose output is something of word size or smaller," and "in the lexicon" means not "stored in longterm memory" but rather "involving principles that build things of word size or smaller." That is, "lexical" in these terms really refers to the *grammatical* notion of *word*, not to the notion of the lexicon as stored information.

3.2. Semiproductive morphology

The situation is quite different with semiproductive morphology, where only partial regularities are to be found. A typical case is the irregular forms of the English past tense. There are various generalizations, for example that irregularity is confined to monosyllabic verbs (plus bi- and trisyllabic verbs that begin with the quasi-prefixes *a-*, *be-*, *for-*, *over-*, and *under-*), and that many irregular verbs form their past tenses by changing the vowel. But even among verbs that are phonologically very similar, one must know whether the vowel changes and what it changes to: compare *ring–rang, wring–wrung, spring–sprang, sting–stung, drink–drank, swing–swung, hang–hung,* plus cases that are variable such as *shrink–shrank/shrunk, stink–stank/stunk.* In addition, these are interspersed with homophonous regular cases, such as *hang-hanged* and *ring-ringed* ('put a ring around'). Thus a "lexical rule" of this sort does not apply across the board. Rather, given a stem form that the rule potentially applies to, one must know whether the rule *actually* applies to it.

When a word lacks a specified irregular form for past tense or other inflectional morphology, the inflectional paradigm must still be filled out. For instance, a verb *must* have a past tense form. So in the absence of an irregular form, the regular combinatorial process jumps in. However, in the case of derivational morphology there need be no derived form at all, so the result of a semiproductive process may be just a gap — that is, there may be no regular pattern that serves as default. Consider for example the English denominal verbs formed by zero-affixation, such as *butter (the bread), water (the flowers), paint (the wall), roof (the house).* These exhibit a clear regularity, in that they all mean roughly 'put N on something,' where N is the homophonous noun. But for each individual noun in the language, one needs to know whether it gives rise to such a denominal verb. For example, one only asks someone to *mustard the sandwich* or *door the cabinet* ('put a door on the cabinet') as a metalinguistic joke; speakers know that these forms do not exist.

Derivational morphology raises two further complications. First, deverbal nouns can have a variety of meanings, for instance those in (2.6).

(2.6) 'put N on': butter, water, paint, roof
'take N off': dust (the shelves), scale (a fish), skin (a cat)
'put on N': saddle (a horse), shelve (the books)
'put in N': pocket (the money), bottle (the wine)
'fasten with N': glue, staple, nail, tape
and others

And just as there are homophonous irregular verbs with different past tenses, such as *hang-hung* vs. *hang-hanged* and *ring-rang* vs. *wring-wrung*, there are homophonous denominal verbs. For example, in addition to *dust (the shelves)* 'take dust off', there is *dust (the cake with sugar)* 'put dustlike substance on'; in addition to *roof (the house)* 'put a roof on', my daughters' dialect has *roof (a frisbee)*, 'put/throw onto a roof'. Thus one must know not just *whether* a particular noun has a corresponding denominal verb, but also which variety or varieties of denominal verb it has.

The second complication is that, even if one knows this much, one cannot predict the complete meaning of the denominal verb. To put a clock on a shelf is not to *shelve* it; to just pour wine into a bottle is not to *bottle* it; to spill water on a table is not to *water* it. One cannot *saddle* a table by putting a saddle on it; one cannot *butter* one's toast by laying a stick of butter on it. Every denominal verb has semantic pecularities that are not predicted by the general lexical rule.

The upshot is that the outputs of semiproductive rules must be listed (at least in part) in longterm memory; they cannot be a product of free combination. So in this case the notion of a "lexical rule", a rule applying "in the lexicon", makes sense. Such a rule expresses a generalization in the relationship among pairs of lexical entries. But it does not apply to all entries that satisfy its conditions, nor does it fully predict the information in one of these entries, given the other.

3.3. The necessity of a heterogeneous theory

The conclusion is that the term "lexical rule" has been applied to two distinct phenomena. The principles that express semiproductive generalizations are indeed lexical rules: they relate lexical items to each other, but speakers must learn one by one the lexical items that the rule relates. That is, the rule expresses the *possibility* but not the *existence* or the *details* of forms. By contrast, productive generalizations are the result of free combination of individual morphemes stored as separate lexical items. (This does not preclude high-frequency combinations being stored as well, and there is some evidence that they are, e.g. Baayen et al., 1992; 1993; 2001 (this volume)).

On this proposal, then, *dog* is both a word and a lexical item; *-s* is a lexical item but *not* a word; the regular form *dogs* is a word but not a lexical item, being made out of the lexical items *dog* and *-s*; and the irregular *men* is both a word and a lexical item. What may seem unintuitive here is the inhomogeneity of the solution. Two forms with the exact same syntactic properties, for instance *dogs* and *men*, may have different sources: one is a product of free combination and the other comes from the lexicon.

In fact, most morphological theories have tacitly assumed that there must be a uniform solution for both cases. The consequence has been a continued tension between on one hand "morpheme-based" or "item-and-arrangement" theories such as Zwicky, 1988 and Di Sciullo and Williams, 1987 and on the other hand "lexeme-based" or "word-and-paradigm" theories such as Halle, 1973; Aronoff, 1976, and Anderson, 1992 (also Jackendoff, 1975). Morpheme-based theories are perspicuous for productive morphology and spend most of their effort trying to explain semiproductive phenomena. Lexeme-based theories are good at semiproductive phenomena, where whole words have to be listed, but they force one to believe for instance that the entire Turkish verb paradigm is stored for every verb. Looking at the theories from the very concrete standpoint of storage in the brain, we arrive at the conclusion that both approaches are correct, but each is correct for only part of the lexicon. This is not an optimally elegant solution — but of course it is not clear that the brain is always optimally elegant.

The same split appears among syntactic theories. It has already been mentioned that many theories such as HPSG achieve a homogeneous treatment of morphology by doing it all "in the lexicon." As we have seen, such theories level out the distinction between *words*, a grammatical notion, and *lexical items*, a notion having to do with storage; they treat all words as lexical items. Thus in this respect they parallel the lexeme-based morphological theories. The price is having to claim that the entire paradigm of inflection is present for every word. Late Government-Binding Theory (Baker, 1988, Pollock, 1989) and the Minimalist Program (Chomsky, 1995) level out the distinction in the opposite direction: they treat inflectional affixes as X^0 syntactic categories, hence like words in their potential to project complement and specifier structure. Because they stress the free combination of affixes, they parallel the morpheme-based morphological theories. The price here is complex derivations that reduce a great deal of combinatorial syntactic structure to the observed morphological forms. In both types of theories, part of the problem comes from expecting a homogeneous theory.

The need for a heterogenous theory of morphology has also been the subject of intense dispute in the psycholinguistic and neurolinguistic community. The genesis of the dispute was the claim by Rumelhart and McClelland, 1986 that a connectionist network that performs pattern association could learn the past tense system of English, and would in fact learn it in roughly the way a child does. Pinker and colleagues, in part drawing on work by many others (Pinker, 1999; Pinker and Prince, 1988; 1991 and references therein) have amassed a great deal of experimental evidence against this account, drawing on the statistical distribution of regulars and irregulars, on speakers' judgments and reaction times in producing and recognizing past tenses of known and novel verbs (Bybee and Moder, 1983; Prasada and Pinker, 1993), and on the behavior of agrammatics and individuals with Specific Language Impairment (Gopnik, 1999; Van der Lely, 1999) and with Williams Syndrome (Clahsen and Almazan, 1998). They show that the pattern association account is satisfactory for irregular verbs (here, semiproductive patterns), and even provides considerable insight. But they also show that the formation of regular past tenses is a phenomenon of quite different character, not captured by the Rumelhart and McClelland model nor by subsequent connectionist models in a similar spirit such as those of Plunkett and Marchman, 1991 and Hare et al., 1995. The experiments have been replicated with other inflectional systems where a regular default pattern is overlain by a system of irregularities: German noun plurals (Marcus et al., 1995) and Hebrew noun plurals (Berent et al., 1999). More strikingly, Marcus, 1998; 2001, shows (at least to my satisfaction) that a multilayer network trained by backpropagation is *in principle* incapable of extracting the sort of regularity necessary to account for productive morphology.

Pinker characterizes the productive process of past tense formation as a *rule* that adds *-d* to a stem; his claim is that a network instantiating pattern association cannot learn *rules.* The present account of the productive process is slightly different: I would like to treat it as *free combination* of the lexically stored affix *-d* with a verb stem, in accordance with the affix's structural requirements. Instead of a special rule "Form past tense by adding *-d*", or a somewhat more general rule "Add affixes to stems", there is the maximally simple and general rule *COMBINE* or *UNIFY*. However, even under this interpretation, the argument against the network approach still goes through. Marcus localizes the difficulty for pattern associators in the fact that they cannot encode a *variable*: they cannot say "this generalization applies to anything I encounter that belongs to such-and-such a category, regardless of its other features." In Pinker's characterization, a variable appears in the rule: "To form the past tense of *any verb*, add *-d*." In the present account, the rule has two variables: "Combine *anything* with *anything appropriate*." Furthermore, the lexical item *-d* defines what is appropriate using a variable: "I combine with *any verb*." So the present account presents the same principled difficulties for a network of the usual sort.

I believe the present approach in fact makes clearer what is at stake in this argument. For, as stressed in section 1, it is the principle of free combination that makes language what it is. Connectionist approaches may give us considerable insight into semiproductivity. But if a multilayer network trained by backpropagation in principle cannot account for the regular past tense, there is no hope of scaling up current connectionist solutions to the past tense to the rest of language, where free combination reigns supreme. Rather, the challenge to network approaches is to develop a robust device for encoding variables (one such proposal is Shastri and Ajjanagadde, 1993) — not to continue to try to live without variables. Accepting this challenge could, I believe, lead to far more meaningful dialogue between network modelers and theoretical linguists.

To my knowledge it has not been observed that a heterogeneous morphological theory presents an interesting challenge to acquisition. The child, after all, does not have a "Maxwell's demon" that sorts the words in the environment into regular and semiregular cases. The same morphological relationship (say causative formation) may be productive in one language (e.g. Turkish) but only semiproductive in another (e.g. English). Nor does relatively high frequency signal a regular pattern. For instance, German regular plural nouns are considerably less frequent than irregulars in speech, counting either tokens or types (Marcus et al., 1995). My inclination is to think that the child's brain takes a catholic approach, trying to analyze new morphological patterns both ways at once, and that eventually one mechanism extinguishes the other. But developing such a theory is a topic for future research in acquisition theory and neuroscience. (Some suggestions for the way the difference is represented in the competence theory appear in Jackendoff, 2001.)

4. Idioms

So far we have been investigating lexical items smaller than words, i.e. stems and affixes. As suggested at the end of section 2, the lexicon also embraces items *larger* than words, with idioms as a prime case. This section looks at idioms somewhat more closely. They will lead us on into a more abstract species of lexical item, the *construction*, which we take up in sections 5 and 6.

First of all, it is clear that idioms must be stored in longterm memory. There is no way that one can construct the meaning 'die' by combining the morphemes *kick*, *the*, and *bucket* by regular processes. Moreover, despite a tendency among grammarians to treat idioms as a relatively marginal phenomenon, there are in fact thousands of them – probably as many as there are adjectives. So theories of grammatical structure and processing ignore idioms at their own risk.

Idioms have been problematic to all the successive architectures adopted by Chomsky since *Aspects*. The difficulty lies in the assumption that words are inserted into syntactic trees under lexical categories such as N, V, and Det. The grammar has to generate a VP dominating a V plus a definite NP before inserting *kick*, *the*, and *bucket* individually under V, Det, and N respectively; then the semantic component has to interpret the concatenation of these three words idiomatically. However, the idiomatic interpretation has to come directly from the lexicon, not from the usual compositional process; in the insertion of the words individually, their unity as an idiom has been lost. So how can the lexicon record the idiom as a unit, and how can this unit be inserted into larger combinatorial structures?

One solution (Chomsky, 1981, p.146, note 94) treats *kick the bucket* as a lexical verb rather than a verb phrase, giving it the internal structure shown in (2.7).

(2.7)

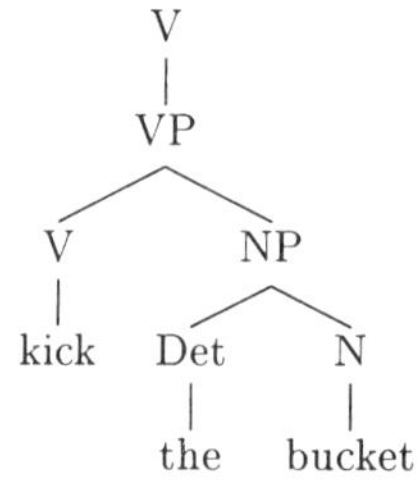

Because (2.7) is dominated by a V node, it can be inserted as a whole into a V position in syntax. It thus can carry its idiomatic information through to the level of semantic interpretation.

Such a solution has a number of fatal difficulties. First, as pointed out as early as Emonds, 1970, there are many discontinuous idioms in which a direct object intervenes between two constituents of the idiom, for example those in (2.8). (Pro_e designates a pronoun that must be coreferential with the subject; pro_i designates a pronoun that must be coreferential with the NP subscripted i.)

(2.8) take NP to task
take NP for granted
show NP the door
give NP the boot
give NP a piece of pro_e's mind
put NP_i in pro_i's place

A structure like (2.7), in which the entire idiom is dominated by V, predicts that these idioms should instead have the form *[*take to task*] *NP*, with the direct object to the right of the entire idiom. One can save the analysis by stipulating that *to task* has to move around the direct object in the course of the syntactic derivation. And then one may try to propose a reason within Universal Grammar that would justify forcing such a movement to take place. However, it is evident that the analysis rapidly becomes forced.[1]

[1] Regretfully, such strategies have become so commonplace in certain circles of generative syntax that many linguists do not recognize their unnaturalness anymore; indeed they may

As hinted at the end of section 2, a second difficulty for an analysis like (2.7) comes from idioms that cannot be shoehorned into a lexical category, for instance those in (2.9).

(2.9) a. The jig is up.
b. That's the way the cookie crumbles.
c. The cat's got NP's tongue.

These are complete sentences; if they were inserted under V, the underlying structure of the sentence would lack a subject and hence be illformed.

The overwhelming generalization about idioms, in fact, is that they have the syntax of garden-variety sentences. A theory with structures like (2.7) has to predict that this garden-variety syntax arises by obligatorily moving everything out from under the VP into — coincidentally — its normal position.

But even this is not enough. There are rare instances of idioms whose syntax is deviant:

(2.10) a. all of a sudden
b. by and large
c. Far be it from NP to VP. (usually NP is *me*)

(2.10a,b) appear in adverbial contexts, but they contain no syntactic structure recognizable from elsewhere in the grammar. (2.10c) is another complete sentence that cannot be stuffed into a V. Its syntax is at best a relic of some earlier stage of English, but of course it is perfectly acceptable in modern speech.

The upshot is that, although idioms must be stored, the way they must be stored cannot be reconciled with a theory in which only individual words are inserted into sentences. The obvious solution is to admit that, for instance, *kick the bucket* is a lexically stored VP. In the approach to the lexicon sketched in section 1, such a solution is quite natural. (2.11) illustrates with the idiom *take to task.*

---

even think highly of the analysis on the grounds that it shows us more about the abstractness of Universal Grammar. Such a stance tends to distance syntactic theory from psycholinguistic and developmental considerations; my overall program (see the introduction) is to try to reduce that distance.

(2.11)

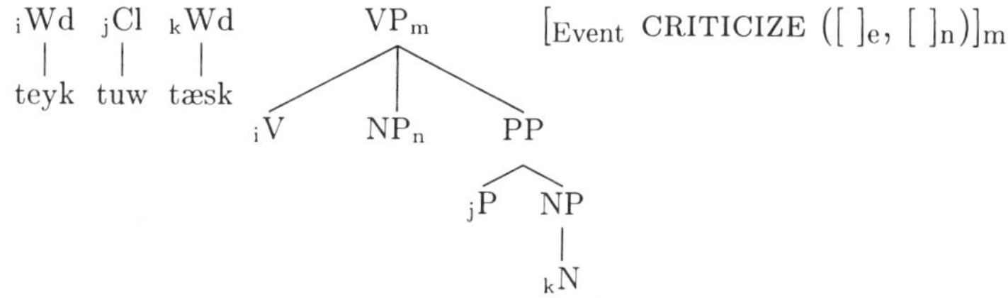

This is somewhat more elaborate than *cat* (example (2.3)), but the similarities are clear. There are two innovations over (2.3). The first is that the subscripts are now bifurcated into pre-subscripts, which denote phonology-syntax connections, and post-subscripts, which denote syntax-semantics connections. This is necessary because an idiom does not have a standard word by word mapping. Here, the first word in phonology maps into the verb, the clitic maps into the preposition, and the second word maps into the noun. However, these do not have meanings of their own: only the whole verb phrase does — it means 'criticize', as notated by the subscript *m*. That is what makes this an idiom.

The other innovation in (2.11) is the subscripts *e* and *n* in the semantic structure. These are subscripted to open argument places in the meaning of the idiom — the "critic" and the "victim." In this notation the subscript *e* is used by convention to link to the "external argument" or subject of the sentence; the subscript *n* links to the direct object position. Thus whatever the meaning of the NPs in subject and object, they come to be linked to these argument positions in the idiom. This aspect of the formalism is necessary for ordinary verbs as well, and a version of it is present in every constraint-based theory of grammar. Notice by the way that its formulation requires variables: the two arguments in the semantic structure and the NP in the syntactic structure.

Now observe how (2.11) accounts for the discontinuity of the idiom. The NP object is provided with no pre-subscript that maps it into a pronounced word. That subscript has to come from the elaboration of the NP in object position into actual words. The fact that the corresponding phonological material will fall between *take* and *to task* comes from the position of the NP in syntactic structure.

Two important questions are always posed of theories of idioms, and they must be addressed here. The first is the classic question of why *kick the bucket* cannot form a passive or other standard deformations – *the bucket was kicked by John* has only the literal interpretation. Chomsky's answer (e.g. in Chomsky, 1981) has been that idioms are somehow "frozen" in their deep structure form, for instance the NP in (2.7) is inaccessible to passive because it is inside the V. However, this also precludes moving the PP *to task* out of V and around the direct object.

Much worse, as pointed out by Nunberg et al., 1994, there are many idioms that appear only in heavily "transformed" versions, for instance the cases in (2.12).

(2.12) NP has it made. [passive]
NP is fit to be tied. [passive]
play hard to get ["tough-movement"]
hard to take ["tough-movement"]
a tough nut to crack ["tough-movement", infinitival relative]
How do you do? [Wh-movement]
(Now) NP_e's got NP_j where pro_e wants pro_j. [Wh-movement, free relative]
NP_e's not what pro_e's cracked up to be. [Wh-movement, free relative]

This shows that idioms must be specified in the lexicon for their *surface structure.* The best way to accomplish this is for the grammar as a whole to check lexical items against surface structures. In a theory with movement rules (e.g. all of Chomsky's theories throughout the years), this amounts to what has been called "late lexical insertion": lexical items are inserted not at the initial point in syntactic generation, but after all movement has taken place. Of course, in a constraint-based theory (such as the alternative theories mentioned in section 1, where surface structure is the only syntactic level there is), lexical checking at surface structure is the *only* option.

There are however idioms that do permit a degree of syntactic freedom, for instance *He let the cat out of the bag* vs. *The cat was let out of the bag*; *We must draw the line somewhere* vs. *The line must be drawn somewhere.* It has frequently been observed (Bresnan, 1978; Ruwet, 1991; Nunberg et al., 1994) that in such idioms, the mobile portion has a sort of metaphorical semantic interpretation: *the cat* is a secret, *the line* is a distinction. By contrast, *the bucket* in *kick the bucket* has no such interpretation. The key to mobility appears to lie in the partially compositional semantics of the idiom. A proper solution is beyond the scope of this paper (but see Jackendoff, 1997a, 166-170, for a proposal).

The other standard question about idioms is more basic: why do virtually all of them have perfectly normal syntactic structure? I would propose an interesting parallel with the discussion in the previous section: apart from their semantics, idioms are like stored regular morphological combinations. A particularly good analogy might be obligatorily plural nouns. For example, *scissors* is morphophonologically regular but does not denote multiple objects (rather an object with multiple parts); and *troops* (in the sense 'soldiers') has no singular form that means 'soldier'. These are morphological idioms with regular morphological form.

Still, the question arises of why there shouldn't be more syntactically *ir*regular idioms like (2.10). One reason is probably that idioms are historical developments from syntactically compositional phrases. Another possibility, suggested by Jackendoff, 1975, is that the general principles of free composition, which govern on-line construction, also place pressure on stored items to conform as well. This can be seen, for instance, in principles of syllable structure, which both constrain the stored words and also enable speakers to syllabify incoming signals on-line. Speakers can also use them to make distinctions among putative words, for example in Halle's well-known example of *blick* (possibly English) versus *bnick* (not English). And they exert a pressure on the phonological form of borrowings; for instance *Dvorak* is pronounced in English with three syllables in order to avoid the onset */dv/*, which is perfectly fine in the original Czech but ungrammatical in English. Under this conception, then, the rare idioms with syntactic violations are rather like the rare words with ungrammatical syllable structure, for example *kvetch* (pronounced /kfɛč/ in my dialect). The claim, then, is that principles of free composition in a sense act also as lexical rules. In the present approach (also in HPSG) this does not seem particularly unnatural; see Jackendoff, 2001 for a slightly more specific proposal. It is perhaps less natural in Pinker's approach, where the two types of principles are more sharply distinguished in formal and functional terms.

More generally, one might wonder whether a structure like (2.11) is too specific. Perhaps, for example, one should remove all indications of syntactic order, since they are predictable from the phrase-structure rules in any event. And perhaps one should replace the phonological information with some sort of pointers to the lexical items *take*, *to*, and *task*, which provide the phonology with no further ado.

However, I would see such moves as reflections of Chomsky's impulse to make the lexicon consist only of exceptions, to make it totally nonredundant. We have already rejected this position in allowing the possibility of stored words with regular morphology, which, since they can be generated by free combination, are totally redundant. In fact the stored regulars yield a good parallel to the situation of idioms in this respect. Parallel to the word order in idioms is the order of stem and affixes in stored regulars, which is also predictable by rule. And parallel to the phonological content of idioms is that of stored regulars, which is completely derivable from their constituents. What would it mean to remove this redundant information from stored regulars? It would be tantamount to deriving them only by rule, which is exactly what is denied in claiming they are stored! I conclude that if such redundancy is tolerable in stored regulars, it should be no problem in idioms.

5. A class of constructional idioms

I now want to move from idioms like those in (2.8) to a broader class of lexically specified VPs that include free variable positions. All the members of this broader class have the syntactic structure shown in (2.13).

(2.13)

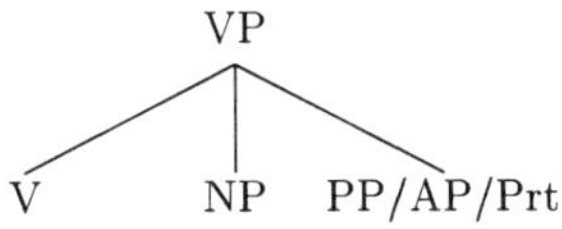

They vary in which parts of the VP are open positions. The idioms in (2.8) are a subclass that has a specified V and a specified PP but leaves the NP open. Notating the specified elements in upper case and the free elements in lower case, we can schematize this subclass as (2.14).

(2.14) [$_{VP}$ V np PP]: take NP to task, put NP$_i$ in *pro*$_i$'s place, ...

The familiar verb-particle idioms such as *look NP up* are a variant of (2.14) in which the PP is replaced by a particle (Prt). There are also many idioms in which the NP and P are specified and the object of the PP is left open:

(2.15) [$_{VP}$ V NP [$_{PP}$ P np]]: take unfair advantage of NP, make much of NP, ...

A much less remarked case (Jackendoff, 1997b) is a class of expressions exemplified by *sing one's head off* and *argue one's heart out.* In these, *NP's head off* and *NP's heart out* are fixed, and *NP* must be a pronoun coreferential with the subject. But the verb is totally free, within pragmatic constraints. One can *talk one's head off; drink one's head off; cook, knit, swim*, or even *program one's head off.* The most striking constraint is that the verb must have no complement of its own: although one can *read one's head off*, one cannot be said to **read mysteries one's head off.* Rather, *head* appears to occupy the direct object position, though it is hardly the object of the verb. And *off* is evidently in the particle position. Another member of this class is *V up a storm*, with the particle in its other possible position.

The meaning of all three of these expressions is roughly 'do to excess.'[2] One would not want to say that all the possible combinations are listed

[2]Some readers might be tempted to think this construction is a "metaphorical resultative." It is not. A genuine resultative such as *pull the bottle's top off* is telic, that is, it describes an

in the lexicon: that would in effect say that every time one learns a new verb V, one also must add to one's lexicon *V* pro_e*'s head off, V* pro_e*'s heart out, and V up a storm.* This situation should sound familiar from the discussion of regular morphology in section 3.1; it argues that we are dealing with free combination of stored elements. One element is the verb. Because of the idiomatic meaning, the other element has to be pro_e*'s head off.* In order to account for the fact that this element occupies positions that would normally be complements of the verb, we have to give it the syntactic structure in (2.16).

(2.16) [$_{VP}$ v NP PRT]: V pro_e's head off, V pro_e's heart out
[$_{VP}$VP v PRT NP]: V up a storm
'V excessively'

That is, these expressions are VPs of the general structure (2.13) in which the NP and PRT are fixed but the V is a free variable.

We should also note the idiom *eat one's heart out*, which has the form of (2.16) but a fixed verb and an idiomatic meaning 'experience envy.'

The next case is the inverse of (2.14): it has a fixed NP and a free V and PP. This is the *way*-construction (Jackendoff, 1990; Marantz, 1992; Goldberg, 1995), exemplified by (2.17). As can be seen, the verb can be just about anything that denotes a continuous process, and the PP can be any expression of path in space, time, or even metaphor.

(2.17) Bill belched his way out of the restaurant.
Frank drank his way across the country.
Sue sang her way through dinner.
Sosa and McGwire have homered their way into the hearts of America.
Chew your way to cleaner teeth. [ad for gum]

Again it is crucial that the verb be intransitive: one cannot **drink beer one's way across the country* or **hit home runs one's way into the hearts of America.* Evidently, parallel to the class in (2.16), pro_e*'s way* occupies direct object position.

The meaning of the construction is roughly 'go along the path PP while/by doing V.' (Goldberg, 1995 has a detailed discussion of the semantics.) Again, it would not make sense to say each verb combines with *way* "in the lexicon" to form an idiom; this would mean that when

event with a definite endpoint. Thus *he pulled the bottle's top off for hours* can only mean repeated removal of the top. By contrast, *he talked his head off* is atelic, that is, it can go on indefinitely. Thus *he talked his head off for hours* does not imply repeated acts of talking.

one learns a new intransitive verb, one also adds to memory its *way* form (in addition to its *heart out* and *up a storm* forms!). Rather, we are again dealing with free combination, this time combining a verb and a PP with a lexical item of the structure (2.18).

(2.18) [$_{VP}$ v NP pp]: V *pro*$_e$'s way PP, 'go PP while/by V-ing'

This construction too has more specialized versions, including *wend one's way PP* (where the verb *wend* occurs only in this construction), *worm one's way PP* (where *worm* occurs as a verb only in this construction), and the metaphorical *sleep one's way to the top.*

The next case is exemplified in (2.19) (more details in Jackendoff, 1997b).

(2.19) We're twisting the night away.
Hank drank the whole afternoon away.
Kathy happily knitted two hours away.

Here the verb is followed by a noun phrase that expresses a time period, plus the particle *away.* Clearly a time period is not a normal object for the verbs in (2.19) — one cannot **twist the night,* **drink the afternoon* (except perhaps metaphorically), or **knit two hours* (except in the different sense *knit for two hours*). Moreover, like the previous cases, the verb cannot take an object of its own: **drink beer the whole afternoon away,* **knit a sweater two hours away.* Thus the time period is occupying direct object position.

The meaning of the construction is roughly 'spend time period doing V'. By now the scenario is familiar: the best account is to say that, instead of the verb taking the object and the particle as free variables, the construction is a VP that takes the verb and the time expression as free variables. The only phonologically specified part of the construction is the particle *away.*

(2.20) [$_{VP}$ v np Prt]: V NP[time expression] away, 'spend NP V-ing'

Again there are specialized cases that use this frame: *while NP[time] away* and *fritter NP away* both have verbs that occur only in this construction (though *fritter* permits a wider range of NPs than just times).

At this point we have seen nearly every possible combination of specified constituents and free variables in structure (2.13). One might wonder whether there is also a situation in which the structure is composed *entirely* of free variables. This appears to be an appropriate solution for the well-known resultative construction, illustrated in (2.21).

(2.21) Wilma watered the tulips flat.
Clyde cooked the pot black.
Drive your engine clean. [ad for gasoline]

Though the verb *water* takes a direct object — the thing on which water is sprinkled — the further result of the tulips becoming flat is not predicted by the verb's meaning. And although one can *cook food* and *drive a car*, one cannot **cook a pot* or **drive a car engine*. Thus there is something special about having a direct object plus a predicate adjective that is not predicted by the verb's meaning.

Various discussions in the literature (e.g. Levin and Rappaport Hovav, 1991) treat the formation of resultatives as a "lexical rule" that changes and/or adds to the argument structure of the verb. Thus in addition to the regular verb *cook NP* 'cause NP to become cooked', there is also "in the lexicon" a further verb *cook NP AP* 'cause NP to become AP by cooking (with it)'. As usual, to say this is "in the lexicon" in the sense "stored in longterm memory" makes the otiose claim that every appropriate verb carries around yet another extra argument structure frame. The present approach (advocated also by Goldberg, 1995 and Jackendoff, 1990) is to say that the meaning of (2.21) is the product of the free composition of a resultative construction with three arguments. The construction itself comprises nothing but a syntactic frame associated with a meaning.

(2.22) [$_{\text{VP}}$ v np ap], 'cause NP to become AP by V-ing ((with) it)'

Notice that this lexical item has no phonology. It is just a pairing of a syntactic and semantic structure. However, this should not be too disturbing. We already know of the existence of other such "defective" lexical items from the discussion of section 1: *hello* and *ouch* lack syntax, and *do*-support *do* and epenthetic *it* lack semantics. So in principle there should be nothing objectionable about a lexical item that lacks phonology.

To sum up, in each of these cases — the *one's head off* construction, the *way*-construction, the *time-away* construction, and the resultative — we have regarded the construction not as a lexical rule that creates new verb argument structures "in the lexicon," but rather as a lexical item in its own right that undergoes free combination with verbs. What makes them unusual is that the verb does not determine the complement structure of the VP. Rather, the construction itself determines the complement structure of the VP, and the verb satisfies a free position in the construction.

We have still omitted one combination of specified and free constituents in (2.13): a specified verb with free NP and PP positions. But this is precisely the case of a verb that strictly subcategorizes obligatory NP and PP complements:

(2.23) $[_{\mathrm{VP}}$ V np pp$]$: put NP PP, place NP PP, etc.

In the *Aspects* framework, subcategorization was regarded as a feature on a verb, say [+__ NP PP] for *put* and *place*; various other approaches have appeared over the years. The present approach suggests that we can analyze *put* as having the lexical structure shown in (2.24).

(2.24)

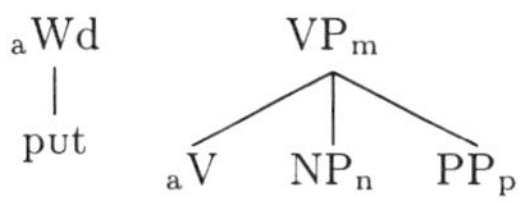

$[_{\mathrm{Event}}\ \mathrm{CAUSE}\ ([\ ]_e, [\mathrm{GO}\ ([\ ]_n, [\ ]_p)])]_m$

This lexical VP shows up phonologically only in the V position (the only syntactic position that has a pre-subscript to phonological structure). So on the surface it looks like it is just a verb. But it is not: it is actually a lexical VP.

To sum up, we have discovered a cline of lexical VPs, going from verbs that obligatorily subcategorize complements, through idioms, through constructional idioms that specify part of the VP's complement, to the resultative. Each step from one to the next is perfectly natural, but at the ends of the cline we have entities that appear entirely different (and have regularly been so analyzed in the literature). This approach permits us to see obligatory subcategorization by a verb, by an idiom, and by a construction as falling under a common formalization: leaving open positions in a lexical VP. (Williams, 1994 and Langacker, 1998 point out the existence of such clines in other areas of the lexicon.)

6. More general considerations

One claim of this analysis, then, is that English has this family of constructional idioms in which the main verb of the sentence serves as an argument. Most of these idioms are not attested in other languages; in fact the resultative, the most intensively investigated of them, seems to appear only in a relatively limited range of languages (Levin and Rappaport Hovav, 1991; however, Toivonen, 1999 finds a close parallel to the *way*-construction in Swedish, using a reflexive instead of *way*).

We can formulate the contextual restrictions on regular affixes using a similar approach. (2.25) shows how the regular past tense might be formalized.

(2.25)

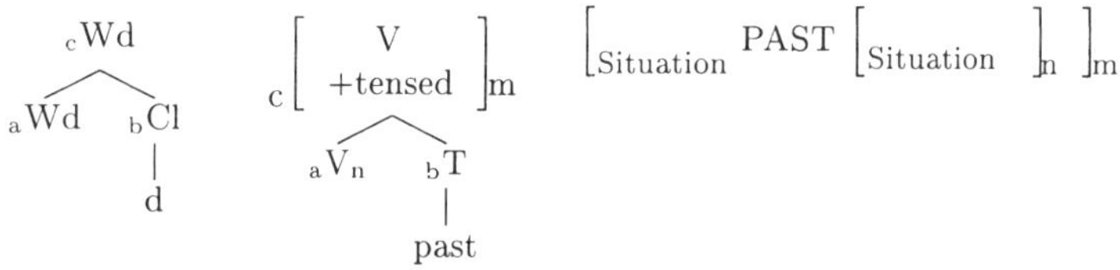

Thus the present framework permits a major unification of regular combinatorial phenomena.[3] Derivational (i.e. Chomskyan) generative grammar has discouraged recognizing constructions as of any theoretical interest, for a principled reason. In this approach, a construction such as passive or question or free relative is the product of a sequence of movement rules applying to an underlying structure. By definition, the application of a movement rule is free — it is determined only by the rule's own input constraints, not by what sequence of prior movements gave rise to that input. Therefore the emergence of a complex construction can be regarded only as the application of a fortuitous sequence of independent movement rules. In other words, constructions must be regarded as epiphenomena: the theoretical interest can lie only in the constraints on application of individual rules.

In the present approach, as we have seen, constructions turn out to be perfectly respectable lexical items that clip together with ordinary words according to ordinary procedures. To see that this is a more effective approach, we observe (with Fillmore et al., 1988) that there are constructions in English that like the idioms in (2.10) are syntactically ill-formed. (2.26) gives examples of two such cases along with their general form. (The notation t_i indicates a trace or gap in the sentence, understood as being satisfied by the comparative phrase.)

(2.26) a. One more beer and I'm leaving.
NP conj S
Culicover, 1972; Culicover and Jackendoff, 1997

b. The more you eat, the fatter you get.
[the [comparative phrase]$_i$ [S ... t_i ...]], [the [comparative phrase]$_j$ [S ... t_j ...]]
Fillmore et al., 1988; McCawley, 1988; Culicover and Jackendoff, 1999

[3]HPSG and Construction Grammar lead to the same conclusion, in a somewhat different formalism. Pollard and Sag, 1994 deals with many of the tricky details of how syntactic combination is accomplished, in such a way that the right lexical features come to be projected to the top of the tree. Much of that machinery appears to be readily adaptable to the present notation.

These are certainly not "core" constructions of English in the sense of Chomsky, 1981, but they are used all the time and must be learned by the child. Universal Grammar must therefore make provision for them. Once one bluntly admits the possibility of such "syntactic junk" in the grammar, it is easier to condone more well-behaved constructional idioms such as those in section 5.

This approach leads to a number of theoretical issues for future research. The first is: How structurally complex can constructions be? This issue has been addressed to some extent in the literature on idioms (e.g. Bresnan, 1982a; Marantz, 1984); I do not know if it has been addressed in terms of the broader class of constructions. An intriguing possibility is to regard poetic meters and verse forms as phonological constructions that must unify with a text. And since we spoke in section 2 of song lyrics as being stored as large lexical items, we might be tempted to include as constructions those song lyrics that contain a variable to be filled creatively in successive verses, for instance the children's game song (2.27).

(2.27) Let everyone VP like me!
Let everyone VP like me!
Come on and join into the game,
You'll find that it's always the same.
(where VP is a one- or two-syllable VP naming an action, e.g. *clap hands, laugh, fall down*)

Another issue is how far the constructional approach extends into "core" grammar. Construction Grammar claims that *all* syntax is built from constructions clipped together. Different versions of Construction Grammar vary as to whether they claim all syntactic structures are form-meaning pairings, and therefore inherently meaningful (Goldberg, 1995, and Langacker, 1987; 1992, tend to think they are; Fillmore and Kay, 1993 are more agnostic). My own preference (Jackendoff, 1996) is to think that not all syntactic configurations are inherently meaningful – that the relation between form and meaning is often more flexible than in constructions like those we have seen here.

The view of constructions as lexical items however suggests an intriguing possibility: that phrase-structure rules may be formulated as lexical constructions. For example, (2.13), the expansion of VP into V plus NP plus PP/AP/Prt, could be a "defective" lexical item that encodes only syntactic structure, with no phonology or semantics. This could be clipped together with other lexical "treelets" (to use a term suggested by Janet Fodor) to form the usual phrase-structure trees. This manner of viewing tree construction begins to blur the distinction between lexical items and what have traditionally been regarded as rules of grammar. It reflects the same spirit as our treating regular morphology in section 3, not in terms of rules that add affixes, but rather as free combination of lexically stored parts. That is, the only "rule of grammar" is UNIFY PIECES, and all the pieces are stored in a common format that permits unification.[4] Ordinary words, which encode word-sized linked units of phonology, syntax, and semantics, are on the other end of a scale (or better, at an opposite corner of a multidimensional space) from phrase-structure rules, which encode phrase-sized pieces of syntax without any associated phonology or semantics. But we can attest every step on the scale in between them – and most of these steps are types of units that have raised difficulties for the standard syntactocentric architecture. It is too soon to tell how this program of unification will work out, but it sets an interesting agenda for future research.[5]

The present approach also has consequences for learnability of grammar. Going back to *Aspects*, the problem of learnability has traditionally been posed as how the child learns the rules of grammar, given knowledge of the words. In the course of time, it has become clear that learning words is itself a phenomenally difficult problem, and that word learning is often aided by knowledge of grammar (e.g. Carey, 1978; Macnamara, 1982; Landau and Gleitman, 1985; Pinker, 1989 and many others). The child learns tens of thousands of words, surely dwarfing the amount of information encoded in rules of grammar.

Of course children have to learn idioms too, which pose all the problems of learning word meanings. But given the present story, from the problem of learning idioms it is only a short step to the problem of learning constructional idioms of the sort discussed in section 5. The meanings of constructional idioms are about as complex as the meanings of words. Consider for instance the *time-away* construction, which

[4]In a sense this proposal thus begins to concur with the Minimalist Program, which creates structure by means of the single operation Merge. A major difference, of course, is that the present approach has no counterpart to the Minimalist Program's Move – not to mention the major architectural differences discussed in section 1.

[5]An important problem that has not to my knowledge been solved satisfactorily is how constructional idioms compose with each other. Examples like (i), a middle construction based on a resultative, and (ii), a relative clause based on a comparative correlative, are sufficiently remote from everyday experience that their constructional properties must be composed on-line.

(i) That pot doesn't cook black so easily.

(ii) This is a book that the more you study, the more confused you get.

In the traditional derivational formalism, of course, constructions like these arise from the successive application of movement rules. But successive application is not available in a constraint-based formalism.

means roughly 'spend time wastefully or frivolously doing something.' This meaning is comparable in complexity and subtlety to, say, *procrastinate*, 'spend time wastefully in order to avoid doing something', and so it should not be more difficult to learn (however children manage to do it!). On the other hand, the grammatical structure of a construction might be more difficult to learn than that of a word because it has more variables in it and less overt phonology to mark its presence. Going further, from constructions to phrase-structure rules and productive morphology is again only a short formal step, so the problems of learnability for these phenomena might come to take on a different complexion, closer to the problem of word learning.

Above all, what I would like the reader to take away from the present essay is the importance of psychological considerations in the theory of grammar. By taking very seriously the question of what is stored and what is computed on-line, we have managed to justify a major reorganization of the theory of grammar. If this is letting the theory of performance intrude on the theory of competence, so be it. For my own taste, such interaction between the two theories is the proper way for linguistic research to proceed in the future.

Acknowledgments

The material developed here has benefited from numerous opportunities I have had to present it in talks, not the least of which was the Conference on Storage and Computation in Utrecht on which the present volume is based. I am indebted to Sieb Nooteboom and the rest of the UiL OTS staff for making that conference such a rewarding experience. Of all the interesting questions and comments I have had to field, I want to single out a very perspicuous remark by Steve Pinker that enabled me to see the scope of the unification achieved in section 5. Adele Goldberg has been an unending source of wisdom and enthusiasm on constructions for the past ten years. Marc Hauser, Heike Wiese, and the editors have offered useful comments on an earlier version of the paper. Above all, I am overwhelmingly grateful to the Wissenschaftskolleg zu Berlin, where the text of this article was written during my 1999-2000 residence as a Fellow.

This research was also supported in part by NIH Grant DC03660 to Brandeis University. A slightly different version of this chapter appears as part of chapter 6 of my *Foundations of Language* (Oxford University Press, 2001).

References

Anderson, S. R. (1992). *A-morphous morphology*. New York: Cambridge University Press.

Aronoff, M. (1976). *Word formation in generative grammar*. Cambridge, MA: MIT Press.

Baayen, R.H., Levelt, W., and Haveman, A. (1993). Research reported in annual report of the Max-Planck Institut für Psycholinguistik, 6. Technical report, Nijmegen: Max-Planck Institut.

Baayen, R.H., Van Casteren, V. C., and Dijkstra, T. (1992). Research reported in annual report of the Max-Planck Institut für Psycholinguistik, 28. Technical report, Nijmegen: Max-Planck Institut.

Baayen, R. H., Schreuder, R., De Jong, N. H., and Krott, A. (2001). Dutch inflection: The rules that prove the exception. *This volume.*

Baker, M. (1988). *Incorporation: A theory of grammatical function changing*. Chicago: University of Chicago Press.

Berent, I., Pinker, S., and Shimron, J. (1999). Default nominal inflection in Hebrew: Evidence for mental variables. *Cognition*, 72:1–44.

Berko, J. (1958). The child's learning of English morphology. *Word*, 14:150–177.

Bloomfield, L. (1933). *Language*. London: George Allen & Unwin Ltd. 7th printing 1962.

Bresnan, J. W. (1978). A realistic transformational grammar. In Halle, M., Bresnan, J. W., and Miller, G., editors, *Linguistic theory and psychological reality*, pages 1–59. Cambridge, MA: MIT Press.

Bresnan, J. W. (1982a). Control and complementation. In Bresnan, J. W., editor, *The mental representation of grammatical relations*, pages 282–390. Cambridge, MA: MIT Press.

Bresnan, J. W., editor (1982b). *The mental representation of grammatical relations*. Cambridge, MA: MIT Press.

Bybee, J. and Moder, C. (1983). Morphological classes as natural categories. *Language*, 59:251–270.

Carey, S. (1978). The child as word learner. In Halle, M., Bresnan, J. W., and Miller, G., editors, *Linguistic theory and psychological reality*, pages 264–293. Cambridge, MA: MIT Press.

Chomsky, N. (1957). *Syntactic structures*. The Hague: Mouton.

Chomsky, N. (1965). *Aspects of the theory of syntax*. Cambridge MA: MIT Press.

Chomsky, N. (1981). *Lectures on government and binding*. Dordrecht: Foris.

Chomsky, N. (1995). *The minimalist program*. Cambridge, MA: MIT Press.

Chomsky, N. and Halle, M. (1968). *The sound pattern of English.* New York: Harper & Row.

Clahsen, H. and Almazan, M. (1998). Syntax and morphology in Williams syndrome. *Cognition*, 68:167–198.

Culicover, P. (1972). OM-sentences. *Foundations of Language*, 8:199–236.

Culicover, P. and Jackendoff, R. (1997). Semantic subordination despite syntactic coordination. *Linguistic Inquiry*, 28:195–217.

Culicover, P. and Jackendoff, R. (1999). The view from the periphery: The English correlative conditional. *Linguistic Inquiry*, 30:543–571.

Dalrymple, M., Kaplan, R., Maxwell, J. T., and Zaenen, A., editors (1995). *Formal issues in Lexical-Functional Grammar.* Stanford: CSLI Publications.

Deacon, T. (1997). *The symbolic species.* London: Allen Lane, the Penguin Press/New York: Norton.

Di Sciullo, A. M. and Williams, E. (1987). *On the definition of word.* Cambridge, MA: MIT Press.

Edelman, G. (1992). *Bright air, brilliant fire; On the matter of the mind.* London: Penguin Books/New York: Basic Books.

Elman, J., Bates, E., Johnson, M., Karmiloff-Smith, A., Parisi, D., and Plunkett, K. (1996). *Rethinking innateness. A connectionist perspective on development.* Cambridge, MA: MIT Press.

Emonds, J. E. (1970). *Root and structure-preserving transformations.* PhD thesis, MIT.

Fillmore, C. and Kay, P. (1993). *Construction Grammar coursebook.* Berkeley: Department of Linguistics, University of California, Berkeley.

Fillmore, C., Kay, P., and O'Connor, M. C. (1988). Regularity and idiomaticity in grammatical constructions: The case of *let alone. Language*, 64:501–538.

Goldberg, A. (1995). *Constructions: A Construction Grammar approach to argument structure.* Chicago: University of Chicago Press.

Goldsmith, J. (1976). *Autosegmental phonology.* PhD thesis, MIT. Distributed by Indiana University Linguistics Club, Bloomington.

Gopnik, M. (1999). Some evidence for impaired grammars. In Jackendoff, R., Bloom, P., and Wynn, K., editors, *Language, logic, and concepts*, pages 263–283. Cambridge, MA: MIT Press.

Hale, K. and Keyser, S. J. (1993). On argument structure and the lexical expression of syntactic relations. In Hale, K. and Keyser, S. J., editors, *The view from Building 20*, pages 53–109. Cambridge, MA: MIT Press.

Halle, M. (1973). Prolegomena to a theory of word-formation. *Linguistic Inquiry*, 4:3–16.

Halle, M., Bresnan, J., and Miller, G., editors (1978). *Linguistic theory and psychological reality*. Cambridge, MA: MIT Press.

Hankamer, J. (1989). Morphological parsing and the lexicon. In Marslen-Wilson, W., editor, *Lexical representation and process*, pages 392–408. Cambridge, MA: MIT Press.

Hare, M., Elman, J., and Daugherty, K. (1995). Default generalization in connectionist networks. *Language and Cognitive Processes*, 10:601–630.

Jackendoff, R. (1975). Morphological and semantic regularities in the lexicon. *Language*, 51:639–671.

Jackendoff, R. (1978). Grammar as evidence for conceptual structure. In Halle, M., Bresnan, J., and Miller, G., editors, *Linguistic theory and psychological reality*, pages 201–228. Cambridge, MA: MIT Press.

Jackendoff, R. (1983). *Semantics and cognition*. Cambridge, MA: MIT Press.

Jackendoff, R. (1990). *Semantic structures*. Cambridge, MA: MIT Press.

Jackendoff, R. (1996). Conceptual semantics and cognitive semantics. *Cognitive Linguistics*, 7:93–129.

Jackendoff, R. (1997a). *The architecture of the language faculty*. Cambridge, MA: MIT Press.

Jackendoff, R. (1997b). Twistin' the night away. *Language*, 73:534–559.

Jackendoff, R. (2001). *Foundations of language*. Oxford: Oxford University Press.

Katz, J. and Fodor, J. (1963). The structure of a semantic theory. *Language*, 39:170–210.

Katz, J. and Postal, P. M. (1964). *An integrated theory of linguistic descriptions*. Cambridge, MA: MIT Press.

Lakoff, G. (1987). *Women, fire, and dangerous things*. Chicago: University of Chicago Press.

Landau, B. and Gleitman, L. (1985). *Language and experience: Evidence from the blind child*. Cambridge, MA: Harvard University Press.

Langacker, R. (1987). *Foundations of cognitive grammar*, volume 1. Stanford: Stanford University Press.

Langacker, R. (1992). The symbolic nature of cognitive grammar: The meaning of *of* and *of*-periphrasis. In Pütz, M., editor, *Thirty years of linguistic evolution*, pages 483–502. Amsterdam/Philadelphia: John Benjamins.

Langacker, R. (1998). Conceptualization, symbolization, and grammar. In Tomasello, M., editor, *The New Psychology of Language*, pages 1–39. Hillsdale, NJ: Erlbaum.

Levin, B. and Rappaport Hovav, M. (1991). Wiping the slate clean: A lexical semantic exploration. *Cognition*, 41:123–151.

Liberman, M. and Prince, A. (1977). On stress and linguistic rhythm. *Linguistic Inquiry*, 8:249–336.

Macnamara, J. (1982). *Names for things.* Cambridge, MA: MIT Press.

Marantz, A. (1984). *On the nature of grammatical relations.* Cambridge, MA: MIT Press.

Marantz, A. (1992). The *way*-construction and the semantics of direct arguments in English: A reply to Jackendoff. In Stowell, T. and Wehrli, E., editors, *Syntax and the lexicon*, volume 26, pages 179–188. San Diego: Academic Press.

Marcus, G. (1998). Rethinking eliminative connectionism. *Cognitive Psychology*, 37:243–282.

Marcus, G. (2001). *The algebraic mind.* Cambridge, MA: MIT Press.

Marcus, G., Brinkmann, U., Clahsen, H., Wiese, R., and Pinker, S. (1995). German inflection: The exception that proves the rule. *Cognitive Psychology*, 29:186–256.

McCarthy, J. (1982). Prosodic structure and expletive infixation. *Language*, 58:574–590.

McCawley, J. D. (1988). The comparative conditional construction in English, German, and Chinese. In *Proceedings of the 14th Annual Meeting of the Berkeley Linguistics Society*, pages 176–187. Berkeley: Berkeley Linguistics Society.

Nunberg, G., Sag, I., and Wasow, T. (1994). Idioms. *Language*, 70:491–538.

Partee, B. (1975). Montague grammar and transformational grammar. *Linguistic Inquiry*, 6:203–300.

Partee, B., editor (1976). *Montague Grammar.* New York, Academic Press.

Pinker, S. (1989). *Learnability and cognition: The acquisition of argument structure.* Cambridge, MA: MIT Press.

Pinker, S. (1999). *Words and rules.* Weidenfeld & Nicholson/New York: Basic Books.

Pinker, S. and Prince, A. (1988). On language and connectionism: Analysis of a parallel distributed processing model of language acquisition. *Cognition*, 26:195–267.

Pinker, S. and Prince, A. (1991). Regular and irregular morphology and the psychological status of rules of grammar. In *Proceedings of the 17th Annual Meeting of the Berkeley Linguistics Society*, pages 230–251. Berkeley: Berkeley Linguistics Society.

Plunkett, K. and Marchman, V. (1991). U-shaped learning and frequency effects in a multi-layered perceptron: Implications for child language acquisition. *Cognition*, 49:21–69.

Pollard, C. and Sag, I. (1994). *Head-Driven Phrase Structure Grammar.* Chicago: University of Chicago Press.

Pollock, J.-Y. (1989). Verb movement, universal grammar, and the structure of IP. *Linguistic Inquiry*, 20:365–424.

Prasada, S. and Pinker, S. (1993). Similarity-based and rule-based generalizations in inflectional morphology. *Language and Cognitive Processes*, 8:1–56.

Rumelhart, D. and McClelland, J. (1986). On learning the past tense of English verbs. In McClelland, J., Rumelhart, D., and the PDP Research Group, editors, *Parallel distributed processing*, volume 2, pages 216–271. Cambridge, MA: MIT Press.

Ruwet, N. (1991). *Syntax and human experience.* Chicago: University of Chicago Press.

Sadock, J. (1991). *Autolexical syntax.* Chicago: University of Chicago Press.

Shastri, L. and Ajjanagadde, V. (1993). From simple associations to systematic reasoning: A connectionist representation of rules, variables, and dynamic bindings using temporal synchrony. *Behavioral and Brain Sciences*, 16:417–494.

Spencer, A. (1991). *Morphological theory.* Oxford: Blackwell.

Toivonen, I. (1999). The directed motion construction in Swedish. Ms., CSLI, Stanford.

Van der Lely, H. (1999). Learning from grammatical SLI. *Trends in Cognitive Sciences*, 3:286–288.

Van Valin, R. and LaPolla, R. (1997). *Syntax: Structure, meaning and function.* Cambridge: Cambridge University Press.

Williams, E. (1994). Remarks on lexical knowledge. In Gleitman, L. and Landau, B., editors, *The acquisition of the lexicon*, pages 7–34. Cambridge, MA: MIT Press.

Zwicky, A. (1988). Morphological rules, operations and operation types. In *Proceedings of the Eastern States Conference on Linguistics*, volume 4, pages 318–334.

II

ACCESSING REGULAR AND IRREGULAR WORD FORMS

Chapter 3

DUTCH INFLECTION: THE RULES THAT PROVE THE EXCEPTION

Harald Baayen,
Robert Schreuder,
Nivja de Jong
and Andrea Krott

Abstract This chapter addresses the balance of storage and computation in the mental lexicon for fully regular and productive inflectional processes in Dutch. We present evidence that both regular inflected nouns and regular inflected verbs show clear and robust effects of storage, but that at the same time on-line parsing also plays a role. We argue that the balance of storage and computation cannot be predicted on the basis of economy of linguistic description. Instead, a range of cognitive and linguistic factors are crucial determinants.

Keywords: Morphological processing, frequency effects, dual route modelling, inflection, regularity, economy of description, defaults.

1. Introduction

This chapter addresses the issue of the balance of storage and computation for regular inflected words in Dutch in language comprehension. Traditionally, this question has not been an issue in linguistics. Ever since Bloomfield, 1933, the lexicon has been the repository of idiosyncracies. Listing in the lexicon is restricted to monomorphemic words and to complex words that are not predictable by rule, whether at the level of form or at the level of meaning. For linguistics as a descriptive discipline, this approach is justified, as the listing of complex words sharing features that can be predicted by rule implies the loss of generalizations.

In computational linguistics, practical considerations have led researchers to store the shorter complex words in their parsing programs in order to minimize the costs of having to analyze — on-line — such often highly

S. Nooteboom et al. (eds.), Storage and Computation in the Language Faculty, 61–92.

ambiguous and frequent forms. In recent computational approaches such as data-oriented parsing (Bod, 1998) and lazy learning (Daelemans et al., 1999), extensive storage of regular words and multi-word structures is used to optimize on-line performance. In these approaches, the data are the primary source of information, and no attempt is made to extract explicitly from the data rules for analysing unseen constructions.

In psycholinguistics, the complete range of possible trade-offs between storage and computation has found its defenders. Butterworth, 1983 was the first to formulate the hypothesis that complex words in a language such as English are extensively stored in the mental lexicon, and that parsing is a back-up analogical procedure used only for the rare instances in which novel forms are encountered. Connectionist models of the kind advocated by Seidenberg, 1987 are implementations of this position using a framework in which distributed data storage takes place without any role for explicit morphological rules. Effects of morphological structure observed in on-line processing experiments are, in this approach, an epiphenomenon of statistical regularities between input and output patterns. The opposite extreme has been defended by Pinker, 1991; Marcus et al., 1995; Clahsen et al., 1997 and Clahsen, 1999. Their approach assumes that Bloomfield's position is an adequate characterization of the balance of storage and computation in human language processing. An intermediate position has led to the formulation of a parallel dual route model (Schreuder and Baayen, 1995), in which rules and memory-based retrieval operate in parallel.

The aim of the present chapter is to address the question of the balance of storage and computation for regular inflected words. Authors such as Pinker, Marcus, Clahsen, and also Jaeger et al., 1996 have argued that regular and irregular inflected complex words are processed differently by the brain, irregulars being handled by memory-based retrieval, and regulars being handled by rule (but see Plunkett and Juola, 1999, and Seidenberg and Hoeffner, 1998, for alternative interpretations of the data). One of the arguments used by Pinker and Clahsen concerns the occurrence of frequency effects for complex words, which they argue to be restricted to irregular complex words.

There are two distinguishable token frequency effects. The Surface Frequency Effect concerns the finding that the frequency of occurrence of a complex word such as *walks* can be an important predictor of response latencies in a variety of word recognition tasks. The Base Frequency Effect concerns the observation that the frequency of the lexeme *walk*, i.e., the summed token frequency of *walk* and all its inflectional variants, can also be an important predictor of such response latencies. The effects of Surface Frequency and Base Frequency are independent, as shown by

Taft, 1979 and Burani et al., 1984 for English and Italian inflected words. The existence of a Surface Frequency Effect is generally interpreted as evidence for storage of the inflected word as a whole at some level of representation. The existence of a Base Frequency Effect indicates that at some point during lexical access the base word itself has been accessed. The claim advanced by Pinker and Clahsen is that for regular inflected words only Base Frequency Effects should be observed and no Surface Frequency Effects.

Our research, however, has revealed very reliable Surface Frequency Effects for regular inflected words. For Dutch, Italian, and English, regular noun plurals show substantial Surface Frequency Effects (Baayen et al., 1997a; 1997b; Sereno and Jongman, 1997; and Allegre and Gordon, 1999. In Finnish, such an effect has been reported for regular partitive noun plurals, even though Finnish is a language with a very rich morphology (Bertram et al., 2000b). In Dutch, furthermore, fully regular comparatives have been found to show Surface Frequency Effects (Bertram et al., 2000c). These results call into question the idea that the economy of linguistic description, which requires maximization of rule-based description and minimization of list-based description, can be mapped directly onto the domain of lexical processing in the mental lexicon. In the cognitive domain, it is not a priori self-evident that the costs of processing by rule are less than the costs of storage (Frauenfelder and Schreuder, 1992). The storage capacity of the human brain is enormous (Landauer, 1986), and it is well known from various cognitive domains (e.g., hand reaches, Rosenbaum et al., 1992, and arithmetic, Rickard et al., 1994) that storage may take over when computations become complex and time-consuming. In the domain of morphological processing, storage might likewise be a useful mechanism complementing rule-based access.

Moreover, from a more general linguistic point of view, storage for regular noun plurals as observed by Baayen et al., 1997b is not that surprising either. Tiersma, 1982 has pointed out that high-frequency plural forms are what he called locally unmarked. Normally, plurals are formally and semantically marked with respect to their singulars, as in the case of *nose* versus *noses*. On the other hand, plurals that are much more frequently used than their corresponding singulars tend to be semantically unmarked. For instance, *eyes* and *feet* are unmarked in the sense that they represent the default occurence of the objects they refer to. Tiersma shows that locally unmarked plural nouns serve as attractors in language change, which implies that such nouns must have been stored in the mental lexicon. Cross-linguistically, it is precisely the locally unmarked plural forms that emerge as simplex forms in languages such as Bari (Eastern Nilotic), which uses a singulative suffix to derive the singular form of a monomorphemic semantic plural noun (e.g., *kuru*, 'worms', *kuru-töt*, 'worm', Dimmendaal, 1987).

Clahsen et al., 1997, however, have suggested another reason why effects of storage might have been observed for Dutch noun plurals, namely, their supposed irregularity. Clahsen and his colleagues argue that a more subtle notion of regularity is called for than the one used in traditional grammars (Clahsen et al., 1997, p.208). In order to ascertain whether the plural noun suffixes of Dutch fall into what they call the regular cluster, the properties of Dutch noun plurals would have to be checked against a reference list of linguistic criteria for regularity as proposed by Marcus et al., 1995, p.197. In this approach, the traditional notion of regularity has been replaced by the notion of default. Default forms are said to be free of morphological restrictions and lexical governance, they are claimed to attract members of non-default classes in historical change. Loan words and marginal forms such as acronyms and abbreviations are also analyzed to fall into default classes.

Other scholars have likewise questioned the regularity of the Dutch plural suffixes (Gordon, 1985; Pinker and Prince, 1988; 1991), on the basis of the occurrence of Dutch noun plurals in compounds, and on the basis of the plurals being rival affixes.

In what follows, we will examine this important alternative explanation for why storage effects in lexical processing might arise: irregularity. If it is indeed the case that some form of irregularity is the driving force behind any storage in the mental lexicon, then irregularity would overrule more general cognitive considerations concerning the balance of storage and computation in general. Before assigning primacy to irregularity as the driving force behind lexical storage, we should consider in detail whether it is linguistically justified to describe Dutch noun pluralization as in some sense irregular. In section 2, we therefore examine noun plural formation in Dutch with respect to the notion of default developed by Marcus et al., 1995. We will show that the system of noun pluralization is regular, and that native speakers of Dutch coin new noun plurals exactly as predicted. In section 3, we will proceed to show that Surface Frequency Effects may also appear for fully regular verbal inflections which can only be described as default suffixes. At the same time, we will show that these Surface Frequency effects can occur simultaneously with Base Frequency effects, suggesting that storage and computation are not mutually exclusive. In the General Discussion, we will integrate our findings from the regular nominal and regular verbal inflectional domains, and we will trace some of the resulting theoretical consequences.

2. Dutch noun plurals

In this section, we first present an outline of the rules governing the distribution of the plural suffixes in Dutch. We then proceed to show that speakers of Dutch apply these rules consistently without problems to phonotactically legal pseudowords, which illustrates that pluralization is indeed rule-governed.

2.1. The rules

There are three plural suffixes in Dutch: *-en*, *-s*, and *-eren*. The latter suffix occurs only in 15 nouns, and need not concern us here.

There are five factors that determine the distribution of *-en* and *-s*, both of which are fully productive. The main factor is the phonological structure of the base word: *-s* appears after unstressed syllables, and *-en* appears after stressed syllables. From the phonological point of view, *-s* and *-en* are in complementary distribution, and can be considered synchronically as suppletive forms. There are some further phonological restrictions: Words ending in a full stressed vowel often select *-s* rather than *-en*, which may be due to avoid a sequence of two non-homorganic vowels: *pa's*, 'dads'. Furthermore, if a word already ends in an *-s*, the appropriate suffix is *-en*: *cactussen.*

A second important factor is morphological in nature. Some suffixes always require *-en*, e.g., *-ing*, '-ing', other suffixes only take *-s*, e.g., the diminutive suffix *-tje*, while yet others allow both, e.g., *-isme*, '-ism'.

Third, loan words select *-s*, e.g., *stations, trams, jeeps.*

Fourth, the *-s* tends to be selected for persons as opposed to things, especially in the case of homonyms: *portiers*, 'doorkeepers' versus *portieren*, 'car doors'.

Fifth, both suffixes are possible for nouns ending in a schwa (*kade*: *kades, kaden*, 'quay'); more formal registers prefer the suffix *-en*.

The existence of choice for words ending in a schwa can be understood in terms of the general preference for disyllabic trochees in Germanic (see Booij, 1998, for an account in terms of optimality theory). Both *kades* and *kaden* as plural forms of *kade* satisfy this rhythmic constraint (Van Haeringen, 1947) of Dutch. There are words for which the first factor (the rhythmic principle) clashes with the fourth factor, which specifies *-s* as the choice for person names. In such cases, both suffixes can be used: *directeur*, 'director', has as plural forms both *directeurs* (by factor 4) and *directeuren* (by factor 1).

Finally, there are also some exceptions to these rules, such as *wonder*, 'miracle', which has as its plural *wonderen* instead of *wonders.* In a linguistic description, these exceptions can be handled by listing, just as the irregular plurals in *-eren* must be listed.

In sum, *-en* and *-s* are typical rival suffixes in the sense of Van Marle, 1986. Each suffix has its own specific input domain, defined on several dimensions: phonology, morphology, semantics, and register. On each dimension, there is a regular division of labor between the two suffixes, although the overall outcome of their affixal rivalry may lead to both suffixes being acceptable for particular subdomains.

Having outlined the system of Dutch plural formation, we now consider whether the notion of default in the sense of Marcus et al., 1995 and Clahsen et al., 1997 can be applied to the complementary distribution of Dutch noun plurals. The study of Marcus et al., 1995 contrasts irregular inflection with regular inflection for German. This study claims that the German *-s* plural is the default, that because it is the default it is processed by rule, while all other German noun plurals fall outside the regularity cluster and are processed by means of retrieval from memory. The use of the term default for a particular morphological operation that can be used when other morphological operations with idiosyncratic input domains do not apply has a long history that goes back to Panini, and that has been formalized in morphological theory as the elsewhere condition (Kiparsky, 1973; 1982). Marcus et al., 1995 and Clahsen et al., 1997 use the notion of default to denote the elsewhere condition, and by taking the default to be prototypically regular, non-default operations now fall outside the regularity complex and become in some sense irregular. This amounts to the idea that whenever more than one affix is available for the realization of an inflectional function, only one of these affixes can be truly regular.

Is this notion of default applicable to the Dutch noun plurals? According to Marcus et al., 1995, a default suffix is marked by a wide range of different but converging properties:

First, the default affix is used for words that do not have an entry in the mental lexicon. By this criterion, however, both *-en* and *-s* are defaults. Nonwords such as *snarp* and *krilgem* pluralize as *snarpen* and *krilgems* by factor 1.

Second, the default affix is selected for expressing a more specialized meaning than carried by the irregular form, e.g, hanged *for a form of execution instead of* hung. According to this criterion, the *-s* would be the default, as it intrudes into the phonological input domain of *-en* to denote persons (*portiers*, 'door keepers', compare *portieren*, 'car doors').

Third, the default is the affix to attach to non-canonical roots: onomatopeia, quotations, surnames, acronyms, unassimilated borrowings. As we have seen, *-s* is used in Dutch for unassimilated borrowings, but here we should keep in mind that many loan words may be borrowed together with their plural form, which, in the case of borrowings from English or French, already may have a plural in *-s*. Moreover, the *-en* is not available as a noun plural for loan words, because it functions as a verbal ending both for indigenous verbs and for loan words: the conversion verb *trammen* means 'to go by tram' and *computeren* means 'to use a computer', while *trams* and *computers* are the plurals of *tram* and *computer*. Hence, the force of the argument that *-s* would be the default because it attaches to loan words is unclear.

Both *-s* and *-en* attach to surnames. When proper names are pluralized, the phonological form of the base determines the choice of suffix: *de Neit-en*, *de Levelt-s*. Often, the rhythmic principle applies (e.g., *PA-BOs*, *HATten*), but equally often both plural suffixes can be used. This criterion does not allow us to select either affix as the default.

Fourth, the default suffix attaches to words that normally do not undergo inflection. In Dutch, the rhythmic principle again determines the choice: *of-en*, 'ifs', *maar-en*, 'buts', *buitens*, 'outs', and *binnens*, 'ins'. This suggests again that there is no simple default in Dutch.

Fifth, exocentric formations require the default suffix. Again, the rhythmic principle determines the choice between *-s* and *-en*, and not default status. For instance, the noun *schip* has the irregular plural *schepen*. However, the plural of *schip* when mentioned meta-linguistically rather than used is *schippen*, not *schips*. When a word such as *lepel*, 'spoon', is to be pluralized when mentioned instead of used, its plural will not differ from the standard plural, *lepels*. Similarly, we have two *Mercedes-CLen* and three *Citroen-Saxo's*.

Sixth, under memory failure, the default affix is used. Although we have no concrete data on speech errors for Dutch noun plurals, our intuition is that the rhythmic principle is so strong that for monomorphemic words errors will be few and evenly balanced between *-en* and *-s*.

Summing up, there are two pieces of evidence that suggest that *-s* might be the default in Dutch, namely, its use for loan words, and its use to denote persons, but these two criteria are not compelling, and they are counterbalanced by massive evidence that *-en* shares all other default properties with *-s*. We conclude that the Dutch plural system does not have a clear default in the sense of Marcus et al., 1995 or Clahsen et al., 1997. In fact, the six clusters of criteria provide an elegant series of lithmus tests for productive regularity once 'default' is replaced by 'regular'. Both *-en* and *-s* are regular fully productive suffixes in this sense.

However, Pinker and Prince, 1991 argue that the complementary distribution of *-en* and *-s* in Dutch indicates that these suffixes would not have unrestricted productivity. It is unclear to us in what sense this would call the regularity of the Dutch plural system into question. The complementary distribution of rival affixes has indeed been interpreted as qualitatively restricting productivity (Schultink, 1961; Booij, 1977; Van Marle, 1985), but quantitatively these qualitative restrictions have little or no weight. For instance, the verb-forming prefix *ver-* attaches to verbs (*verslaan*, 'to beat', from *slaan*, 'to hit'), to nouns (*verhuis*, 'to move house', from *huis*, 'house'), and to adjectives (*vergroot*, 'to magnify', from *groot*, 'big') and occurs with some 950 formations in the CELEX lexical database (Baayen et al., 1995). In terms of its input domain, the suffix *-heid* ('-ness' in English) is far more restricted in that it attaches only to adjectives. Nevertheless, 3017 formations in *-heid* are attested in CELEX. Even though *ver-* has fewer restrictions as to word category than *-heid*, which would predict that *ver-* should be more productive than *-heid*, the reverse holds: *-heid* is more productive than *ver-*. Clearly, the number of qualitative restrictions has little to say about how often an affix is used or might be used potentially in the language (see Baayen, 1992; 1993; Baayen and Renouf, 1996, for detailed discussion).

Therefore, the simple fact that *-en* and *-s* are in regular complementary distribution cannot by itself constitute evidence for or against the regularity or default status of *-s* or *-en*. In fact, the traditional notion of being in complementary distribution is perpendicular to the notion of regularity. The complementary distribution of the English plural suffix *-s/-z/-iz* has, as far as we know, never been proposed as evidence that this suffix and its phonological alternants should be classified as irregular or outside a regularity complex.

In the light of these considerations, we conclude that Dutch noun plurals in *-en* and *-s* are fully regular. Hence, we maintain that the experimental evidence reported in Baayen et al., 1997b shows that fully regular inflected words can be stored in the mental lexicon.

2.2. The rules applied

In order to make sure that the rules governing the distribution of the plural suffixes *-s* and *-en* described above are truly predictive, we carried out a simple production experiment in which participants had to build plural forms for pseudoword singulars.

Experiment 1

Method

Participants. 49 participants, mostly undergraduates at Nijmegen University, were paid to take part in this experiment. All were native speakers of Dutch.

Materials. We constructed 80 pseudowords, none of which violated the phonotactic rules of Dutch. In order to test the rhythmic principle, 10 of these were stressed one-syllable pseudowords (e.g., *dréip*) whose plural suffix is predicted to be *-en*, and 10 were two-syllable pseudowords with an unstressed final syllable (e.g., *wórkel*) whose plural suffix is predicted to be *-s*. Ten pseudowords were two-syllable words ending in schwa whose plural, according to the rhythmic principle, can be built with either *-(e)n* or *-s*. Ten two-syllable pseudowords with an unstressed final syllable ended with the consonant *s*. These words are predicted to take *-en* as plural suffix. Ten words ended in a full stressed vowel, 5 ending in *-ee* (e.g., *stree*), and 5 ending in *-a* (e.g., *kna*). The rhythmic principle predicts the plural suffix *-en*, but the suffix *-s* is also possible in order to avoid a sequence of two non-homorganic vowels. To test the morphological factor we created 10 pseudowords for three kinds of derived words: *-ing* derivations (e.g., *bestroet-ing*) whose plural suffix should be *-en*, *-tje* derivations (e.g., *kloer-tje*) whose plural suffix should be *-s*, and *-isme* derivations (e.g., *kad-isme*) whose plural suffix can be either *-en* or *-s* according to the rhythmic principle. The materials are listed in Appendix A. Word stress was not indicated in the test materials, as all words were patterned on the germanic word-initial stress pattern, and as the only set with real orthographic ambiguity (the set with two syllable pseudowords ending in a final *s*) are, because of the final *s*, words which must pluralize in *-en* independent of the stress pattern assigned.

*Procedure.*The experiment was a paper and pencil task. Participants were asked to write down the plural forms for a list of pseudowords. The experiment lasted approximately 5 minutes.

Results and discussion

In our analysis, we counted only responses built with the plural suffixes *-en* or *-s*, not including 72 (1.8%) responses which were mostly constructed with latinate plural suffixes, which we regarded as errors. (Such latinate plurals were produced for pseudowords ending in, e.g., *us*, a nominative singular ending in Latin.) Table 3.1 shows the number of responses for the nine experimental conditions.

In the experimental conditions for which the plural suffix *-en* was expected, participants used this suffix for 96.3% up to 100% of the pseudo-

Table 3.1. Experiment 1: Number and percentage of pseudoword plurals in *-s* and *-en*.

condition	*expected suffix*	*S*	*%S*	*EN*	*%EN*
dréip	*-en*	18	3.7	469	96.3
wórkel	*-s*	469	97.9	10	2.1
bástus	*-en*	0	0	445	100
bestroet-ing	*-en*	5	1.0	484	99.0
kloer-tje	*-s*	488	99.6	2	0.4
kna	both	198	81.1	46	18.9
stree	both	73	29.8	172	70.2
stape	both	144	29.6	343	70.4
kad-isme	both	120	24.9	362	75.1

singulars to create a plural noun. When the plural suffix *-s* was expected, 97.9% up to 99.6% of the plural forms were indeed built with *-s*. In the case where both suffixes are possible, the preference for one particular suffix was never greater than 81.1%. The suffix *-en* was used more often when the pseudoword ended in a schwa (70.4%), the full vowel *e* (70.2%), or in the suffix *-isme* (75.1%). When the pseudoword ended in *a*, participants preferred an *-s* (81.1%).

For the first 5 conditions in Table 3.1, the choice of plural suffix is deterministic according to the rules. This is reflected in the behavior of our participants, who selected the predicted suffix for 2355/2390 = 98.5% of the pseudo singulars. For the remaining four vowel-final conditions, both plural endings are possible in principle, and again this is what we find in our data. We observe that *-s* appears to be the preferred choice (81%) for words in *a*, while words in *-e* and schwa as well as words in *-isme* select *-en* for roughly 70% of the pseudowords. Note that variability of suffix choice for the subsets of pseudowords labelled 'both' in Table 3.1, for which the rules of plural formation in Dutch are non-deterministic, is of another order of magnitude (*-s* is selected in 30% up to 80% of the pseudowords) than the variability that is not predicted by the rules (100% - 98.5% = 1.5% with the incorrect suffix, calculated for the first 5 sets in Table 3.1 jointly). Also note that *-s* is the dominant choice for one of the non-deterministic subdomains (final *a*), while *-en* is the dominant choice for the other non-deterministic subdomains. This shows that it is impossible to designate *-en* or *-s* as default on the basis of overall dominance in the non-deterministic subdomains.

In order to ascertain whether the observed differences are reliable, we used a classification and regression tree analysis (Breiman et al., 1984) to predict the choice of plural suffix from the independent variables Rhythmic Principle (stressed or unstressed final syllable), Morphology (*-ing*, *-tje*, *-isme* or monomorphemic), and Phonology (final *a*, *e*, final schwa, final s, or other). Using 10-fold cross-validation and cost-complexity pruning (Venables and Ripley, 1994), we obtained a classification tree which identified the sets separated by horizontal lines in Table 3.1 as statistically reliable distinct subclasses.

The fact that participants are able to form plural forms for pseudo-singulars according to the rules for plural formation in Dutch confirms that the system of plural formation in Dutch is truly fully regular and productive.

In the next section we will present experimental evidence that not only fully regular noun plurals are stored, as shown by Baayen et al., 1997b, but that also fully regular inflected verbs which have no rival 'suppletive' affix in the language reveal substantial effects of storage. At the same time, we will argue that the very same data also shed light on the circumstances under which the parsing route will contribute effectively to lexical access.

3. Dutch verbal inflections

We have seen that there are no compelling linguistic reasons to assume that the Dutch noun plural suffixes are in some sense irregular. In fact, it has proved to be very difficult to designate either suffix as being or not being a default. In this section we report three visual lexical decision experiments concerning verbal morphological inflectional processes for which the question of default status does not arise, simply because there are no rival morphological processes in the language realizing the same semantic and syntactic functions. Is it possible to observe Surface Frequency Effects for inflected words of this kind?

The first experiment investigates the perfect participle, which in Dutch is formed by the circumfix *ge- -D*, where /D/ represents an alveolar stop that is realized either as a /d/ or as a /t/ depending on the phonological context. In our experiment, we have used only words that are written in the orthography with a final *d*: *gewandeld*, 'walked'. We have used a simple factorial design in which two sets of words are compared: words with on average a high Surface Frequency, and words with on average a low Surface Frequency. The two sets of words were matched with respect to Base Frequency and Family Size, the number of derived words and compounds in which the base word appears as a constituent (see Schreuder and Baayen, 1997; Bertram et al., 2000a; De Jong et al., 2000). If Surface Frequency plays a role during lexical processing, then a difference in the mean reaction times for the two groups should be observed, with shorter response latencies for the words with the higher Surface Frequencies, which would indicate that these regular participles are stored in the mental lexicon.

The second experiment applies the same experimental design to the plural past tense suffix *-Den*, using only words in which the /D/ is realized orthographically and phonologically as *-d*: *wandelden*, 'we/you/they walked'. The third experiment similarly studies the present participle suffix *-end*, as in *wandelend*, 'walking'. None of these experiments contained any irregular complex word whatsoever.

Experiment 2

Method

Participants. 25 participants, mostly undergraduates at Nijmegen University, were paid to take part in this experiment. All were native speakers of Dutch.

Materials. We selected 60 regular perfect participles with the circumfix *ge- -d* (e.g., *gegrijnsd*, 'grinned') from the CELEX lexical database, which is based on a corpus of 42 million wordforms. Thirty of these participles had a high Surface Frequency with an average of 18.34 (range 4.52–70.24, $\hat{s}$ 15.03), and 30 had a low Surface Frequency with an average of 0.94 (range 0.00–12.40, $\hat{s}$ 2.52) per million. The two sets were matched for Base Frequency (high: mean 118.44, range 9.76–430.88, $\hat{s}$ 118.18; low: mean 118.23, range 10.36–430.69, $\hat{s}$ 116.60), Family Size (high: mean 51.8, range 1–243, $\hat{s}$ 55.3; low: mean 50.9, range 3–282, $\hat{s}$ 57.7), and for mean length in letters (high: 7.9, low: 7.7). Note that matching for base frequency implies implicitly that other variables correlating with base frequency, such as number of senses, concreteness, and age of acquisition, are also controlled for between the high and low Surface Frequency groups. We added 38 monomorphemic words (mostly verbs) and 76 inflected verbs in the third person singular. Each word was paired with a pseudoword with the same morphological structure which did not violate the phonotactic rules of Dutch. The experiment was preceded by 32 practice trials. There was a short pause after the practice session, and once during the experiment. In total, the experiment lasted about 20 minutes. The experimental materials are listed in Appendix B.

*Procedure.*Participants were tested in noise-proof experimental rooms. They were asked to decide as quickly and accurately as possible whether a letter string appearing on the computer screen was a real Dutch word. Each stimulus was preceded by a fixation mark in the middle of the screen for 50 ms. After 500 ms, the stimulus appeared at the same position. Stimuli were presented on Nec Multisync color monitors in white lowercase 36 point Helvetica letters on a dark background and they remained on the screen for 1500 ms. The maximum time span allowed for response was 2000 ms from stimulus onset.

Results and discussion

The participants performed the experiment with an error rate less than 13%. Table 3.2 lists mean reaction times and mean error scores for the two experimental conditions. The participles with a high Surface Frequency elicited reliably shorter response latencies ($t1(24) = -12.00$, $p < 0.005$; $t2(58) = -6.74$, $p < 0.005$), and less erroneous responses ($t1(24) = -7.25$, $p < 0.005$; $t2(58) = -4.97$, $p < 0.005$) than those with a low Surface Frequency. Clearly, this experiment shows that in Dutch regular participles can be stored in the mental lexicon.

Base Frequency and Surface Frequency are correlated variables in our materials. Pooling the words of the high and low Surface Frequency sets, we observe that the Pearson correlation between Base Frequency and Surface Frequency equals $r = 0.246$, $t(58) = 1.93$, $p = 0.03$ (one-tailed test). Given the strong negative correlation of Surface Frequency with the reaction times ($r = -0.730$; $t(58) = -8.14$, $p < 0.005$), one would expect a negative correlation of Base Frequency with reaction time as well (see, e.g., Bertram et al., 2000c). However, there is no such correlation for Base Frequency ($r = -0.0005$; $t < 1$). We therefore inspected the partial correlation of Base Frequency and reaction time, partialling out the correlation of reaction time with Surface Frequency. This partial correlation turned out to be positive and, surprisingly, reliable: $r = 0.27(t(57) = 2.12$, $p = 0.04)$ (two-tailed test). This positive correlation shows that response latencies to the perfect participle become longer when its base is more frequent.

How can we explain this unexpected result? Two possible explanations suggest themselves. First, we may be observing an effect of competition between the access representation of the base word *wandel* (a free form in Dutch) and that of the participle, *gewandeld*. Access representations are modality specific representations of the form of words, either their orthographic shape or their phonological form. In many current models of word recognition, access representations enter into a process of competition for recognition. In this competition process, access representations that are similar to each other and to the target inhibit each other. Thus, the competition process is a selection mechanism for weeding out irrelevant but similar forms (see, e.g., Grainger and Jacobs, 1996). In this framework, higher-frequency base words might lead to more severe competition between the access representations of *wandel* and *gewandeld*, resulting in a positive correlation between Base Frequency and reaction time. This explanation runs into the problem, however, that under strict lexical competition, i.e., competition in which there is only one winning lexical candidate, one would expect symmetrical effects. If anything, one would expect the lower-frequency full-form to suffer more from the competition than the higher-frequency base, instead of the observed reverse. In the model for morphological segmentation developed by Baayen et al., 1999b; Baayen and Schreuder, 1999, and Baayen and Schreuder, 2000, however, there is no substantial competition between base and full form because the two routes work together rather than against each other. In this parallel dual route model, the observed positive correlation of Base Frequency and reaction time cannot be explained at the access level.

A second explanation locates the effect at a deeper, central level than that of the form-based access representations. The central level is the level where semantic and syntactic representations are activated, the level also at which alternative parses have to be weighted. In our parallel dual route model, access representations of affixes provide access to their syntactic and semantic properties before base words and full forms, due to their very high frequencies of use. (For evidence of this early availability of affixes in visual word recognition, see Bertram et al., 2000a, and De Jong et al., 2000.) Likewise, base words often become available before full-form representations, again due to their higher frequency. A full segmentation of the input, e.g., *ge-wandel-d*, may therefore become available for central processing before the full form itself. This complete segmentation, however, contains a sub-parse that is incompatible with the correct parse: *ge-wandel* is an iterative action noun formed by prefixing the category-changing prefix *ge-*. Possibly, the incongruity of the sub-parse *ge-wandel* with the correct parse *ge-wandel-d* causes uncertainty at the central level of lexical processing that slows down responses based on the parsing route: More frequent base words will become available more quickly, leading to an earlier onset of uncertainty, and hence to longer response latencies and a positive correlation of Base Frequency with reaction time.

This second explanation receives further support from a more detailed analysis of the data, as not all participles have a corresponding form with *ge-*. In contrast to the pair *ge-wandel* and *ge-wandel-d*, participles such as *gedoemd* ('doomed') and *gestoeld* ('based on') do not have parallel

Table 3.2. Mean response latencies and error proportions for the regular perfect participles of Experiment 2 (means by participants).

		RT	$\hat{s}$ *RT*	*Error*	$\hat{s}$ *Error*
Perfect participles	High Surface Frequency	594	79.88	0.04	0.05
	Low Surface Frequency	702	95.38	0.19	0.14

forms with *ge-*. Interestingly, the subset of items for which a parallel form with *ge-* exists or is an easily interpretable possible form reveal a reliable positive partial correlation of Base Frequency and response latency ($r = 0.33$, $t(32) = 1.96$, $p = 0.03$, one-tailed test), while the corresponding partial correlation for the remaining items is not reliable ($r = 0.15$, $t(22) = 0.73$, $p = 0.24$, one-tailed test). This confirms the hypothesis that the existence of a parallel form with *ge-*, or the plausibility of such a form, slows down response latencies in visual lexical decision.

Summing up, we have observed a 100 ms effect of Surface Frequency for a suffix that has no suppletive rival affix and that must be considered to be a default in the sense of Marcus et al., 1995. This shows unambiguously that Surface Frequency Effects cannot be used as a lithmus test for (ir)regularity. Interestingly, the very same data suggest that parsing is also going on for our experimental materials. The parsing route runs into problems, however, possibly at the access level, but more likely at a more central level of processing.

The present strong effect of storage for Dutch participles contrasts with results reported by Baayen et al., 1997a for inflected past tense plural verbs with the suffix *-en* in Dutch and by Bertram et al., 2000c for the singular past tense suffix *-te* in Dutch. Both studies report the complete absence of an effect of Surface Frequency. In fact, these authors hypothesize that while inherently inflected words may be stored (e.g., noun plurals), contextually inflected words such as person and number agreement marking on verbs are not stored (see Booij, 1993, for the distinction between contextual and inherent inflection). The present effect of Surface Frequency for our Experiment 2 may therefore have two sources. On the one hand, it may arise due to the parsing problem mentioned above. On the other hand, it may arise from the kind of word formation involved. Perfect participles are not prototypical inflected forms, as they often are used as adjectives and may acquire various idiosyncratic shades of meaning (e.g., *gezien* 'seen', has the additional meanings of being 'welcomed' and 'honored'). When we allow ourselves to assume that the perfect participle instantiates inherent inflection, the inconsistency with earlier results is resolved.

Returning to the question of the usefulness of the notion default, it might be argued that the notion of default comes into play primarily for the most prototypical kinds of inflection, i.e., contextual inflection, more than for less prototypical inflection such as the perfect participle. The next experiment therefore considers the plural past tense suffix *-den* as in *wandel-den*, 'we, you, they walked', which realizes not only tense (inherent inflection) but also number marking (contextual inflection).

Experiment 3

Participants. 28 participants, mostly undergraduates at Nijmegen University, were paid to take part in this experiment. All were native speakers of Dutch.

Materials. We selected 44 inflected past tense plural verbs with the suffix *-den* from the CELEX lexical database (e.g., *wandelden*, 'walked'). Twenty-two of these verbs had a high Surface Frequency with an average of 10.09 (range 0.55–38.29, $\hat{s}$ 9.99), and 22 had a low Surface Frequency of 0.30 (range 0.05–1.33, $\hat{s}$ 0.37). We matched the two sets of verbs with respect to Base Frequency (high: mean 156.24, range 3.12–863.24, $\hat{s}$ 223.96; low: mean 157.08, range 2.98–829.83, $\hat{s}$ 222.86), Family Size (high: mean 42.5, range 2–255, $\hat{s}$ 59.4; low: mean 38.6, range 2–309, $\hat{s}$ 67.7), and mean length in letters (high: 7.5, low: 8.0). We added 50 present participles with the equally regular inflectional suffix *-end*, serving as a separate experiment to be discussed below, and 90 inflected verbs in the third person singular. Each word was paired with a pseudoword with the same morphological structure which did not violate the phonotactic rules of Dutch. The experiment was preceded by 30 practice trials. There was a short pause after the practice session, and once during the experiment. In total, the experiment lasted about 20 minutes. The materials are listed in Appendix C.

Procedure. The procedure was identical to that of Experiment 2.

Results and discussion

One participant performed the experiment with an error rate of more than 15%, and was excluded from further analyses. Table 3.3 lists mean reaction times and mean error scores for the two experimental conditions. The verbs with a high Surface Frequency elicited reliably shorter response latencies ($t1(26) = -11.21$, $p < 0.005$; $t2(42) = -4.57$, $p < 0.005$), and less erroneous responses ($t1(26) = -4.83$, $p < 0.005$; $t2(42) = -2.71$, $p = 0.01$), than those with a low Surface Frequency.

Table 3.3. Mean response latencies and error proportions for the plural past tense inflections of Experiment 3 (means by participants).

		RT	$\hat{s}$ *RT*	*Error*	$\hat{s}$ *Error*
Past plural inflections	High Surface Frequency	586	59.8	0.07	0.06
	Low Surface Frequency	680	72.3	0.18	0.10

Even though *-den* is more contextual in nature than the perfect participle, and even though it is a default suffix in the absence of a suppletive rival affix, we observe a substantial effect of Surface Frequency that is also supported by a post-hoc correlation analysis ($r = -0.67$, $t(42) = -5.83$, $p < 0.005$).

Bertram et al., 2000c did not observe an effect of Surface Frequency for the singular past tense suffix *-te*. They show that derivational affixes reveal very reliable effects of Surface Frequency for the same range of Surface Frequencies where *-te* reveals only an effect of Base Frequency. Their data show that Surface Frequency Effects arise more easily with derived words than with contextually inflected words. However, the frequency contrast in their Experiment 1 was much smaller (5.3 versus 1.4 per million) than the contrast in the present experiment (10.1 versus 0.3 per million). The present experiment shows that, surprisingly, Surface Frequency Effects may even emerge for contextual inflection when the frequency contrast becomes large enough, even though *-den* is a suffix that is not in complementary distribution with other suffixes. For a similar recent finding for the inflectional suffix for the third person singular in the present tense paradigm, see Schreuder et al., 1999).

In the present experiment, Base Frequency revealed a reliable correlation with reaction time in the expected direction ($r = -0.31$, $t(42) = -2.09$, $p = 0.04$). However, as Surface Frequency and Base Frequency are strongly correlated for our materials ($r = 0.40$, $t(42) = 2.79$, $p = 0.008$), we also ran a partial correlation analysis of Base Frequency and reaction time, partialling out the correlation of Surface Frequency and reaction time. This partial correlation turned out not to be reliable ($r = -0.06$, $t < 1$). The present experiment, therefore, does not provide evidence for an independent contribution of Base Frequency. At the same time, it is not the case that a high Base Frequency leads to longer response latencies as observed in Experiment 2. This is what one would expect, as there is no parsing conflict for verbs ending in *-den*. Even when *den* is analyzed as a sequence of two morphemes, the past tense marker *-de* and the plural marker *-(e)n*, the two subparses *wandelde* and *wandelden* are not in conflict with respect to the word category of the input as is the case for the perfect participle (verbal for *gewandeld* and nominal for *gewandel*).

Our last experiment considers the Dutch present participle, which is formed by suffixation of *-end* (*wandelend*, 'walking'). The present participle is fully regular and productive, it is again a suffix without a suppletive rival suffix, and hence a default. However, it is also a form that is not often used in informal registers. It might be the case that, due to its lower frequency of use, the Surface Frequency Effect may be reduced or even absent for this suffix. Conversely, we expect the parsing route to play a more effective role for these lower-frequency inflected words.

Experiment 4

Participants. 28 participants, mostly undergraduates at Nijmegen University, were paid to take part in this experiment. All were native speakers of Dutch.

Materials. We selected 50 present participles with the inflectional suffix *-end*. Twenty-five of these present participles had a high Surface Frequency with an average of 5.83 (range 1.57–24.12, $\hat{s}$ 5.54), and 25 had a low Surface Frequency with an average of 0.21 (range 0.05–0.81, $\hat{s}$ 0.20). The two sets were matched for Base Frequency (high: mean 84.59, range 7.67–384.98, $\hat{s}$ 85.83; low: mean 85.12, range 7.55–400.55, $\hat{s}$ 90.38), Family Size (high: mean 33.9, range 2–251, $\hat{s}$ 54.2; low: mean 37.1, range 2–243, $\hat{s}$ 57.4), and for mean length in letters (high: 8.1, low: 7.7). We added 44 inflected past tense plural verbs with the suffix *-den*, which served as Experiment 3 above, and 90 inflected verbs in the third person singular. Each word was paired with a pseudoword with the same morphological structure which did not violate the phonotactic rules of Dutch. The experiment was preceded by 30 practice trials. There was a short pause after the practice session, and another short pause during the experiment. In total, the experiment lasted about 20 minutes. The materials are listed in Appendix D.

Procedure. The procedure was identical to that of Experiment 2.

Results and discussion

One participant made over 15% erroneous responses and was excluded from further analyses. Table 3.4 lists the mean reaction times and error scores for the two experimental conditions. The present participles with a high Surface Frequency elicited significantly shorter response latencies than the present participles with a low Surface Frequency ($t1(26) = -9.28$, $p < 0.005$; $t2(48) = -5.51$, $p < 0.005$). The differences in error scores were also reliable ($t1(26) = -6.86$, $p < 0.005$; $t2(48) = -3.55$, $p < 0.005$).

Table 3.4. Mean response latencies and error proportions for the present participles of Experiment 4 (means by participants).

		RT	$\hat{s}$ *RT*	*Error*	$\hat{s}$ *Error*
Present participles	High Surface Frequency	582	59.12	0.03	0.04
	Low Surface Frequency	660	70.68	0.13	0.08

Even though the contrast between the high and low Surface Frequency conditions is substantially reduced compared to the contrasts in the previous experiments (5.83 versus 0.21 in Experiment 4, compared to 10.09 versus 0.30 in Experiment 3 and 18.34 versus 0.94 in Experiment 2), we still observe a large 78 ms effect of Surface Frequency that is supported by a post-hoc correlation of Surface Frequency with reaction time as well ($r = -0.58$, $t(48) = -5.00$, $p < 0.0005$).

Interestingly, Surface Frequency and Base Frequency are not reliably correlated in the experimental materials of Experiment 4 ($r = 0.08$, $t(48) = 0.54$, $p = 0.590$), while at the same time Base Frequency and reaction time emerge as reliably correlated ($r = -0.28, t(48) = -2.03, p = 0.048$). Apparently, present participles with a high Base Frequency are responded to more quickly than present participles with a low Base Frequency. We interpret this to indicate that not only the full-form representations of the present participles are activated, but that during the parsing process the lexical representations of the base verbs themselves are activated as well. In other words, for the present participles, which tend to be lower-frequency forms, the parsing route also contributes effectively and independently of the full-form route to the process of lexical access.

The results of this experiment show, again, that complex words with a suffix that does not have rival suffixes may reveal clear Surface Frequency Effects. The balance of storage and computation for *-end* is not determined by its position on the regular–irregular scale, but by the balance in the frequencies of use of the base words and the participles themselves.

4. General discussion

This study addresses the balance of storage and computation for fully regular Dutch inflected words. Whereas Marcus et al., 1995 and Clahsen et al., 1997 claim that the balance of storage and computation crucially depends on an affix having default status, i.e., it being prototypically regular to the exclusion of any other rival affix, our data show that the default status of affixes is irrelevant and that the linguistic desideratum of economy of description cannot be mapped directly onto cognitive models of lexical processing. Instead, the balance of storage and computation is determined by a wide range of linguistic *and* cognitive factors such as frequency of occurrence, computational complexity, and the relative costs of storage and computation in the mental lexicon.

Our argument against the projection of linguistic economy of description onto lexical processing is based on two sets of observations. The first set of observations concerns the formation of plural nouns in Dutch. A linguistic analysis of the regular and productive rival suppletive suffixes *-en* and *-s* shows that both can be considered to be prototypically regular and productive. They share most properties ascribed to default affixes by Marcus et al., 1995. A production experiment shows that participants can attach both suffixes to pseudowords, exactly as predicted from the regular complementary distribution of these suffixes. This experiment confirms that *-en* and *-s* are fully productive regular suffixes. Nevertheless, plural nouns in Dutch reveal substantial effects of Surface Frequency (Baayen et al., 1997a), which indicates that many regular plurals have their own full-form access representations in the mental lexicon. Fully regular inflected words can be stored in the mental lexicon, even though they are prototypically regular.

The second set of observations concerns three verbal inflectional suffixes in Dutch, all of which have no suppletive rival affix and must therefore be considered to be prototypically regular. For the perfect participle *ge- -d*, the plural past tense suffix *-den*, and the present participle *-end*, we again observed substantial effects of Surface Frequency of some 80–100 ms. This shows that unambiguous default status does not imply the absence of storage in the mental lexicon. These results are in line with those obtained for the second and third person present tense suffix *-t* (*wandel-t*, 'you walk, he walks') studied by Schreuder et al., 1999, which likewise revealed a strong effect of Surface Frequency, and which is a prototypically contextual inflection.

Considered jointly with previous results for morphological processing in the visual modality (e.g., Sereno and Jongman, 1997; Taft, 1979; Burani et al., 1984; Allegre and Gordon, 1999), we conclude that, at least for the visual modality, the notion of default is not a good predictor of the balance of storage and computation in Dutch. In a descriptive sense, an affix can be the default affix among a set of rival affixes, but this does not imply that the other rival affixes cannot be prototypically regular as well.

Effects of full-form storage for inflected words indicate that at some level of representation knowledge about the combined occurrence of the inflectional affix and its base word is stored. Our hypothesis is that the appropriate level of representation for the storage effects observed in the present experiments is that of the access representations, the level of representation at which form information is stored. Especially in the case of contextual inflection, words probably do not have their own separate central, semantic representations as well.

Evidence supporting this hypothesis concerns the absence of an effect of Surface frequency for plural verb forms in visual lexical decision and its presence in progressive demasking. Plural nouns matched with these verbs in Surface Frequency showed an effect in both tasks (Baayen et al., 1997b; 1999a). Progressive demasking is a task that is especially sensitive to the form properties of words, and applied to plural nouns and verbs it reveals Surface Frequency effects for both, which we interpret as arising at the level of orthographic form. By contrast, lexical decision is a task that is not only sensitive to form, but also to meaning. For the relatively small contrast in Surface Frequency used in the above studies (high: 27 per million; low: 7 per million; a difference of roughly a factor 4 that contrasts with the much larger differences used in the experiments in the present paper, factors ranging from 18 to 30), visual lexical decision is not sensitive enough to pick up effects of storage at the form level, not for the verbs nor for the nouns. However, because noun plurals have their own semantic representations (see Baayen et al., 1997b, for arguments that noun plurals instantiate inherent inflection similar to derivation), visual lexical decision latencies still reflect the difference between low and high frequency representations at the central level. In other words, verb plurals have full-form access representations, but no separate central representations (in line with the Augmented Addressed Morphology model of Caramazza et al., 1988; Laudanna and Burani, 1985), while nouns have representations at both levels. Note that the contrasts in Surface Frequency used in the present experiments are apparently large enough to be picked up by visual lexical decision, even in the absence of separate semantic representations for inflected verb forms in the central mental lexicon.

It might be argued that effects of storage of regular complex inflected words might only be observed when high-frequency forms are contrasted with low-frequency forms. In fact, Allegre and Gordon, 1999 argue, on the basis of frequency counts from the Brown corpus (1 million tokens, Kučera and Francis, 1967), that full-form frequency effects in English do not occur below a frequency threshold of 6 per million. However, it remains to be seen to what extent the small corpus size underlying the counts used by Allegre and Gordon is responsible for their findings. In Dutch, regression analyses using frequency counts based on a corpus with 42 million word tokens, suggest that a discrete frequency threshold, if it exists at all, should be positioned at a much lower frequency. A dataset illustrating this point is the experiment in part reported in Schreuder et al., 1999, which concerns the inflectional forms for the first and third person singular in the present tense paradigm of Dutch, *denk*, 'I think', and *denk-t*, 'he/she thinks'. This study reports a factorial contrast between high and low surface frequency inflected forms, covering a wide frequency range for both the surface frequency of the inflected forms and the frequency of the base words.

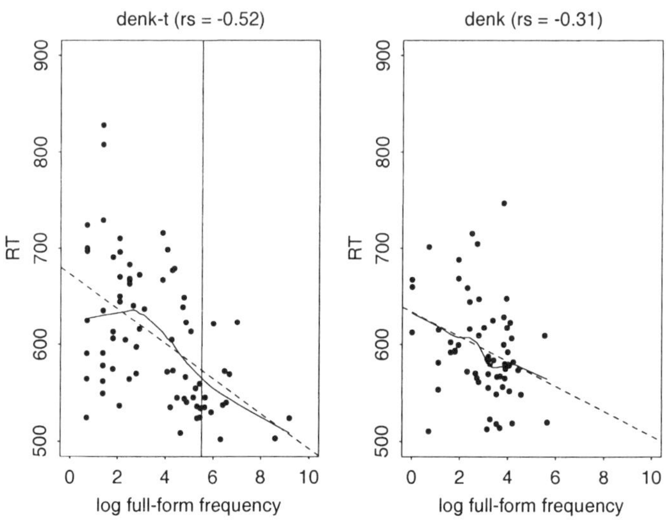

Figure 3.1. Response latency (RT) as a function of log Surface Frequency for monomorphemic inflectional forms (right panel) and bi-morphemic inflectional forms (left panel). The dashed line represents a linear regression line, the solid line a non-parametric regression curve. The vertical line in the left panel represents the frequency threshold of 6 per million proposed by Allegre and Gordon, 1999.

Figure 3.1 provides scatterplots for the simplex singular forms ('denk') in the right panel and for the complex third person forms ('denk-t') in the left panel. The dashed lines represent linear regression lines. Because the variance increases for decreasing frequency, we have also checked the correlational structure of RT and log surface frequency by means of a non-parametric regression technique, resulting in the solid lines, and by means of Spearman correlation analyses. For the simplex inflectional forms, $r_s = -0.31$, for the complex inflectional forms, $r_s = -0.52$. The parametric and non-parametric analyses present very similar regression patterns, allowing us to also check the partial correlations for the complex inflectional forms. When RT is correlated with log Surface Frequency when log Base Frequency is partialled out first, a fully reliable correlation is obtained ($r = -0.44$, $t(71) = -4.17$, $p < 0.001$), and similarly the correlation between log Base Frequency and RT remains reliable when Surface Frequency is partialled out ($r = -0.29$, $t(71) = -2.62$, $p < 0.01$). Again, we find that both storage and computation independently contribute to the lexical processing of complex regular inflected forms. Interestingly, it emerges from these data, which allow us to observe independent effects of Surface Frequency and Base Frequency, that a cut-off point at 6 per million (highlighted by the solid vertical line in the left panel of Figure 3.1) as suggested by Allegre and Gordon, 1999 is much too high. If we trust the non-parametric regression line, a cut-off point might come into play around a frequency of 0.3 per million. Due to the large variance in the RTs for low frequencies, it remains unclear whether this cut-off point might be even lower. Frequency counts based on substantially larger corpora are required to settle this possibility.

Our findings have two main theoretical consequences. First, our data show that those who wish to argue against connectionist models or machine-learning based models (see Daelemans et al., 1995, for a computational model for morphology based on extensive storage in machine learning) cannot buttress their arguments with the claim that regular inflected words are never stored in the mental lexicon. Second, the present findings shift the focus of research from the question whether regular forms may or may not be stored to the question what factors might determine the balance of storage and computation.

This balance is not determined by linguistic regularity as such, but by a range of factors, such as frequency of use, the costs of storage, the costs of computation, and modality (Frauenfelder and Schreuder, 1992). First consider frequency of use. The three experiments with Dutch inflectional forms reported above show a pervasive effect of the frequency of the inflected form itself. However, when this Surface Frequency is relatively low, as for the Dutch present participles in Experiment 4, the frequency of use of the base word emerges as a second factor in visual lexical decision. The balance of storage and computation is clearly co-determined by the balance of Surface Frequency and Base Frequency.

Next, consider the costs of storage. The storage capacity of the human brain is enormous (Landauer, 1986), and probably more than large enough to allow storage of all commonly used complex words in languages with simple morphological systems such as English or Dutch. For languages such as Turkish or Finnish, in which one base can appear in thousands of other complex words, extensive storage may overtax human memory, and it may also be inefficient due to increasing retrieval times from memory. Not surprisingly, Niemi et al., 1994 report that full-form storage in Finnish is restricted to the domain of word formation. In their experiments, inflected words do not reveal any Surface Frequency Effects.

Costs are associated not only with storage, but also with computation. When morphological parsing is computationally intensive, lexical processing may be speeded up when a full-form representation is available. Such a full-form representation may provide a pointer to the correct syntactic and semantic representations in the central mental lexicon. In the parallel dual route model of Schreuder and Baayen, 1995, Baayen et al., 1997b, and Baayen et al., 1999b, the direct route, using the full-form representation, may complete lexical access long before the parsing route, which uses the constituents, especially when the parsing route is slowed down due to ambiguities. One such ambiguity is caused by affixal homonymy. Bertram et al., 2000b report that the Finnish partitive plurals with the suffix *-jA*, which also forms agent nouns, show clear effects of Surface Frequency. Apparently, on-line resolution of affixal homonymy is so expensive in real time that lexical access is completed more efficiently on the basis of the full form. A second kind of ambiguity arises when incompatible parses are present, as in Experiment 2, where we studied perfect participles in *ge-X-d*, which contain a regular derivational sub-parse in *ge-X*. For these participles, we observed an inhibitory effect of a high Base Frequency, which suggests that the parsing route has difficulties in resolving the morphotactic ambiguity. More in general, storage may enhance the parsing of longer complex words and the resolution of parsing ambiguities, as shown for our parallel dual route model by Baayen and Schreuder, 2000.

Modality (visual and auditory word recognition versus word production) plays an important role as well with respect to the balance of storage and computation. In speech production, inflected words have been argued to be assembled on-line (Roelofs, 1996; Janssen, 1999), driven by the semantics of the base word and the requirements of the syntactic context. In order to avoid overregularizations, precedence mechanisms are required that give priority to existing irregular forms over possible but unused regular forms. In language comprehension, by contrast, such a precedence mechanism is not required. When reading a regular present participle such as *wandel-end* ('walking'), the combination of constituents is already legitimate. Instead of having to assemble the correct form, the correct form is available in the input and has to be used as efficiently as possible to access the correct meaning, using both the full form and the constituents.

Note that we do not claim that regular and irregular forms are processed in exactly the same way by the brain. What we do claim is that, e.g., neurophysiological evidence in favor of a processing dissociation should not be interpreted in terms of a dissociation of storage (for irregulars only) and computation (for all regulars).

From our point of view, the claim advanced by Marcus et al., 1995 that the German noun plural suffix *-s* is the default and the one and only plural suffix for which rules are involved during lexical processing is rather counterintuitive for language comprehension. This claim entails that a mere 7% of German plural noun types and a mere 2% of German plural noun tokens would be processed by rule (see Table 5 in Clahsen, 1999). This would imply an exceptional degree of storage for German, even though a great many German noun plurals are completely regular from the perspective of language comprehension. For instance, given access representations for the *-en* and *-e* German plural suffixes as well as central representations that link these access representations to the syntactic and semantic representations of noun plurals, plural forms such as *Frauen* ('women') and *Hunde* ('dogs') can be readily parsed into their constituents. Not surprisingly, non-native speakers of German tend to have few difficulties with understanding German plurals while at the same time they may experience considerable difficulties to produce the correct plural forms. These considerations lead us to expect that upon careful examination the parsing route will be found to contribute more substantially to the lexical access of German noun plurals than Marcus et al., 1995 suggest.

Our examination of a range of fully regular and productive inflectional rules of Dutch shows that regularity and storage are not incompatible with each other. This insight cannot be gained by generalizing from a default affix with a quantitatively weak position in the language, such as the German plural in *-s*. For such an affix, high-frequency formations are atypical, and the likelihood that effects of full-form storage can be observed experimentally is small. For more productive inflectional affixes that give rise to more and higher frequency forms, storage in the mental lexicon is easier to observe. Although Marcus et al., 1995 and Clahsen et al., 1997 claim that the case of the German *-s* plural proves the rule that only default affixes are accessed on the basis of computation, the Dutch rules of noun and verb inflection suggest that this claim is based on an exception.

Acknowledgments

This study was financially supported by the Dutch Research Council NWO (PIONIER grant to the first author). Requests for reprints should be addressed to R. H. Baayen, Interfaculty Research Unit for Language and Speech, University of Nijmegen, P.O.Box 310, 6500 AH Nijmegen, The Netherlands.

References

Allegre, M. and Gordon, P. (1999). Frequency effects and the representational status of regular inflections. *Journal of Memory and Language*, 40:41–61.

Baayen, R. and Schreuder, R. (2000). Towards a psycholinguistic computational model for morphological parsing. In *Philosophical Transactions of the Royal Society (A: Mathematical, Physical and Engineering Sciences)*, volume 358, pages 1–13.

Baayen, R. H. (1992). Quantitative aspects of morphological productivity. In Booij, G. E. and Van Marle, J., editors, *Yearbook of Morphology 1991*, pages 109–149. Dordrecht: Kluwer Academic Publishers.

Baayen, R. H. (1993). On frequency, transparency, and productivity. In Booij, G. E. and Van Marle, J., editors, *Yearbook of Morphology 1992*, pages 181–208. Dordrecht: Kluwer Academic Publishers.

Baayen, R. H., Burani, C., and Schreuder, R. (1997a). Effects of semantic markedness in the processing of regular nominal singulars and plurals in Italian. In Booij, G. E. and Van Marle, J., editors, *Yearbook of Morphology 1996*, pages 13–34. Dordrecht: Kluwer Academic Publishers.

Baayen, R. H., Dijkstra, T., and Schreuder, R. (1997b). Singulars and plurals in Dutch: Evidence for a parallel dual route model. *Journal of Memory and Language*, 36:94–117.

Baayen, R. H., McQueen, J., Dijkstra, A., and Schreuder, R. (1999a). Dutch inflectional morphology in spoken- and written-word recognition. Submitted.

Baayen, R. H., Piepenbrock, R., and Gulikers, L. (1995). *The CELEX lexical database (CD-ROM)*. Philadelphia: Linguistic Data Consortium, University of Pennsylvania, PA.

Baayen, R. H. and Renouf, A. (1996). Chronicling The Times: Productive lexical innovations in an English newspaper. *Language*, 72:69–96.

Baayen, R. H. and Schreuder, R. (1999). War and peace: morphemes and full forms in a non-interactive activation parallel dual route model. *Brain and Language*, 68:27–32.

Baayen, R. H., Schreuder, R., and Sproat, R. (1999b). Modeling morphological segmentation in a parallel dual route framework for visual word recognition. In van Eynde, F. and Gibbon, D., editors, *Lexicon Development for Speech and Language Processing*. Dordrecht: Kluwer Academic Publishers.

Bertram, R., Baayen, R. H., and Schreuder, R. (2000a). Effects of family size for derived and inflected words. *Journal of Memory and Language*, 42:390–405.

Bertram, R., Laine, M., Baayen, R. H., Schreuder, R., and Hyönä, J. (2000b). Affixal homonymy triggers full-form storage even with inflected words, even in a morphologically rich language. *Cognition*, 74:b13–b25.

Bertram, R., Schreuder, R., and Baayen, R. H. (2000c). The balance of storage and computation in morphological processing: the role of word formation type, affixal homonymy, and productivity. *Journal of Experimental Psychology: Memory, Learning, and Cognition*, 26:1–23.

Bloomfield, L. (1933). *Language*. London: Allen and Unwin.

Bod, R. (1998). *Beyond grammar: An experience-based theory of language*. Stanford, CA: CSLI publications.

Booij, G. E. (1998). Phonological output constraints in morphology. In Kehrein, W. and Wiese, R., editors, *Phonology and morphology of the Germanic Languages*, pages 143–163. Tübingen: Max Niemeyer Verlag.

Booij, G. E. (1977). *Dutch morphology. A study of word formation in Generative Grammar*. Dordrecht: Foris.

Booij, G. E. (1993). Against split morphology. In Booij, G. E. and Van Marle, J., editors, *Yearbook of Morphology 1993*, pages 27–49. Dordrecht: Kluwer Academic Publishers.

Breiman, L., Friedman, J., Olshen, R., and Stone, C. (1984). *Classification and regression trees*. Belmont, CA: Wadsworth International Group.

Burani, C., Salmaso, D., and Caramazza, A. (1984). Morphological structure and lexical access. *Visible Language*, 18:342–352.

Butterworth, B. (1983). Lexical representation. In Butterworth, B., editor, *Language production*, (Vol. II): Development, Writing and Other language Processes, pages 257–294. London: Academic Press.

Caramazza, A., Laudanna, A., and Romani, C. (1988). Lexical access and inflectional morphology. *Cognition*, 28:297–332.

Clahsen, H. (1999). Lexical entries and rules of language: a multi-disciplinary study of German inflection. *Behavioral and Brain Sciences*, 22:991–1060.

Clahsen, H., Eisenbeiss, S., and Sonnenstuhl-Henning, I. (1997). Morphological structure and the processing of inflected words. *Theoretical Linguistics*, 23:201–249.

Daelemans, W., Berck, P., and Gillis, S. (1995). Linguistics as data mining: Dutch diminutives. In Andernach, T., Moll, M., and Nijholt, A., editors, *CLIN V, Papers from the 5th CLIN meeting*.

Daelemans, W., Zavrel, J., Van der Sloot, K., and Van den Bosch, A. (1999). TiMBL: Tilburg memory based learner reference guide 2.0. Technical report, Tilburg University.

De Jong, N. H., Schreuder, R., and Baayen, R. H. (2000). The morphological family size effect and morphology. *Language and Cognitive Processes*, 15:329–365.

Dimmendaal, G. J. (1987). Drift and selective mechanisms in morphological changes: the Eastern Nilotic case. In Ramat, A. G., Carruba, O., and Bernini, G., editors, *Papers from the 7th international conference on historical linguistics*, pages 193–210. Amsterdam: John Benjamins.

Frauenfelder, U. and Schreuder, R. (1992). Constraining psycholinguistic models of morphological processing and representation: The role of productivity. In Booij, G. E. and Van Marle, J., editors, *Yearbook of Morphology 1992*, pages 165–183. Dordrecht: Kluwer Academic Publishers.

Gordon, P. (1985). Level-ordering in lexical development. *Cognition*, 21:73–93.

Grainger, J. and Jacobs, A. M. (1996). Orthographic processing in visual word recognition: A multiple read-out model. *Psychological Review*, 103:518–565.

Jaeger, J., Lockwood, A. H., Kemmerer, D. L., Van Valin, R. D., and Murphy, B. (1996). A positron emission tomographic study of regular and irregular verb morphology in English. *Language*, 72:451–497.

Janssen, D. (1999). *Producing past and plural inflections*. PhD thesis, University of Nijmegen.

Kiparsky, P. (1973). Elsewhere in phonology. In Anderson, S. R. and Kiparsky, P., editors, *A Festschrift for Morris Halle*, pages 93–106. New York: Holt, Rinehart & Winston.

Kiparsky, P. (1982). From cyclic phonology to lexical phonology. In Van der Hulst, H. and Smith, N., editors, *The structure of phonological representations*, pages 131–176. Dordrecht: Foris.

Kučera, H. and Francis, W. N. (1967). *Computational analysis of present-day American English*. Providence, RI: Brown University Press.

Landauer, T. K. (1986). How much do people remember? Some estimates of the quantity of learned information in long-term memory. *Cognitive Science*, 10:477–493.

Laudanna, A. and Burani, C. (1985). Address mechanisms to decomposed lexical entries. *Linguistics*, 23:775–792.

Marcus, G., Brinkman, U., Clahsen, H., Wiese, R., and Pinker, S. (1995). German inflection: The exception that proves the rule. *Cognitive Psychology*, 29:189–256.

Niemi, J., Laine, M., and Tuominen, J. (1994). Cognitive morphology in Finnish: foundations of a new model. *Language and Cognitive Processes*, 9:423–446.

Pinker, S. (1991). Rules of language. *Science*, 153:530–535.

Pinker, S. and Prince, A. (1988). On language and connectionism. *Cognition*, 28:73–193.

Pinker, S. and Prince, A. (1991). Regular and irregular morphology and the psychological status of rules of grammar. In *Proceedings of the 1991 meeting of the Berkeley Linguistics Society*.

Plunkett, K. and Juola, P. (1999). A connectionist model of English past tense and plural morphology. *Cognitive Science*, 23:463–490.

Rickard, T. C., Healy, A. F., and Bourne Jr., E. (1994). On the cognitive structure of basic arithmetic skills: Operation, order, and symbol transfer effects. *Journal of Experimental Psychology: Learning, Memory, and Cognition*, 20:1139–1153.

Roelofs, A. (1996). Serial order in planning the production of successive morphemes of a word. *Journal of Memory and Language*, 35:854–876.

Rosenbaum, D. A., Vaughan, J., Barnes, H. J., and Jorgensen, M. J. (1992). Time course of movement planning: Selection of handgrips for object manipulation. *Journal of Experimental Psychology: Learning, Memory, and Cognition*, 18:1058–1073.

Schreuder, R. and Baayen, R. H. (1995). Modeling morphological processing. In Feldman, L. B., editor, *Morphological Aspects of Language Processing*, pages 131–154. Hillsdale, NJ: Lawrence Erlbaum.

Schreuder, R. and Baayen, R. H. (1997). How complex simplex words can be. *Journal of Memory and Language*, 37:118–139.

Schreuder, R., De Jong, N. H., Krott, A., and Baayen, R. H. (1999). Rules and rote: beyond the linguistic either-or fallacy. *Behavioral and Brain Sciences*, 22:1038–1039.

Schultink, H. (1961). Produktiviteit als morfologisch fenomeen. *Forum der Letteren*, 2:110–125.

Seidenberg, M. (1987). Sublexical structures in visual word recognition: Access units or orthographic redundancy. In Coltheart, M., editor, *Attention and Performance XII*, pages 245–263. Hove: Lawrence Erlbaum Associates.

Seidenberg, M. and Hoeffner, J. (1998). Evaluating behavioral and neuroimaging data on past tense processing. *Language*, 74:104–122.

Sereno, J. and Jongman, A. (1997). Processing of English inflectional morphology. *Memory and Cognition*, 25:425–437.

Taft, M. (1979). Recognition of affixed words and the word frequency effect. *Memory and Cognition*, 7:263–272.

Tiersma, P. M. (1982). Local and general markedness. *Language*, 58:832–849.

Van Haeringen, C. B. (1947). *De meervoudsvorming in het Nederlands.* Mededelingen der Koninklijke Nederlandse Akademie van Wetenschappen, Afd. Letterkunde. Nieuwe Reeks.

Van Marle, J. (1985). *On the Paradigmatic Dimension of Morphological Creativity.* Foris, Dordrecht.

Van Marle, J. (1986). The domain hypothesis: the study of rival morphological processes. *Linguistics*, 24:601–627.

Venables, W. N. and Ripley, B. D. (1994). *Modern Applied Statistics with S-Plus.* Springer, New York.

Appendix

Appendix A

Experiment 1, number of responded plural suffixes (-s, -en, others)
Stressed one-syllable pseudowords:
dreip (3, 46, 0); luif (1, 48, 0); stril (2, 47, 0); treig (3, 45, 1); horp (2, 47, 0); driem (1, 48, 0); grijk (1, 48, 0); krons (1, 48, 0); pruit (0, 49, 0); moek (4, 43, 2).
Two-syllable pseudowords with an unstressed final syllable:
workel (49, 0, 0); drimmel (46, 1, 2); straggem (39, 4, 6); merkel (48, 1, 0); brezem (46, 1, 2); griekel (48, 1, 0); struimel (48, 0, 1); kloegel (48, 1, 0); zoppel (48, 1, 0); dreigel (49, 0, 0).
Two-syllable pseudowords ending in schwa:
bame (20, 29, 0); kule (21, 28, 0); klijze (5, 44, 0); broele (16, 33, 0); stape (12, 37, 0); kloge (11, 37, 1); pliete (11, 37, 1); vule (19, 30, 0); loeke (16, 32, 1); hoele (16, 36, 0).
Two-syllable pseudowords with an unstressed final syllable ending in the consonant -s:
bastus (0, 43, 6); muidus (0, 45, 4); briegus (0, 45, 4); klogus (0, 44, 5); stroebas (0, 49, 0); gienus (0, 44, 5); klettus (0, 43, 6); dietus (0, 42, 7); brenkis (0, 45, 4); glostis (0, 45, 4).
Pseudo words ending in a fully stressed vowel e or a:
kna (39, 10, 0); kra (39, 10, 0); pla (41, 7, 1); wa (39, 10, 0); za (40, 9, 0); dee (13, 36, 0); bee (22, 27, 0); kee (17, 32, 0); stree (9, 40, 0); vlee (12, 37, 0).
Pseudo words ending in the suffix -ing:
bestroeting (0, 49, 0); ontdruibing (1, 48, 0); herbanzing (1, 47, 1); begrijking (0, 49, 0); ontvloding (0, 49, 0); herbrekking (0, 49, 0); bepoesting (0, 49, 0); ontloeding(0, 49, 0); herstranking (2, 47, 0); beklusting(1, 48, 0).
Pseudo words ending in the suffix -(t)je:
megje (49, 0, 0); bralkje (49, 0, 0); bunkeltje (49, 0, 0); strimseltje (48, 1, 0); noogje (49, 0, 0); frienkje (49, 0, 0); braantje (49, 0, 0); gruimseltje (49, 0, 0); lannertje (49, 0, 0); kloertje (48, 1, 0).
Pseudo words ending in the suffix -isme:
kadisme (16, 36, 0); mylisme (10, 39, 0); microtalisme (12, 35, 2); tellinisme (13, 36, 0); heminisme (12, 36, 1); idiokatisme (12, 34, 3); exhilisme (13, 36, 0); profemisme (11, 38, 0); eudadisme (13, 35, 1); meteolyisme (11, 37, 1).

Appendix B

Experiment 2, Past participles with a high Surface Frequency
geleverd (delivered) 585, gedoofd (extinguished) 630, gemiddeld (mediated) 636, gedoemd (doomed) 675, gedraaid (turned) 551, geleerd (learned) 531, gescheurd (ripped) 633, geboeid (chained) 580, geregeld (arranged) 672, geplaagd (teased) 535, gestuurd (sent) 529, gemengd (mingled) 618, gepleegd (committed) 596, gebouwd (built) 580, gegooid (thrown) 606, gesteund (supported) 618, geerfd (inherited) 731, gerekend (calculated) 661, gedroomd (dreamed) 622, geklemd (clasped) 600, gehinderd (impeded) 601, gekoppeld (coupled) 569, gefaald (failed) 586, gewisseld (swapped) 522, gespeeld (played) 566, gelegd (put) 600, gemarteld (tortured) 591, getrouwd (married) 559, geweigerd (refused) 532, gevuld (filled) 556.

Experiment 2, Past participles with a low Surface Frequency
getraand (teared) 857, gegeurd (smelled) 861, gegrijnsd (smirked) 664, gesneld (hurried) 733, gekleurd (colored) 565, gekreund (moaned) 630, gecirkeld (circled) 674, gesuikerd (sugared) 684, gepeperd (peppered) 629, gezweefd (floated) 636, gevuurd (fired) 585, getafeld (dined) 729, geleegd (emptied) 626, gebeterd (improved) 700, genaamd (named) 705, gemodderd (messed around) 779, geboterd (buttered) 687, geboerd (burped) 773, gestoeld (based) 784, geruwd (roughened) 834, gewankeld (staggered) 661, gevlamd (flamed) 676, gedokterd (acted as a doctor) 750, gewinkeld (shopped) 753, geboomd (poled) 834, gestoomd (steamed) 671, gespeld (spelled) 746, geborreld (bubbled) 700, geraamd (estimated) 681, gewaterd (watered) 642.

Appendix C

Experiment 3, Past plural verbs with a high Surface Frequency
gloeiden (glowed) 589, wisselden (swapped) 592, dwaalden (wandered) 541, vormden (formed) 566, breiden (knitted) 605, renden (ran) 539, spanden (stretched) 629, meenden (thought) 590, redden (saved) 551, dartelden (romped) 686, trilden (trembled) 630, vulden (filled) 641, speelden (played) 527, zeulden (dragged) 647, groeiden (growed) 538, wandelden (walked) 585, streelden (carressed) 540, hoorden (heard) 563, zweefden (floated) 530, noemden (named) 599, voerden (feeded) 608, dromden (swarmed) 761.
Experiment 3, Past plural verbs with a low Surface Frequency
peinsden (pondered) 655, jammerden (moaned) 573, bezigden (employed) 734, pelden (pealed) 646, zegenden (blessed) 709, zuiverden (purified) 614, nummerden (numbered) 810, filterden (filtered) 956, oogden (eyed) 647, regelden (arranged) 633, zoogden (breastfed) 693, wortelden (took root) 673, huisden (were housed) 697, nodigden (requested) 630, snelden (hurried) 690, schilden (peeled) 653, strandden (stranded) 674, stilden (stilled) 727, ruzieden (quarreled) 674, vaagden (faded) 723, scheelden (differed) 683, hongerden (starved) 611.

Appendix D

Experiment 4, Present participles with a high Surface Frequency
weifelend (wavering) 663, draaiend (turning) 550, handelend (trading) 638, kreunend (moaning) 559, steunend (supporting) 548, wankelend (staggering) 587, juichend (jubilating) 572, aarzelend (hesitating) 627, brandend (burning) 536, zwijgend (being silent) 556, huiverend (shivering) 577, huilend (crying) 564, dreigend (threatening) 564, dwingend (forcing) 578, dansend (dansing) 582, wachtend (waiting) 537, piepend (sqeeking) 623, donderend (thundering) 701, fluitend (whistling) 530, zuchtend (sighing) 537, drinkend (drinking) 582, vloekend (cursing) 574, leunend (leaning) 636, druipend (dripping) 619, blinkend (blinking) 599.
Experiment 4, Present participles with a low Surface Frequency
bouwend (building) 739, sleurend (dragging) 628, hechtend (attaching) 615, hijsend (hoiling) 619, haastend (hurrying) 619, louterend (ppurifying) 783, voegend (joining) 689, neigend (inclining) 592, luidend (sounding) 656, pleitend (pleading) 663, sterkend (strengthening) 687, gooiend (throwing) 670, vangend (catching) 659, barstend (bursting) 646, wensend (wishing) 617, wringend (wringing) 714, leidend (leading) 608, koersend (setting course) 751, regenend (raining) 670, schetsend (sketching) 646, rimpelend (wrinkling) 676, wemelend (teeming) 860, kleurend (coloring) 647, startend (starting) 574, wijdend (consecrating) 685.

Chapter 4

WORDS, RULES AND STEMS IN THE ITALIAN MENTAL LEXICON

Tessa Say
and Harald Clahsen

Abstract Psycholinguistic evidence from different sources (child language acquisition data and experimental data from adult native speakers) indicates that stem formation and inflectional processes in Italian show a distinction between rule-based and memory-based processes. The findings are interpreted as providing cross-linguistic support for the dual-mechanism model.

Keywords: Stem formation, rule-based processes, memory-based processes, dual-mechanism model, lexicon, verb inflection.

1. Introduction

Recent psycholinguistic studies on the processing and acquisition of morphologically complex words have provided evidence for the view that the mental grammar has a dual structure with two distinct representational mechanisms, a set of lexical entries that are (associatively) listed in memory, and a set of symbolic operations to form larger linguistic expressions from items in the lexicon. Most of the psycholinguistic evidence for such a *dual-mechanism model* comes from inflectional phenomena in two closely related languages, English and German; see Pinker, 1999 and Clahsen, 1999 for reviews.

Consider, for example, errors children produce in acquiring the English past tense. Marcus et al., 1992 found that only one type of inflectional error is productive in English, overapplications of the regular past tense affix *-ed* to irregular stems (**go-ed*, etc.). Overapplications of irregular patterns (**brang*, **wope*) are much less frequent and systematic (see also Xu and Pinker, 1995). Marcus et al. also found that irregular verbs are sensitive to frequency and similarity: children make inflectional er-

S. Nooteboom et al. (eds.), Storage and Computation in the Language Faculty, 93–129.

rors more often with low-frequency irregular verbs, and they make fewer overregularization errors with irregular verbs that fall into families with more numerous and higher-frequency members. The same pattern of errors was found in two inflectional systems of German, past participles and noun plurals (Clahsen et al., 1992; Clahsen and Rothweiler, 1993). Overextensions of the irregular participle ending (*-n*), for example, were extremely rare in German. In contrast, regular inflection (past participle *-t*, noun plural *-s*) were overgeneralized more extensively and were not sensitive to phonological similarity (see also Weyerts and Clahsen, 1994; Bartke et al., 1996 for supporting experimental evidence).

Studies on morphological processing in adult native speakers using different experimental paradigms (e.g. lexical decision, priming, elicited production, sentence matching, event-related potentials) have also provided evidence for the dual-mechanism model (Pinker, 1999; Clahsen, 1999). Consider, for example, results from priming experiments. In such studies, stimulus pairs are presented to subjects, and the researcher manipulates the relation between them. The task is usually to make a lexical decision to the second presentation. If the second presentation (the target) is identical to the first presentation (the prime), e.g. *walk* followed by *walk*, access to its lexical representation is facilitated, reflected in a faster response time. Stanners et al., 1979 found an equivalent amount of facilitation when the prime was a regularly inflected past tense form (*walked*) and the target its stem (*walk*). That is, a regular past tense form fully primes its corresponding stem form. Irregular past tense forms, on the other hand, primed their stems less effectively than did the stem itself, e.g. *sing* was primed to a much lesser extent by *sang* than by *sing*. All subsequent experiments have confirmed Stanners et al.'s finding of full priming for regularly inflected words (Kempley and Morton, 1982; Napps, 1989; Fowler et al., 1985; Marslen-Wilson et al., 1993). It has been noted, however, that in English regular past tense forms are often orthographically and phonologically more similar to their base forms than are irregular past tense forms (*walked* → *walk* versus *taught* → *teach*) and that these different form properties may account for full priming of regular and reduced priming of irregular past tense forms (see Rueckl et al., 1997, among others). On the other hand, priming is absent from phonologically related pairs (e.g. *market* does not prime *mark* (Münte et al., 1998; see also Marslen-Wilson et al., 1994), indicating that the priming effects obtained for regular past tense forms do not merely reflect phonological similarities. For German, Sonnenstuhl et al., 1999 have recently found regular/irregular differences in priming experiments with past participles despite the fact that the phonological and orthographical distance between the participle forms and their corresponding stem forms they tested was identical for both regular and irregular verbs.

For example, an irregular participle such as *geschlafen* 'slept' is as similar to its base form (*schlaf-*) as a regular participle (e.g. *geöffnet* 'opened') is to its base stem (*öffn-*), yet despite these formal similarities the regular form produced full priming, and the irregular one did not. Whereas these results cannot be accounted for in terms of formal (prime-target) overlap, they receive a straightforward explanation from a dual-mechanism model: regularly inflected forms are decomposed and directly access their stems, hence the full priming effects in the experiments; irregularly inflected forms have their own lexical representations distinct from, albeit related to, their stems, hence the lack of full priming.

Despite the considerable body of evidence from, in particular, English and German, there are many reasons to extend research to a wider range of languages. Principally, both English and German belong to the same language family — Germanic; any generalizations emerging from these languages may well be due to the specific characteristics of this family and not to truly universal properties of language. Study of Italian represents an extension of the research on the dual-mechanism model to the Romance languages. Apart from having a much richer verbal morphology than either English or German, Italian presents a further interesting dimension, the presence of morphological classes or conjugations. The question this poses for the dual-mechanism model is how to deal with a system where on the one hand a regular, productive class (conjugation 1) contrasts with non-productive or semi-productive classes (conjugations 2 and 3) within which regular and irregular inflections are distinguished. As will be seen, by isolating those aspects of word formation which pertain to class membership, i.e. thematic vowel affixation or stem formation, from those aspects which are the domain of inflection proper, the dual-mechanism model is able to account for the subtleties of Italian verb formation.

In the next section, we discuss different linguistic treatments of the Italian verbal system, focussing on past participles and past definite (preterite) forms. In the empirical parts of our study, we investigate data from Italian child language and present different kinds of experimental data from adult Italian speakers.

2. Verb inflection in Italian

2.1. A descriptive overview

According to traditional descriptive grammars (for example, Serianni, 1988; Sensini, 1988) Italian has three morphological classes, or conjugations, identified by the thematic vowel (TV) which appears between the verb root and the inflectional endings. First conjugation verbs have the TV *-a-*, e.g. *parl-**a**-re* 'to speak', second conjugation verbs have the TV *-e-*, e.g. *tem-**e**-re* 'to fear', and third conjugation *-i-*, e.g. *dorm-**i**-re* 'to sleep'. The first conjugation is by far the largest class of verbs (1,709, 73% [1]), almost all of which are regular. Only three 1st conjugation verbs have irregularly inflected verb forms, *andare* 'to go', *dare* 'to give', *stare* 'to stay'. Although *fare* 'to make, to do' is traditionally included in this class, its paradigm indicates that it more properly belongs to the second conjugation (e.g. imperfect (1sg.) *facevo*, past definite (2sg.) *facesti*, imperfect subjunctive (sg.) *facessi*), the infinitive being irregular. The first conjugation is also the only class which is truly productive; neologisms and foreign loan words all fall into this class. The second conjugation has far fewer members (403, 17%), which are for the most part irregular (around 95%). The third conjugation is the smallest class (238, 10%) and is mostly regular (around 10% of its verbs are irregular). Its members include verbs derived from adjectives and nouns, usually with the addition of a prefix, for example: *inverdire* 'to become green' (from *verde* 'green'), *arricchire* 'to become rich' (from *ricco* 'rich'), although it is doubtful whether new words are still generated in this way (see Dressler and Thornton, 1991, p.5; Orsolini et al., 1998, p.429, fn 1)).

Regularly inflected verb forms consist of a root, which carries semantic information, plus (in most cases) a thematic vowel, plus an inflectional ending encoding some or all of the categories of person, number, tense, aspect and mood (and gender in the case of past participles in certain contexts). The root together with the thematic vowel is traditionally referred to as the stem. Most inflected forms are stem-based (e.g. *parl-a-vo* 'I was speaking') but some are root-based (e.g. *parl-o* 'I speak'). A subset of 3rd conjugation verbs have stems augmented with *-sc-* in forms where stress would otherwise fall on the root (e.g. *finìsco* 'I finish' from *finire* vs. *sènto* 'I feel' from *sentire*), but are otherwise perfectly regular. Regular past participles are formed by adding the participial suffix *-t-* to the verb stem, with the further addition of an agreement marker (*-o* is the default masculine singular form); Table 4.1 provides examples from each conjugation. Irregular past participles are characterized by phonologically modified stems, absence of the TV, and exhibit one or other of the endings *-(s)s-* or *-(t)t-* (gender/number agreement markers are as in regular past participles). Examples are given in Table 4.2.

[1]Calculations are made on the basis of just those verbs listed in the two largest frequency dictionaries of Italian, Bortolini et al., 1971 and De Mauro et al., 1993, each based on a corpus of 500,000 words.

Table 4.1. Regular Italian past participles.

conjugation	*root*	*tv*	*part.*	*gen/num*	*gloss*
1st	parl-	a	-t	-o	spoken
2nd	tem-	u*	-t	-o	feared
3rd	dorm-	i	-t	-o	slept

* -u- is considered an allomorph of the second conj TV -*e*-.

Table 4.2. Irregular Italian past participles.

	Past Participle	*Infinitive*	*gloss*
Forms in -s-:	preso	prendere	'to take'
	apparso	apparire	'to appear'
Forms in -ss-:	discusso	discutere	'to discuss'
	messo	mettere	'to put'
Forms in -t-:	vinto	vincere	'to win'
	aperto	aprire	'to open'
Forms in -tt-	scritto	scrivere	'to write'
	detto	dire	'to say'

The regular past definite (= preterite) paradigm for the 1st conjugation verb *parlare* is shown in Table 4.3. Regular 2nd and 3rd conjugation paradigms differ only in the TV (e.g. 1sg *tem-e-i*, *dorm-i-i*) and in the 3sg suffixes, e.g. 2nd conjugation *temè*, 3rd conjugation *dormì*. The 1sg, 3sg and 3pl forms of some 2nd conjugation regular verbs may take an augmented stem, e.g. *temei/temetti* 'I feared'. Both forms are considered regular, although that with the augment is generally preferred unless the root ends in -t (e.g. *potei/*potetti* 'I was able'). Irregular past definite forms, which occur only in the 1sg, 3sg and 3pl, are characterized by alternations in the verb stem and in the case of the 3pl, an irregular ending, as illustrated by the verb *prendere* 'to take' in Table 4.4.

For a given verb the irregular past participle and past definite stems may or may not be the same; cf. for example, *presi* 'I took', *preso* 'taken' (from *prendere*) and *ruppi* 'I broke', *rotto* 'broken' (from *rompere*). Irregular past definite forms and past participles are also characterized by

Table 4.3. The regular past definite paradigm (1st Conjugation).

1sg.	parl-a-i	*1pl.*	parl-a-mmo
2sg.	parl-a-sti	*2pl.*	parl-a-ste
3sg.	parl-ò	*3pl.*	parl-a-rono

Table 4.4. Irregular past definite paradigm (2nd conjugation).

1sg.	presi	*1pl.*	prend-e-mmo
2sg.	prend-e-sti	*2pl.*	prend-e-ste
3sg.	prese	*3pl.*	presero

having stress on the root, while in regularly inflected verb forms, stress falls on the TV. Irregular forms never carry a theme vowel (apparent exceptions, such as *venuto* from *venire* or *assistito* from *assistere* exhibit an anomalous theme vowel), nor do their inflectional endings vary according to conjugation membership (cf. *tenere* 'to hold', *tenni* 'I held' and *venire* 'to come', *venni* 'I came').

2.2. Linguistic accounts of Italian verb morphology

The linguistic representation of inflected verb forms is controversial. Basically, there are three proposals:

(4.1) a. Regular and irregular forms are derived by rule.

b. Regulars and irregulars are listed.

c. Regulars are derived by rule, irregulars are listed.

De Boer, 1981 proposed a standard Generative phonology account of Italian inflection with suffixation rules for regular and irregular inflection and morphophonological rules for alternant stems. The lexical entry is assumed to be the root and regular past participles, for example, are formed by (a) suffixing the TV to the root to form the stem, and (b) attaching the participial suffix *-t-* to the verb stem; for second conjugation participles, an additional allomorphy rule applies to the TV ($e \rightarrow u$). Irregular past participles are also generated by rules; morphophonological rules derive alternant roots from the base form (= the regular root), suffixation rules add the inflections. In our terms, De Boer's account is an example of (1a), i.e. a uniquely rule-based approach to inflectional morphology.

A radically different alternative has been proposed by Burzio, 1998. He assumes (following Bybee, 1995) that all morphologically complex words are stored whole with morphological relationships expressed as correspondences between words or word fragments which share sound and meaning. With these assumptions, Burzio's account is an example of (1b). Burzio argues that past participles are in direct correspondence with their infinitival stems in Italian. In the framework of Optimality Theory ('OT', Prince and Smolensky, 1993), this is captured by segmental and metrical faithfulness constraints which operate on both stems and affixes. For first conjugation participles, such as *parl-ato* 'spoken', segmental faithfulness is always ranked above metrical faithfulness, hence they never exhibit stem or affix allomorphy. For second and third conjugation participles the ranking is not fixed: regular participles have segmental faithfulness ranked higher, while for irregulars metrical faithfulness takes precedence over segmental faithfulness. Burzio's account depends on alternant stems arising from the normal phonological constraints of Italian and on the fact that the vast majority of 2nd conj verbs with irregular past participles have infinitives with stressed roots (e.g. *vìncere* 'to win' vs. regular *temère* 'to fear'). For example, a constraint disallowing adjacent stressed syllables prevents the regular participial ending being attached to a stressed root (**vìncúto*); instead an alternant syncopated suffix (*-t(t)-* or *-s(s)-*) is resorted to which triggers phonological modification of the stem to prevent an illicit consonant cluster (**vìncto* → *vìnto*). However, not all irregular past participles can be motivated in this way. For example, *pre-so* (from *prend-ere* 'to take') need not lose the *-n-* of its stem to satisfy the phonological constraints of Italian, (**prenso* is a perfectly acceptable phonological form in Italian), yet it does. Other irregular participles also feature an unmotivated vowel change: *esigere-esatto* 'to demand-demanded', *fondere-fuso* 'to melt-melted'. Phonologically unmotivated forms account for 38% of irregular past participles,[2] and as such represent a by no means marginal phenomenon. These examples show that Burzio's account of Italian past participle formation does not explain the full range of data.

In contrast to these accounts which deal with regular and irregular inflection in the same way, Vogel, 1993 argued that regularly inflected verb forms are rule-generated while irregulars have their own lexical entries.

[2] Counting only those verbs listed in Bortolini et al., 1971 and De Mauro et al., 1993, excluding compounds.

She assumes the lexical entry to be the verb stem (e.g. *parla-*) with a vowel deletion rule to account for root-based inflected forms. Regular past participles are formed by affixation of the participial suffix *-t-* to the verb stem plus suffixation of the appropriate gender/number marker. Irregular verbs, on the other hand, have their alternant stems listed alongside their regular stems in the lexicon (e.g. *pres-* is listed along with *prende-*), and irregular past participles (and past definites) are formed by affixation of the appropriate gender/number (or person/number) markers to the alternant stem.

These linguistic analyses may be adopted as the basis for different psycholinguistic accounts of morphological processing in Italian, although it should be pointed out that the authors themselves do not necessarily claim psychological reality for the linguistic procedures they propose. Given this proviso, analyses by De Boer, 1981 and Burzio, 1998 may be considered single mechanism models in that irregular and regular past participle inflections are accounted for in a uniform way ('rules' for De Boer and 'stored forms subject to output-to-output constraints' for Burzio). Vogel posits two different mechanisms for (participle) inflection, listed alternant stems for irregulars (e.g. *pres-*) and a suffixation rule ('Add *-t*') for regulars. None of the accounts, however, distinguishes between different mechanisms for stem formation in the various conjugations. De Boer derives stem forms of 1st, 2nd and 3nd conjugation verbs via concatenative rules, whereas Vogel and Burzio assume them all to be stored. However, as will be shown in the next section, the first conjugation stands apart from the second and third conjugations in many ways and this needs to be accounted for.

2.3. Analyzing Italian verb stems

The first conjugation is the only class which shows unrestricted productivity. It is also 'regular' in the sense of Bybee, 1995, in that it is the pattern "with the least allomorphy in affix and stem" (p.452). With the exception of three verbs of this class, first conjugation verbs have entirely regular paradigms and exhibit no stem allomorphy, while the majority of second conjugation verbs and a significant minority of third conjugation verbs have irregularities in their paradigms. There is also evidence to indicate that the first conjugation is the default class; default being "the pattern that applies when all else fails" (Bybee, 1995, p.252). Note that productivity and default, although they often coincide, do not express the same concept. Non-default processes differ from default processes in that the former are constrained in some way. For example, the 3rd conjugation used to have a process of forming inchoatives from adjectives;

that it failed to apply beyond this restricted domain indicates that the 3rd conjugation is not a default class. The first conjugation on the other hand shows unrestricted productivity and can accommodate any type of root. If the criteria put forward by Marcus et al., 1995, p.197 for default status with respect to inflectional processes are applied, where appropriate, to the morphological verb classes of Italian, it turns out that the relevant categories apply almost always to the first conjugation, as illustrated by the examples in Table 4.5.

The common property that holds together the various circumstances in Table 4.5 is that access to memorized verbal stem forms is prevented and that therefore the default 'elsewhere' process has to apply. For neologisms and foreign loans, this is obvious as they do not have stored lexical entries. Onomatopoeia are stretches of sound that lack canonical entries, and derived verbs are based on a different grammatical category, adjective or noun for example, which does not have an entry as a verbal stem or root; see Marcus et al., 1995 for further discussion. As the list shows, non-suffixed neologisms, loan words, deadjectivals and denominals fall into the first conjugation. In addition, Italian has a range of verb modifying suffixes all of which assign the resultant verb to the first conjugation (e.g. *dormire* 'to sleep', *dormicchiare* 'to snooze'). Neither the second nor the third conjugation ever applies under the default circumstances listed in Table 4.5. (As already mentioned in section 2.1, 3rd conjugation deadjectivals and denominals are probably no longer productive in Italian). Another characteristic of 1st conjugation verb roots is their phonological heterogeneity, compared to 2nd and 3rd conjugation verb roots which fall into fairly constrained phonological patterns.

These differences between the productive, default 1st conjugation and the unproductive, non-default 2nd and 3rd conjugations recall the differences between regular and irregular inflection. Given that it is the TV (or the verb stem) which characterizes each conjugation, we might consider whether a distinction between rule-based and stored forms also arises at this level paralleling the distinction between regular and irregular inflection. From this perspective, a 1st conjugation stem formation rule (*Add -a-*) could apply to any verbal root in Italian to form a regular stem. Like any other default rule, it would apply under 'elsewhere conditions', i.e. unless blocked by some listed (2nd or 3rd conjugation) stem. The rule operates on any root belonging to the syntactic category [+V], and would not be constrained by phonological or semantic properties. It is therefore based on a symbolic category in the same way as an inflectional rule, such as *Add -ed* in English past tense formation. The difference between stem formation and inflectional rules is that the latter are markers of morphosyntactic properties, such as tense, case,

Table 4.5. Default categories for Italian verbal conjugations.

foreign loan words	*scioccare* 'to shock' *dribblare* 'to dribble' (in football) *boicottare* 'to boycott'
neologisms	*silurare* 'to torpedo' *emarginare* 'to put aside' *tifare* 'to be a supporter/fan of'
deadjectival verbs	*falsare* 'to falsify' (from *falso* false) *calmare* 'to calm' (from *calmo* 'calm') [but also *arricchire* 'to enrich' (from *ricco* 'rich'), *ingiallire* 'to turn yellow' (from *giallo* 'yellow')]
denominal verbs	*fumare* 'to smoke' (from *fumo* 'smoke'), *contattare* 'to contact' (from *contatto* 'contact') silenziare 'to silence' (from *silenzio* 'silence')
onomatopoeia	although there is a tendency to form onomatopoeic verbs as compounds of the type [*fare* + noun] ('to make' + noun) for example: *fare bum* 'to go bang', *fare qua qua* 'to quack', *fare un tonfo* 'to thud, splash', the following are also found: *tonfare, sguazzare, schizzare, spruzzare* 'to splash' *cinguettare* 'to tweet', *gracchiare* 'to croak', *sgranocchiare* 'to crunch'‡

‡ Lepschy and Lepschy, 1979, 28 cite some fieldwork of De Amicis in which natives of Florence were asked for the word to describe the sound of freshly baked bread between the teeth: all 12 responses (for example *croccare, sgrigliolare, sgricchiolare* etc.) are verbs of the first conjugation.

number, etc., whereas stem formation rules reflect neither the syntactic nor the semantic system. They are rather — as Aronoff, 1994, p.58 put it — 'part of the abstract and unmotivated morphological machinery of language'. In contrast to 1st conjugation stems, 2nd and 3rd conjugation stems might not be rule-based, but rather stored in the lexicon, which would account for the fact that they do not turn up in default circumstances.

In the remainder of this article, we investigate psycholinguistic evidence from different sources (child language, adult processing) with respect to the question of how Italian verb forms are represented in the mental lexicon. In section 3, we will discuss evidence from previous studies. Experiments testing the hypothesized differences in Italian stem formation, and the differences between regular and irregular inflection are reported in sections 4 and 5 respectively. It will be argued that the evidence supports the distinction between stored lexical entries and combinatorial operations for both stem formation and inflectional processes.

3. Psycholinguistic studies of Italian verb inflection

To date there is a small body of psycholinguistic evidence concerning the mental representation and processing of Italian verb forms. In this section, we present some of the main findings from previous studies addressing this issue which, as will be seen, are by no means consistent.

3.1. Morphological processing in adults

Caramazza et al., 1988 found that in a lexical decision task the degree of morphological structure played a role in non-word recognition which they interpret as evidence for morphological decomposition of regularly inflected verb forms. Non-words with morphological structure (real stem + real suffix in illegal combination) took significantly longer to reject than non-words with only partial (real stem + non-suffix or non-stem + real suffix) or no morphological structure. Caramazza et al. argued that structures with partial morphological structure can be quickly rejected as no access unit will be found for one of the morphemes. Words comprised of real morphemes, on the other hand, activate access units for their component parts, but at a later stage the illegal combination is recognized and the word rejected, hence the slower response times. Non-words with no morphological structure attempt a whole word look-up and fail but because no parsing is involved the process of rejection is the fastest.

Two further experiments carried out by Caramazza et al., 1988 are claimed to provide evidence for inhibitory links between regular stems and the affixes of those forms which are irregular, preventing overgeneralization of regular forms. This mechanism is similar to the blocking device posited in dual-mechanism models of inflection, Marcus et al., 1992; Kiparsky, 1982 (the 'elsewhere condition') and Pinker, 1984 (the 'uniqueness principle'), all of which ensure that specific forms take precedence over general forms. Caramazza et al. found that overregularized past participles such as **corr-uto* (from *correre* 'to run' — the correct form is *corso*) took longer to reject as non-words than forms such as **copr-uto*

(3rd conjugation stem (from *coprire* 'to cover') + 2nd conjugation suffix). In both cases the component morphemes exist and will therefore activate their respective access representations. However, **copr-uto* will be rejected more quickly as it comprises incompatible morphemes whereas *corruto*, consisting of compatible morphemes, will be rejected only after further processing accesses the inhibitory links.

Although these studies provide evidence that regularly inflected word forms are processed via their constituent morphemes, the focus on nonwords leaves open the question of whether real words are similarly processed.

Regular/irregular differences were also found by Cappa and Ullman, 1998 in a study of Italian patients with Alzheimer's disease in which the patients performed worse at producing irregular present tense and past participle forms of 2nd conjugation verbs than regular 1st conjugation verb forms. This is in line with the observation that English-speaking Alzheimer patients are worse at irregular than regular past tense production (Ullman et al., 1997) and suggests a regular/irregular distinction for verb forms in Italian.

In contrast, Orsolini and Marslen-Wilson, 1997 argued that their findings provide support for single-mechanism models of Italian. In their first experiment, the priming abilities of regularly and irregularly inflected past definite forms were tested. They found that irregular forms prime both regularly and irregularly inflected morphologically related items (e.g. *preso-prendere* 'taken-to take' and *preso-presero* 'taken-they took') as effectively as regular prime/target pairs (e.g. *amato-amare* 'loved-to love') which lead Orsolini and Marslen-Wilson, 1997, p.21 to conclude that both regularly and irregularly inflected verb forms are rule-based.

In their second experiment, past participles were elicited to novel verbs (with varying degrees of similarity to existing items) presented in infinitival form, to investigate the generalization properties of regular and irregular inflectional patterns. The conditions tested were: (i) novel verbs with high similarity to existing irregular verbs of the 2nd conjugation and to existing regular verbs of the 3rd conjugation (e.g. novel *frendere* and *affertire* based respectively on existing *prendere* 'to take' and *avvertire* 'to advise') and (ii) novel verbs with low similarity to existing irregular verbs of the 2nd conjugation and existing regular verbs of the 3rd conjugation, (e.g. novel *carripere* and *probucire*)[4]. They found

[4]Although three degrees of phonological similarity were compared in this experiment — 'high', 'root' and 'low' — only the high and low similarity conditions will be discussed here as the results from the intermediate 'root' condition add nothing further to (nor detract from) the present discussion.

that for both regular 3rd conjugation verbs and irregular 2nd conjugation verbs, the low similarity condition elicited significantly fewer expected responses, i.e. regular 3rd conjugation past participles in the former case and irregular past participles in the latter case, than in the high similarity condition. Thus, it seems as if the generalization properties of both regular and irregular patterns are sensitive to phonological similarity, indicating that they are not rule-based.

The two experiments therefore appear to produce conflicting results: the priming results indicate decomposition of regular and irregular forms, while the elicitation results indicate whole-word storage of regulars and irregulars. However, Orsolini & Marslen-Wilson's interpretations did not take into account the distinction between stem formation and inflection. In their priming study, Orsolini & Marslen-Wilson collapsed 1st and 3rd conjugation stems into one 'regular' condition. Recall from section 2.3, however, that only the 1st conjugation exhibits default properties and is fully productive. It is possible that these differences yield different priming patterns for 1st and 3rd conjugation forms which are masked by collapsing them into one experimental condition. Moreover, because an identity repetition condition was not included it is not possible to ascertain whether the results indicate full or partial priming effects. Only full priming would indicate a common underlying lexical entry. With respect to their second experiment, only 2nd and 3rd conjugation verbs were tested using stem-based presentation forms (= infinitives). As pointed out in section 2.3, stems of both these conjugations could be lexically stored rather than rule-based, and hence similarity effects would be expected in both cases. It is only the default class (= 1st conjugation) which should be entirely insensitive to similarity effects. Hence, the significant difference between the high and low similarity conditions for 3rd conjugation verbs may reflect properties of stored stems, rather than of stored inflected forms.

3.2. Evidence from child language

There is one study, Orsolini et al., 1998, specifically investigating the acquisition of past definites and past participles in Italian children with respect to the controversy between dual and single mechanism models of inflection. They assume an interpretation of the dual-mechanism model for Italian whereby the 2nd conjugation, being non-productive, yields inflected verb forms which are all listed, while 1st and 3rd conjugations, being productive, have rule-based inflected forms. Let us consider this assumption and their acquisition data in some detail.

In their first study, Orsolini et al. investigated the spontaneous production of past definite forms in 100 children, age range 4;4 - 10;5, 20 per age group. The children were asked to tell the 'Frog story' from a picture book containing 24 pictures. Of the 1282 past definite tokens obtained from the speech of 74 children (the remaining 26 children did not produce any), 48 were erroneous and formed the basis of their analysis; 9 of these were imperfect subjunctive forms, probably resulting from local dialect influence (see Orsolini et al., 1998, p.438), and will not be discussed further. Orsolini et al. found that most errors were overapplications of 2nd conjugation non-productive (hence listed) past definite patterns, while defaults, i.e. 1st conjugation forms, are rarely overapplied. This, they claim, shows that the dual-mechanism model does not hold for Italian and they suggest instead that a connectionist account would be a more appropriate characterisation of Italian verbal inflection.

The trouble with this account is that it confuses the properties of conjugation membership with those of inflectional processes and assumes that a verb class which is unproductive will have only listed inflections, yet in neither case is there a direct mapping between the two sets of properties in Italian. For example, although the 2nd conjugation is not productive as a class, verbs belonging to this class may nonetheless be subject to rule-based inflectional processes. From a dual-mechanism perspective, one would expect that with respect to inflection only the irregular forms (irrespective of conjugation class membership) are listed, while regularly inflected verb forms (of all classes) are rule-based.

To get a clearer picture, we have reanalyzed Orsolini et al.'s data and present in Table 4.6 a breakdown of the erroneous past definite forms (imperfect subjunctive responses are excluded). The top half of the table shows errors with irregular verbs, the bottom half errors with regular verbs.

Three types of error were found: (i) *irregularizations* refer to overapplications of an irregular inflectional pattern, e.g. **vise* for *vide* (from *vedere* 'to see'); (ii) *specific regularizations* refer to forms with a regular conjugation-specific suffix instead of the required irregular form, e.g. **cadè* instead of *cadde* (from *cadere* 'to fall'), **venì* instead of *venne* (from *venire* 'to come'); (iii) *default regularizations* refer to incorrect assignment of the default (1st conjugation) suffix to a 2nd or 3rd conjugation verb, e.g. **cadò* for *cadde*, **dormò* for *dormì*. Table 4.6 shows that almost all errors occur on irregular verbs and that regularizations clearly outnumber irregularizations. More importantly, Orsolini et al. point out that while regularizations are unconstrained by phonological similarity, irregularizations are analogy-based, for example **visse* or **vise* for *vide*

Table 4.6. Errors on irregular and regular verbs in children's spontaneous data (Adapted from Orsolini et al. 1998).

Irregular verbs	*4yrs*	*5yrs*	*6yrs*	*8yrs*	*10yrs*
Irregularizations e.g. **vise* for *vide*	0	5	1	5	0
Specific regularizations e.g. **prendè* for *prese*	2	8	2	5	7
Default regularizations e.g. **cadò* for *cadde*	0	1	0	0	0

Regular verbs	*4yrs*	*5yrs*	*6yrs*	*8yrs*	*10yrs*
Irregularizations	0	0	0	0	0
Default regularizations e.g. **dormò* for *dormì*	1	2	0	0	0

'she saw' (from vedere), on analogy with *visse* 'she lived' (from *vivere*) and possibly *mise* 'she put' (from *mettere*) — forms which have very high frequencies in the child's environment. Note that these are what have been termed 'product-oriented' generalisations (e.g. Bybee, 1995), i.e. they are based on similarities between past definite forms rather than similarities in base stem to alternant stem mappings. In contrast, regularization errors, the vast majority of which are cases of **cadè* for *cadde* 'she fell', **venì* for *venne* 'she came', cannot be analogy based as there are no similar sounding existing regular verbs of the appropriate conjugation. Moreover, most of the errors occur with idiosyncratic irregulars (e.g. *cadde*, *venne*) and rarely with verbs with past definites in *-s-*; in other words it is the irregulars with low type frequency patterns which are more vulnerable to error. Finally, we note from Table 4.6 that default regularizations are only found in the youngest children, indicating that while children continue making inflectional errors up to (at least) 10 years, they seem to learn class membership earlier. This is perhaps not surprising given that class membership involves only a three-way distinction, available from every verb form that contains a TV, while the inflectional system involves around 40 forms for regulars alone, many of them less readily available than *-a-*, *-e-* or *-i-* stems.

The second experiment Orsolini et al. carried out was a sentence completion task designed to elicit past participles as well as past definites of irregular 2nd conjugation and regular 3rd conjugation verbs. 60 children were tested, 5, 6 and 8 year olds, 20 per age group. The verbs chosen (20 irregular 2nd conj. verbs, 10 regular 3rd conj. verbs) were all familiar to the children. All children achieved high correctness scores (mean 93%) with participles of both conjugations, whereas performance with past definites was worse overall, especially for the younger age groups. The error patterns were the same as those found in the first study. Again, irregularizations were rare (= 6% of all errors) and applied only to phonologically similar items. Regularizations, on the other hand, accounted for more than 90% of the errors.

These data show that Italian children overgeneralize regular patterns to irregular items, whereas generalizations of irregular patterns to regular verbs are rare or non-existent and are based on phonological similarity. Moreover, members of family clusters with low type frequencies are most susceptible to overregularization. Thus Italian past definites and past participles show the same asymmetry with respect to the generalisation of regular and irregular patterns as do English past tenses (Marcus et al., 1992) and German participles (Clahsen and Rothweiler, 1993) and provide cross-linguistic support for the dual-mechanism model.

Taken together, the picture we get from previous psycholinguistic studies of Italian verbs is not entirely clear. It is true that the data from Italian child language discussed in this section show a qualitative distinction between the generalization properties of regular and irregular inflection, but as pointed out in section 3.1, the experimental evidence from adult native speakers appears to be less clear. We have attributed the inconsistencies across experiments to the fact that the distinction between stem formation and inflection has not been taken into account. Consequently, we have designed new experiments to investigate potential distinctions between rule-based and memory-based representations for both stem formation and inflection. The results of these experiments will be reported in the following sections.

4. Experiment 1: Generalization properties of stem forms

The purpose of this experiment is to determine the generalization properties of the various conjugation classes in Italian by investigating circumstances under which a novel verb may be assimilated into one or other of them. Presentation forms were root-based (present tense 1sg., 2sg. or 1pl), having no TV to indicate conjugation membership, thus providing only phonological cues for analogical processes. The task, formation of the past participle, requires subjects to assign each novel root to one of the conjugations in order that a stem may be formed upon which the participle in turn may be formed. It is this process of conjugation assignment, or stem formation, as opposed to the process of inflectional affixation, which we are interested in here. By including a true 'no similarity' condition (i.e. neither morphological nor phonological cues), a proper testing ground for conjugation default status is presented. If, as hypothesized in section 2.3, 1st conjugation stems are rule-based and 2nd and 3rd conjugation stems are lexically stored, we would expect that the 1st conjugation, being the default class, will accept verbs regardless of their phonological properties, while the 2nd and 3rd conjugations will only accept verbs bearing phonological similarities to existing items of these classes. Furthermore, if 2nd and 3rd conj. stem forms are stored, we would expect frequency effects for these classes, i.e. novel verbs that are phonologically similar to existing high frequency verbs will be accepted more easily into the appropriate conjugation class, whereas those based on low frequency verbs will be more susceptible to default (1st conj.) classification.

4.1. Materials

A total of 82 novel verbs were devised, divided amongst the various conditions as shown in Table 4.7; see Say, 1999 for a full item list. The criterion for establishing similarity was rhyme. A novel verb was considered similar to an existing verb, if it shared the final vowel and consonant(s) of the root. Rhymes were also chosen to be exclusive to each condition as far as possible. The rhyme *-end*, for example, is not only highly frequent in irregular second conjugation verbs (e.g. *prend-ere* 'to take', *attend-ere* 'to wait for', *difend-ere* 'to defend' etc), it is also almost entirely absent from regular second conjugation verbs and from both regular and irregular verbs of the first and third conjugations. Where it was not possible to maintain complete exclusiveness, it was ensured that a particular rhyme found outside the category which it typified occurred only in low frequency verbs. For the 'no similarity' condition, novel verbs were created with stems that consisted of odd sounding but phonologically legal strings. These were all checked against an inverse dictionary of Italian (Thornton et al., 1994) to ensure that no existing verb of any conjugation shared the same root final vowel and consonant(s).

The novel verbs were presented in sentences in either a first singular (e.g *cendo*), second singular (e.g. *cendi*) or first plural (*cendiamo*) present tense form. These are forms in which the TV is not present, giving no cue to class membership. All novel verbs in condition 4 were presented in 1pl

Table 4.7. Experimental conditions with example stimuli, corresponding existing verbs, and number of verbs per condition.

Condition	*Novel verb*	*Existing verb*	*No.*
1. Similarity to irregular 2nd conj.	cendiamo	prendiamo 'we take'	20
2. Similarity to irregular 3rd conj.	suffriamo	soffriamo 'we suffer'	10
3. Similarity to regular 2nd conj.	bremiamo	temiamo 'we fear'	20
4. Similarity to regular 3rd conj.	rinferiamo	riferiamo 'we refer'	20
5. No similarity	zuisdiamo		12
		Total	82

present tense form (e.g. *perferiamo*) because the 1sg and 2sg forms of regular 3rd conjugation verbs take the stem augment -sc- (for example, *riferisco*) which would indicate their class membership.

Half of the verbs in conditions 1, 3 and 4 were based on high frequency rhymes, the other half on low frequency rhymes. It was not possible to have a high and a low frequency condition for irregular third conjugation verbs, as these all have high frequencies (hence half the number of stimuli in this condition), and of course it is not possible to manipulate frequency with respect to non-rhyming novel verbs. To establish rhyme frequency, both the type frequencies of particular patterns and the token frequencies of individual verbs displaying those patterns were taken into account. Type frequencies were based on verbs listed in one or both of the major frequency dictionaries of Italian (Bortolini et al., 1971; De Mauro et al., 1993), while token frequencies were calculated from the combined counts of these verbs. Firstly, all verbs of the second conjugation and of the third conjugation were grouped according to root rhyme to obtain a rhyme type frequency. For example, 32 second conjugation verbs have a basic root ending in *-end-* and a past participle based on an alternant stem ending in *-eso* (such as *prend-ere/preso* 'to take-taken', *tend-ere/teso* 'to stretch-stretched'). Secondly, a rhyme lemma frequency was obtained by adding together the lemma frequencies of all the verbs conforming to a given pattern. The combined lemma frequencies of all 32 irregular second conjugation verbs with a regular root *-end-* and a past participle in *-eso*, for instance, comes to 3,408 per million. The motivation for this was that a novel verb with a root ending in *-end-* could not be said to be based on any single verb but rather rhymed with all 32 verbs of this family group, and as such the frequencies of all of these verbs should be taken into account. A corresponding rhyme past participle frequency was obtained by adding together the past participle frequencies of all the verbs sharing a given pattern.

Novel 'high frequency' verbs were based on rhymes having a mean type frequency of 11.7, a mean lemma frequency of 1387.2 and a mean past participle frequency of 455.2. Novel 'low frequency' verbs were based on rhymes with a mean type frequency of 1.9, a mean lemma frequency of 28.5 and a mean past participle frequency of 4.5.

4.2. Method

40 subjects, adult native Italian speakers aged between 16 and 46 years (mean age 18;10, 24 female and 16 male), carried out the experiment. Subjects were given a booklet on each page of which was printed a pair of sentences. The first sentence contained a novel verb printed in bold type. The second sentence had a blank space which subjects were instructed to fill in with a past participle form of the novel verb. The following is an example pair of sentences:

(4.2) Oggi **praino** con mio fratello
Ieri ho _______ con i miei amici
(*Today I* **praino** *with my brother*
Yesterday I have _______ *with my friends*)

The presence of the auxiliary verb (*ho* 'I have') in the second sentence makes it clear that a past participle is required in the space. A few of the verbs were used transitively, and in these cases the direct object was also a novel noun in order to avoid semantic associations being made. Subjects were instructed that there was no correct or incorrect answer but that they were to write down the form of the verb which they felt 'sounded right'. The order of sentences was pseudo-randomized so that no two verbs of the same condition appeared consecutively. All subjects saw all stimuli.

A number of responses were excluded from the analysis. These were illegible responses or forms which could not be identified as past participles as well as responses involving regular participle endings (including TV, e.g. *-a-to*, *-i-to* or *-u-to*) on modified or truncated stems (e.g. *endiato* from *edend-o*); in these latter cases, it is not clear whether they should be counted as regular forms or irregularizations. The results from one subject were discarded as he had misunderstood the instructions and incorrectly completed the experiment. Moreover, one stimulus from condition 3 was discarded from all subjects due to a printing error in the booklet. The responses that had to be excluded from the analysis made up 5% of the entire data set.

4.3. Results

A summary of the elicited participle forms, expressed as percentages of all responses to each condition, is presented in Table 4.8. Column 2 shows the percentage of responses which were regular first conjugation forms in *-a-to*, the second column regular second conjugation forms in *-u-to*, the third column regular third conjugation forms in *-i-to*, and the final column irregularizations. The figures in bold italics highlight the predicted responses.

Table 4.8. Participle forms of novel verbs by condition (expressed as percentages).

Condition / *Response type*	*I* (*-a-to*)	*II* (*-u-to*)	*III* (*-i-to*)	*Irreg.*
1. Similar to irreg. II	59	7	3	***31***
2. Similar to irreg. III	71	4	4	***21***
3. Similar to reg. II	54	***38***	1	8
4. Similar to reg. III	62	1	***35***	1
5. No similarity	***90***	4	4	2
All conditions	64	12	11	12

Note firstly the very high percentages of first conjugation forms (*-a-to*) in all conditions - 64% of responses overall. It is the form found almost exclusively in the no similarity condition, and in the other conditions it accounts for between 54% and 71% of responses. These observations confirm the status of the first conjugation as the default. Otherwise responses are as predicted: irregular novel verb types elicit irregular participles, and regular second and third conjugation types elicit regular second and third conjugation participles respectively. What is crucial here is that regular 2nd and 3rd conjugation forms only turn up in the expected context and almost never in other conditions. This is in marked contrast to the first conjugation form which turns up everywhere. To see the different generalization properties more clearly, consider Table 4.9 which shows the extent to which a given response type occurs in its expected context ('expected' defined in terms of phonological similarity for 2nd and 3rd conj. forms) compared with the extent to which the same response type occurs in all the remaining conditions. The last column, then, indicates the extent to which a given stem generalizes to contexts outside its normal range, i.e. beyond similarity.

It is clear that only first conjugation forms generalize freely to all contexts: the difference between the rate of 57% for these and the rate

Table 4.9. Generalization properties of past participle forms.

Type of Response	*Expected context*	*All other contexts*
Reg. 1st Conj. (*-a-to*)	90%	57%
Reg. 2nd Conj. (*-u-to*)	38%	4%
Reg. 3rd Conj. (*-i-to*)	35%	3%
Irregularizations	28%	4%

of 4%, 3% and 4% for second and third conjugation forms and irregular forms respectively is statistically highly significant ($p < .0001$).

Consider now potential frequency effects in stem formation. Table 4.10 presents a breakdown by frequency for conditions 1, 3 and 4, expressed as percentages of total responses to each condition. As previously mentioned, it was not possible to break down condition 2 into high and low frequency. Expected responses are shown in bold italics.

Table 4.10. Responses to conditions 1, 3 and 4 broken down according to frequency (expressed as percentages).

Condition	*Freq.*	*Conj. I (-a-to)*	*Conj. II (-u-to)*	*Conj. III (-i-to)*	*Irregs.*
1. Irregular II	High	60	11	1	***28***
	Low	57	3	6	***34***
3. Regular II	High	43	***45***	2	10
	Low	65	***31***	1	4
4. Regular III	High	55	2	***41***	2
	Low	69	1	***30***	1

As can be seen from Table 4.10, in conditions 3 and 4 the high frequency condition elicits a higher percentage of expected responses than the low frequency condition. A pair-wise comparison using a Tukey test showed that the differences between the high and low conditions were statistically significant in both cases ($p < 0.05$). Frequency effects are indications of associative processes, hence the finding that novel verbs with phonological similarities to existing high frequency verbs will be accepted more easily into the appropriate conjugation than those similar to existing low frequency verbs supports the view that stem forms of 2nd and 3rd conjugation verbs are stored in associative memory.

The surprising result is that there was no frequency effect for novel verbs that were based on existing irregular 2nd conjugation verbs. Table 4.10 shows that the low-frequency condition elicited even slightly more irregularizations, but the difference between the high and low frequency conditions is not statistically significant. One explanation for this may be that the low frequency base verbs are more consistent than the high frequency base verbs. Several of the novel verb forms that were used for the high frequency irregular 2nd condition were based on the subclass of verbs which have roots in -*end*, and past participles in -*eso*. Exceptions to this pattern are the 2nd conjugation verb *vendere* 'to sell' (and its compound *rivendere* 'to resell') with the regular past participle *venduto*, and the 1st conjugation verb *rammendare* 'to darn' with the past participle *rammendato*. On the other hand, there were no exceptions to patterns of the low frequency base verbs. The phonological cohesiveness of the low frequency clusters may account for the low percentage of conjugation-specific regularizations (= 3%, see Table 4.10), while the lesser phonological cohesiveness of the high frequency clusters may have provoked the higher percentages of conjugation-specific regularizations with these (= 11%).

4.4. Discussion

An elicitation task has been reported in which subjects were required to produce past participles to novel verbs with similarity to existing regular or irregular verbs of the 2nd and 3rd conjugations and with no similarity to any existing items. It was found that almost all the no similarity items and a significant proportion of the novel verbs in all other conditions were assigned to the 1st conjugation, while the 2nd and 3rd conjugations assimilated novel verbs only if these bore phonological similarity to existing items. Thus, a marked contrast was shown between the generalization abilities of the 1st conjugation and those of the 2nd and 3rd conjugation; regular 2nd and 3rd conjugation stems pattern with irregular stems in opposition to the 1st conjugation. This finding is in line with the observation of Orsolini and Marslen-Wilson, 1997 that both 2nd and 3rd conjugation forms exhibit similarity effects. Taken together, these findings provide support for a dual-mechanism account of stem formation, with 2nd and 3rd conjugation stem forms being lexically stored and 1st conjugation stems formed by affixation.

5. Experiment 2: Event-related potentials to violations of Italian past participles

In this section, we will present results from an experiment using event-related brain potentials (ERPs) to investigate past participle formation in Italian. Before presenting the experimental design and results, we will provide some background information focussing on the use of ERPs in the psycholinguistic study of morphological processing.

5.1. ERPs and morphological processing

Active neurons in the brain produce electrical activity which can be measured by electrodes placed on the scalp. Psycholinguists are concerned with isolating the electrical activity associated with a specific task - the event-related potentials - from background activity with the aim of identifying the electrical components associated with a given linguistic stimulus (for reviews see Osterhout and Holcomb, 1995; Kutas and Van Petten, 1994). While many of the techniques involved in psycholinguistic research are only able to measure the end-result of the task (e.g. lexical decision, probe recognition, sentence matching), this technique has the advantage of being able to measure linguistic processes as they actually occur. The limitations of this technique lie in the fact that it has poor spatial resolution and therefore extreme caution must be taken in drawing conclusions about the localization of brain functions from this technique.

One particular component is of interest here: the LAN (left anterior negativity). This early negative component with a left anterior distribution has been associated with violations of morpho-syntactic rules in a range of languages, for example, violations of subject-verb agreement (**you goes*, see Münte et al., 1993; Osterhout and Mobley, 1995), number errors in Turkish (Münte et al., 1995), phrase-structure violations in English (Neville et al., 1991) and in German (Friederici et al., 1996) and ungrammatical *wh* questions (Kutas and Kluender, 1994).

With respect to inflectional morphology, ERP studies on English (Newman et al., 1999) and German (Penke et al., 1997; Weyerts et al., 1997) showed that violations or misapplications of regular inflection elicited a LAN. Penke et al., 1997 compared ERPs to participles with correct regular affixes (*getanz-t* 'danced') and correct irregular affixes (*gelad-en* 'loaded') with ERPs to incorrectly affixed participles, that is, regular verbs with the irregular inflection (**getanz-en*) and irregular verbs with the regular inflection (**gelad-et*). No significant differences were observed between the correct and incorrect regulars, but incorrectly affixed irregular participles produced a widespread negativity which was most prominent over the left anterior region (i.e. a LAN) when compared with correct irregulars. This effect was also obtained by Weyerts et al., 1997 for overapplications of regular *-s* plurals. These ERP results were taken as indication of different neuronal processes for regular and irregular morphology. That is, misapplication of regular inflection is akin to morpho-syntactic violation in that two legal components appear in illegal combination, and hence a LAN in both cases. irregulars, on the other hand, are not decomposed into stem and affix, and hence irregularizations do not produce effects typical of rule violations (LAN).

Another component identified as an electrophysiological marker of grammatical anomaly is the P600 or syntactic positive shift (SPS), a positive going waveform occurring between around 300 and 900ms post stimulus onset with a centro-parietal-maximum scalp distribution. This component has been found to occur in violations of verb subcategorisation (Osterhout and Holcomb, 1992), phrase-structure anomalies and agreement violations (Hagoort et al., 1993). Experimental results indicate that the P600 component is sensitive not just to ungrammatical structures, but also to sentences that are difficult to parse. It appears therefore to be associated with the inability of the parser to continue to assign the preferred structure in the face of a syntactically anomalous element in the sentence. The LAN and the P600 appear to be related in that the former often precedes the latter in cases of morpho-syntactic anomaly (see Neville et al., 1991; Kutas and Kluender, 1994; Friederici et al., 1996).

The present experiment makes use of the ERP violation paradigm to investigate the representation of Italian verb forms; see also Gross et al., 1998.

5.2. Materials

Critical stimuli were 1st, 2nd and 3rd conjugation past participles matched for lemma and past participle frequency. These comprised 110 regular 1st conjugation verbs (mean lemma frequency 35.47 per million, past participle frequency 8.64 per million[5]), 110 regular 3rd conjugation verbs (mean frequencies 36.87 & 8.85) and 110 irregular 2nd conjugation verbs (mean frequencies 34.31 & 8.85). In addition 330 fillers were devised with the following characteristics:

- 55 correct infinitives, e.g. *lambire* 'to lick';

[5] These figures are based on combined counts from Bortolini et al., 1971 and De Mauro et al., 1993.

- 55 incorrect infinitives, e.g. *riconoscire* (from *riconoscere* 'to recognize');

- 110 past definite forms, e.g. *succedemmo* 'we succeeded';

- 110 present tense forms, e.g. *insistiamo* 'we insist'.

A further 130 common nouns served as response targets; see Say, 1999 for a complete item list.

Inflectional violations were created by incorrect suffixation of the 1st conjugation TV and the regular participial inflection to the regular stems of 2nd conjugation verbs having irregular past participles, for example, **prend-a-to* instead of *preso* 'taken'. Stem formation errors were obtained by interchanging the TVs of 1st and 3rd conjugation past participles, for example **parl-i-to* instead of *parl-a-to* 'spoken' and **dorm-a-to* instead of *dorm-i-to* 'slept'.

Two stimulus lists were constructed such that each critical item appeared in its correct form in one list and in its incorrect form in another list, with correct and incorrect forms balanced across both lists. Half the subjects saw one list, the other half saw the other list. Thus, no subject saw any critical item in both its correct and incorrect form, and each subject saw a total of 790 stimuli. A summary of the breakdown of each stimulus list, with examples, is shown in Table 4.11. A further 20 practice items were devised, of the same types as those in the stimulus lists, and were presented to the subjects prior to the start of the experiment.

Table 4.11. Summary of stimulus list for ERP study.

Stimulus		*Example*	*Number*
Critical	1st conj. correct	*amato* 'loved'	55
	1st conj. incorrect	*rubito* (from *rubato* 'stolen')	55
	3rd conj. correct	*pulito* 'cleaned'	55
	3rd conj. incorrect	*ferato* (from *ferito* 'wounded')	55
	2nd conj. correct	*sospeso* 'suspended'	55
	2nd conj. incorrect	*prendato* (from *preso* 'taken')	55
Fillers	correct infinitives	*lambire* 'to lick'	55
	incorrect infinitives	*riconoscire* (from *riconoscere* 'to recognize')	55
	past definites	*succedemmo* 'we succeeded'	110
	present tenses	*insistiamo* 'we insist'	110
Targets	nouns	*paese* 'village, country'	130
		Total	*790*

5.3. Method

Twelve healthy native Italian speakers participated in the experiment, eight women and four men, ages ranging from 22 to 35 years. Stimuli were presented one word at a time in the centre of a computer screen. Each word was presented for 300 ms. with a random onset asynchrony of 1400-2200 ms. The subjects' task was to read the words silently and to respond to the presentation of a noun by pressing a button with the dominant hand. EEG activity was recorded at all standard sites of the 10/20 system plus 10 additional intermediate sites (total 29) using tin electrodes mounted in an electrocap with reference electrodes placed on both mastoid processes. The electro-oculogram was recorded for artefact correction purposes. The biosignals were amplified (bandpass 0.01-100 Hz) and digitised with 4 ms resolution. After artefact correction for eye blinks using a spatial filter, ERPs were averaged for 1024 ms epochs beginning 100 ms prior to presentation of the stimuli. Mean-amplitude measures were taken in the 250-500ms and 500-750ms time windows and subjected to measures of analysis of variance. Separate analyses were done for midline (Fz, Cz, Pz), parasagittal (F1/2, F3/4, C3/4, P3/4, O1/2) and temporal (F7/8, T3/4, T5/6) electrode rows. The ERP-recordings produced 29 triplets of graphs such as those shown in Figure 5.3 below. Fig. 5.3 shows the electrical activity recorded at the frontal midline electrode Fz for each condition during the recording period, starting 100 ms. before stimulus presentation and ending after 800 ms.

5.4. Results

Figure 5.3 shows the grand average ERPs for one of the three midline electrodes (Fz), where the effects are most pronounced. As these graphs indicate, a clear effect of incorrectness is only found with the regularized irregular verbs. This is manifested in a more negative waveform for incorrect irregulars beginning 250 ms. post stimulus onset. This effect is much smaller in the waveforms of 1st and 3rd conjugation verb forms; incorrect 1st and 3rd conjugation verbs also produced more negative waveforms, but the differences are statistically non-significant. The results of an analysis of variance for each verb type revealed main effects of correctness in both the 250-500 ms and the 500-750 ms. time windows for irregular verbs, but not for regular 3rd conjugation verbs and for regular 1st conjugation verbs; see Gross et al., 1998 and Say, 1999 for further details.

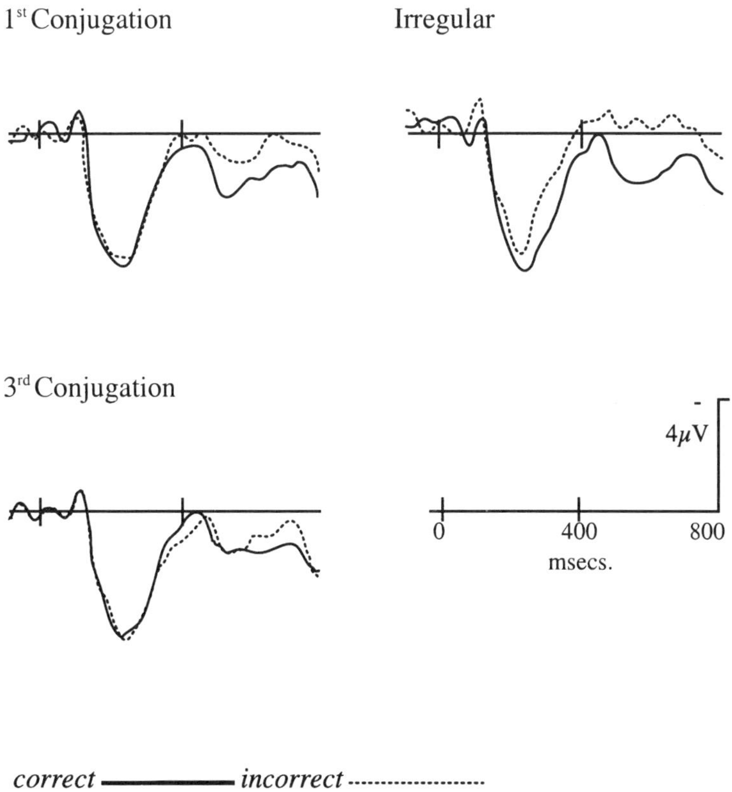

Figure 4.1. Grand average (n=12) for midline electrode Fz.

5.5. Discussion

We found that incorrect irregulars resulting from overapplications of regular inflection, e.g. **prendato* *'taked' instead of the correct *preso* 'taken', gave rise to a significant ERP effect, namely an early negativity. By contrast, we did not find a P600 effect for the incorrect items, which may seem surprising given the wide range of conditions that elicit this component. Note, however, that the P600 has been interpreted as reflecting reanalysis or repair processes on a *sentential level*, but that in our study a simple word list containing incorrect participles was used which does not involve any sentential processing.

The early negativity for overapplications of regular inflection in Italian is similar to the effect found for incorrect irregular inflection in German, although it should be noted that the scalp distribution of the negativities in the Italian study is different from that found in German. In the Italian ERP experiment, violations of regular inflection produced a negativity which was most pronounced at the midline and parasagittal electrode sets (Fz, Pz and Cz). In the German studies, effects were also found at these sites, but the most pronounced effects were found at the left anterior site (F7).

In contrast to violations of regular inflection, stem violations did not produce a statistically reliable ERP effect in our study. That is, participle forms with the correct inflectional ending (= -*t*-) and incorrect theme vowels, e.g. **parlito* (instead of *parlato* 'spoken') and **dormato* (instead of *dormito* 'slept'), elicited similar ERP waveforms to the corresponding correct forms. The lack of a stem-violation effect in the ERP study might be attributed to the task assigned to subjects, which was to identify nouns from the stimulus list. Note that the word structure of nouns in Italian is different from that of verbs: whereas inflected verbs generally consist of a root, a theme vowel and an inflectional ending (*parl-a-to* 'spoken'), noun inflections are attached directly to the root, e.g. *tavol-o* - *tavol-i* 'table-Masc.Sg. - table-Masc.Pl.'. In order to identify nouns from the stimulus list, it is therefore sufficient to monitor the items only with respect to inflectional endings and corresponding roots. The form of the theme vowel, however, is likely to receive much less attention, as it does not provide any cue for solving the experimental task, i.e. detecting an Italian noun; hence the lack of a significant effect for stem violations. Moreover, if this account is correct, the negativity elicited by incorrect irregulars, e.g. **prendato* instead of the correct irregular form *preso* 'taken', is clearly due to overapplication of -*t*- affixation, and not to the incorrect TV.

In order to elicit ERP effects of stem violations, one would have to assign subjects a task that encourages them to process the form of the verb stimuli (including their TVs) in more detail. This issue has recently been addressed in a similar ERP study on Catalan past participles (Rodriguez-Fornells et al., 1999). Stem and participle formation in Catalan are very similar to Italian. Catalan has three morphological classes, as well as a regular -*t* participle ending and irregular participles, e.g. regular 1st conj. *cant-a-t* 'sung', regular 2nd conj. *tem-u-t* 'feared', regular 3rd conj. *part-i-t* 'left', irregular 2nd conj. *admes* 'admitted' (from *admettre*). The Catalan study also employed the ERP violation paradigm, but in this study correct and incorrect participles were presented embedded in sentences within short stories. The subjects' task was to respond to questions regarding the contents of the stories. This task encourages subjects to process the form of the verb stimuli at the same level of detail as other stimuli and to analyze incorrect forms. The results showed that overregularization of the 1st conj. theme vowel *-a-* to a verb form that requires a 2nd or 3rd conjugation form, e.g. **dorm-a-t* instead of the correct *dorm-i-t* or **tem-a-t* instead of *tem-u-t* produced an early negativity that was more significant on the left side of the brain, in other words a LAN. On the other hand, incorrect 1st conjugation forms in which the correct theme vowel (*-a-*) was replaced with the 3rd conjugation form (*-i-*), e.g. **parl-i-t* instead of *parl-a-t*, did not yield a LAN effect. Taken together, these findings indicate that 1st conjugation stem formation (but not 3rd conjugation stem formation) is rule-based in Catalan. In this study the incorrect participles elicited P600 effects which might be taken to result from the fact that (in contrast to the Italian study) the participles in the Catalan study were presented in sentences (rather than in a word list) and hence required processing at the sentential level.

Comparison of the two studies is suggestive, although further research on Italian using experimental designs which focus subjects' attention on processing the verb forms are required to clarify the issue.

6. General discussion

The question of how morphologically complex forms are mentally represented has stimulated a number of linguistic and psycholinguistic studies. In studies of English and German, dissociations have been found between regular and irregular inflection in human language processing, in language disorders and in child language development (see Pinker, 1999, Clahsen, 1999 for review). These findings have been interpreted in terms of a dual-mechanism model according to which regular and irregular inflections are based on different mental representations, irregulars being stored as entries in the lexicon, regulars being computed by combinatorial rules. The purpose of the present study was to investigate Italian verbs with respect to this distinction.

An important property of Italian is that inflection is root-based or stem-based, whereas in English it is by default word-based. That is, inflectional affixes in Italian are combined with stems, which in turn are combinations of TVs and roots which cannot form words on their own, e.g. **parl-*, **cred-*, and **fin-* are illicit words in Italian. This is different from English where verbs and nouns typically have one single uninflected base form, e.g. *walk, rat*, etc., which forms a perfectly legal word and to which inflectional affixes are directly attached. Thus, in examining Italian verb forms, we need to study the issue of storage versus combinatorial mechanisms with respect to both the representation of stems and the representation of inflected word forms.

6.1. On the representation of stem forms in Italian

The structure of stem forms is controversial in the linguistic literature. While De Boer, 1981 posits regular stems of the 1st, 2nd and 3rd conjugations to be generated by rules which affix the theme vowel to the root, Vogel, 1993 assumes them all to be stored. For Burzio, 1998, although the whole word is stored, the surface fragments (ibid. p.85) that comprise it are (a) the root and (b) the inflectional ending which incorporates the TV.

None of these approaches posits different mechanisms for stem formation in the various conjugations. In section 2.3, however, we saw that the first conjugation stands apart from the second and third conjugations in many ways. In elicited production tasks (see sections 3.1 and 4), similarity and frequency effects were found in the formation of 2nd conjugation and 3rd conjugation stems from novel verbs: 2nd and 3rd conjugation stems generalize to novel verbs only if these are phonologically similar to existing items of these classes, and novel items that rhyme with existing high frequency verbs will be accepted more easily into the corresponding conjugation class than items that rhyme with existing low frequency verbs of the same class. In contrast to 2nd and 3rd conjugation stems, we found that 1st conjugation stems generalize to novel items which bear no similarity whatsoever to existing forms. Thus, any kind of phonological shape can form a 1st conjugation stem, provided that it is a verbal root, i.e. is an exemplar of the category [+V].

The distinction between the 1st conjugation on the one hand and the 2nd and 3rd conjugations on the other hand appears to parallel the distinction between regular rule-based inflectional processes and stored irregulars, and indeed the results of the elicitation task reported in section 4 are consistent with the hypothesis that 1st conjugation stems are rule-based while 2nd and 3rd conjugation stems are stored.

Nonetheless, from the perspective of traditional accounts of Italian grammar, it seems odd that a highly irregular class of verbs such as the 2nd conjugation should be assigned the same status as a mostly regular class such as the 3rd conjugation. Furthermore, the 2nd conjugation is unproductive while the 3rd conjugation had (until recently) a productive deadjectival verb formation process. However, while the 3rd conjugation is mostly regular it is no more predictable than the 2nd conjugation. It encompasses two types of verbs: those that take an infix *-isc-* in forms in which stress would otherwise be on the root (e.g. *finire* 'to finish', *fin-isc-o* 'I finish') and those that do not. Thus the information that a given verb belongs to the 3rd conjugation is insufficient to determine the stem forms and inflections that it will take. In this it patterns with the 2nd conjugation and contrasts with the predictable 1st conjugation. Furthermore, that each conjugation comprises predominantly either regular or irregular verbs ceases to be surprising if we do not look on irregularity as some kind of aberration in the language but rather just another way of encoding grammatical information (see Maiden, 1992). Indeed it may even be the preferred option. Whether a class of verbs is characteristically regular (1st and 3rd conjugations) or whether it is characteristically irregular (2nd conjugation) may, theoretically, be independent of whether it is productive.

Given these considerations and the empirical evidence presented in sections 3.1 and 4, we maintain the hypothesized distinction between 1st conjugation stem forms, on the one hand, and 2nd and 3rd conjugation stems on the other, such that the latter are lexically stored, while the former are rule-based.

6.2. Regular and irregular inflection

Linguistic treatments of Italian inflection have given conflicting accounts of regular and irregular verb inflections. As pointed out in section 2.2, De Boer, 1981 argued that both regular and irregular inflections are controlled by rules in Italian, while Burzio, 1998 suggested that all inflected word forms are lexically listed. In contrast to these models, Vogel, 1993 proposed different representations for regulars and irregulars; the latter are assumed to be lexically stored, while regularly inflected words are claimed to be based on affixation rules.

Psycholinguistic evidence in support of a dual-mechanism account of inflection along the lines of Vogel, 1993 comes from the child language data discussed in section 3.2 and from the results of the ERP study in section 5. Recall that incorrect irregular participles of Italian produced a significant negativity in the ERP study, and that this effect was similar to what was found for incorrect irregular participles and noun plurals of German (despite different scalp distributions in the two languages). With respect to child language, the data discussed in section 3.2 show that Italian children generalize regular patterns to irregular items, but generalization of irregular patterns to regular verbs is rare or nonexistent. Moreover, similarity and frequency effects were found only for irregulars, but not for regularly inflected verb forms. More inflectional errors were found with low frequency irregulars than with high-frequency irregulars, and children overapply irregular patterns only to phonologically similar items whereas overapplications of the regular patterns are not constrained by similarity. These results are familiar from studies of the acquisition of the English past tense (Marcus et al., 1992) and of German participles (Clahsen and Rothweiler, 1993). The dual-mechanism model provides a straightforward explanation: irregulars are stored in associative memory, hence their sensitivity to frequency and similarity; regularly inflected words are computed by symbolic rules, and hence they may generalize freely and regardless of similarity and frequency.

7. Conclusion

The psycholinguistic evidence put forward in this article indicates that in Italian (as in English and German), irregularly inflected words show effects of associative storage (similarity, frequency). Regulars, on the other hand, do not depend on stored representations of inflected word forms, but rather involve rule-based processes such as stem+affix decomposition. It is clear, for example, from the generalization properties of regular inflections, that subjects do not have to rely on stored versions of regularly inflected words in making use of the rule. A similar distinction also arises with respect to stem formation in Italian. We found evidence that 1st conjugation stems behave differently to 2nd and 3rd conjugation stems, suggesting that the former may be rule-based and the latter lexically stored.

Stem formation and inflectional affixation are clearly related in that both are necessary for word formation in the Italian verbal system. However, we have shown that it is essential to bear in mind the different contribution each process makes in word formation. At one end of the scale are 1st conjugation verb forms which are completely rule-based: a rule for stem formation and rules for inflectional affixation. At the other end of the scale are irregular forms *of any conjugation* which are stored and subject neither to stem formation rules nor to inflectional rules. Regular forms of the 2nd and 3rd conjugation represent the middle ground: inflectional rules apply to stored stem forms. The distinction between rules and storage is therefore more complex in Italian verbs than in morphological systems which present just the simple binary distinction between regular and irregular inflection such as English past tense and German past participle forms. We have shown that the dual-mechanism model is able to account for this. Of course further investigation of other languages with more fine-grained distinctions in their morphological systems is necessary to decide the universal status of the dual-mechanism model. Our work in this regard may be seen as exploratory rather than conclusive.

Acknowledgments

The research in this article has been supported by a NATO Collaborative Research grant and an ESRC postgraduate training scholarship. Earlier presentations were given in 1997 and 1998, at the LAGB meeting (University of Hertfordshire), the Frontiers in Morphology meeting (University of Essex), the MRC Cognitive and Brain Science Unit (University of Cambridge), the Centre for Speech and Language (Birkbeck College, London) and at the Cognitive Science Colloquium (University of Hamburg). Our thanks to the organizers and the participants of these meetings for discussions and helpful suggestions. We are also grateful to Wolfgang U. Dressler, William Marslen-Wilson, and Dieter Wunderlich for comments on an earlier version of this paper.

Corresponding author: Harald Clahsen, Department of Linguistics, University of Essex. Tel: +44/1206/87-2228; Fax: +44/1206/87-2085; email: harald@essex.ac.uk

References

Aronoff, M. (1994). *Morphology by itself. Stems and inflectional classes.* Cambridge, MA: MIT Press.

Bartke, S., Marcus, G., and Clahsen, H. (1996). Acquiring German noun plurals. In MacLaughlin, D. and McEwen, S., editors, *Proceedings of the 19th Annual Boston University Conference on Language Development.* Somerville, MA: Cascadilla Press.

Bortolini, U., Tagliavini, C., and Zampolli, A. (1971). *Lessico di frequenza della lingua italiana contemporanea.* Milan: Garzanti.

Burzio, L. (1998). Multiple correspondence. *Lingua*, 104:79–109.

Bybee, J. (1995). Regular morphology and the lexicon. *Language and Cognitive Processes*, 10:425–455.

Cappa, S. and Ullman, M. (1998). A neural dissociation in Italian verbal morphology. *Journal of Cognitive Neuroscience SS*, 53.

Caramazza, A., Laudanna, A., and Romani, C. (1988). Lexical access and inflectional morphology. *Cognition*, 28:297–332.

Clahsen, H. (1999). Lexical entries and rules of language: a multidisciplinary study of German inflection. *Behavioral and Brain Sciences*, 22:991–1013.

Clahsen, H. and Rothweiler, M. (1993). Inflectional rules in children's grammars: evidence from the development of participles in German. *Yearbook of Morphology 1992*, pages 1–34.

Clahsen, H., Rothweiler, M., Woest, A., and Marcus, G. (1992). Regular and irregular inflection in the acquisition of German noun plurals. *Cognition*, 45:225–255.

De Boer, M. (1981). The inflection of the Italian verb: a generative account. *Journal of Italian Linguistics*, 2:55–93.

De Mauro, T., Mancini, F., Vedovelli, M., and Voghera, M. (1993). *Lessico di frequenza dell'italiano parlato*. Milan: Etas Libri.

Dressler, W. and Thornton, A. M. (1991). Doppie basi e binarismo nella morfologia italiana. *Rivista di Linguistica*, 2:3–22.

Fowler, C., Napps, S., and Feldman, L. (1985). Relations among regular and irregular morphologically related words in the lexicon as revealed by repetition priming. *Memory and Cognition*, 13:241–255.

Friederici, A., Hahne, A., and Mecklinger, A. (1996). Temporal structure of syntactic parsing: early and late event-related brain potential effects. *Journal of Experimental Psychology: Learning, Memory and Cognition*, 22:1219–1248.

Gross, M., Say, T., Kleingers, M., Münte, T. F., and Clahsen, H. (1998). Human brain potentials to violations in morphologically complex Italian words. *Neuroscience Letters*, 241:83–86.

Hagoort, P., Brown, C., and Groothusen, J. (1993). The syntactic positive shift (SPS) as an ERP measure of syntactic processing. *Language and Cognitive Processes*, 8:439–483.

Kempley, S. and Morton, J. (1982). The effects of priming with regularly and irregularly related words in auditory word recognition. *British Journal of Psychology*, 73:441–454.

Kiparsky, P. (1982). From cyclic phonology to lexical phonology. In Van der Hulst, H. and Smith, N., editors, *The structure of phonological representations (Part 1)*. Dordrecht: Foris.

Kutas, M. and Kluender, R. (1994). What is who violating: A reconsideration of linguistic violations in light of event-related brain potentials. In Heinze, H.-J., Münte, T., and Mangun, G., editors, *Cognitive electrophysiology*. Boston: Birkhäuser.

Kutas, M. and Van Petten, C. (1994). Psycholinguistics electrified. In Gernsbacher, M., editor, *Handbook of psycholinguistics*. London: Academic Press.

Lepschy, A. L. and Lepschy, G. (1979). *The Italian language today*. London: Hutchison University Library.

Maiden, M. (1992). Irregularity as a determinant of morphological change. *Journal of Linguistics*, 28:285–312.

Marcus, G., Brinkmann, U., Clahsen, H., Wiese, R., and Pinker, S. (1995). German inflection: The exception that proves the rule. *Cognitive Psychology*, 29:186–256.

Marcus, G. F., Pinker, S., Ullman, M., Hollander, M., Rosen, T., and Xu, F. (1992). Overregularization in language acquisition. *Monographs of the Society for Research in Child Development*, 57(4). Serial No. 228.

Marslen-Wilson, W., Hare, M., and Older, L. (1993). Inflectional morphology and phonological regularity in the English mental lexicon. In *Proceedings of the Fifteenth Annual Conference of the Cognitive Science Society*. Princeton, N.J.: Laurence Erlbaum Associates.

Marslen-Wilson, W., L. Tyler, R. W., and Older, L. (1994). Morphology and meaning in the English mental lexicon. *Psychological Review*, 101:3–33.

Münte, T., Heinze, H.-J., and Mangun, G. (1993). Dissociation of brain activity related to syntactic and semantic aspects of language. *Journal of Cognitive Neuroscience*, 5:335–344.

Münte, T. F., Anvari, E., Matzke, M., and Johannes, S. (1995). Brain potential correlates of number errors in the Turkish language. *Neuroscience Letters*, 199:57–60.

Münte, T. F., Say, T., Clahsen, H., Schiltz, K., and Kutas, M. (1998). Decomposition of morphologically complex words in English: Evidence from event-related brain potentials. *Cognitive Brain Research*, 7:241–253.

Napps, S. (1989). Morphemic relationships in the lexicon: are they distinct from semantic and formal relationships? *Memory and Cognition*, 17(6):729–739.

Neville, H., Nicol, J., Barss, A., Forster, K., and Garrett, M. (1991). Syntactically based sentence processing classes: evidence from event-related brain potentials. *Journal of Cognitive Neuroscience*, 3:151–165.

Newman, A., Izvorski, R., Davis, L., Neville, H., and Ullman, M. (1999). Distinct electrophysiological patterns in the processing of regular and irregular verbs. Poster presented at the Cognitive Neuroscience Society Annual Meeting, Apr. 11-13, Washington, DC.

Orsolini, M., Fanari, R., and Bowles, H. (1998). Acquiring regular and irregular inflection in a language with verb classes. *Language and Cognitive Processes*, 13:425–464.

Orsolini, M. and Marslen-Wilson, W. (1997). Universals in morphological representation: Evidence from Italian. *Language and Cognitive Processes*, 12:1–47.

Osterhout, L. and Holcomb, P. (1992). Event-related brain potentials elicited by syntactic anomaly. *Journal of Memory and Language*, 31:785–806.

Osterhout, L. and Holcomb, P. (1995). Event-related potentials and language comprehension. In Rugg, M. and Coles, M., editors, *Electrophysiology of mind: event-related brain potentials and cognition.* Oxford: Oxford University Press.

Osterhout, L. and Mobley, L. (1995). Event-related brain potentials elicited by failure to agree. *Journal of Memory and Language*, 34:739–773.

Penke, M., Weyerts, H., Gross, M., Zander, E., Münte, T., and Clahsen, H. (1997). How the brain processes complex words: an ERP-study of German verb inflections. *Cognitive Brain Research*, 6:37–52.

Pinker, S. (1984). *Language learnability and language development.* Cambridge, MA: Harvard University Press.

Pinker, S. (1999). *Words and rules.* London: Weidenfeld & Nicholson.

Prince, A. and Smolensky, P. (1993). Optimality theory: constraint interaction in generative grammar. Ms., Rutgers University, New Brunswick, and University of Colorado, Boulder.

Rodriguez-Fornells, A., Clahsen, H., Lleó, C., Zaake, W., and Münte, T. (1999). Event related brain responses to morphological violations in Catalan. *Essex Research Reports in Linguistics*, 27:49–75.

Rueckl, J., Mikolinski, M., Raveh, M., Miner, C., and Mars, F. (1997). Morphological priming, fragment completion, and connectionist networks. *Journal of Memory and Language*, 36:382–405.

Say, T. (1999). *The mental representation of Italian verbal morphology: evidence for the dual-mechanism model.* PhD thesis, University of Essex, UK.

Sensini, M. (1988). *La grammatica della lingua Italiana, dell'italiano scritto e parlato.* Milan: Mondadori.

Serianni, L. (1988). *Grammatica Italiana: Italiano comune e lingua letteraria.* Turin: UTET.

Sonnenstuhl, I., Eisenbeiss, S., and Clahsen, H. (1999). Morphological priming in the German mental lexicon. *Cognition*, 72:203–236.

Stanners, R., Neiser, J., Hernon, W., and Hall, R. (1979). Memory representation for morphologically related words. *Journal of Verbal Learning and Verbal Behavior*, 18:399–412.

Thornton, A., Iacobini, C., and Burani, C. (1994). *Una base di dati sul vocabolario di base della lingua italiana.* Rome: Istituto di Psicologia del Consiglio Nazionale delle Ricerche.

Ullman, M., Corkin, S., Pinker, S., Coppola, M., Growdon, J., and Locascio, J. (1997). Which neural structures subserve language? Evidence from inflectional morphology. *Journal of Cognitive Neuroscience*, 9:289–299.

Vogel, I. (1993). Verbs in Italian morphology. In: Booij, G.E. and Van Marle, J. editors. *Yearbook of Morphology 1993*, pages 219–254. Dordrecht: Kluwer Academic Publishers.

Weyerts, H. and Clahsen, H. (1994). Netzwerke und symbolische Regeln im Spracherwerb: Experimentelle Ergebnisse zur Entwicklung der Flexionsmorphologie. *Linguistische Berichte*, 154:430–460.

Weyerts, H., Penke, M., Dohrn, U., Clahsen, H., and Münte, T. (1997). Brain potentials indicate differences between regular and irregular German noun plurals. *NeuroReport*, 8:957–962.

Xu, F. and Pinker, S. (1995). Weird past tense forms. *Journal of Child Language*, 22:531–556.

III

CHANGING THE RULES

Chapter 5

THE BALANCE BETWEEN STORAGE AND COMPUTATION IN PHONOLOGY

Geert Booij

Abstract This article discusses two kinds of phonological evidence concerning the balance between storage and computation: allomorphy and phonological change. It is shown that even allomorphs that can be derived by a productive phonological rule are sometimes stored in lexical memory because these allomorphs are preserved although the relevant phonological process has been lost. Phonological processes that are subject to lexical diffusion also require lexical storage of the effects of these processes. This implies that the notions 'underlying form' and 'lexically stored form' should not be equated: surface forms are stored, and underlying forms are computed when they are needed for coining new words.

Keywords: Allomorphy, Auslautverhaertung, final devoicing, lexical diffusion, Optimality Theory, paradigmatic leveling, phonological change, rule opacity, underlying form, vowel lengthening, vowel reduction.

1. Introduction

The dominant view in classical generative phonology with respect to the kind of phonological information that is stored in the lexicon, can be summarized as follows: what can be computed should not be stored (cf. Kenstowicz, 1994, p.60). This view implies that predictable information about words is omitted from lexical representations. In case there are alternations in the shape of morphemes, the preferred solution is to assume one underlying form for all alternants, listed in the lexicon, and to derive the different surface allomorphs by means of one or more phonological rules. This kind of lexicon can be characterized as the Bloomfieldian lexicon, since Bloomfield, 1933, p.274 defined the lexicon as "a list of basic irregularities".

S. Nooteboom et al. (eds.), Storage and Computation in the Language Faculty, 133–156.

This view of the division of labour between lexicon and grammar has come under attack from a number of different perspectives. First, this view suffers from what has been called the 'rule/list fallacy' by Langacker, 1987, p.29: it is not necessarily the case that what can be computed by rule, should not also be stored in the lexicon. In the realm of morphology, Jackendoff, 1975 already argued that morphological rules have in principle two functions: they create new forms, but they can also function as redundancy rules with respect to existing complex words listed in the lexicon. This also applies to syntactic rules, for instance the rule of NP formation for English. There are adjective + noun phrases that function as names such as *yellow pages, red tape, green card, black hole, hard disk, little toe* which have an unpredictable meaning aspect, and hence have to be listed in the lexicon (Jackendoff, 1997, Chapter 7). Nevertheless, there is also a productive syntactic rule of English that creates new NP's that consist of an adjective and a noun.

This issue is quite an actual one for our view of the nature of the language faculty. In a recent paper, Clahsen, 1999 argues in favour of a dual structure of the human language faculty, a lexicon and a set of rules. His view is based on the analysis of inflectional rules of German, and he argues that it is only irregularities that are listed: regular forms are always derived by rule. As I pointed out in my commentary on this paper (Booij, 1999), this position cannot be completely correct. For instance, past participles of Dutch that are fully regular from the formal point of view must nevertheless be stored because of semantic irregularities. Examples of such participles are *gezet* 'fat' (from the verb *zetten* 'to put)', and *gesmeerd* 'fast, fluent' (from the verb *smeren* 'to smear'). The meanings of these participles are not predictable from their verbal stems, and therefore, they have to be lexically stored. Note, however, that this does not weaken Clahsen's view of the language faculty: his basic point is that there are rules besides lexical representations (contra the connectionist view), but in order to maintain that position he does not have to take the position that the outputs of regular processes are never stored.

There is also a wealth of psycholinguistic evidence that predictable information is sometimes stored in the lexicon. For instance, in the area of morphology, Baayen et al., 1997 showed that in Italian completely regular but frequent plural forms of nouns are stored in lexical memory.

In the realm of phonology similar considerations apply. A clear example is syllable structure. In most phonological analyses it is assumed that syllable structure should not be encoded in the lexical representation of words because it is fully predictable from the segmental structure of a word. The basic reasoning behind this view is that we should account for the fact that in most cases syllable structure is not distinctive; hence it should not be stored. However, there is psycholinguistic evidence that the syllable templates of words are stored independently from their segmental structure. In speech errors one often finds that segments are exchanged that occupy the same position in syllable structure, for instance the onset position, as in the speech error *peel like flaying* instead of *feel like playing*. This shows that syllable structure must be lexically represented independently from segmental structure (Levelt, 1992, p.9-10).

The lexical presence of syllable structure is also presupposed in linguistic analyses of stress patterns that make use of the concept of syllable extrametricality. For instance, in Polish, a language with penultimate stress, there are a few words with antepenultimate stress, such as *uniwérsytet* 'university'. The last syllable of this word has to be marked as extrametrical in the lexicon in order to derive the correct stress pattern of this word. This implies that at least the last syllable (*tet*) is present as such in the lexicon. That is, the lexical presence of predictable syllable structure is implied by the necessity of lexical markings for stress.

In this article I will focus on two kinds of phonological evidence that throw light on the balance between storage and computation in the lexicon: allomorphy and phonological change. As to allomorphy, I will argue in section 2 that in many cases the surface allomorphs of a morpheme cannot be derived by phonological rule, and hence have to be stored in the lexicon, because there are no productive phonological rules that account for that allomorphy. In section 3 I will take a more radical step and argue that even when alternations are fully predictable by means of general and productive phonological rules, the facts of phonological change suggest that the outputs of such rules may nevertheless be stored in lexical memory. Both kinds of phenomena show that much more is lexically represented than what is assumed in classical generative phonology.

2. Allomorphy

Allomorphy is the phenomenon that morphemes exhibit certain alternations in form. The traditional generative approach is assuming one underlying form for a morpheme, and to compute the surface allomorphs by means of a set of rules.

In quite a number of cases, however, the actual variation in form, though predictable, is specific for only one or a small set of morphemes. For example, the Dutch diminutive suffix exhibits five surface forms, *-tje*,

-je, -pje, -kje and *-etje*. These five forms can be derived by rule from one underlying form by means of rules (cf. Trommelen, 1984, Booij, 1995). However, these rules have to mention the feature [+ diminutive] in their structural description because it is only the diminutive morpheme that triggers these rules. That is, they are, in terms of Anderson, 1974, morpholexical rules, and stand in opposition to phonological rules whose application is triggered by phonological conditions only, the so-called automatic phonological rules.

Recently, the insight has re-emerged that output constraints are essential for a proper account of phonological regularities. In Optimality Theory, such output constraints are seen as a set of universal constraints, ranked on a language-specific basis. This poses a problem for a phonological analysis of allomorphy because the equivalent of morpholexical rules in OT-phonology is a morpheme-specific ranking of constraints. Although the possibility of morpheme-specific constraint ranking is accepted by some linguists (cf. Plag, 1998; Raffelsiefen, 1999), it is quite implausible from the learnability point of view. Therefore, Mester, 1994, Kager, 1996, and Booij, 1998 proposed analyses in which the different allomorphs of a morpheme are lexically listed, and the choice of the correct allomorph follows from the set of ranked output constraints.

Let us make the discussion of this issue more concrete by having a look at the Dutch nominal suffix allomorphs *-er* /ər/ and *-aar* /aːr/ '-er'. Historically, both derive from the Latin suffix *-arius*. Synchronically, they are in complementary distribution: *-aar* occurs after verbal and nominal stems ending in schwa plus a coronal sonorant consonant, *-er* occurs in all other cases, except after /r/ where a third allomorph *-der* is chosen:

(5.1)	*stem*	*noun*
	luist[ə]r 'to listen'	luister-aar 'listener'
	twijf[ə]l 'to doubt'	twijfel-aar 'doubter'
	rek[ə]n 'to compute'	reken-aar 'computer'
	bel 'to ring'	bell-er 'ringer'
	spin 'to spin'	spinn-er 'spinner'
	klier 'to nag'	klier-der 'nagger'

Attempts to derive one of the allomorphs from the other have always caused problems: if /ər/ is the underlying form we need a rule that changes a schwa into /aː/ but this rule should apply to this suffix only. If we want to derive /ər/ from /aːr/ by means of a rule of vowel reduction that changes the full vowel /aː/ into a schwa, the problem arises that, although there is a rule of vowel reduction in Dutch (cf. Booij,

1995), it never applies to the last syllable of a word, whereas here the relevant vowel does form part of the last syllable. Therefore, we have to conclude that both allomorphs are to be listed in the lexicon. Thus, they function as competing suffixes, and the choice is made in terms of optimal outputs. In this case, the relevant output condition is that of Optimal Parsing: preferably, a word is parsed into trochaic feet. Given a verbal stem such as *bedel* /beːdəl/, the addition of the suffix *-er* would result in a rhythmic lapse because it will create a sequence of two unstressed syllables, of which the second cannot be parsed into a foot, and hence remains unparsed. On the other hand, if we add *-aar*, the syllable corresponding to this suffix can form a foot of its own because it has a full vowel, and hence it will have two feet, (beːdə) and (laːr).

The nice point of this solution is that, unlike the common underlying form approach, it also explains the reason behind the complementary distribution of these two suffixes: it is no coincidence that *-aar* is chosen after a stem that ends in a syllable headed by schwa because that is the only way to avoid a rhythmic lapse. In an approach in which we derive one allomorph from the (underlying form of) the other, there is no explanation of why the nature of the last vowel of the stem (full vowel versus schwa) plays a crucial role as a trigger of the alternation (Booij, 1998).

In sum, what I have done here so far is giving theoretical and empirical reasons for lexical listing of two allomorphs. Their status has thus become that of two competing affixes with a phonological similarity. Diachronically, there is a phonological relation between the two, but synchronically, this is no longer the case. This implies that as far as the balance between storage and computation in phonology is concerned, we move into the direction of storage: both allomorphs have to be stored, they have become competing morphemes.

This analysis is confirmed by the fact that the suffix *-aar* exceptionally also occurs in other phonological environments, i.e. after a syllable with a full vowel, as in *ler-aar* /leːraːr/ 'teacher' and *dien-aar* /dinaːr/ 'servant'. This is to be expected if *-aar* is a suffix of its own because affixes sometimes appear with other types of bases than the regular ones. Similarly, a number of diminutive nouns exhibit the 'wrong' allomorph, for instance *bruggetje* 'small bridge' (diminutive of *brug* 'bridge') instead of the regular *brugje*. Such a situation could never arise if the surface forms of the diminutive suffix were derived by automatic phonological rules. Thus, the existence of exceptional forms supports the individual listing of the five allomorphs of the diminutive suffix.

The implication is that an account of allomorphy in terms of derivation from a common underlying form is only possible if the rules that compute the surface form are real phonological generalizations, that is: automatic phonological rules.

A shift of the burden of information for alternation patterns from rules towards the lexicon can also be found in Ortmann's analysis of consonant epenthesis in High Alemannic (Ortmann, 1998). In this dialect of German, spoken mainly in Switzerland, the consonant /n/ occurs after a set of vowel-final words, if the next word is vowel-initial, as in

(5.2) grösser wie-n-i 'taller than I'
bi-n-ene 'with them'

Historically, this /n/ is comparable to the intrusive /r/ in English: originally it was a word-final segment that was deleted before a consonant, and kept before a vowel. Synchronically, this /r/ has been reanalyzed in many varieties of English as an epenthetic /r/. In the German case, however, the occurrence of /n/ is lexically restricted. Ortmann's conclusion therefore is that the /n/ has to be present in the underlying representation. In other words, lexical storage of this /n/ is required.[1] The output condition onset ('do not have an empty onset') will then select the /n/-final allomorph before a vowel-initial word in the same phonological phrase. In short, this is a case where from a diachronic point of view there is a shift of information to the lexicon: the alternation between word-final /n/ and zero was once computable by rule, but now it has to be encoded in the lexicon. What is left for computation is the selection of the correct allomorph for each context, a selection performed by the universal constraint Onset. In other words, these German facts can be analyzed similarly to the lexically governed allomorphy of the English indefinite article *a/an* where the output condition Onset will prefer *an* before a vowel-initial word because the /n/ will fill the onset of the first syllable of the next word.

Another argument for the lexical listing of allomorphs in allomorphy that is governed by the Onset constraint (of which we saw an example for High Alemannic in the preceding paragraph), can be found in the French liaison facts (cf. Clements and Keyser, 1983). A word like *petit* 'small' has two surface forms, [pti] and [ptit]:

[1] Ortmann's specific solution is that the /n/ is treated as a floating segment not associated to a syllable position. If the next word begins with a vowel, it provides an empty onset position, to which the /n/ can be attached under resyllabification within the phonological phrase (Ortmann, 1998, p.67). Since the notion 'floating segment' requires the assumption of an independent X-tier in lexical representations to which not necessarily all segments are linked, and thus forms an addition to the theoretical machinery of phonology, I prefer a more straightforward solution, in line with what has been said above: the relevant words have two lexically listed allomorphs, one vowel-final and the other /n/-final.

(5.3) petit ami [ptit ami] 'little friend'
petit garçon [pti garsõ] 'little boy'

This alternation cannot be accounted for in terms of a word-final consonant deletion rule, but is best accounted for in terms of the word *petit* having two allomorphs, one with, and one without final /t/. The allomorph ending in /t/ is chosen if that /t/ can be attached to the empty onset position of the next vowel-initial word. Indeed, the syllable division of *petit ami* is (/pti/)(/ta/)(/mi/). In other words, it is the lexicon that accounts for the alternation between /t/ and zero, rather than a phonological rule or constraint. In sum, the adjective *petit* has two allomorphs, *peti* and *petit*, and selection of the right allomorph is done by the output condition Onset.

This allomorph selection interpretation of liaison is supported by the observation that there is a number of words for which the two allomorphs are phonologically too different to share an underlying form. A clear example is *beau* 'beautiful', which has the allomorph *bel* before a vowel-initial word; clearly, the form *bel* cannot be derived from *beau* by means of a phonological rule of French:

(5.4) un beau garçon 'a beautiful boy'
un bel ami 'a beautiful friend'

The stem *bel* also occurs in the feminine form *belle*, as in *une belle amie* 'a beautiful girl-friend'. The same universal output condition Onset will select *bel* as the optimal allomorph before vowel-initial words since it will result in the syllable sequence (/bɛ/)(/la/)(/mi/), with no empty onsets, whereas *beau ami* would have the syllable pattern (/bo/)(/a/)(/mi/), with a second syllable with an empty onset.[2]

The conclusion of this section is that there is a strong linguistic evidence for lexical storage of phonologically similar allomorphs of words, instead of deriving them from one common underlying form. This implies a shift from computation to storage with respect to the division

[2]This is an argument against the floating consonant analysis of word-final consonants of Clements and Keyser, 1983 because their analysis cannot generalize over *petit/peti* and *bel/beau*. In Perlmutter, 1998, an attempt is made to reduce the degree of lexical information required here by considering *bel* as identical to the feminine form of the adjective, *belle*. He then argues that the prosodic output condition Onset is ranked higher than the morphological Agreement condition that requires agreement in gender between a head noun and its modifying adjective. However, as Janda, 1998 pointed out in a commentary on Perlmutter's paper, there is no general principle for French that states that the agreement requirement can always be ignored in order to satisfy Onset, and that the possibility of using an allomorph that is similar to the feminine form is lexically governed, and also differs for different varieties of French. Therefore, for each word that exhibits C/V allomorphy, the allomorphs must be stored in the lexicon.

of labour between the phonological component and the lexicon. In the next section I will show how phonological change further strengthens this conclusion.

3. Phonological change

The main idea of this section is that phonological change provides a window on what is lexically stored versus what is computed by rule. In the previous section, we dealt with a number of alternations that have to be stored instead of being computed. In all of these alternations we have to do with alternations between phonemes or between phonemes and zero. What about allophonic properties? The traditional position in generative phonology is that allophonic properties are not lexically represented because they are predictable. There is, however, evidence, that even allophonic properties can be stored because they can survive after loss of the rule that accounted for that allophony.

A relevant case is that of vowel lengthening in open syllables in Early Middle Dutch. This process affected both simplex nouns and complex nouns, and even word+clitic combinations.

(5.5)	a.	*simplex nouns*	
		name 'name'	n[aː]me
		smake 'taste'	sm[aː]ke
		stave 'staff'	st[aː]ve
	b.	*singular*	*plural*
		sch[ɪ]p 'ship'	sch[eː]p-en
		w[ɛ]g 'way'	w[eː]g-en
		h[ɔ]l 'hole'	h[oː]l-en
		oorl[ɔ]g 'war'	oorl[oː]g-en
		d[ɑ]g 'day'	d[aː]g-en
	c.	*word + clitic*	
		saetic /sɑt ɪk/	[saːtɪk] 'sat I'

The singular-plural pairs in (5.5b) have been preserved in modern Dutch. This process of vowel lengthening is a manifestation of a much more general tendency in Germanic languages that stressed syllables must be heavy, i.e. cannot end in a short vowel, but contain minimally either a long vowel or a short vowel followed by a consonant (also known as Prokosch' Law).

In the first stage of this process in Early Middle Dutch (cf. Van Loon, 1986, p.89), the lengthening of the vowel was an allophonic process. In the course of time (probably in the 12th century), however, the lengthened vowel was phonemicized, i.e. became an underlying long vowel. How do we know this?

The first evidence concerns short vowels followed by geminate consonants. These were protected from lengthening because the first half of the geminate closes the syllable. In the 12th century, degemination took place. Yet, the short vowels that thus ended up in open syllables, did not lengthen anymore, and so we find many words with short vowels followed by only one consonant such as *wikke* [ʋɪkə] 'vetch'. That is, the following development took place:

(5.6)	VCV	> V:CV (predictably long vowel)		> V:CV (phonemic long vowel)	
	VCCV	> VCCV (predictably short vowel)		> VCV (phonemic short vowel)	

These changes are illustrated by the following minimal pair (Van Loon, 1986, p.89):

(5.7)	/ʋɪka/ 'week'	/ʋɪkə/	/ʋeːkə/ (lengthened /ɪ/= /eː/)
	/ʋɪkkia/ 'vetch'	/ʋɪkkə/	/ʋɪkə/

The classical generative interpretation of this kind of phonemicization is as follows: the initial change is the addition of a rule of degemination to the phonological system of the adult speakers. This rule of degemination made the alternation between long and short vowels in the output forms opaque: vowel lengthening is ordered before degemination, and this is a non-bleeding order. The next generation of language users therefore interpreted the length contrast as a phonemic contrast, and hence the length contrast became part of the lexical representation. In addition, the process of vowel lengthening in open syllables disappeared.

A second kind of evidence for the phonemicization of these initially allophonic contrasts for simplex nouns is provided by the later process of schwa apocope (13th century). This phonological change did not affect the length of the vowel in the simplex nouns ending in schwa: after apocope the vowels of words such as *naam* 'name' (<name) and *smaak* 'taste' (<smake) stayed long. Again, vowel lengthening became opaque, and the next generation had to store the vowel length as part of the lexical representation. The phonemicization process even led to doublets such as *bar* 'raw' – *baar* 'ready (money)' and *staf* 'staff' – *staaf* 'bar', a process that can be expected given the phonemicization of vowel length.

This account in terms of rule opacity does not explain, however, why the alternation between long and short vowels was kept in certain cases such as those in the singular-plural pairs in (5.5b) above. When vowel lengthening disappeared, the length alternation should also have disappeared. The fact that it was kept for a number of words shows that in these cases the plural forms must have been stored in their phonetic form, with a long vowel in the stressed syllable, at a time when the alternation was still governed by a phonological rule. In addition, it also shows that plural forms of nouns can be lexically stored, a conclusion that is confirmed by recent psycholinguistic evidence, as I already mentioned above (cf. Baayen et al., 1997).

The traditional generative account of this change would read as follows. Each new generation of speakers has to discover the rules of its native language on the basis of the phonetic outputs encountered. First, they will simply store the phonetic output forms of words. Once they have discovered the phonological regularities involved, they will replace each set of related phonetic output forms with one common underlying phonological form (so-called restructuring). If, for some reason, a particular phonological regularity (such as vowel lengthening in open syllables, the process discussed here) is not grasped by the new generation, there will be no restructuring: the stored phonetic forms will remain memorized as is, and if new words or word forms are coined, they will not be affected by that rule. Hence, the rule disappears, and only those words for which the different surface form had already been stored in lexical memory will keep that alternation.

However, this reasoning clearly presupposes that output forms are stored in the initial stages of acquisition. The question then is, why native speakers would change, and even erase that information about output forms in a later stage of acquisition, once they have discovered the phonological regularity involved. Given the vastness of human memory, there is no reason not to keep that information in lexical memory, and to use the phonological rule that can be discovered on the basis of related output forms for the computation of the phonetic shape of new words and word forms only. Thus, we get a natural division of labour between storage and computation: output forms, once heard, may be stored, and rules, once discovered, are used to interpret phonetically similar forms as instantiations of the same morpheme, and for the computation of the phonetic forms of new words.

For those words where there was no alternation involved, such as the words *weke* versus *wikke* given in (5.7) the assumption of storage in memory of the output forms by adult speakers is also necessary. Only if we assume that predictable length differences are stored, can we explain why the rule of degemination was added to the adult grammar: the addition of degemination has been made possible by the length difference, because the latter could now serve to keep words phonetically distinct. The language user is able to survey and inspect the phonetic output forms of words in his memory, and can thus conclude that the distinction between single and geminate consonants is redundant given a concomitant distinction in vowel-length. The emergence of degemination can therefore be seen as the result of storage in speakers' memory of output forms. Similarly, the possibility of schwa apocope may also be seen as the result of storage of the phonetic output forms: since the vowel-length distinction was kept in memory, the word-final schwa could disappear. This then made it necessary to consider vowel length as information that is part of the lexical representation.

Given this analysis, we avoid constructing a complete gap between two generations of language speakers, and are not forced to assume that language change is only caused by the imperfect learning of the next generation that has to acquire the language on the basis of outputs. Language change is also an effect of the adult language user who is able to analyze the phonetic forms of words which are accessible in his memory.

The consequence of the loss of transparency of a phonological process (rule opacity) is that it is no longer possible to compute or store an underlying form for a word that differs from its phonetic form. A distance between phonetic form and underlying form is only possible in the case of surface-true transparent processes. In the case at hand this means that the plural forms of these nouns, with their long vowels, must be stored, also for new generations, since their phonetic forms cannot be computed.

Since the output form of the singular noun is the basis for computing the underlying form, the input for morphological operations, it is the short vowel that appears in such cases:

(5.8)	*singular noun*	*plural noun*	*derived word*	
	gebr[ɛ]k 'handicap'	gebr[eː]ken	gebr[ɛ]kkig	'handicapped'
	h[ɔ]l 'hole'	h[oː]len	h[ɔ]lletje	'diminutive'
	sch[ɪ]p 'ship'	sch[eː]pen	sch[ɪ]pper	'skipper'
	g[ɔ]d 'god'	g[oː]den	g[ɔ]ddelijk	'divine'
	sp[ɛ]l 'game'	sp[eː]len	sp[ɛ]lletje	'diminutive'
	w[ɛ]g 'road'	w[eː]gen	w[ɛ]ggetje	'diminutive'

In a number of cases the alternation that existed between singular and plural nouns disappeared after the loss of the rule of vowel lengthening (so-called analogical or paradigmatic leveling). This applies to, for instance, the following Dutch nouns which have a short vowel in their last syllable in both singular and plural forms:

(5.9)	bisschop 'bishop'	bisschoppen
	lek 'leak'	lekken

gemak 'ease' gemakken
straf 'punishment' straffen

The traditional interpretation of these facts is that since the plural forms of these words were not stored, the regular forms with short vowels will show up after the loss of the rule of vowel lengthening. However, since the position is taken here that plural forms can be stored in their output form, the following interpretation is called for: the original plural forms of these words with long vowels did have a lexical representation of their own, but their frequencies, and thus their resting level of activation was not high enough to block the formation of a regular plural form without vowel lengthening, i.e. on the basis of the underlying form of the singular noun. This is also the point of view defended in Wetzels, 1981, p.95-97 and Wetzels, 1984, p.595 as to analogical leveling: analogical leveling is nothing else but the application of productive rules that are not blocked by the existence of stored forms.

3.1. Automatic rules and lexical storage

So far, our findings with respect to the lexicalization of vowel lengthening are in line with the conclusion of Wetzels mentioned above. However, he argued that paradigmatic leveling only takes place if rules are no longer automatic phonological rules, and hence require storage of allomorphs. Only if rules are no longer phonologically conditioned will the different allomorphs of a morpheme be lexically stored, which then may give rise to leveling by using the 'wrong' allomorph. Since, according to Wetzels, the outputs of automatic phonological rules are not stored, they will not lead to paradigmatic leveling. For instance, the alternations created by the automatic rule of devoicing of obstruents in coda position have, with a few exceptions to be discussed below, not been leveled in Dutch. Therefore, we will now have a more detailed look at coda devoicing.

It is an uncontroversial assumption within mainstream generative phonology that the effects of automatic neutralization rules are not encoded in lexical representations. For instance, Kenstowicz and Kisseberth, 1979, p.49 argue on the basis of the Russian rule of word-final devoicing of obstruents that it would be wrong to list both the allomorph with a voiced obstruent and the one with a voiceless obstruent in the lexicon, and to assume a selection rule for the allomorphs stated as follows:

(5.10) "If a morpheme has alternants that differ with respect to the voicing of a final obstruent, select the alternant with a final voiceless obstruent when the morpheme appears at the end of a word; otherwise, select the alternant with a voiced obstruent."

The authors then add that the "basic criticism is that this sort of analysis fails to adequately characterize the rule-governed nature of the voicing alternation in Russian" (p. 49). That is, such an analysis implies that two rules have to be assumed for Russian, a phonological rule of devoicing, and a morphological rule of allomorph selection.

Language change again provides a window on this issue: if we do not lexically store the outputs of a neutralization rule (with the effect that each output is a possible underlying form), we predict that paradigmatic leveling will not take place. I will therefore have a look at a process similar to Russian devoicing, coda devoicing of obstruents in Dutch. Final devoicing in Dutch is a productive generalization: voiced obstruents cannot occur in codas. If there are two allomorphs for a lexical item with an alternation between a voiced and a voiceless obstruent, it is generally assumed that the underlying form that is stored, is the form that ends in a voiced obstruent. If this voiced obstruent ends up in coda position, it is devoiced by the rule of final devoicing:

(5.11) rib [rɪp] / ribben [rɪbən] 'rib, sg/pl'
hoed [hut] / hoeden [hudən] 'hat, sg/pl'
slaaf [slaːf] / slaven [slaːvən] 'slave, sg/pl'
kiez [kis] / kiezen [kizən] 'molar, sg/pl'
vlieg [vlix] / vliegen [vliɣən] 'fly, sg/pl'

Interestingly, in some cases the alternation is lost. For instance, although we have the alternation *hand/handen* [hɑnt]/[hɑndən], there is an idiomatic phrase *bijdehand* 'lit. at the hand, bright' that functions as an adjective. One of its inflected forms in prenominal position is *bijdehante*, i.e. there is no alternation between voiced and voiceless obstruent anymore.

In Van Loey, 1964, p.54 the rise of forms such as *bijdehante* is interpreted as a case of paradigmatic leveling (analogy), which would suggest that the allomorph [hɑnt] of *hand* is stored. However, the problem for this account is that it does not explain why paradigmatic leveling almost never takes place with respect to effects of final devoicing. Another interpretation is therefore called for: the language learner only computes an underlying form that differs from the phonetic one if (i) the two words involved are related, and (ii) the two surface forms are relatable by means of a transparent rule. In the case of *bijdehand*, this adjective has no transparent formal relation to the word *hand* 'hand' with its plural form *handen*, and thus it will be stored with a final /t/. In other words, we can only get underlying forms that differ from the surface forms if there is a transparent morphological relation between the words in which the different allomorphs occur (cf. Wetzels, 1981). Thus, the form *bijdehante* is not a counterexample to the claim made by Wetzels, 1981 that automatic phonological rules do not lead to leveling.

Another interesting case is the word *stad* [stɑd] 'town' with the irregular plural form *steden* [steːdən]. The plural noun not only exhibits vowel lengthening, but also vowel quality change, from /aː/ to /eː/. Consequently, the underlying form of *stad* is apparently computed as /stɑt/, as shown by new coinings such as the verb *statten* 'to do shopping in town' derived through conversion form the noun *stad* 'city', and the inhabitant name *Lelystatter* derived from the toponym *Lelystad*.

A similar phenomenon can be seen in Afrikaans for a number of nouns that have plural forms with lengthened vowels in Dutch. Apparently, the distance between *smid* 'blacksmith' and *smeden* (plural), for instance, is too large for speakers of Afrikaans, and thus they do not conclude to a common stem /smɪd/. Thus, the lexical form of *smid* will be /smɪt/ rather than /smɪd/, and consequently the regular plural *smitten* has arisen.

(5.12)	*Dutch*:	*Afrikaans*:	
	smid [smɪt]	smit [smɪt]	'smith, sg'
	smeden [smeːdən]	smitten [smɪtən]	'smith, pl'

The point here is that precisely the nouns with the unproductive vowel length alternation exhibit paradigmatic leveling with respect to the still transparent rule of coda devoicing.

In the case of the words with the vowel length alternation discussed above, there is also internal evidence for the storage of the effect of coda devoicing in the lexical entry, because vowel length plays a role in the distribution of fricative consonants. The generalization is that /v/ and /z/ only occur after long vowels, the *v/z*-constraint.[3]

[3]There are four exceptions: the loan words *mazzel* 'good luck', *puzzel* 'puzzle', *razzia* 'idem', and the name for railway kiosks *wizzl*, a form intentionally coined as a marked form with a high attention value.

Interestingly, we find the following alternations

(5.13) *nouns*

graf [ɣrɑf]	graven [ɣraːvən]	'grave, sg/pl'
hof [hɔf]	hoven [hoːvən]	'court, sg/pl'
glas [ɣlɑs]	glazen [ɣlaːzən]	'glass, sg/pl'
staf [stɑf]	staven [staːvən]	'staff, sg/pl'
verlof [vərlɔf]	verloven [vərloːvən]	'permission, sg/pl'

verbs, past tense, sg/pl

las [lɑs]	lazen [laːzən]	'read'
genas [ɣənɑs]	genazen [ɣənaːzən]	'cured'
gaf [ɣɑf]	gaven [ɣaːvən]	'give'
vergaf [vərɣɑf]	vergaven [vərɣaːvən]	'forgave'

noun-verb pairs

draf [drɑf] 'trot'	draven [draːvən]	'to trot'
lof [lɔf] 'praise'	loven [loːvən]	'to praise'

In all these cases, short vowels are followed by a voiceless fricative, whereas long vowels are followed by a voiced fricative. In other words, all allomorphs obey the constraint on the distribution of /v/ and /z/. In these cases, the voicelessness of the final obstruent is also part of the underlying form, although this information is predictable, and although these obstruents alternate with voiced ones. We know this on the basis of the forms of complex words derived from such nouns: these words are derived either from a form with short vowel + voiceless obstruent, or from a form with long vowel + voiced obstruent; the combination short vowel + voiced obstruent does not occur:

(5.14)

—	gl[aː]zenier 'stained glass artist'	*glazzenier
h[ɔf]elijk 'polite'	h[oː]veling 'courtier'	*hovveling
best[ɑf]ing 'staff'	st[aː]ven 'to prove'	*bestavving
l[ɔf]elijk 'praiseworthy'	l[oː]ven 'to praise'	*lovvelijk

On the other hand, if the noun ends in a stop or a velar fricative, this restriction does not apply, and morphology can apply to underling forms with a voiced stop:

(5.15)	*singular*	*plural*	*derived word*	
	god	goden	g[ɔ]ddelijk	'divine'
	bad	baden	b[ɑ]dderen	'to bathe'
	weg	wegen	w[ɛ]ggetje	'small road'

The v/z-constraint thus restricts the distance between phonetic form and underlying form.

Van Loey, 1964, p.54-55 also mentions a number of cases in which leveling in favour of the allomorph with voiceless obstruent took place, where no additional alternations are involved that make the two allomorphs different in other respects as well. Examples from 17th century Dutch are:

(5.16` gewaet 'dress' / gewaden 'pl.' > gewaeten
cieraet 'ornament'/ cieraden 'pl.' > cieraeten

In these cases the allomorphs with final [d] have been restored in modern Dutch.

There are also cases in present-day Dutch of this kind of leveling. An example is the adjective *boud* 'bold'. Originally, the inflected form of this adjective is *boude*, but most speakers of Dutch say *boute*, which shows that the alternation d/t has been leveled out. What these examples show is that leveling in favour of the allomorph with voiceless obstruent is possible. This kind of leveling can be due to imperfect learning: the language user did not yet compute the correct underlying form of the noun on the basis of the alternation between singular and plural form, although the alternation is transparent. Therefore, the underlying form is identical to the phonetic form of the singular noun.

We may thus hypothesize that we store phonetic forms and that underlying forms are computed on the basis of stored phonetic forms (a similar position is taken in Leben, 1979). Underlying forms will only differ from phonetic forms in so far that difference follows from transparent phonological rules. If the distance between two forms is too big either semantically (the case of *bijdehand*) or because the formal differences are too big (*stad-steden* and the Afrikaans cases), the underlying forms will not differ from the surface forms. A structural constraint such as the Dutch *v/z*-constraint will also block the computation of an underlying form that is different from the surface form of a word, even though there is an automatic alternation involved.

3.2. Lexical diffusion

In the early stages of generative phonology, phonological change was seen as the addition of a rule at the end of the grammar. That is, the lexical representations do not change, but the corresponding surface form is affected by the application of the added rule. It is only the new generation that will have different lexical representations with the effect of the added rule lexically encoded, except when it is a rule that creates alternations. In the latter case, lexical representations will not necessarily change.

A problem for this view is that phonological changes in progress often affect lexical representations but are also simultaneously the source of phonological alternations. For instance, Dutch is subject to a process of /d/-weakening in which intervocalically, /d/ is replaced with the glide /j/ before a following, suffix-initial schwa (Booij, 1995, p.90). This causes alternations of the following type:

(5.17) goed 'good', inflected form goed-e,
phonetic form [ɣudə] or [ɣujə]
rood 'red', inflected form rod-e,
phonetic form [roːdə] or [roːjə]

Application of this allomorphy creating rule of /d/-weakening is lexically governed. For instance, it does not apply to the plural form of *hoed-en* 'hats' [hudən]: the phonetic form [hujən] is impossible. Weakening also applies optionally to the derived adjective *goed-ig* 'good-natured' [ɣudəx] or [ɣujəx], but obligatorily to the derived noun *goeierd* [ɣujərt] 'good-natured person': the form [ɣudərt] is impossible. But other adjectives with stem-final /d/ do not always allow weakening; the adjective *wreed* 'cruel', for instance, does not have the inflected form [wreːjə] for *wrede*, the only form possible is [wreːdə]. Similar observations apply to processes such as /d/-deletion in Dutch (Booij, 1995, p.90). The lexically governed nature of these alternations implies that they must be stored lexically, even in the case of morphologically completely regular inflected forms of adjectives such as *goed-e*.

The facts of *d*-weakening support the claim of Kiparsky, 1988; 1995 that it is lexical, i.e. neutralizing rules that exhibit lexical diffusion, since the distinction between /d/ and /j/ is phonemic in Dutch. What is essential from the perspective of this paper is that they support the view that information provided by rule and information that is lexically stored are not exclusive with respect to each other.

These allomorphy facts imply that the recognition system of the language user must have a certain robustness because (s)he has no problems in relating *goed* to *goeie* and *goeierd* notwithstanding the phonological differences in the lexical representation of the shared part of these words, the lexical morpheme *goed*. That is, apparently the phonetic forms of a morpheme do not have to be computed by rule from a common underlying form in order to be recognizable as allomorphs of that morpheme (contra Lahiri and Marslen-Wilson, 1992).

In the case of /d/-deletion an intervocalic /d/ is deleted, and replaced with a predictable hiatus filling glide. For instance, the inflected adjective *oud-e* 'old' can be pronounced as [ɑudə] or [ɑuʋə]. Both forms must be stored because it cannot be predicted which forms allows for *d*-deletion. The phonetic difference even correlates with a semantic difference in the case of the A+N phrases *oude hoer* [ɑudəhuːr] 'old whore' (the literal meaning) versus *ouwe hoer* [ɑuʋəhuːr] 'talkative person'.

Labov, 1981; Labov, 1994 proposed to distinguish two types of phonological change: change that is phonetically gradual, and affects all relevant words, and change that is phonetically abrupt, replaces a phoneme with another one, and is lexically gradual, i.e. exhibits lexical diffusion. Kiparsky, 1988 argued that the distinction between phonetically gradual and phonetically abrupt changes coincides with the distinction between postlexical and lexical phonological rules. The rules of /d/-weakening and /d/-deletion can indeed be considered lexical rules since they are neutralizing. As expected, they have exceptions, and thus exhibit lexical diffusion. Lexical diffusion always creates surface opacity for rules since the speaker will find forms that have not undergone the rule. Therefore, as stated above, opacity will lead to lexical storage in the sense that for each phonetic form of such words a distinct lexical entry has to be created. This in its turn explains why semantic distinctions may correlate with phonological differences, as in the pair *oude hoer* / *ouwe hoer* discussed above.

What about the effects of postlexical rules? The usual assumption (cf. Kiparsky, 1988, p.399) is that the effects of such rules are not encoded in lexical representations. In recent work, Bybee (to appear, a) has questioned these assumptions. She argues that a change may be both phonetically and lexically gradual. This implies that the effects of such gradual changes must be lexically stored, in the lexical representations of individual words.

Vowel reduction in Dutch (Booij, 1982; 1995; Van Bergem, 1995) is a potentially interesting phenomenon in this respect because it has both lexical and postlexical properties. The basic generalization is that at the phonetic level all unstressed vowels are affected by reduction in the sense that their actual realisation can be quite far away from the target values of the acoustic parameters of these vowels (Van Bergem, 1995). In addition, there is a lexical process of vowel reduction of vowels in unstressed (non-word-final) syllables that has already affected many words whose full vowels have been replaced with schwa, for instance:

(5.18) tel*e*vísie 'television'
álg*e*bra 'algebra'
ser*e*náde 'serenade'
r*e*cláme 'publicity'
b*e*tón 'concrete'
rep*e*títie 'rehearsal, test'
conf*e*réntie 'conference'

Morover, there is also a large number of words that exhibit vowel reduction in more casual speech only, i.e. there is still alternation:

(5.19) banáan 'banana' [baːnaːn] / [bənaːn]
polítie 'police' [poːlisi] / [pəlisi]
minúut 'minute' [minyt] / [mənyt]

These facts of vowel reduction nicely fit into Kiparsky's two-stage theory of phonological change: "...the phonetic variation inherent in speech, which is blind in the neogrammarian sense, is selectively integrated into the linguistic system and passed on to successive generations of speakers through language acquisition" (Kiparsky, 1995, p.642). Vowel reduction, originally a purely phonetic process motivated by ease of articulation, could become a lexical rule, subject to lexical diffusion, because the schwa is a phoneme. As a lexical rule, it can be seen as a process in which the place of articulation features of vowels in unstressed syllables are removed from the lexical representations of words; subsequently, a default rule will fill in the relevant features of the schwa (cf. Kiparsky, 1995, p.642-47 for this interpretation of lexical diffusion). Simultaneously, vowel reduction is a postlexical rule applying to vowels in syllables without lexical stress, and a process of phonetic implementation for vowels (even those with lexical stress) that are not stressed in a particular utterance.

The alternation between full vowel and schwa is also visible in related pairs of words that differ in whether the relevant vowel is stressed or not; if the vowel is unstressed it can reduce, but also be pronounced as a full vowel:

(5.20)	a	p*e*rsóon 'person'	pèrs*o*néel 'staff'
		p*e*rcént 'procent'	pèrc*e*ntáge 'id.'
		p*a*stóor 'priest'	pàst*o*ráal 'pastoral'
	b	proféet 'prophet'	pròf*e*téer 'to prophesy'
		juwéel 'juwel'	jùw*e*líer 'jeweler'
		gêne 'embarrasment'	g*e*nánt 'embarrassing'

The words in (5.20a) exhibit optional reduction, whereas in those in (5.20b) the vowel in italic can only be realized as schwa. That is, the words in (5.20a) are subject to the postlexical rule of vowel reduction whereas the words in (5.20b) exhibit lexical diffusion effects. This implies that a morpheme like *juweel* will have two different lexical representations, /jyʋeːl/ when it is an independent word, and /jyʋəl/ when occuring in *juwelier*. This does not cause any computational problem since words are the units of storage, and thus the two allomorphs will automatically appear in the right context. The only problem that the language user has to solve here, is the recognition problem: how can both forms be recognized as forms of the same morpheme (a prerequisite for the semantic analysis)? But this is part and parcel of commanding a language since allomorphy that is not reducible to one underlying form is a widespread phenomenon, as we saw above (cf. also Booij, 1997a; 1997b; 1998).

Van Bergem, 1995 rightly qualifies this process of vowel reduction as a sound change in progress, which came into being due to interpretation by the native speaker of acoustic vowel reduction as a process of replacement of full vowel with schwa. It also exhibits lexical diffusion, since in some words the unstressed vowel can only be realized as a schwa, as we saw above. Furthermore, this kind of reduction is boosted by high frequency: in high frequency words unstressed vowels are reduced more easily and more frequently than in low frequency words. This is to be expected since vowel reduction reduces lexical contrasts, and thus impedes word recognition. High frequency, on the other hand, boosts recognition, and can thus compensate for the negative effects of vowel reduction.

The question then arises if the postlexical rule of optional vowel reduction in unstressed syllables is phonetically gradual, or should be interpreted as the replacement in lexical representations of the full vowel with schwa by means of a phonological rule, just as in the case of the lexical rule of vowel reduction. If the first position is taken, this may have the further implication that the degree of reduction of the vowel is encoded in lexical representation. This position is argued for in Bybee (to appear, a, b) for some other cases of reduction, and implies that details of the phonetic realization of phonemes are lexically specified. Can we say something about this on the basis of Dutch vowel reduction?

The data in Van Bergem, 1995, p.21 show that there is a positive correlation between frequency and acoustic parameters: in high frequency words the formant values for the unstressed vowel are farther away from the target values than in low frequency words. Moreover, this correlates with how native speakers perceive these vowels: "the average number of schwa responses increases when the spectral distance between the test vowel and its target increases" (Van Bergem, 1995, p.125). These results are explained if the growing distance between the acoustic parameters of unstressed vowels in words of high frequency and those of the non-reduced correlates is lexically encoded: each time a vowel is reduced, its formant values move away from those of the unreduced vowel. This is the kind of explanation advocated in Bybee (to appear, a). The theoretical implication of this step is that lexical representations are not redundancy-free as far as phonetic details are concerned, a position also defended by Ohala and Ohala, 1995.

This position as to the lexical specification of vowel reduction effects is supported by the observation that data concerning optional vowel reduction can be obtained by means of introspection: native speakers of Dutch systematically know that certain words are more susceptible to vowel reduction than other. For instance, they know that the /i/ in *minuut* is susceptible to reduction, whereas the /i/ in *pilóot* 'pilot' is not. This suggests that such information is stored in memory.

The conclusion to be drawn is that phonological rules may be productive and automatic, and yet at least some of their outputs are lexically stored because the process exhibits lexical diffusion. In addition, it seems that phonetic details concerning the pronunciation of vowels can be stored, given the facts concerning the gradual erosion of unstressed vowels. Note, however, that this kind of stored information does not necessarily lead to a proliferation of distinct underlying forms (in the sense of 'bases for morphological operations') for a morpheme. This is a crucial difference between lexical and postlexical rules: it is only the effects of lexical rules that may lead to more than one underlying form for a particular morpheme.

4. Conclusions

In this chapter, we saw that the standard view in generative phonology of the balance between storage and computation has to be reconsidered: there is a wealth of evidence for the position that predictable information is stored in the lexicon. First, recent theoretical developments in phonology imply that the allomorphs of morphemes are stored in the lexicon to a much higher degree than previously assumed. Secondly, data concerning phonological change show that computable information concerning the phonetic realization of morphemes has nevertheless to be stored lexically. I also proposed that with respect to the relation between underlying form and phonetic form we should take a radical step: it is not the phonetic form that is computed by the speaker, but rather the underlying form. Like storage in general, storage of phonetic forms of words will speed up processing; it is only when we coin a new word that computation of the underlying form of the base word is necessary.

These conclusions do not refute the position that the human language faculty has a dual structure: a lexicon with stored representations and rules. The native speaker does need rules for the perception and production of novel forms. What, however, these conclusions do refute is the position that computation and storage of information with respect to the same process or regularity are mutually exclusive.

Acknowledgments

I would like to thank my colleagues Jaap van Marle, Piet van Reenen, and Leo Wetzels, and the anonymous referee for their comments on an earlier draft of this paper.

References

Anderson, S. (1974). *The organization of phonology.* New York etc.: Academic Press.

Baayen, H., Burani, C., and Schreuder, R. (1997). Effects of semantic markedness in the processing of regular nominal singulars and plurals in Italian. In Booij, G. and Van Marle, J., editors, *Yearbook of Morphology 1996*, pages 13–34. Dordrecht: Kluwer.

Bloomfield, L. (1933). *Language.* London: Allen & Unwin.

Booij, G. (1982). Fonetische en fonologische aspecten van klinkerreductie. *Spektator*, 11:295–301.

Booij, G. (1995). *The phonology of Dutch.* Oxford: Clarendon Press.

Booij, G. (1997a). Allomorphy and the autonomy of morphology. *Folia Linguistica*, 31:25–56.

Booij, G. (1997b). Autonomous morphology and paradigmatic relations. In Booij, G. and Van Marle, J., editors, *Yearbook of Morphology 1996*, pages 35–53. Dordrecht/Boston: Kluwer.

Booij, G. (1998). Prosodic output constraints in morphology. In Kehrein, W. and Wiese, R., editors, *Phonology and morphology of the Germanic languages*, pages 1–20. Tübingen: Niemeyer.

Booij, G. (1999). Lexical storage and regular processes. *Behavioural and Brain Sciences*, 22:1016.

Bybee, J. (to appear, a). Lexicalization of sound change and alternating environments. In Pierrehumbert, J. and Broe, M., editors, *Papers in Laboratory Phonology*, volume V. Cambridge: Cambridge University Press.

Bybee, J. (to appear, b). The phonology of the lexicon: evidence from lexical diffusion. In Barlow, M. and Kemmer, S., editors, *Usage-based models of language.*

Clahsen, H. (1999). Lexical entries and rules of language: a multidisciplinary study of German inflection. *Behavioural and Brain Sciences*, 22:991–1013.

Clements, G. N. and Keyser, S. J. (1983). *CV Phonology*. Cambridge MA: MIT Press.

Jackendoff, R. (1975). Semantic and morphological regularities in the lexicon. *Language*, 51:639–671.

Jackendoff, R. (1997). *The architecture of the language faculty*. Cambridge MA: MIT Press.

Janda, R. (1998). Comments on the paper by Perlmutter. In Lapointe, S., Brentari, D., and Farrell, P., editors, *Morphology and its relation to Syntax*, pages 339–359. Stanford: CSLI.

Kager, R. (1996). On affix allomorphy and syllable counting. In Kleinhenz, U., editor, *Interfaces in phonology*, pages 151–171. Berlin: Akademieverlag.

Kenstowicz, M. (1994). *Phonological theory*. Cambridge MA: Blackwell.

Kenstowicz, M. and Kisseberth, C. (1979). *Generative phonology*. New York: Academic Press.

Kiparsky, P. (1988). Phonological change. In Newmeyer, F., editor, *Linguistics, the Cambridge Survey*, volume 1, pages 363–415. Cambridge: Cambridge University Press.

Kiparsky, P. (1995). The phonological basis of sound change. In Goldsmith, J., editor, *The handbook of phonological theory*, pages 340–370. Cambridge MA: Blackwell.

Labov, W. (1981). Resolving the neo-grammarian hypothesis. *Language*, 57:267–309.

Labov, W. (1994). *Principles of linguistic change. Internal factors*. Oxford: Blackwell.

Lahiri, A. and Marslen-Wilson, W. (1992). Lexical processing and phonological representation. In Docherty, G. and Ladd, D. R., editors, *Papers in Laboratory Phonology II, Gesture, Segment, Prosody*, pages 229–254. Cambridge: Cambridge University Press.

Langacker, R. (1987). *Foundations of Cognitive Grammar. Vol 1. Theoretical Prerequisites*. Stanford Calif.: Stanford University Press.

Lapointe, S. G., Brentari, D. K., and Farrell, P. M., editors (1998). *Morphology and its relation to syntax*. Stanford: CSLI.

Leben, W. (1979). The phonological component as a parsing device. In Dinnsen, D., editor, *Current approaches to phonological theory*, pages 174–201. Bloomington and London: Indiana University Press.

Levelt, W. J. M. (1992). Accessing words in speech production: Stages, processes and representations. *Cognition*, 42:1–22.

Mester, A. (1994). The quantitative trochee in Latin. *Natural Language and Linguistic Theory*, 12:1–61.

Ohala, J. and Ohala, M. (1995). Speech perception and lexical representation: the rule of vowel nasalization in Hindi and English. In Connell, B. and Arvaniti, A., editors, *Papers in laboratory phonology*, volume IV, pages 41–60. Cambridge: Cambridge University Press.

Ortmann, A. (1998). Consonant epenthesis: its distribution and phonological specification. In Kehrein, W. and Wiese, R., editors, *Phonology and morphology of the Germanic languages*, pages 51–76. Tübingen: Niemeyer.

Perlmutter, D. (1998). Interfaces: explanation of allomorphy and the architecture of grammars. In Lapointe, S., Brentari, D., and Farrell, P., editors, *Morphology and its relation to syntax*, pages 307–338. Stanford: CSLI.

Plag, I. (1998). Morphological haplology in a constraint-based morphophonology. In Kehrein, W. and Wiese, R., editors, *Phonology and morphology of the Germanic languages*, pages 199–215. Tübingen: Niemeyer.

Raffelsiefen, R. (1999). Phonological constraints in English word formation. In Booij, G. and Van Marle, J., editors, *Yearbook of morphology 1998*, pages 225–87. Dordrecht: Kluwer.

Trommelen, M. (1984). *The syllable in Dutch. With special reference to diminutive formation.* Dordrecht: Foris.

Van Bergem, D. (1995). *Acoustic and lexical vowel reduction.* PhD thesis, Univ. of Amsterdam.

Van Loey, A. (1964). *Schönfeld's historische grammatica van het Nederlands.* Zutphen: Thieme.

Van Loon, J. (1986). *Historische fonologie van het Nederlands.* Leuven/Amersfoort: Acco.

Wetzels, L. (1981). *Analogie et lexique. Le problème de l'opacité en phonologie generative.* PhD thesis, Catholic University Nijmegen.

Wetzels, L. (1984). Paradigm leveling in Latin and Old French: A critical view of rule inversion. In Baldi, P., editor, *Papers from the XIIth Linguistic Symposium on Romance Languages*, pages 579–599. Amsterdam: Benjamins.

Chapter 6

COMPUTATION AND STORAGE IN LANGUAGE CONTACT

Pieter Muysken

Abstract This paper argues that some cases of intrasentential code-switching cannot be accounted for in strictly computational terms, but must involve the storage of bilingual patterns. These can involve stored bilingual equivalence mappings, and bilingual grammatical structures. The cases analyzed are Moroccan Arabic/French demonstrative + noun combinations, and bilingual verbal compounds in the Indic languages.

Keywords: Intra-sentential code-switching, bilingualism, bilingual equivalence, Moroccan Arabic, French, verbal compounds, Indic languages, Sarnami Hindustani, Dutch.

1. Introduction: computation and storage in language-contact Research

In language-contact research, the issue of storage and computation is normally seen in terms of the demarcation between clause-level and word-level phenomena. We find computation at the level of the clause (intrasentential code-switching), storage at the level of the word (word borrowing). In the case of word borrowing, foreign words are adopted into the native lexicon. In the case of code-switching the combination of two grammars and vocabularies is computed in producing a mixed sentence. Thus it is easy to chararacterize, at least from the perspective of the researcher, the word *autootje* in (6.1) as a French lexical borrowing, but now a Dutch noun:

S. Nooteboom et al. (eds.), Storage and Computation in the Language Faculty, 157–179.

(6.1) Wat een te gek autootje (pronounced: ['ɑutotjə])
'What a terrific car.'

It is only one word, it is pronounced with a Dutch dipthong on the basis of its spelling, it has the Dutch diminutive suffix here and the concomitant specifically Dutch neutral gender. It is used very frequently and it is the word used most when referring to cars. It is probably recognized as Dutch by most speakers, and though it has not undergone any semantic changes that could easily have been the case. There is also a more 'French' pronunciation, however, the slightly more posh ['oːtoːtjə], but that fits perfectly within the Dutch phonological system as well. Lexical borrowing is a quite frequent phenomenon, though Haugen, 1956, p.65 suggests that most published accounts of borrowing exaggerate the extent of it, since they are written either to warn against it or to amuse.

Compare in contrast a sentence with French/Dutch code-switching:

(6.2) Ze geven niet ge- uh .. niet genoeg *pour cette jeun.. jeunesse*

'They do not uh ... care [give] enough for this ... youth.'
(French/Dutch; Treffers-Daller, 1994, p.213)

The italicized French fragment in (6.2) has not become part of the Dutch lexicon morphologically, or phonologically, or semantically. Notice that in Dutch the preposition selected by the verb *geven* would be *om* rather than the equivalent of the French *pour* that we find here, *voor*.

While the contrast between (6.1) and (6.2) is clear both conceptually and empirically, there turn out to be more complex cases. Phonological integration is variable with borrowing, and in code-switching both phonologies can be active to some extent. Thus phonological criteria do not help in deciding what is borrowed and what is switched. The empirical data (for instance a transcript of recorded bilingual language use) do not always allow us to make a distinction for each single switch, particularly because many single elements are switched, and these could also be incorporated as borrowings. Consider cases such as the following, recorded by Jeanine Treffers-Daller in French/Dutch bilingual families living in Amsterdam:

(6.3) Oh, Micheline, je viens pas au club parce qu'il faut que j'aille au *oogarts* [standard French: *chez le* ...].
'Oh, Micheline, I can't come to the club because I have to go to the ophtalmologist.'

(6.4) Il y a du *bloot* qui est joli et du *bloot* qui n'est pas joli.
'There is /nude/ that is nice and /nude/ that is not nice.'
(French/Dutch; Treffers-Daller fieldwork data)

Notice that in these cases the alien element is not really culture-specific, although it may be so within the family ambience concerned. Furthermore, the words are perfectly integrated morpho-syntactically (notice the use of *au* and *du*, as in French, in (6.3) and (6.4)), but not phonologically. We really have no criteria to determine whether it is code-switching or borrowing, and often the term *nonce-borrowing* is used to describe such cases. Poplack has argued in many of her publications that generally the introduction of single elements should be viewed as borrowing rather than switching (e.g. Poplack and Meechan, 1995), though this remains controversial. Thus, we now have three categories: borrowing, code-switching, and nonce-borrowing.

Formally, these categories can be represented as follows. Code-switching can be conceived of as inserting words with different language indices, marked with *p* and *q* subscripts, into a phrase-structure (6.5a), in which the brackets labelled C mark the clause level, while lexical borrowing can be seen as using formatives (Fr) within an alien word structure (6.5b), in which the brackets labelled W mark the word level. The word structure behaves externally like an element from the host language and may also contain formatives $\mathrm{Fr_q}$ from the host language:

(6.5) a. $[_{\mathrm{C}}\ \mathrm{W}_{..\mathrm{p}}\ \mathrm{W}_{..\mathrm{q}}\ ]$ above-word or clause level
b. $[_{\mathrm{W}}\ \mathrm{Fr_p}\ (\mathrm{Fr_q})\ ]$ below-word level

I will use the term sublexical for switching below the level of insertion of a word into a syntactic tree; and the term supralexical for switching at the level of insertion in a tree and in the syntactic projection of a word. Thus a word can be inserted into a syntactic tree as, say, a Dutch item, even though some of its components are French.

Thus we have to decide whether a particular language-contact phenomenon occurs at the supralexical or sublexical level, in the sense just described. However, researchers have also taken into account whether an element is listed (DiSciullo and Williams, 1989) or not. The dimension of listedness refers to the degree to which a particular element or structure is part of a memorized list which has gained acceptance within a particular speech community.

Both lexical borrowing and the creation of new words through morphological derivation and lexical coining involve the dimension of listedness. Therefore we can compare the phenomena associated with lexical borrowing to those associated with word creation. It has often been noted that lexical borrowing, in contrast with code-switching, involves gradual semantic specialization over time, blurring of morpheme boundaries, lexical unpredictability, etc. These strikingly resemble the properties of derivational morphology. Both can be viewed as the consequences of lexicalization and storage typical of sublexical structures. It may be possible to integrate lexicalization into derivation and language-contact even further, e.g. if we assume that there is a progressive linking of new forms to established (mono-morphematic) word shapes in the mental lexicon in both cases.

We can arrange linguistic elements, then, on two scales: computed versus stored, and syntactic or supralexical versus sublexical. Jackendoff, 1975 and others have pointed out, of course, that these two dimensions are not entirely separate. The sublexical mode is primarily reproductive (listed or stored), the supralexical, syntactic, mode primarily creative or computed. Nonetheless, there are many languages, e.g. polysynthetic and agglutinative languages, in which processes of word formation are regularly used to produce novel formations. Similarly, there are phrase-structure configurations, most clearly idioms and collocations, which are to some extent reproductive. In the model of Construction Grammar, a much larger set of phrase-structure configurations is assumed to be listed (Goldberg, 1995). For this reason, it is better to see these dimensions as separate.

When we classify language-contact phenomena in terms of these dimensions, the following picture emerges:

(6.6)

	computed	*stored*
supralexical	code-switching (a)	??? conventionalized code-switching (b)
sublexical	nonce loans (c)	established loans (d)

Most code-switchings are spontaneously computed in discourse, (6.6a). The phenomenon of nonce loans, (6.6c), was first described by Haugen, 1950 and has recently been taken up in work of Sankoff and Poplack, 1984: elements are borrowed on the spur of the moment, without having any status yet in the receiving speech community. Finally, established loans, (6.6d), are a familiar phenomenon. Now, how about category (6.6b): conventionalized code-switching? As said before, code-switching is generally analyzed as having the ordinary, supralexical, productive properties of syntax.

The contribution of this paper is to argue that some instances of code-switching have features that must be analyzed in terms of storage, constituting examples of (6.6b). I want to present two cases, both classics in the code-switching literature: Moroccan Arabic demonstratives and bilingual verbal compounds in the Indic languages. In both cases, I want to claim, the well-formedness of the bilingual sentences cannot simply be computed from the properties of the contributing languages, and must be stored in some kind of bilingual grammar.

The argument has four parts. Section 2 surveys where we stand in terms of the research on constraints on code-switching. Then, in section 3, I discuss code-switching involving Moroccan Arabic demonstratives, followed by the case of Surinam Hindustani bilingual verb cases in section 4. Finally, these two cases will be compared in the light of the previous discussion.

2. Code-switching research

I cannot even begin to summarize the development of code-switching research in general here, not even that part that has focussed on grammatical processing. However, it is necessary to outline some of the general background assumptions and research methodologies in this field, as well as some of the main findings and points of disagreement.

Most researchers in this area have based their work on a combination of quantitative and structural analysis of utterances in recorded spontaneous bilingual in-group conversations, generally involving quite fluent bilinguals. Introspection or experimental data have played a marginal role so far. While individual code-switches may serve a variety of pragmatic functions, sometimes it is the code-switching speech style as such that seems to be a stylistic or conversational marker. Occasionally, word finding problems play a role in the production of a particular switch, but code-switching goes much beyond word-finding problems. Indeed, often bilingual equivalents in the two languages occur in the same conversation and are uttered by the same speaker. Code-switching is acquired quite early on in some bilingual settings and does not necessarily lead to interference in simultaneous bilingual acquisition. It often is a fairly automatic process and may but need not involve pausing, hesitation, or self-repair.

There has been less agreement on the grammatical and psycholinguistic mechanisms involved in bilingual processing. A first bone of contention was already mentioned in the introductory paragraph above: are single foreign words occurring productively in bilingual discourse single word code-switches or nonce borrowings? A second important area of controversy concerns the nature of the constraints on the code-switching process. My own view is that different constraints operate to different degrees in different settings and for different language pairs, and thus complement each other (Muysken, 2000).

There is a growing body of work that argues that "...code-switching utterances are constrained by the same set of mechanisms as those which govern monolingual utterances" (Chan, 1999, p.1). Thus the well-formedness of code-switched sentences is assumed to be computed by the bilingual speaker on the basis of the properties of the two languages involved in code-switching, and possibly even just on the basis of UG and two participant lexicons. This approach was implicit in earlier generative work by e.g. Bentahila and Davies, 1983; Woolford, 1983 and DiSciullo et al., 1986, but has become much more explicitly formulated and formally implemented in work from the last decade Pandit, 1990; Mahootian, 1993; MacSwan, 2000; Chan, 1999; Boeschoten and Huybregts, 1997. This line of research is most often associated with the minimalist approach in generative grammar (Chomsky, 1995). A typical example is MacSwan, 2000, who relies on feature matching between the two languages to explain the following contrast in Nahuatl-Spanish code-switching:

(6.7) * *no* nitekititoc

no	ni-tekiti-toc
not	1s-work-DUR

'I am not working.'

(6.8) amo *estoy trabajando*

amo	estoy	trabaja-ndo
not	be.PR.1s	work-DUR

'I am not working.'

(Nahuatl/Spanish; MacSwan, 2000)

Even though the order of negation and the verb in both languages is similar, example (6.7) is not allowed while (6.8) is. MacSwan explains this by arguing that Spanish *no* in (6.7) is a clitic, while Nahuatl *amo* in (6.8) is not, citing independent syntactic evidence for this. The Spanish clitic *no* requires quite specific syntactic features on its host element, not matched by the Nahuatl verb. In contrast, *amo* requires very general features on its host, namely that it is a predicate.

This approach assumes that there is no such thing as a bilingual grammar, but only the computational matching of two lexicons to produce bilingual, code-switched, sentences. In this paper I do not want to argue against this type of approach to code-switching in general. I think it is a logical one and appropriate for quite a few cases. It would be highly redundant to assume that bilinguals had a special grammar stored away somewhere, to be used only when they produce bilingual sentences.

In the two cases I want to focus on, I will be claiming that in fact there is such a thing as a bilingual grammar, kept in storage for bilingual sentences. It is put into operation when the well-formedness of the bilingual sentences cannot simply be computed from the properties of the contributing languages. Before presenting these two cases, however, it is necessary to sketch the proposed computational constraints on the code-switching process in a bit more detail as a backdrop to the ensuing discussion.

We may summarize the constraints on intra-sentential code-switching proposed as specific ways of circumventing a general constraint that blocks code-switching altogether:

(6.9) $* \quad X_p \quad Y_q$ (where *p* and *q* are language indices)

A first way to circumvent the constraint is word-order matching (Poplack, 1980; Woolford, 1983):

(6.10) Constraint (6.9) does not hold where the order of the categories X and Y is identical in both languages P and Q.

Word-order matching plays an important role. Generally switching becomes easier when the two languages have equivalent constituent order at the place where the switch takes place (Poplack, 1980; Woolford, 1983). In examples like the following, switching is quite easy because the word orders of the two languages involved match, as can be seen from the translations in square brackets:

(6.11) Any way, *yo creo que las personas* [I think that the persons] who support *todos estos grupos como los* [all these groups like the] Friends of the Earth *son personas que* [are persons that] are very close to nature.

'Anyway, I believe that the people who support all these groups like the Friends of the Earth are people who are very close to nature.'

(Gibraltar Spanish/English; Moyer, 1992, p.437)

A second condition favoring code-switching is the absence of *syntagmatic coherence* (Bentahila and Davies, 1983; DiSciullo et al., 1986; Belazi et al., 1994. Generally switching becomes easier when the elements on both sides of the switch site do not show a tight syntagmatic relationship, defined in terms of subcategorization (Bentahila and Davies,

1983), government (DiSciullo et al., 1986), or selection by a functional category (Belazi et al., 1994):

(6.12) Constraint (6.9) only holds where

a. Where X subcategorizes for Y (Bentahila & Davies)

b. Where X governs Y (Di Sciullo, Muysken & Singh)

c. Where X is a functional element and selects Y (Belazi, Rubin & Toribio)

Thus switches at the clausal periphery, created through adjunction rather than selection, are much more productive. Some typical examples:

(6.13) Aller à l'hôpital *toch niet*?

'Going to the hospital,/ you don't mean?'

(French/Dutch; Treffers-Daller, 1994, p.213)

(6.14) *Les femmes et le vin*, ne ponimayu.

'Women and wine, I don't understand.'

(French/Russian; Timm, 1978, p.312)

In (6.13) the tag *toch niet* is clearly separate from the main part of the clause, and in (6.14) the French object of the Russian verb is put at the periphery through fronting.

Third, code-switching involves the maintenance of *matrix-language integrity*. Integrity is maintained when the rules of the matrix language determine the overall structure and categorial make up of a clause (Myers-Scotton, 1993; Pandit, 1990; Mahootian, 1993; Sebba, 1998), and inserted elements have the same category as native language elements.

(6.15) Constraint (6.9) does not hold when the matrix language is determined by X and Y corresponds to a matrix language category. (Sebba, Myers-Scotton, Pandit, Mahootian)

In the following example the inserted elements fit into the structure of the overall clause since they share the categorial make-up of matrix elements and occur in the position of native elements:

(6.16) Ngai yew *krampen* in nga *buik*.
'**I have** cramps in **my** stomach.'

(Chinese/Dutch; Tjon, 1988, p.8)

Content elements such as nouns, here Dutch words in a Chinese clause can freely be taken from another language. The function words and the morpho-syntax come from the matrix language.

While these constraints are interrelated and may be partly reduced to each other, it is fair to say that together they represent the main findings so far about what constrains the process of bilingual sentence production.

In the next two sections I will illustrate bilingual patterns created and then stored to comply with these constraints.

3. Moroccan-Arabic determiners

The first case of storage I want to discuss involves Moroccan Arabic demonstratives in code-switching settings involving French and Dutch. Bentahila and Davies, 1983 made an important contribution to the code-switching literature when they pointed out the contrast in (6.17), and gave a principled explanation for it:

(6.17) a. dak la chemise
that the shirt

b. * dak chemise

(Moroccan Arabic/French; Bentahila and Davies, 1983)

All relevant examples encountered in Moroccan Arabic/French bilingual speech are of the (6.17a) type; the (6.17b) type does not occur. After Arabic demonstratives the French article is obligatory in switches. The same holds for French nouns occurring after the indefinite determiner *wahed* 'one'. This type of pattern was the basis for Bentahila and Davies' **subcategorization constraint**: the demonstrative *dak* and the indefinite determiner *wahed* subcategorize for a definite article (often *l*) + noun combination in Arabic, it also needs one in a switched constituent involving a French noun. The subcategorization constraint follows from two formal principles mentioned in the previous section: the principle of matrix language integrity (cf. (6.15) above) in a selection context. This selection can be analyzed in terms of subcategorization (cf. (6.12a) above) or selection by a functional head (cf. (6.12c) above). The presence of *la* in (6.17a) then serves to satisfy the categorial requirements of Arabic *dak*. If *la* were absent, both the constraint of matrix language integrity and that of selection by a functional head would be violated. Notice that there is word-order matching here (cf. (6.10) above): both in Arabic and French the demonstrative precedes the noun. Word-order conflicts cannot be the source of the unacceptability of (6.17b).

Nait M'Barek and Sankoff, 1988, p.148 show that this pattern also holds for 91% of the cases in their bilingual Moroccan Arabic/French corpus (and claim that the remaining 9% are true nonce-borrowings). An example from their corpus is:

(6.18) *le* *charme* walla **hadik** *la* *particularité* dyal *les*
the charm or that the particularity of the
Clubs *Meds*
Club Meds
'The charm or rather that specific character of the Club Meds.'
(Moroccan Arabic/French; Nait M'Barek and Sankoff, 1988, p.149)

This example resembles (6.17a) in that *la particularité* follows an Arabic demonstrative, *hadik*. However, the well-formedness of (6.17a) crucially depends on the recognizablity of French *la* as an element satisfying the featural requirement of the Arabic demonstrative, i.e. as a marker of definiteness.

As Nortier, 1990, p.199 points out, there is a discrepancy between the way French articles are treated in French noun phrases incorporated into Moroccan Arabic (Bentahila and Davies, 1983 and other sources), and the way Dutch articles are treated when Dutch nouns occur in Arabic. The pattern opposite to (6.17) is found in Moroccan Arabic/Dutch switching, where we have (data and analysis by Nortier, 1990):

(6.19) a. * dik het gesprek
this the conversation

b. dik gesprek (Moroccan Arabic/Dutch)

In these bilingual speech data the (6.19a) type is absent and the (6.19b) type abundant. After *wahed* 'one' and Arabic demonstratives such as *dik*, the Dutch article is forbidden, while the article was obligatory in the context of Moroccan Arabic/French code-switching.

This contrast forces us to look at differences between Dutch and French articles in more detail and consider the issue of storage of bilingual patterns. The findings for noun phrases in both language pairs after a demonstrative, a preposition, or without either demonstrative or preposition can be summarized as follows (Nortier, 1990, p.201), where # is the switch site:

(6.20)

		MA/F	MA/D
a.	wahed/dem art # N	yes	yes
b.	wahed/dem # art N	yes	no
c.	wahed/dem # [0] N	no	yes
d.	P art # N	?	yes
e.	P # art N	yes	no
f.	P # [0] N	no	yes
g.	# art N (subj)	yes	yes
h.	# art N (obj)	yes	yes

The two data sets correspond where a French or Dutch bare noun is inserted after an Arabic article (6.20a), or where a Dutch or French noun phrase occurs in subject or object position (6.20g,h). After an Arabic preposition (6.20e,f) or demonstrative (6.20b,c), a Dutch article is not allowed, while a French one is obligatory here. In Muysken, 2000 I argue that this contrast can be explained by assuming that French articles are, and Dutch articles are not, stored in a bilingual grammar as equivalent to Moroccan Arabic articles by bilingual speakers.

I assume that Moroccan Arabic has a category of DNG-P (definiteness/number/gender phrase) headed by the article *l* and that French articles are considered appropriate heads of this phrase as well in bilingual language use, but not Dutch articles:

(6.21) $[_{\mathrm{DP}}$ wahed/dak,dik/0 $[_{\mathrm{DNG-P}}$ $\mathbf{l}_{ma}$/**le,la**$_{fr}$ $[_{\mathrm{NP}}$ Noun]]]

Since prepositions are proclitic elements in Moroccan Arabic, they also require an appropriate nominal complement, in this case one with a definite article head. This explains the grammaticality contrasts in (6.20e,f). The structure of the Moroccan Arabic prepositional phrase can be represented as follows:

(6.22) $[_{\mathrm{PP}}$ P $[_{\mathrm{DNG-P}}$ l_{ma}/le,la$_{fr}$ $[_{\mathrm{NP}}$ Noun]]]

Heath, 1989 has shown that the Moroccan Arabic/French code-switching pattern in (6.17) has developed over a century and that the present-day pattern actually was not the original one. In an earlier stage, French nouns were incorporated into Arabic only sporadically and with great difficulty: *le/la* were not yet recognized as potential equivalents of the Arabic definite markers.

The Dutch pattern remains a bit of a mystery. We can explain why (6.19a), with the Dutch article *het*, is unacceptable: it is not stored in bilingual grammar as equivalent to Arabic *l*. However, why we can have (6.19b), without any article, still requires an explanation. In many code-switching contexts, there is a null-form strategy as a way of reconciling incompatibilities in feature requirements between languages (Muysken, 2000), sometimes termed 'suspension of syntax'. One possibility is that this null-form strategy emerges through the adjunction of the alien noun to a DP containing and empty nominal position, possibly a small *pro*.

Returning to the issue of storage and computation, what is stored then in the case of Moroccan Arabic demonstratives is the equivalence between the French determiner, which can have the shapes *le*, *la*, and *les* on the one hand, and the Arabic definite marker *l*, which can also take several forms depending on its phonological context, on the other. That this equivalence is not automatic can be seen from the fact that the Dutch determiners *de* and *het* are not considered equivalent to the Moroccan Arabic definite marker, and from the fact that the equivalence was only established over time. We can find post-hoc explanations for this discrepancy between French and Dutch:

- French articles are semi-obligatory and omni-present in discourse;
- French articles are proclitic;
- the French article in its reduced form *l'* resembles the canonical form of the Arabic determiner *l*.

Dutch articles lack these features. However, none of these post-hoc explanations, however plausible they may be, amounts to an automatic computational equivalence between Arabic and French. At best, they pave the way for a stored equivalence mapping in bilingual grammar.

It remains to be seen whether there ever is automatic equivalence between categories of two languages. This question involves at least four subquestions:

(a) Does UG provide a universal set of grammatical categories for the languages of the world?

(b) Does this set exhaust the categories that exist in the world's languages?

(c) How do bilingual speakers (children/adults) match specific items across language boundaries in terms of the universal set of categories?

(d) How do bilingual speakers (children/adults) match specific items across language boundaries for those categories not included in the universal set?

This issue is extremely complicated and has a number of typological and psycholinguistic dimensions.

Here, a tentative 'no' is given in response to question (b), and for question (d) it is claimed that bilingual speakers have to store equivalence matches in their bilingual grammar, based possibly on accidental factors.

4. Bilingual compound verbs

In this section I want to argue that in addition to equivalence matches stored in bilingual grammars (section 3), specific constructions also need to be stored. Thus we have another case where intra-sentential code-switching does not proceed in terms of simple computation. The case at hand is bilingual verbal compounds.

In a great many language pairs, involving Tamil, Hindi, Farsi, Turkish, and Greek, as well as other languages we find bilingual compound verbs consisting of a lexical verb from another language coupled with a verb meaning 'do' or 'be' from the native language. Consider first some examples from Sarnami Hindustani, an Indic language spoken in Surinam and also among part of the Surinamese-origin population in the Netherlands:

(6.23)	a.	*onti* kare hunt do	'to hunt'	Sranan/Sarnami
	b.	*train* kare train do	'to train'	English/Sarnami
	c.	*bewijs* kare prove do	'to prove'	Dutch/Sarnami
				(Kishna, 1979)

In these examples the Sarnami 'do' verb *kare* is combined with a non-native verb.

The pattern is extremely productive and has been extensively analyzed in the code-switching literature (cf. Romaine, 1995; Backus, 1996; Boumans, 1998; Muysken, 2000). In most of this literature, the reasoning adopted is the following: the native languages involved (Hindi, Turkish, etc.) invariably have noun + light verb compounds, in which the noun carries the lexical information and the verb makes it into a predicate. Semantically, the noun functions as the object of the verb. This pattern, it is claimed, is simply extended in the verb + verb compounds that occur in bilingual settings, bearing witness to the computational adaptability of native patterns to contact settings.

I want to argue against this analysis here. Instead, I want to claim that a fundamentally new structure has emerged, stored as such in bilingual grammar, even though its origin lies in the native pattern. The new structure involves the adjunction of an alien element to a native verb:

(6.24)

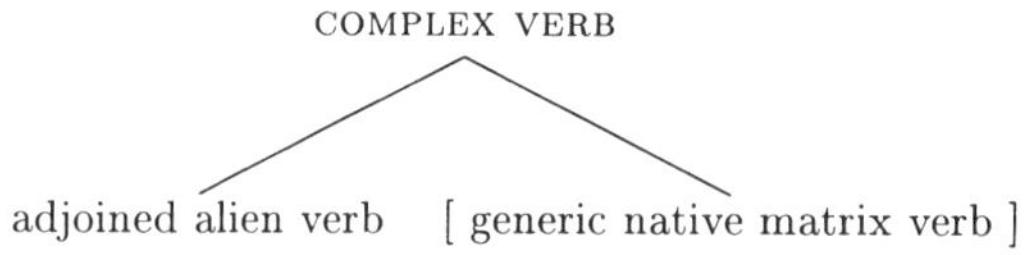

Here the adjoined verb further specifies the nature of the action generically indicated by the native verb.

Thus I assume the following reinterpretation of the structure as the result of the emergence of the bilingual varieties:

(6.25) a. **native** (selection): [$\text{love}_{\text{noun}}$ do] 'to perform love'
⇒
b. **bilingual** (adjunction): [$\text{love}_{\text{verb}}$ [do]] 'to do something (namely loving)'

In the native pattern (6.25a) the content noun is the selected object of the matrix verb, while in the bilingual pattern the content element is adjoined to the matrix verb, specifying the content of the action.

In what follows I will adduce evidence, drawn from Sarnami Hindustani/Dutch bilingual speech but generalizable to other cases, for the structure in (6.24) and the reinterpretation process in (6.25).

First of all, the Sarnami helping verb can have any type of element adjoined to it, even if verbs are most frequent. There is no categorial selection by a head, as would be expected in a complementation structure:

(6.26)

mixed compound	**gloss**	**meaning**	**Dutch X =**
luk ho:ve	'succeed be'	'succeed'	V
uit ja:	'out go'	'go out'	P
over a:ve	'over come'	'come over, migrate'	P
tegen rahe	'against be'	'be against'	P, Adv
geboren bhaili	'born be'	'I am born'	Part
schoon-maak kare	'clean make do'	'clean'	A+V
propaganda kare	'propaganda do'	'make propaganda'	N
koffer pak kare	'suitcase pack do'	'pack a suitcase'	N+V

This categorially indiscriminate relationship is not found in complement structures, but is typical of loose adjunction structures.

In the native pattern the only possibilities are noun + verb compounds. In the bilingual varieties the largest group are verb + verb structures. Still, there is no evidence of nominalization of the non-native verb. Five arguments can be given for this.

First, if the non-native verbs were treated as nouns, we would also expect many non-native nouns to occur in this position, as in the original pattern. While non-native nouns are not excluded, they are certainly not very frequent here. The verb kare takes nouns only infrequently. In Kishna's corpus there are 12 Dutch nouns, 5 Dutch adjectives, 13 Dutch adpositions, and 100 Dutch verbs combined with a Sarnami matrix verb.

Second, in Dutch prefixed verb stems cannot act as nominalized elements (*de handel* 'the trade, activity' versus **de be-handel* 'the treatment'). Prefixed verb stems freely occur in these bilingual structures, however:

(6.27)	ver=ken kare	verkennen	'explore'
	be=handel kare	behandelen	'treat'
	ver=wijs kare	verwijzen	'refer'

Third, in Dutch learned verb stems cannot act as nominalized elements (*de loop* 'the run' versus **de marcheer* 'the march'). Learned stems freely occur in these bilingual structures, however:

(6.28)	solliciteer kare	solliciteren	'apply for a job'
	discrimineer kare	discrimineren	'discriminate'
	forceer kare	dwingen	'force'

Fourth, while the Dutch verbs that occur in these structures occasionally have the infinitival form (17 infinitives versus 82 stem forms), suggesting that they are nominalized, there is no evidence for a systematic pattern of nominalization. Stem forms are in the majority.

Fifth, the adjoined verb can be finite in form, having undergone "verb second" and occuring to the left of the separable particle:

(6.29)	*leg uit* kare	(cf. Du uit-leggen)	'explain (lit. lay out)'
	vraag aan kare	(cf. Du aan-vragen)	'request (lit. ask to)'

This finite form is incompatible with the idea that these structures are nominalized.

Taking these five arguments together, there is absolutely no evidence that these elements are nominalized complements of the helping verb.

Yet another feature of these structures suggesting modification rather than complementation is that there is a tendency towards semantic congruence of the Sarnami helping verbs with the element that specifies them. Non-agentive Dutch predicates like *het lukt* 'it succeeds' and *flauw (vallen)* 'to faint' occur with Sarnami 'be', while agentive predicates such as *overplaatsen* 'to transfer someone' and *schoonmaken* 'to clean' occur with Sarnami 'do':

(6.30)	a.	*luk* ho:ve	lukken	'succeed (impersonal)'
		flauw ho:ve	flauw vallen	'faint'
	b.	*overplaats* kare	overplaatsen	'transfer'
		schoon-maak kare	schoonmaken	'clean'

The semantic congruence on the agentivity parameter suggests that the non-native verb makes the meaning of the native auxiliary explicit.

However, with nouns this relation does not hold necessarily. Thus agentive *kare* 'do' sometimes yields an inactive predicate when combined with a noun:

(6.31)	*bijles* kare	extra class	'follow extra classes' (not: teach extra classes)
	operatie kare	operation	'undergo an operation' (not: operate)

Again: these interpretations are unexpected if we have a verb + complement relation here.

The left-most element is sometimes a phrase rather than a word: *zielig gezicht kare* 'put on a sad face'. In a true compound only words are allowed (or other compounds), but not phrases. Notice we cannot argue here that *zielig* 'sad' is outside of the compound, since it only functions as the pre-nominal modifier.

A final argument for an adjunction structure is that there is no absorption of the transitivity properties of *kare*. The ensuing verb retains the possibility of selecting an object, while the native noun + helping verb combinations are never transitive.

A much more complete account of these structures is given in Muysken, 2000, but I hope to have adduced sufficient evidence for an adjunction rather than a complementation analysis of complex bilingual verbs. This analysis admittedly is unexpected, particularly since these complex verbs are not productively attested in native languages. All the languages under consideration have noun + verb compounds, but none has verb + verb constructions. In fact, I have encountered no non-contact language yet anywhere which has these verb + verb compounds.

Several questions need to be settled at this point: first the compound status of the verbal complexes involved. Second, the reason why these adjunctions emerged at all.

How do we know that we are really dealing here with a compound construction rather than an auxiliary + infinitive construction? This question can be best answered by contrasting the Sarnami Hindustani/Dutch case with the Moroccan Arabic/Dutch data analyzed by Boumans, 1998. These contain many cases of the helping verb *der* 'do':

(6.32)

ka-**ndir**-ha	*elke*	*keer*	*uitstellen*
1-do-3	every	time	postpone

'I postpone it every time.'

(Moroccan Arabic/Dutch; Boumans, 1998)

In this example, in contrast with the Sarnami cases, it is plausible to assume that the Dutch fragment is a bare VP that is used as a complement to the Moroccan Arabic helping verb.

There are at least four differences between the two data sets. First of all, in the Moroccan Arabic case, there is often much more Dutch material than just a verb. This was already evident in (6.32), where *elke keer* 'every time' modifies the infinitive *uitstellen* 'postpone', and also is evident in examples such as:

(6.33)

ana	kunt	ndir	*twijfelen*	*of*	*ik*	*ook*
I	1sg.was	1sg.do	doubt	whether	I	also

psychologie	*ging*	*studeren*
psychology	would	study.'

'I doubted whether I would study psychology.'

(Moroccan Arabic/Dutch; Boumans, 1998)

Second, the Moroccan Arabic case involves only one helping verb, *der*. There is no agentivity restriction. A non-agentive verb like *voelen* 'feel' can occur with it freely:

(6.34)

ma	ka-t-dir-ha	š	*voelen*?
NEG	DUR-2sg-do.IMPF-F	NEG	feel

'Don't you feel it?'

(Moroccan Arabic/Dutch; Boumans, 1998)

Third, the Moroccan Arabic verb and the Dutch element need not be adjacent, while this is obligatory in the Sarnami cases:

(6.35)

ka-t-dir	mʔa-hum	*voetballen*?
DUR-2-do.IMPF	with-3pl	football

'Do you play football with them?'

(Moroccan Arabic/Dutch; Boumans, 1998)

Fourth, in the Moroccan Arabic case, the Dutch verb always has the infinitive ending *-en*, while in the Sarnami cases, Dutch verb stems or finite forms are frequent.

All these facts suggest that *der* is an inflection-carrying helping verb in these structures taking an at least partly Dutch verb-phrase complement, in contrast with the Sarnami Hindustani verbal compounds. There are a great many languages with auxiliary + verb phrase-structures of different kinds, to be sure. Possibly in some cases an auxiliary + verb phrase combination is lexicalized, as in Flemish Dutch *gaan slapen* 'go sleep', which can even be combined with a new auxiliary as in *gaan gaan slapen* 'go go sleep'. There is no evidence, to my knowledge, that these patterns are productive, however.

How did the bilingual compounds emerge? In the case of the Sarnami Hindustani community, no work has been done on earlier stages of language-contact, but we do have some evidence from the Turkish bilingual community, where the same structures occur. In the case of Turkish/Dutch bilingual speech, the data in Backus, 1996 show that first generation migrants tend to have Dutch noun + Turkish verb combinations, and younger migrants Dutch verb + Turkish verb combinations. Thus, older speakers fit Dutch nouns into Turkish following the pattern available in the native language, while younger speakers expand the inventory of Dutch elements in Turkish to verbs.

The adoption of Dutch verbs into the native Turkish noun + verb structures is blocked, however, by the principle of Matrix-Language Integrity (6.15) in a selection context as in (6.12), since Turkish (like Sarnami Hindustani) allows no verbs here. The requirements of Matrix-Language Integrity were circumvented through adjunction within the bilingual community, creating a structure where feature compatibility became irrelevant. Again, there is word-order matching here (cf. (6.10) above): Turkish and Sarnami Hindustani take their complements on the left.

It is important to realize that the absence of verb + verb constructions in native Turkish and Sarnami Hindustani does not constitute an accidental gap in the grammatical patterns of these languages. In all the cases known to me, the native pattern involves a noun + verb combination, and the bilingual pattern is unique in allowing verb + verb combinations. The reason for the absence of the pattern in monolingual speech is straightforward if we make the following claim:

(6.36) Categorially specific patterns are transmitted in L1 acquisition as selected structures, involving a head + complement relation.

Head + complement relations are constrained by something like the Unlike Category Condition (Hoekstra, 1984), which block a head and a complement from having the same categorial feature specification, in this case [+V].

5. What can we learn from these two examples?

Several researchers, and most recently Sebba, 1998, have pointed to the dynamic charactér of language-contact situations: in different stages of language-contact across time, bilingual speakers behave differently. The reason for this is that bilingual language use does not only involve computation, but storage as well. What exactly is stored?

In the Moroccan-Arabic cases what is stored is a cross-linguistic equivalence: within the bilingual community the convention is established and transmitted that French *le/la* is equivalent to Moroccan Arabic *l*. Numerous cases of such conventionalized equivalences can be encountered: between case markers and adpositions, between classes of conjunctions and complementizers, between stative verbs and predicate adjectives, etc.

The verbal compound data constitute a second type of stored innovation, namely of a bilingual structure. What makes this structure so special is that we do not find it in monolingual speech.

The two types of stored patterns are part of the bilingual grammar stored by speakers of specific bilingual communities. The first one involves knowledge of two languages, the second one involves a structure not found in native languages, though very frequent in bilingual settings. They share the feature that they develop within a speech community over time, and may well be part of adult-to-adult rather than adult-to-child language transmission.

Together they show that linguistic knowledge may involve more than knowledge of UG (parametrized or not) and of individual lexicons. It also involves secondary knowledge of equivalences and patterns of usage, secondary knowledge that may be acquired by adults rather than by children. Thus there is a link between research on bilingual speech and that on adult second language learning that Harald Clahsen and I have argued for (Clahsen and Muysken, 1986). What the nature is of this secondary knowledge and how it interacts with primary, UG-linked, knowledge is an issue for further research. Two formal features of this secondary knowledge may be tentatively postulated. The first is **locality**, a feature of all language-specific knowledge, to be sure (Emonds, 1973). The second is the availability of structures resulting from **adjunction**, a basic type of non-grammatical or pre-grammatical structure (Bickerton, 1990).

At least two types of future research are called for to corroborate the tentative suggestions made in this paper of stored bilingual equivalences and adjunction structures. First, patterns of transmission in bilingual families need to be studied. How are equivalences between elements in two languages acquired by bilingual children? When do children start using verb + verb compounds? While some data are available on bilingual acquisition in Turkish/Dutch, Sarnami Hindustani/Dutch, Moroccan Arabic/Dutch and Moroccan Arabic/French bilingual families, these have not been systematically studied yet with respect to these linguistic variables.

Second, the implicit claim is made here that some code-switching patterns are like pidgin patterns in involving stored structures created by adult bilinguals. Thus a systematic search of pidgins involving typologically diverse language pairs would be illuminating to see whether they contain similar types of verb + verb compounds and whether they show bilingual equivalences. In fact, there is a long tradition in pidgin and creole research arguing that one of the crucial factors involved in pidgin genesis is the establishment of such equivalences (cf. e.g. Kouwenberg, 1992).

Acknowledgments

This short paper is dedicated to the memory of Teun Hoekstra, who encouraged me at various points to pursue this topic further from a more theoretical perspective. I also want to thank participants at the Utrecht meeting, particularly Harald Clahsen, and the editors of this volume for their comments. Needless to say, I am much indebted to my friends in the code-switching community, particularly Ad Backus, Rik Boeschoten, Jacomine Nortier and Rajendra Singh, for discussions on these topics, although they may not share the views expressed here. The Sarnami data are drawn from the corpus of lexical interferences collected by Sita Kishna, 1979. (1s = first person singular; AC = accusative case; PR = progressive aspect; NEG = negation marker).

References

Backus, A. (1992). *Patterns of language mixing. A study in Turkish-Dutch bilingualism.* Wiesbaden: Otto Harassowitz.

Backus, A. (1996). *Two in one. Bilingual speech of Turkish immigrants in the Netherlands.* PhD thesis, Katholieke Universiteit Brabant. Tilburg: Tilburg University Press, Studies in Multilingualism 1.

Belazi, H. M., Rubin, E. J., and Toribio, A. J. (1994). Code-switching and X-bar theory: The functional head constraint. *Linguistic Inquiry*, 25:221–238.

Bentahila, A. and Davies, E. D. (1983). The syntax of Arabic-French code-switching. *Lingua*, 59:301–330.

Bickerton, D. (1990). *Language and species.* Chicago: University of Chicago Press.

Boeschoten, H. E. and Huybregts, R. (1997). Code switching without switching codes. Presented at the TULP workshop on code switching and language change, Tilburg University, 15-16 May, 1997.

Boumans, L. (1998). *The syntax of code switching. Analysing Moroccan Arabic/Dutch conversation.* PhD thesis, Katholieke Universiteit Nijmegen. Tilburg: Tilburg University Press, Studies in Multilingualism 12.

Chan, B. H.-S. (1999). Aspects of the syntax, production and pragmatics of code-switching, with special reference to Cantonese-English code-switching. Unpublished doctoral dissertation, University College London.

Chomsky, N. (1995). *The minimalist program.* Cambridge, MA: MIT Press.

Clahsen, H. and Muysken, P. (1986). The availability of universal grammar to adult and child learners: a study in the acquisition of German word order. *Second language research*, 2:93–119.

Di Sciullo, A.-M., Muysken, P., and Singh, R. (1986). Code-mixing and government. *Journal of Linguistics*, 22:1–24.

Di Sciullo, A.-M. and Williams, E. (1989). *On the definition of word.* Cambridge, MA: MIT Press.

Emonds, J. E. (1973). *A transformational grammar of English.* New York: Academic Press.

Goldberg, A. E. (1995). *Constructions. A construction grammar approach to grammatical structure.* University of Chicago Press.

Haugen, E. (1950). The analysis of linguistic borrowing. *Language*, 26:210–231.

Haugen, E. (1956). *Bilingualism in the Americas: a bibliography and research guide.* Publication 26 of the American Dialect Society. Birmingham, Ala.: University of Alabama Press.

Heath, J. (1989). *From code-switching to borrowing. A case study of Moroccan Arabic.* Library of Arabic Linguistics, Monograph No 9. London: Kegan Paul International.

Hoekstra, T. (1984). Transitivity. Grammatical relations in government-binding theory. Unpublished doctoral dissertation, Rijksuniversiteit Leiden.

Jackendoff, R. (1975). Morphological and semantic regularities in the lexicon. *Language*, 51:639–671.

Kishna, S. (1979). Lexicale interferentie in het Sarnami. Unpublished master's thesis in linguistics. Universiteit van Amsterdam.

Kouwenberg, S. (1992). From OV to VO. Linguistic negotiation in the development of Berbice Dutch Creole. *Lingua*, 88:263–300.

MacSwan, J. (2000). The architecture of the bilingual language faculty: evidence from intrasentential code switching. *Bilingualism: Language and Cognition*, 3:37–54.

Mahootian, S. (1993). A null theory of codeswitching. Unpublished doctoral dissertation. Northwestern University.

Milroy, L. and Muysken, P., editors (1995). *One speaker, two languages. Cross-disciplinary perspectives on code-switching.* Cambridge: Cambridge University Press.

Moyer, M. (1992). Analysis of code-switching in Gibraltar. Unpublished doctoral dissertation. Universitat Autònoma de Barcelona.

Muysken, P. (2000). *Bilingual speech: a typology of code-mixing.* Cambridge: Cambridge University Press.

Myers-Scotton, C. (1993). *Duelling languages. Grammatical structure in codeswitching.* Oxford: Clarendon Press.

Nait M'Barek, M. and Sankoff, D. (1988). Le discours mixte Arabe / Français: des emprunts ou alternances de langue. *Canadian Journal of Linguistics / Revue Canadienne de Linguistique*, 33:143–54.

Nortier, J. (1990). *Dutch-Moroccan Arabic code-switching among young Moroccans in the Netherlands.* Dordrecht: Foris.

Pandit, I. (1990). Grammaticality in code-switching. In Jacobson, R., editor, *Code-switching as a world-wide phenomenon*, pages 33–69. New York: Peter Lang.

Paradis, M., editor (1978). *Aspects of bilingualism.* Columbia, S.C.: Hornbeam.

Poplack, S. (1980). Sometimes I'll start a sentence in Spanish Y TERMINO EN ESPAÑOL. *Linguistics*, 18:581–618.

Poplack, S. and Meechan, M. (1995). *Patterns of language mixture: nominal structure in Wolof-French and Fongbe-French bilingual discourse.* Cambridge: Cambridge University Press.

Romaine, S. (1995). *Bilingualism.* Oxford: Blackwell, second edition.

Sankoff, H.D. and Poplack, S. (1984). Borrowing: the synchrony of integration. *Linguistics*, 22:99–136.

Sankoff, H.D., Poplack, S., and Vanniarajan, S. (1990). The case of the nonce loan in Tamil. *Language Variation and Change*, 2:71–101.

Sebba, M. (1998). A congruence approach to the syntax of code-switching. *International Journal of Bilingualism*, 2:1–20.

Timm, L. A. (1978). Code-switching in war and peace. In Paradis, M., editor, *Aspects of bilingualism*, pages 302–315. Columbia, S.C.: Hornbeam.

Tjon, S. (1988). Conversationele codewisseling bij Chinese jongeren. Seminar paper, Chinese Department. Rijksuniversiteit Leiden.

Treffers-Daller, J. (1994). *Mixing two languages, French-Dutch contact in a comparative perspective.* Berlin: Mouton de Gruyter.

Woolford, E. (1983). Bilingual code-switching and syntactic theory. *Linguistic Inquiry*, 14:520–536.

IV

PRONOUNCING SPOKEN WORDS

Chapter 7

STORAGE AND COMPUTATION IN SPOKEN WORD PRODUCTION

Ardi Roelofs

Abstract This chapter addresses the storage/computation issue in spoken word production. It is argued that word production is characterized by a storage versus computation trade-off that not only varies over the ensemble of planning stages but also within stages. Based on previous experience, the word production system has various aspects of words already prepared and stored away. To use such preparations, the system must access memory, retrieve the prepared material, and adapt it to the word at hand. The chapter reviews the WEAVER++ model of word production, spells out the model's stance on the storage/computation trade-offs, and describes relevant empirical evidence.

Keywords: Conceptual preparation, lemma retrieval, morphophonological encoding, phonetic encoding, underspecification, WEAVER++.

1. Introduction

The production of spoken words is one of our most highly exercised psychomotor skills. In normal conversation we produce about 2 to 3 words, which is about 4 syllables or 10 speech segments, per second (Levelt, 1989). This means that already with one hour talking per day, we produce 3 to 4 million word tokens, or over 5 million syllable tokens, per year. Statistics have shown that native speakers of English or Dutch produce over 80 percent of these tokens using no more than 500 different syllables, although these languages have over 10,000 different syllables (see Levelt et al., 1999b, for details). It seems therefore plausible that speakers have a memory store of motor programs for frequently used syllables and that only programs of low frequency are computed when needed. Quite impressively, in producing these large numbers of words to express our thoughts, we make only a few errors, namely about 1 error

S. Nooteboom et al. (eds.), Storage and Computation in the Language Faculty, 183–216.

per 1,000 words that are spoken (Levelt, 1989). An important question is what information is retrieved from memory, or is computed, to achieve the mapping of intended concepts onto motor programs for the corresponding words. And how are the concepts prepared from which words are accessed? Do speakers assemble message concepts for words out of a, possibly universal, vocabulary of primitive concepts (Bierwisch and Schreuder, 1992) or do they retrieve concepts for words from a store of prefabricated lexical concepts (Roelofs, 1992; 1997a)? The latter idea of retrieving stored lexical concepts seems plausible given that conceptually driven word retrieval does not appear to proceed by trial-and-error. Word meanings typically evade definition (e.g., Fodor et al., 1980), but speakers apparently know exactly what conceptual information to prepare to access words efficiently.

In this chapter, I address the issue of storage versus computation in spoken word production. I restrict myself to production in languages such as Dutch and English whose adult speakers typically produce word forms they have spoken before. By contrast, in languages such as Finnish and Turkish, the production of novel word forms is the rule rather than the exception (e.g., Hankamer, 1989; Koskenniemi, 1984). It is difficult to assess the relative merits of storage and computation without an explicit computational framework (e.g., Sandra, 1994). Therefore, I use a concrete model of spoken word production as a guideline for my discussion. The model is WEAVER++ (Levelt et al., 1999a; 1999b; Roelofs, 1992; 1993; 1996b; 1996c; 1997c; 1998), which is a comprehensive, computational model of lexical access. Until recently, models of production have been designed to account for speech errors, which constitute the traditional database for production research and modeling (e.g., Dell, 1986; 1988; 1975; 1980; Shattuck-Hufnagel, 1979; Stemberger, 1985). In recent years, however, researchers have started to use chronometrical techniques and have collected latency data on production. The WEAVER++ model recognizes the key insights from speech errors, but has specifically been designed to provide a unifying account of the increasing body of chronometrical data.

I start by describing a general theoretical framework for lexical access and indicate how access happens in WEAVER++ (for an extensive review, see Levelt et al., 1999a; 1999b). In the model, a distinction is made between conceptual preparation, lemma retrieval, and word-form encoding, with the encoding of forms further divided into morphological, phonological, and phonetic encoding. For each of these levels of word planning, I discuss a number of theoretical and empirical arguments concerning storage and computation. But before reviewing the planning stages and the arguments, it is important to be clear about the goals.

Whereas linguistic models are designed to account for facts about language competence or knowledge per se, psycholinguistic models such as WEAVER++ aim at explaining facts about language performance such as how this knowledge is computed or stored in memory and, in case of storage, how it is accessed by speakers. WEAVER++ has been designed to account for facts about mental processes and representations, such as how long it takes to plan a particular type of word. Psycholinguistic models and linguistic models commonly play under different sets of rules. Linguistic models typically try to eliminate as much redundancy in representations as possible and try to capture redundancy in a rule. But this is usually not a major theoretical concern in developing a psycholinguistic model. On the contrary, psycholinguists often hold that when speakers can memorize a certain piece of knowledge, especially when it is frequently used, there is no reason to compute it, even when this would mean that redundant information is stored in memory. I indicate why certain design decisions have been taken in developing WEAVER++ and review relevant empirical evidence.

The view that I advocate is one in which storage versus computation in word production is not an all-or-none matter. Instead, word production can be characterized by a storage versus computation *trade-off*. Planning a word calls forth some mixture of computation and retrieval from storage. That mix not only varies over the ensemble of planning stages but also within stages. Based on previous experience, the word production system has various aspects of words already prepared and stored away. To use such preparations, the system must access memory, retrieve the prepared material, and then adapt it as appropriate to the word at hand. Stored are high-frequency aspects of words that take considerable time to assemble or aspects that are difficult or impossible to derive by rule. What is computed are aspects that are easy to derive by rule or aspects that are inherently context dependent. The WEAVER++ model captures these trade-offs in a particular way. It implements lexical knowledge symbolically as rules and stored facts but also has an activation process that determines which facts and rules get deployed for particular words.

2. Planning stages in speech production

Following most language production theories, the WEAVER++ model instantiates the assumption that speaking starts with conceptualization (but see Dennett, 1991). Conceptualization processes plan messages, which are conceptual structures to be conveyed to reach the communicative goal. Messages in WEAVER++ make explicit the intended lexical concepts and their relationships. Lexical concepts are concepts that correspond to the meaning of words. Next, formulation processes take the message, retrieve appropriate words for the lexical concepts, and build syntactic and morphophonological structures, resulting in a phonetic plan for the utterance. Phonetic plans in WEAVER++ make explicit motor programs for the syllables in the utterance. Finally, articulation processes execute the motor programs, which yields overt speech.

Lexical access in WEAVER++ consists of two consecutive stages, namely lemma retrieval and word-form encoding, which are stages of access that are part of the formulation stages of syntactic and morphophonological encoding, respectively (see Caramazza, 1997, for a proposal without lemma retrieval, and a comment on this proposal by Roelofs et al., 1998). In lemma retrieval, a message concept is used to retrieve a lemma from memory, which is a representation of the syntactic properties of a word, crucial for its use in sentences. For example, the lemma of the word *to evade* says that it is a transitive verb and specifies which syntactic environment the word requires. Lemma retrieval makes these properties available for syntactic encoding processes. Furthermore, lemmas contain slots for the specification of abstract morphosyntactic parameters such as aspect (progressive, perfect), tense (past, present), number (singular, plural), and person (first, second, third). In word-form encoding, the lemma and the information in the slots are used to retrieve the morphophonological properties of the word from memory in order to construct an appropriate articulatory program. For example, for first-person present tense *evade* the morpheme <evade> and the segments /ɪ/, /v/, /eɪ/, and /d/ are retrieved and a phonetic plan for [ɪ.'veɪd] is generated.

Figure 7.1 illustrates the stages of access in WEAVER++. Assume a speaker wants to convey the concept TO EVADE and wants to refer to it as an ongoing activity. Expressing this requires mapping the lexical concept EVADE(X,Y) onto the articulatory program for the form *evading*. First, the lemma retriever takes EVADE(X,Y) and delivers the lemma of *evade*. This includes making available the word class and subcategorization features. In order to derive the appropriate word form, progressive [ɪ.'veɪ.dɪŋ] instead of, for example, first-person present tense [ɪ.'veɪd] or past tense [ɪ.'veɪ.dɪd], the lemma retriever has to inspect the message for the relevant temporal information (not shown in Figure 7.1) and has to fill the corresponding morphosyntactic slots. (I ignore for present purposes that in English, the progressive is a two-word form of a verb, consisting of the auxiliary *be* followed by the present participle of the verb. Thus, the slot value "progressive" will have to lead to the retrieval of the lemma of the auxiliary. I refer to Levelt, 1989, and Levelt et al.,

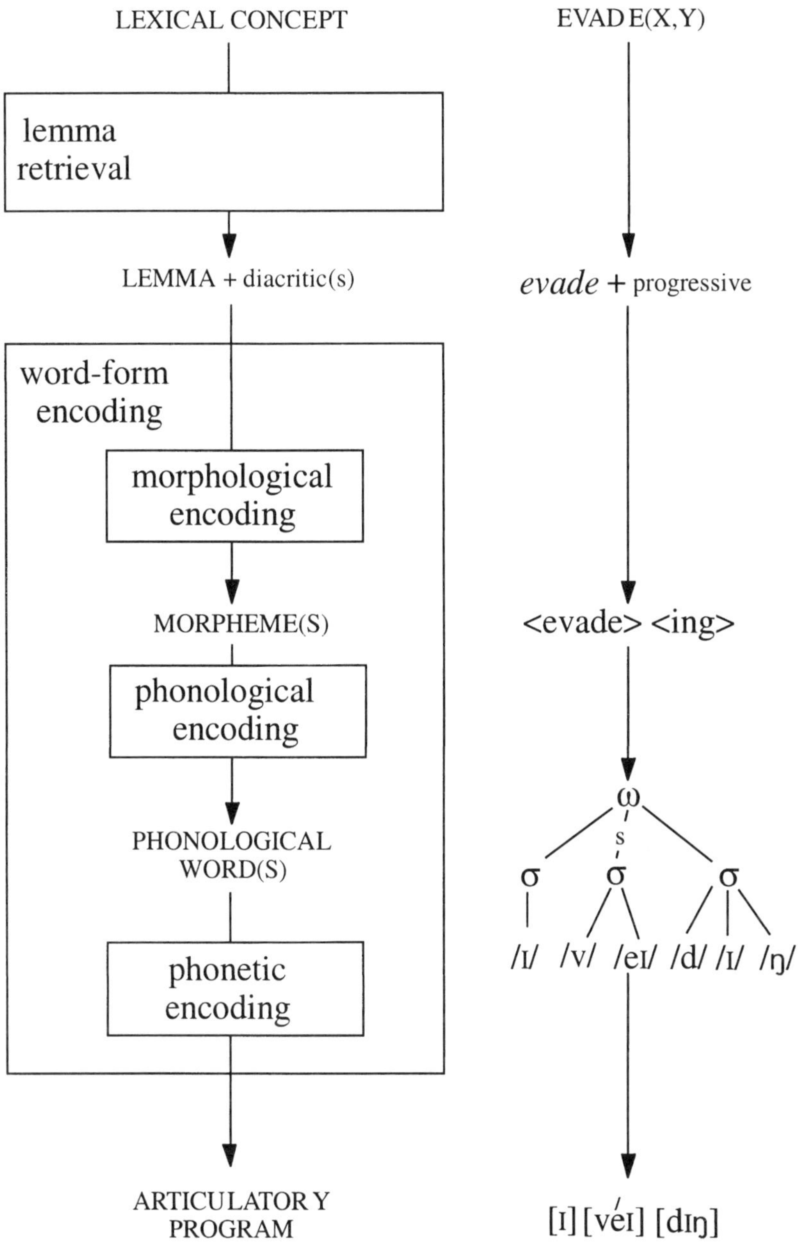

Figure 7.1. Stages of lexical access in WEAVER++.

1999b, for discussion.) The lemma plus slot values are then input to word form encoding. The articulatory program is derived in three major steps, namely morphological, phonological, and phonetic encoding (cf. Dell, 1986; Levelt, 1989). The morphological encoder takes the lemma of *evade* plus the slot value for "progressive" and produces the stem morpheme <evade> and affix <ing>. The phonological encoder takes these morphemes and produces a phonological word representation, which makes explicit the syllables and the stress pattern. This representation describes the progressive form of *evade* as a phonological word (ω) consisting of three syllables, the second carrying word accent(s). The first syllable (σ) has /ɪ/ as nucleus. The second, stressed syllable has /v/ as onset and /eɪ/ as nucleus. The third syllable has /d/ as onset, /ɪ/ as nucleus, and /ŋ/ as coda. Finally, the phonetic encoder takes this phonological word representation, accesses a store of learned motor programs for syllables (Levelt and Wheeldon, 1994), and delivers the corresponding articulatory program for [ɪ.'veɪ.dɪŋ].

3. Storage or computation?

3.1. A case for storage in conceptual preparation and lemma retrieval

Linguistic models often represent lexical concepts by conceptual features. These features make explicit the systematic semantic relations between words or between the meaning and the syntactic properties of a word (cf. Jackendoff, 1990). For example, speakers know that the words *bachelor* and *spinster* contrast in meaning because the former has the conceptual feature MALE and the latter has not. It is a psycholinguistic issue, however, whether the message representation of a lexical concept literally consists of nothing but the concept's features. In a decompositional view on memory representation, *bachelor* would be represented in the message by features like UNMARRIED(X), HUMAN(X), ADULT(X), and MALE(X). By contrast, in a non-decompositional view, *bachelor* would be represented by the abstract representation or "chunk" BACHELOR(X). In that view, the representation BACHELOR(X) would point to and give access to conceptual features such as UNMARRIED(X) in long-term memory but would not contain these features as proper part. Note that chunking involves recoding, which is sometimes overlooked. For example, Jackendoff, 1990, p. 38 assumes that one can have chunks without a loss of information. However, the chunk BACHELOR(X) is assumed to replace a set of conceptual features. A chunk is a memory code that gives access to the memory codes it replaces (like a speed dial button on a telephone, e.g., M8 might stand for the telephone number

3521911), but the chunk does not contain these other codes as proper part. Otherwise, chunks would not have the computational advantages they have. For example, chunks may reduce the load on short-term memory and demands on attention, because instead of several elements (e.g., UNMARRIED(X), HUMAN(X), ADULT(X), and MALE(X)) only a single element (i.e., BACHELOR(X)) has to be kept in short-term memory (or "M8" instead of "3521911"). Note that the representation BACHELOR(X) is redundant from a linguistic point of view. Whether such redundant representations are stored with words in memory is, however, a perfectly valid empirical issue from a psycholinguistic point of view (see Roelofs, 1997a, for discussion).

In lemma retrieval, a message concept has to be mapped onto the lemma of a word in memory, for which there are two main theoretical options (Levelt, 1989; 1992; Roelofs, 1992; 1997a). On the one hand, the message encoder may compute a message concept for a word using a vocabulary of conceptual primitives, and the lemma retriever may access lemmas on the basis of the temporarily assembled set of primitive concepts (cf. Bierwisch and Schreuder, 1992). On the other hand, the message encoder may include lexical concepts in the message as ready-made wholes and lemmas may be accessed from these wholes (cf. Fodor et al., 1980). For example, Dell and colleagues (Dell, 1986; 1988; Dell and O'Seaghdha, 1992) assume that the mental lexicon is an associative network in which nodes for conceptual features (e.g., IS-TO AVOID(X,Y), IS-TO ESCAPE(X,Y), etc.) are connected to lemmas (e.g., *evade*). The lemma of *evade* is retrieved by activating a set of conceptual features such as IS-TO AVOID(X,Y), IS-TO ESCAPE(X), and so forth. Thus, in this view, message concepts for the retrieval of words are assembled. Although a speaker has stored in memory which conceptual features go with which lemmas, the message encoder computes concepts for word retrieval by activating a set of conceptual features corresponding to the intended thought. By contrast, under the non-decompositional account, the message encoder prepares a message by retrieving lexical concepts as chunks such as EVADE(X,Y). The lemma of *evade*, then, is retrieved on the basis of the chunk EVADE(X,Y) instead of features such as IS-TO AVOID(X,Y), IS-TO ESCAPE(X), and so forth. These features are connected to the chunk EVADE(X,Y) in memory, and support thought and reasoning, but are not involved in the actual retrieval of lemmas. Note that the functional role of lexical concepts (part of conceptual processes) and lemmas (part of syntactic encoding) is very different.

The computation of message concepts for words, as defended by Bierwisch and Schreuder, 1992, confronts models with a number of problems concerning convergence that have not been appropriately dealt with yet (see Levelt, 1989, and Roelofs, 1992; 1993; 1996a; 1997a, for extensive discussion). Although solutions have been proposed within a decompositional framework for some of the problems (e.g., Bierwisch and Schreuder, 1992; Bowers, 1999; Caramazza, 1997; Zorzi and Vigliocco, 1999), none of the proposals solves the class of problems as a whole. The convergence problems are (1) how to correctly dissect a thought into lexical concepts during message encoding, (2) how to avoid retrieving hyponyms or hyperonyms along with or instead of the intended words, and (3) how to correctly retrieve a single word instead of several words for a synonymous phrase, or vice versa. I discuss these problems in turn.

In preparing concepts for the retrieval of words, the message encoder has to know which sets of conceptual features correspond to the meaning of words, since only "lexical concepts" can be verbalized by single words. If there is no match, the retrieval system would halt and no word would be retrieved. This is the dissection problem in message encoding (Levelt, 1992). For example, the thought MALE PARENT corresponds to a single lexical concept but the thought YOUNG PARENT does not. The dissection problem is nontrivial because word meanings typically evade definition (e.g., Fodor et al., 1980). What further complicates matters are set inclusions. For example, the set of features of a specific word such as *father* contains the features of its hyperonym *parent* as a proper subset (i.e., *father* has all the features of *parent* plus a few extra ones, for example indicating the sex). Which features should be activated in retrieving a lemma and which subset of features to retrieve its hyperonyms? The hyperonymy problem concerns how to avoid retrieving the word *parent* along with or instead of its hyponym (the retrieval target) *father*. Several models suffer from this problem (e.g., Miller and Johnson-Laird, 1976). But the opposite hyponymy problem also haunts models. For example, in a spreading activation network like that proposed by Dell and O'Seaghdha, 1992, the conceptual primitive PARENT(X,Y) is linked to both the lemma node of *parent* and that of *father*. So in activating PARENT(X,Y) to retrieve *parent*, both *parent* and *father* will attain the same level of activation. This problem may perhaps be solved by tuning the strength of the connections between conceptual features and lemmas. The feature PARENT(X,Y) should be strongly connected to *parent* but weakly to *father*. This would certainly seem to be an improvement but it does not solve all problems. The word *father* and the phrase *male parent* are synonymous. The word-to-phrase synonymy problem concerns how to avoid retrieving *father* along with or instead of *male* and *parent* for the phrase *male parent*, or vice versa. Tuning connection strengths is insufficient to solve this problem, because the same primitives are involved in producing the single word and the phrase. Perhaps this problem may be solved by sequentially activating the conceptual primitives in producing a phrase. This would seem to be an option in theory but it runs into empirical difficulties. There is empirical evidence that suggests that lemmas making up a phrase are planned in parallel (Meyer, 1996).

In summary, conceptually preparing lemma retrieval may involve assembling message concepts out of a vocabulary of primitive concepts. Alternatively, messages may be prepared by retrieving stored lexical concepts. Consequently, lemmas may be retrieved in a conceptually decomposed or non-decomposed fashion. Existing decompositional theories fail to account for convergence in conceptually driven lemma retrieval. This argues for storing rather than computing lexical concepts and for conceptually non-decomposed rather than decomposed lemma retrieval.

3.2. A case for computation in morphophonological encoding

Most existing models assume that word forms are stored in memory as sequences of syllable nodes and that each consonant is stored as an onset or coda (e.g., Dell, 1986; 1988; Shattuck-Hufnagel, 1979). For example, Dell (Dell, 1986; 1988) assumes that the form lexicon is a network that contains nodes for morphemes (e.g., <evade>), syllables (e.g., /ɪ/ and /veɪd/), segments (marked for syllable position, e.g., /onset v/, /nucleus eɪ/, and /coda d/), and phonological features (e.g., voiced). Furthermore, there are nodes that specify the abstract CV structure of a word (Dell, 1988). However, by storing syllable structures these models run into difficulties because syllabification is context dependent. Often the syllabification of segments ignores morpheme and word boundaries in that a segment of one morpheme or word is syllabified with an adjacent morpheme or word. This may occur in the production of polymorphemic words or connected speech (cf. Levelt, 1989; Roelofs, 1997c). By rigidly storing words as sequences of syllable nodes and storing each consonant as an onset or coda, these models have a difficult time dealing with the flexibility of syllable membership. As of yet, this problem has not been solved within these models (see Roelofs, 1997b, for extensive discussion).

Consider, for example, the production of the progressive form *evading*. The progressive form is created by adding <ing> to the stem <evade>. The resulting form is syllabified as (ɪ)$_{\sigma}$(veɪ)$_{\sigma}$(dɪŋ)$_{\sigma}$. Thus, juxtaposing *-ing* to the stem changes the syllabification of /d/. This segment occupies a coda position in *evade*, syllabified as (ɪ)$_{\sigma}$(veɪd)$_{\sigma}$, but an onset position in *evading*. Or consider the production of connected speech. For example, in producing "evade it", *it* may be adjoined to *evade*. This yields the new phonological word *evadit*, which is syllabified as $(\text{ɪ})_\sigma(\text{veɪ})_\sigma(\text{dɪt})_\sigma$. In models that store syllable structures, however, segments are marked for syllable position, so we have /coda d/ for *evade*. Models like Dell's (Dell, 1986; 1988) prohibit selecting this coda node for an onset position, which would be required for the production of *evading* and *evadit*.

The syllabification across morpheme and word boundaries asks for computing rather than storing syllable structures, as argued by Levelt, 1992 and Roelofs, 1997b. The computation of syllable structures has consequences for the design of other aspects of the production system, namely it requires morphologically decomposed form entries for languages such as Dutch. Morphological structure is needed, because several morphemes are separate domains of syllabification (cf. Booij, 1995). In Dutch, this holds for prefixes such as *ver-* and *ont-* and suffixes such as *-achtig*, but not for suffixes such as *-ing* and *-en*. For example, without morphological structure, the /t/ of the Dutch prefix *ont-* of *ontwijken* 'evade' would incorrectly be syllabified with the base *wijken* following the maximal onset principle. Some morphemes such as the plural suffix *-en* are not independent domains of syllabification. For example, the /k/ in *ontwijken* is syllabified with *-en*. Morphological complexity can play a role in form planning without having a synchronic semantic motivation. Morphemes may be separate domains of syllabification independent of semantic transparency. For example, the /r/ of the opaque prefixed verb *verijdelen* 'frustrate' is syllabified with the prefix *ver-* and not with the base as the maximal onset principle would predict. In form planning, morphology appears to operate "by itself" (cf. Aronoff, 1994). In WEAVER++, morphology is "word based" in that no attempt is made to derive the morphemes of a word from its meaning. Which morphemes make up the stem of words is stored by connecting morpheme nodes to lemmas in memory. In planning a derivationally complex word or compound, the stem morphemes are simply accessed from the lemma and used to assemble the word form (see Levelt et al., 1999b, for extensive discussion).

3.3. A case for storage in phonetic encoding

The phenomenon of syllabification across morpheme and word boundaries requires that "phonological syllables" are computed during production rather than stored with words in memory. This corresponds to linguistic models, which derive syllable structures by rule. However, since speakers use only a few hundred different syllables for most of their talking, there is not much use for them in constructing all articulatory programs ("phonetic syllables") from scratch time and again.

Thus, it is plausible to assume that in phonetic encoding, the motor programs are typically not computed but retrieved (for an extensive discussion, see Levelt, 1989; 1992; Levelt et al., 1999b; Levelt and Wheeldon, 1994). Learned motor programs must present a set of retrieval cues to higher-level processes so that the appropriate programs can be accessed. Ideally, these retrieval cues constitute a reasonably small set. Levelt (Levelt, 1992; Levelt and Wheeldon, 1994) has proposed that the retrieval cues for articulatory programs are the phonological syllables that are constructed as part of phonological word representations. Programs that are not stored will be computed on the basis of the information in the phonological word representation. Syllabary access translates an abstract phonological representation into a context-dependent phonetic representation that can guide articulation. For example, the articulatory program for *evade* [ɪ.'veɪd] comprises motor programs for the syllables [ɪ] and [veɪd], where [ɪ] and [veɪd] stand for packages of gestural scores for the articulatory movements to be made. A score specifies the gestures and their temporal relationships (e.g., Browman and Goldstein, 1986; Levelt, 1989; 1992). Scores make explicit articulatory tasks, such as lip protrusion and lowering of the jaw. The details of the movements realizing these scores are left to the articulatory system.

To summarize, I have discussed a number of arguments concerning the relative merits of storage and computation. It makes sense to store high-frequency aspects of words that take considerable time to assemble, such as motor programs, and aspects that are difficult or impossible to derive by rule, such as lexical concepts. And it is plausible to compute those aspects of words that are easy to derive by rule and aspects that are inherently context-dependent, such as syllabifications. In the next section, I discuss in some detail how the trade off between storage and computation has been captured in the WEAVER++ model.

4. The WEAVER++ model

Like many models, WEAVER++ implements the mental lexicon as an associative network of nodes, links, and link labels that is accessed by spreading activation. WEAVER++ deals with the dissection problem, the word-to-phrase synonymy problem, and other convergence problems by assuming that each lexical concept is represented in the network by an independent node (cf. Collins and Loftus, 1975). For example, the network contains the nodes EVADE(X,Y) and AVOID(X,Y) connected by a link labeled IS-TO (to evade something is to avoid something). The node EVADE(X,Y) is connected to the lemma node for *evade*. Conceptually preparing a word consists of selecting lexical concept nodes. Lemmas are accessed from the lexical concept nodes rather than from assemblies of conceptual feature nodes. The model handles the problem of syllabification across morpheme and word boundaries by assuming that syllable positions are not stored with words in memory (e.g., there are no /onset d/ and /coda d/ nodes), but that syllable positions are assigned on-line by a syllabification process (cf. Levelt, 1992). The assignment of segments to syllable positions takes neighboring morphemes and words into account. Syllable positions of segments are computed for phonological words rather than for lexical ones. Finally, the model implements the assumption that speakers have a phonetic syllabary, a store of motor programs for frequently used syllables, which is accessed on the basis of the phonological syllables constructed as part of phonological word representations (Levelt and Wheeldon, 1994).

Words are not planned by a central agent that overlooks the whole process but by several "production rules" that work in parallel on small parts of the word. Production rules are condition-action pairs. If the condition of a rule is met, the action is performed. The production rules are stored with the nodes and have a limited overview only. Activation of nodes in the network triggers production rules that select lemmas and incrementally build phonetic plans by selecting and connecting form nodes. When the activation of a node exceeds threshold, a production rule verifies the link between the node and the selected nodes one level up in the network. Syntactic production rules select the lemma node linked to the target lexical concept node. For example `IF the lemma is linked to the message concept and the activation of the lemma exceeds threshold THEN select the lemma.` Morphological production rules select the morpheme nodes that appropriately encode a selected lemma node and its tense, aspect, and agreement specification. Phonological production rules select the segments linked to the morpheme nodes and prosodify the segments in order to construct phonological word representations. Prosodification consists of syllabification and stress assignment. Finally, phonetic production rules select the syllable program nodes that appropriately encode the constructed phonological syllables, and access the corresponding syllable programs in the syllabary.

Figure 7.2 illustrates the structure of lexical entries in WEAVER++'s associative network. In particular, it shows the memory representation of the word evade. A lexical network with nodes and labeled links is connected to a syllabary with learned motor programs (the syllabary is omitted from Figure 7.2). The lexical network consists of three major strata: a conceptual, a syntactic, and a word-form stratum. The conceptual stratum contains concept nodes and labeled conceptual links. Each lexical concept in the language, for example EVADE(X,Y), is represented

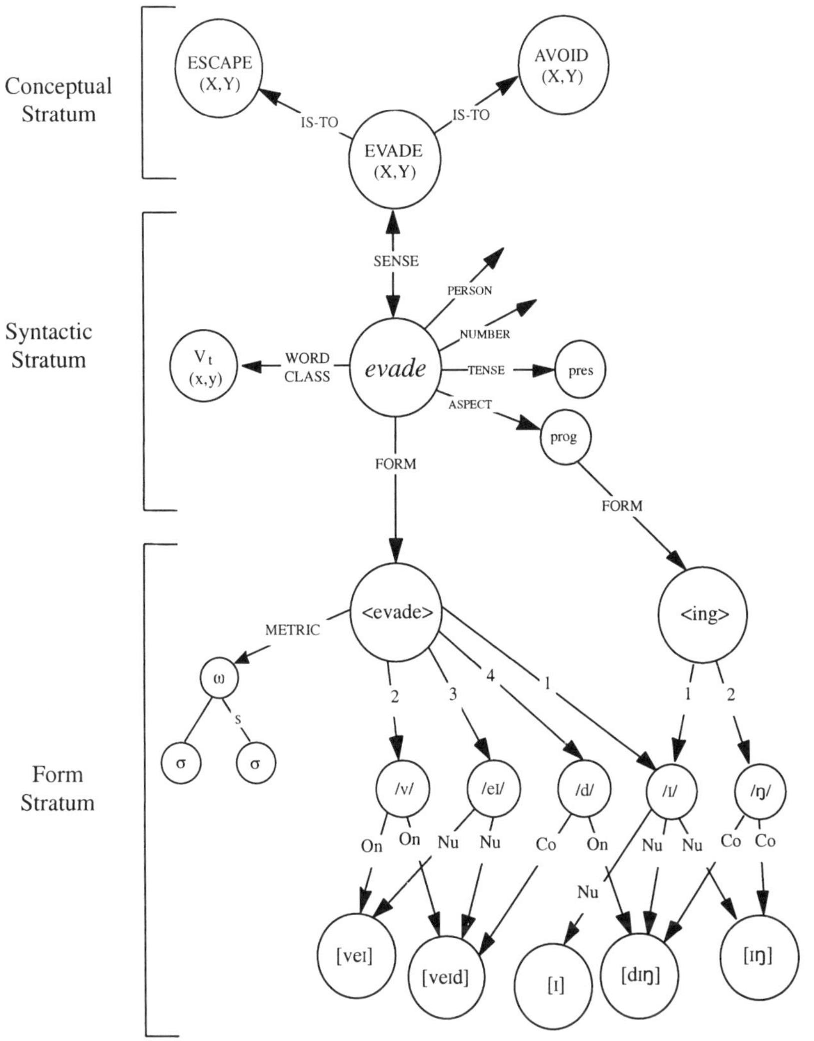

Figure 7.2. Representation of the word "evade" in WEAVER++.

by an independent node. The links specify conceptual relationships. The syntactic stratum contains lemma nodes (*evade*), syntactic property nodes and labeled links (e.g. WORD CLASS: Verb), and slots for the specification of morphosyntactic parameters (e.g., TENSE: present). The word-form stratum contains metrical structure, morpheme, segment, and syllable program nodes and links. Morpheme nodes are connected to a lemma and its diacritics. The links between morphemes and segments specify the serial position of the segments. The links between segments and syllable program nodes specify possible — as opposed to actual — syllabifications. The word-form stratum is connected to a syllabary, storing ready-made motor programs for high-frequency syllables.

The WEAVER++ model implements the claim that lexical concepts are stored in memory rather than computed on-line and that lemmas are retrieved in a conceptually non-decomposed way. That is, for example, the verb *evade* is retrieved on the basis of the chunk EVADE(X,Y) instead of features such as IS-TO AVOID(X,Y), IS-TO ESCAPE(X), and so forth. Retrieval starts by enhancing the level of activation of the node of the target lexical concept. Activation then spreads through the network, each node sending a proportion of its activation to its direct neighbors. The most highly activated lemma node is selected. For example, in verbalizing the thought EVADE, the activation level of the lexical concept node EVADE(X,Y) is enhanced. Activation spreads through the network, whereby the lemma nodes *evade* and *avoid* will be activated, among other nodes. The *evade* node will be the most highly activated node, because it receives a full proportion of the activation of EVADE(X,Y), whereas *avoid* and other lemma nodes receive only a proportion of a proportion of the activation of EVADE(X,Y). Upon verification of the link between the lemma node of *evade* and EVADE(X,Y), this lemma node will be selected.

The basic theoretical claim implemented in WEAVER++ concerning word-form encoding is that lemmas are mapped onto learned syllable-based articulatory programs by rightward incrementally computing morphological and phonological structures. The latter make explicit phonological syllables. These phonological syllables are then used to retrieve stored motor programs from a phonetic syllabary. Figure 7.2 illustrates the form representation of *evade* in WEAVER++. The non-metrical part of the form network consists of three layers of nodes: morpheme, segment, and syllable program "address" nodes. Morpheme nodes stand for roots and affixes. Morpheme nodes are connected to the lemma and its morphosyntactic parameters. For example, the stem <evade> is connected to the lemma of *evade*. A morpheme node points to the segments that make up its underlying form, and, for some words, to its metrical structure. For storing metrical structures, a principle of economy applies. WEAVER++ assumes that the main accent of Dutch (and English) words is on the first syllable containing a full vowel (which holds for more than 90 percent of the word tokens), unless the lexical form representation indicates otherwise (Levelt et al., 1999b). Thus, for polysyllabic words that do not have main stress on the first stressable syllable, the metrical structure is stored as part of the lexical entry, but for monosyllabic words and for all other polysyllabic words, it is not. For example, the metrical structure for *evade* [ɪ.'veɪd] is stored, but for *table* ['teɪ.bəl] it is not. Stored metrical structures describe abstract groupings of syllables (σ) into phonological words (ω). Importantly, it is not specified which segments make up the syllables nor is the CV pattern specified. The links between morpheme and segment nodes indicate the serial position of the segments within the morpheme. Possible syllable positions (onset, nucleus, coda) of the segments are specified by the links between segment nodes and syllable program nodes. For example, the network specifies that /d/ is the coda of [veɪd] and the onset of [dɪŋ]. Segments also point directly to their phonological features (not shown in Figure 7.2), which allows computing motor programs in case there is no stored program in the syllabary.

Encoding starts when a morpheme node receives activation from a selected lemma. Activation then spreads through the network in a forward fashion. The morphological encoder selects the morpheme nodes that are linked to a selected lemma and its parameters. Thus, <evade> and <ing> are selected for *evade* and the specification "progressive". In general, a lemma and its diacritics (e.g., *evade* + "past"; *eat* + "past") correspond to a stem and its affixes (either decomposed <evade> + <ed> or irregular, non-decomposed <ate>) at the word form level. For every word class there is a paradigm, that is, a set of inflectional forms (regular or irregular) that encode the fixed set of grammatical functions specified by the diacritics. Some diacritics obtain their value by agreement with other parts of the utterance (e.g., person, number: *evades* versus *evade*) during the process of syntactic encoding. The stems at the word-form level may be simple or complex. Complex stems may have been created by derivation in the language (i.e., base morphemes plus one or more affixes, e.g., *exhale*) or compounding (i.e., existing words added together, e.g., *afterthought*).

The phonological encoder selects the segments and, if available, the metrical structures that are linked to the selected morpheme nodes. Next, the segments are input to a prosodification process that associates the segments to the syllable nodes within the metrical structure (for "exception" words) or constructs metrical structures based on segmental information. Thus, when stored, metrical structures are retrieved and woven into the phonetic plan, otherwise they are constructed on the spot. The prosodification proceeds from the segment whose link is labeled first to the one labeled second, and so forth. In the prosodification, syllable positions (onset, nucleus, coda) are assigned to the segments following the syllabification rules of the language. Essentially, each vowel and diphthong is assigned to a different syllable node and consonants are treated as onsets unless phonotactically illegal onset clusters arise. In the encoding of *evade*, the /ɪ/ is made nucleus of the first syllable, and the /v/ onset, the /eɪ/ nucleus, and the /d/ coda of the second syllable. The prosodification process provides for cross-morpheme and cross-word syllabification. In planning polymorphemic words or connected speech, the structures of adjacent morphemes or words may be combined. This leads to new phonological words. For example, WEAVER++ may syllabify <ing> with <evade> for the progressive form *evading* or it may prosodify the stem <evade> and <it> together for the cliticization *evadit*. Then, following the maximal onset principle in syllabification (e.g., Goldsmith, 1990), /d/ will be made onset of the third syllable instead of coda of the second syllable, yielding (ɪ)$_\sigma$(veɪ)$_\sigma$(dɪŋ)$_\sigma$ and (ɪ)$_\sigma$(veɪ)$_\sigma$(dɪt)$_\sigma$. In this way, WEAVER++ achieves syllabification across morpheme and word boundaries. Note that, again, a storage versus computation trade-off is involved. For <evade> the metrical structure is stored but for <ing> it is not. In prosodifying <ing> with <evade>, the system retrieves the metrical structure for <evade> and adapts it such that it can accommodate <ing> (i.e., a third syllable node σ is added to the structure).

The phonetic encoder selects the syllable program "address" nodes whose labeled links to the segments correspond with the syllable positions assigned to the segments. For example, [veɪd] is selected for the second phonological syllable of *evade*, because the link between [veɪd] and /v/ is labeled onset, between [veɪd] and /eɪ/ nucleus, and between [veɪd] and /d/ coda. Similarly, the phonetic encoder selects [veɪ] and [dɪŋ] for the progressive form *evading* and [veɪ] and [dɪt] for the form *evadit*. Finally, the phonetic encoder addresses the actual syllable programs in the syllabary, thereby making the programs available to the articulators for the control of the articulatory movements (following Levelt, 1992; Levelt and Wheeldon, 1994). Certain adaptations have to be made to the retrieved motor programs. In particular, the encoder uses the metrical representation to set the programs' parameters for loudness, pitch, and duration. Also, the encoder has to take care of the transitions at syllable boundaries. After making the adaptations, the phonetic plan is ready to govern articulation.

WEAVER++ provides for a suspend/resume mechanism that supports incremental generation of word forms. Incremental planning means that encoding processes are triggered by a fragment of their characteristic input (Levelt, 1989). The three form encoding stages (i.e., morphological, phonological, and phonetic encoding) compute aspects of a word form in parallel from the beginning of the word to its end. For example, syllabification can start on the initial segments of a word without having all of its segments. Only initial segments and, for some words, the metrical structure are needed. When given partial information, computations are completed as far as possible, after which they are put on hold. The computed representation is buffered until the missing segments are available and syllabification can continue. When given further information, the encoding processes continue from where they were left.

5. Storage in conceptual preparation and lemma retrieval

A first test of a model is to see whether it accords with existing data. Below I show that the claim of storage of lexical concepts and non-decomposed retrieval correctly predicts several empirical findings on spoken word production. The findings are from "picture-word interference" experiments. Speakers have to name pictured objects while simultaneously trying to ignore written words superimposed on the pictures. The measurement of interest is the speech onset latency, that is, the difference in time between picture onset and production onset. Elsewhere (in Roelofs, 1992), I have shown by computer simulation that WEAVER++ explains, among other phenomena, the classical semantic effects of picture and word distractors in picture naming, picture categorizing, and word categorizing. Here, I want to concentrate on those aspects of these findings that are particularly relevant for the claim of storage in conceptual preparation and lemma retrieval. In particular, Glaser and Düngelhoff, 1984 and Roelofs, 1992; 1993 have shown that naming is facilitated when the distractors are hyponyms of the target. Glaser and Düngelhoff showed that in picture categorizing, a semantic facilitation effect is obtained from written distractor words. For example, producing the word *furniture* in response to a pictured chair is speeded up by the distractor word *bed* compared to distractor *fish*. Similarly, in word categorizing a semantic facilitation effect is obtained from distractor pictures. For example, producing *furniture* in response to the word *chair* is facilitated by a pictured bed compared to a pictured fish.

Semantic facilitation is not restricted to distractors that are basic object level names such as *chair*, *bed* and *fish*. I have shown (see Roelofs, 1992) that semantic facilitation is also obtained in naming a pictured object, for example, in naming a chair while the distractor words *furniture*, *bed*, or *throne* are superimposed. In addition to the type of distractor, the experiment manipulated the stimulus onset asynchrony (SOA), that is, the time difference between the presentation of the picture and the distractor word. The written distractors were presented 100 msec before (referred to as a negative SOA), simultaneously with, or 100 msec after picture onset (called a positive SOA). The finding was a semantic facilitation effect at the earliest SOA of -100 msec and no effect at later SOAs. Figure 7.3 plots the semantic facilitation effect against SOA. The semantic effect was the same for hyperonym (*furniture*), cohyponym (*bed*), and hyponym (*throne*) distractors compared to unrelated distractors. The bars represent means across these three types of distractor word. Semantic facilitation has also been obtained for hyponym distractor verbs in producing verbs rather than nouns, for example when participants had to say *drink* to a drinking person and ignore the distractors *booze* or *whimper* (Roelofs, 1993).

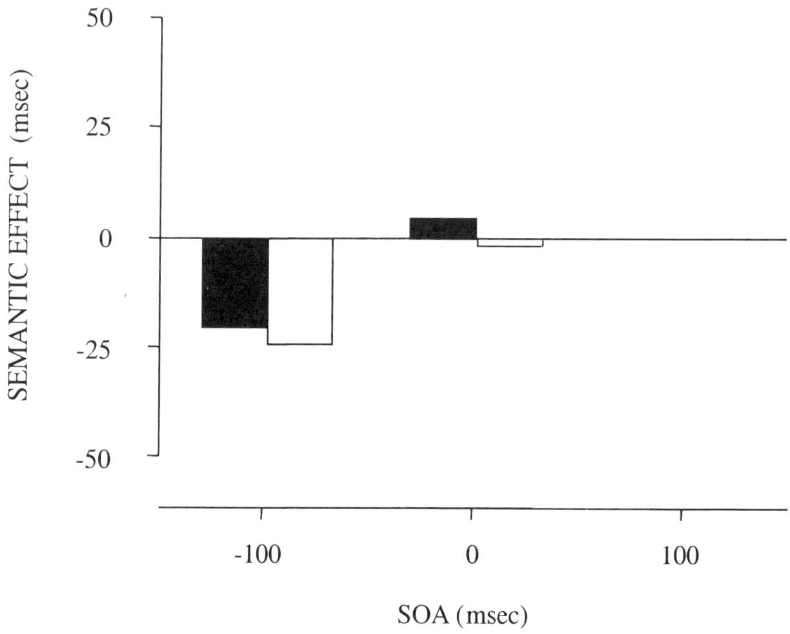

Figure 7.3. The semantic effect for picture naming with written distractor words per SOA: ■ = empirical data (Roelofs, 1992) and □ = predictions by WEAVER++.

Figure 7.3 also shows what WEAVER++ predicts for the noun production experiment. In WEAVER++ a "shortlist" of target lemmas can be defined depending on the task that is set for the retrieval system (e.g., in a categorization task the response set consists of hyperonyms such as *furniture*, *animal*, etc.). Competition is restricted to these shortlisted lemmas. The assumption is that speakers set up the shortlist before an experiment when they receive a booklet with the pictures and names to be used. Thus, in the model, only potential target responses will compete for selection. In case of picture or word categorization, *furniture* and *animal* are the targets and will compete, but *chair, bed, fish*, and *dog* will not. The distractor *bed* superimposed on a pictured chair will activate the target *furniture* via the conceptual network, but *bed* will not be a competitor for *furniture* because *bed* is not a permitted response in the experiment. By contrast, *fish* on a pictured chair will activate *animal*, which is a competitor of the target *furniture*. Thus, semantic facilitation is predicted and this is exactly what is empirically obtained (see Figure 7.3). A chi-square measure of fit showed that the predictions of the model do not differ statistically from the real data.

The semantic facilitation effects in picture and word naming and categorizing demonstrate two important points. First, contrary to what has been suggested in the literature (cf. Caramazza, 1997), the explanation of semantic effects (in picture-word interference) does not require semantic decomposition. What is required is that lemmas of related concepts are connected in memory and this may be achieved by semantic decomposition or by a semantic network as implemented in WEAVER++. Second, the finding of semantic facilitation from hyponyms excludes one type of solution to the hyperonymy problem in lemma retrieval. Bierwisch and Schreuder, 1992 have proposed a decompositional model in which the convergence problem is solved by inhibitory links between hyponyms and hyperonyms (i.e., words inhibit their hyperonyms). For example, in producing *chair*, activating the lemma of *chair* leads automatically to inhibition of the lemma of its hyperonym *furniture*. However, the existence of such inhibitory links predicts semantic inhibition from hyponym distractors (e.g., distractor *throne* should inhibit target *chair*), but facilitation is what has been empirically obtained (empirically, distractor *throne* facilitates the production of *chair*, see Figure 7.3). Also, the finding of semantic facilitation in picture and word categorizing refutes such an inhibitory link between words and their hyperonyms (e.g., between *chair* and *furniture*). In general, these semantic facilitation effects pose difficulty to models in which lemma selection is achieved by hard-wired competition among lemmas, as in the models of Starreveld and La Heij, 1996 and Cutting and Ferreira, 1999. Instead, the facilitation argues in favour of dynamic competition in lemma selection (i.e., the shortlist idea).

It is well known from the literature on human memory that when information is frequently accessed, the retrieval time decreases. This also appears to hold for the retrieval from lexical storage. WEAVER++ accounts for such frequency effects in word production. Frequency effects in the model originate from differences in the speed of applying production rules, which depends on frequency of usage.

Experiments by Jescheniak and Levelt, 1994 have shown that when lemma information such as the grammatical gender of a noun is accessed, a frequency effect is obtained. For example, Dutch participants had to decide on the gender of a picture's name (e.g., they had to decide that the grammatical gender of the Dutch word *tafel* (*table*) is non-neuter), which was done faster for high-frequency words than for low-frequency ones. The effect disappeared with repetition, contrary to a "robust" frequency effect obtained in naming the pictures.

Jescheniak and Levelt provided evidence that the locus of the robust frequency effect is the form level. When participants had to respond to an English probe word by producing its Dutch translation equivalent, the production latency of a low-frequency homophone was determined by the sum frequency of that word and its high-frequency counterpart. For example, participants had to produce the Dutch word *bos* in response to *bunch* (low-frequency reading). The production latencies for these homophones were compared to the latencies for two types of other words. First, there were low-frequency control words whose frequency was matched to that of the low-frequency reading of the homophone. The low-frequency control for *bos* was *hok* (*kennel*). Second, there were high-frequency control words whose frequency was matched to the sum frequency of the low-frequency reading (i.e., *bunch*) and high-frequency reading (i.e., *forest*) of *bos*. The high-frequency control for *bos* was *hoek* (*corner*). Producing the homophones (*bos*) in their low-frequency reading went as fast as producing the high-frequency controls (*hoek*), and it went faster than producing the low-frequency controls (*hok*). Thus, a low-frequency homophone inherits the frequency of its high-frequency counterpart. In WEAVER++, homophones have their form nodes and production rules in common but not the lemma. By sharing form nodes and production rules, a low-frequency homophone inherits the frequency properties of its high-frequency counterpart. This explains the homophone effect observed by Jescheniak and Levelt.

6. Computing morphological structures

In testing for the assembly of morphologically complex forms in production, I have employed the on-line preplanning, or "implicit priming", paradigm developed by Meyer, 1990; 1991. The task falls into the general class of choice-response tasks. Priming and precuing of choice responses has been widely used in studying the advance planning of skilled action. For example, Rosenbaum, 1980 used precuing to control the amount of preparation in arm movement. He manipulated the uncertainty in the specification of arm direction and extent, and observed that as more information was available to allow preparation, movement initiation time decreased. The implicit priming task differs from precuing in that no explicit cues are given in advance but the cue is implicit in the response set. However, the logic is the same in that both implicit priming and precuing allow for preparation of the action. In the implicit-priming paradigm, speakers first have to learn a set of prompt-response pairs and then have to produce the appropriate response when one of the prompts is shown. The big advantage of using paired associates compared to picture naming is that the responses do not have to refer to depictable entities, which gives more freedom in the selection of experimental materials. Roelofs, 1999 showed that implicit priming using paired associates and picture naming gives equivalent results.

An implicit-priming experiment consists of a number of alternating learning and test phases. Before each block of test trials, participants learn a small set of prompt-response pairs such as *street* – *bypath, rule* – *bylaw, show* – *byplay.* During the subsequent test phase, the speakers are shown per trial one of the first words of the pairs, called the prompts (e.g., *rule*), and they have to produce the corresponding second word of the pair as fast as possible without making mistakes (e.g., when presented with *rule* they have to produce *bylaw*). The order of prompts across trials is random. The production latency, the interval between prompt onset on the computer screen and speech onset, is the main dependent variable. There are homogeneous and heterogeneous response sets. In a homogeneous set, the response words share part of their form and in a heterogeneous set they have nothing in common. For example, the responses share the first syllable (*bypath, bylaw, byplay*) or they are unrelated in form (*bypath, misprint, doorstep*). Heterogeneous sets are created by regrouping pairs from different homogeneous sets. Therefore, each word pair is tested both under the homogeneous and the heterogeneous condition, and all uncontrolled item effects are kept constant across these conditions. Each participant is tested on all sets.

In testing sets with monomorphemic words like *bible*, Meyer, 1990; 1991 observed a preparation effect: The production latencies of the words combined in homogeneous sets where they share initial segments (e.g., /baɪ/) were smaller than those of the same words combined in heterogeneous sets. The form overlap between the responses in a homogeneous set apparently allows speakers to preplan part of the responses before the beginning of a trial, whereas such preplanning is not possible in heterogeneous sets. Subsequent studies have tested whether the size of the preparation effect depends on the morphological status of the shared string of segments. WEAVER++ predicts that strings of segments that constitute morphemes should yield larger preparation effects than strings of segments that are not morphemes. For example, the preplanning effect should be larger for the syllable /baɪ/ in response sets including complex words like *bypath* than for /baɪ/ in sets including simple words like *bible*. For monomorphemic words like *bible* consisting of the single morpheme <bible>, sharing the first syllable /baɪ/ allows for phonological preparation only. In contrast, for polymorphemic words like *bypath* consisting of the morphemes <by> and <path>, not only phonological but also additional morphological preparation should be possible, hence the prediction of a much larger preparation effect. The experimental outcomes confirmed the predictions by WEAVER++. In producing disyllabic simple and complex nouns, a larger facilitatory effect was obtained when a shared initial syllable constituted a morpheme than when it did not (Roelofs, 1996c).

WEAVER++ predicts an effect of morpheme frequency. High-frequency morphemes are retrieved faster from memory than morphemes of low frequency, so the benefit from preparation should be larger for low-frequency morphemes than for high-frequency ones. This prediction has been empirically confirmed. For example, in producing compounds in Dutch (Roelofs, 1996b), the facilitatory effect was larger for response sets sharing a low-frequency morpheme like <bloem> (*flower*) — as in *bloemkool* (*cauliflower*) — than for response sets sharing a high-frequency morpheme like <bloed> (*blood*) — as in *bloedspoor* (*trace of blood*). The compounds were matched for word frequency. Also, in producing particle verbs (Roelofs, 1998), the facilitatory effect was larger, for example, for *veeg* (low frequency) in "veeg op" ("clean up") than for *geef* (high frequency) in "geef op" ("give up").

The outcomes of further experiments supported WEAVER++'s claim that forms of morphologically complex words are assembled in a rightward fashion rather than, for example, in parallel (e.g., Stemberger, 1985). In producing complex nouns, no facilitation was obtained for shared noninitial morphemes. For example, no effect was obtained for <rol> in *bijrol* (*supporting role*), *koprol* (*somersault*), *deegrol* (*dough roll*). And in producing prefixed verbs, a facilitatory effect was obtained for the prefix but not for the noninitial base. For example, a facilitatory effect was obtained for the prefix <be> of *behalen* (*to obtain*), but not for the base <halen>.

According to WEAVER++, morphological complexity can play a role in form planning without having a synchronic semantic motivation. Indeed, Roelofs and Baayen, 2001 obtained the effect of morpheme preparation for semantically opaque complex words of Dutch like *bijval* (<bij><val>

applause). In producing simple (*bijbel* <bijbel>) and complex nouns (*bijrol* <bij><rol> and *bijval* <bij><val>), a larger preparation effect was obtained when a shared initial syllable constituted a morpheme than when it did not, replicating Roelofs, 1996c. Importantly, the size of the morphemic effect was identical for semantically transparent complex words (*bijrol*) and opaque complex words (*bijval*), as shown in Figure 7.4. This suggests that morphemes are present in the memory representations of opaque complex words, contrary to what intuition as well as semantic analysis would suggest. The figure also shows the simulation results. Again, there is no statistical difference between model and real data. These findings support WEAVER++'s assumption that form planning is word-based. That is, no attempt is made to derive the morphemes of a word given its meaning. Instead, the morphemes of the stem of derivationally complex words and compounds are stored with the words in memory.

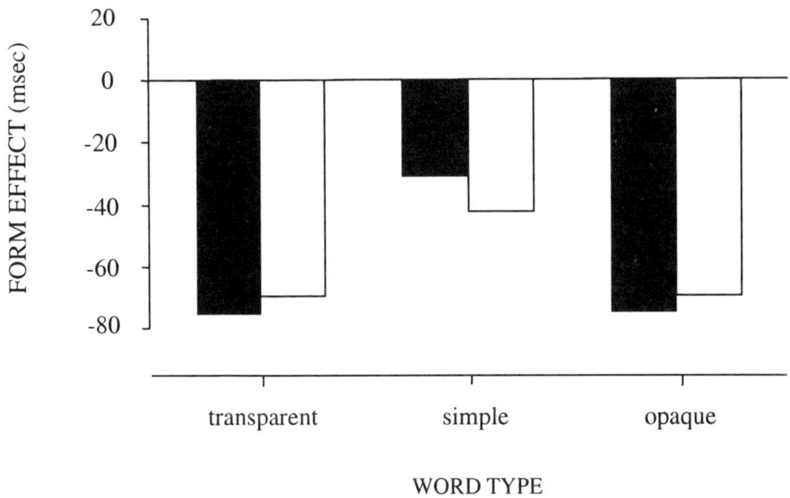

Figure 7.4. Form preparation effect for transparent complex, simple, and opaque complex words: ■ = empirical data (Roelofs and Baayen, 2001) and □ = predictions by WEAVER++.

The studies discussed so far concerned the encoding of complex stems. But how is inflectional encoding achieved? The morphological encoder in WEAVER++ selects the morpheme nodes that are linked to a selected lemma and its morphosyntactic parameters. A lemma and its diacritics may be mapped onto a simple or complex stem and its affixes (e.g., *evade* + "past" is mapped onto the morphemes <evade> and <ed>) or onto an irregular form (e.g., *eat* + "past" is mapped onto the morpheme <ate>).

For regular verbs such as *evade*, linking the stem <evade> to the lemma node of *evade* and the affix <ed> to the diacritic "past" will yield the right result (note that the latter implements a "rule" in that <ed> is selected for a non-progressive form when a lemma's tense parameter is set to "past", independent of the lemma involved). However, for irregular verbs such as *eat*, the diacritic "past" must be linked to the allomorph <ate> and selection of <ed> must be blocked (cf. Pinker, 1994).

Whether inflectional encoding is achieved by retrieving all forms from storage (the "single route" view) or by retrieving irregular forms and computing regular ones (the "dual route" view) is a hotly debated issue (for reviews, see Plunkett, 1995; Pinker, 1994). Evidence for two routes comes from dissociations between performance on regular and irregular forms (see e.g., Pinker, 1994). In WEAVER++ a distinction is made between regular and irregular forms but *both* are produced via an associative network. So the model seems to embrace both sides of the debate. Evidence from the preparation paradigm supports the model. Janssen et al., 2001 observed for Dutch that the effect from preparing a word-initial syllable is much reduced when one of the words in the response set is an inflected verb while the other words are nouns. For example, the effect from sharing the syllable *wa* [wa] in a set including the noun *water* [wa.tər] and the inflected verb *waadde* ([wa.də], the past tense of *waden*, English *wade*) was much less than the effect from sharing *wa* in a set including the nouns *water* and *wapen* (*weapon*). The second syllable /də/ is the past tense suffix of the inflected form *waadde*, whereas the syllable /tər/ has no morphological status in the noun *water*. The reduction of the preparation effect was not observed when the inflected verb in the set was replaced by a homophonous noun (*wade* [wa.də], *shroud*). This suggests that the reduction was not due to the phonological form of the inflected verb itself. There was also no reduction when the past tense form of a strong verb was the odd one out in a set. For example, *kreeg* (past tense of *krijgen*, English *receive*) in a set with *kruin* (*tonsure*) and *krent* (*currant*) did not diminish the preparation effect. This suggests that the reduction is not due to a word class difference (i.e., verb versus noun). Instead, the reduction of the preparation effect must be due to the regular inflectional process itself (see Janssen, 1999; Janssen et al., 2001, for an extensive discussion).

7. Computing phonological structures

WEAVER++ assigns a specific role to metrical structures in syllabification. For words like the trochee *table*, metrical structures are computed on-line, but for words like the iamb *cigar*, metrical structures are stored.

The stored metrical structures specify the stress pattern across syllables, but not the precise CV structure of the syllables as models such as that of Dell, 1988 do. The prosodification process in WEAVER++ associates segments to the syllable nodes within the metrical structure for "exception" words (e.g., *cigar*) or constructs syllable and metrical structures based on segmental information (e.g., for *table*). These claims have been tested in a series of form preparation experiments. I refer to Levelt et al., 1999b; Roelofs, 1997b, and Roelofs and Meyer, 1998 for reviews. In homogeneous sets, the responses shared a number of word-initial segments, whereas in heterogeneous sets they did not. As we saw, earlier research has shown that sharing initial segments reduces production latencies (Meyer, 1990; 1991; Roelofs, 1996c). The crucial manipulation for the current experiments was whether the metrical structure of the words in a set was constant or variable. In metrically constant sets, all responses had the same metrical structure, whereas in metrically variable sets they did not.

A first series of experiments tested (in Dutch) the production of polysyllabic words that do not have main stress on the first stressable syllable such as English *cigar*. According to the model, the metrical structures of these words are not computed but stored in memory. If the responses in a set have different metrical structures, segment-to-frame association cannot take place before the beginning of a trial, and no preparation effect should be obtained. This prediction was tested by comparing the preparation effect for response sets with a constant number of syllables such as {*manier* (*manner*), *matras* (*mattress*), *makreel* (*mackerel*)} to that for sets having a variable number of syllables such as {*majoor* (*major*), *materie* (*matter*), *malaria* (*malaria*)} (respectively, 2, 3, and 4 syllables). In the example, the responses share the first syllable *ma*. Word stress was always on the second syllable. As predicted, a preparation effect was obtained for the metrically constant sets but not for the variable sets. The same predictions were also tested by comparing the preparation effect for response sets with a constant stress pattern such as {*marine* (*navy*), *materie* (*matter*), *malaise* (*depression*), *madonna* (*madonna*)} (all responses having stress on the second syllable) to that for sets having a variable stress pattern such as {*marine* (*navy*), *materie* (*matter*), *manuscript* (*manuscript*), *madelief* (*daisy*)} (first two responses having stress on the second syllable and the last two responses having stress on the third syllable). All response words were trisyllabic. Again, as predicted, a preparation effect was obtained for the constant sets but not for the variable sets. We also tested whether the size of the preparation effect was affected by the constancy versus variability of the CV structure of the response words. We compared the effect of segmental overlap for response sets having a constant CV structure such as {*bres* (*breach*), *bril* (*glasses*), *brok* (*piece*), *brug* (*bridge*)} (responses all CCVC) to that for sets having a variable CV structure such as {*brij* (*porridge*), *brief* (*letter*), *bron* (*source*), *brand* (*fire*)} (responses respectively, CCVV, CCVVC, CCVC, CCVCC). In the example, the responses share the onset cluster *br*. Facilitation from segmental overlap was obtained for both the constant and the variable sets. The size of the preparation effect was the same for both types of set. These results suggest that the stress pattern across syllables but not the exact CV structure is stored, supporting WEAVER++.

A second series of experiments (again in Dutch) tested the production of monosyllabic words and polysyllabic words whose main stress is on the first syllable like English *table*. According to the model, the metrical structures of these words are computed on-line on the basis of retrieved segments. Consequently, preparation of initial segments should now be possible for both metrically constant and variable sets. This prediction was tested by comparing the preparation effect for response sets with a constant number of syllables such as {*borstel* (*brush*), *botsing* (*crash*), *bochel* (*hump*), *bonje* (*fight*)} (all disyllables stressed on the first syllable) to that for sets having a variable number of syllables such as {*borstel*, *botsing*, *bok* (*goat*), *bom* (*bomb*)} (two disyllables stressed on the first syllable and two monosyllables, respectively). In the example, the responses share the onset and nucleus *bo*. As predicted, a preparation effect was obtained for both the constant and the variable sets, and the size of the effect did not differ between the two types of set. The same result is predicted for varying the number of syllables of polysyllabic words with an unstressable first syllable (i.e., words with a schwa as the first vowel) and stress on the second syllable. This was tested by comparing the preparation effect for such words in response sets with a constant number of syllables such as {*gebit* (*teeth*), *gezin* (*family*), *getal* (*number*), *gewei* (*antlers*)} (all disyllables having stress on the second syllable) to that for sets having a variable number of syllables such as {*geraamte* (*skeleton*), *getuige* (*witness*), *gebit*, *gezin*} (two disyllables stressed on the second syllable and two trisyllables stressed on the second syllable, respectively). As predicted, the same preparation effect was obtained for the constant and the variable sets.

In summary, preparation of word initial segments for words with irregular stress depends on all words in a set having the same stress pattern across syllables but not on having the same CV structure. For words with regular stress, sharing the metrical structure is not necessary for preparation. These findings support WEAVER++.

According to WEAVER++ response preparation critically depends on shared segments rather than shared articulatory movements or phonological features. In support of this, it has been shown empirically that preparation requires that the responses share their initial segments fully and that sharing features only does not allow for preparation (Roelofs, 1999). For example, the initial segment of the words *boat*, *bird*, and *boy* is the same, whereas the initial segment of the words *paint*, *boat*, and *bird* is the same except for one feature, namely voicing (i.e., /b/ is voiced, /p/ is voiceless). However, a preparation effect was only obtained for the sets with full segment overlap, but no effect was observed at all (not even a reduction of latencies) for the sets with feature overlap. The same result has been obtained in comparing sets of disyllabic words sharing the first syllable fully (e.g., *te* in *tennis*, *terrace*, *teddy*) and sets of disyllabic words whose first syllable differs in one feature only (e.g., *devil*, *tennis*, *teddy*). Although syllables were shared except for one feature in the first segment, this feature difference completely blocked preparation. Also, the same results were obtained when words were produced in response to pictured objects, and when place of articulation rather than voicing was manipulated (e.g., /m/ versus /n/). The special status of identity suggests that segments are planning units ("chunks") independent of their features. The findings support segmental models such as WEAVER++, but they argue against models without an explicit representation of segments, such as the model proposed by Dell et al., 1993.

8. Phonetic access and underspecification

After phonological structures have been computed, the phonetic encoder in WEAVER++ accesses stored motor programs for the phonological syllables or, if no such program is stored, computes motor programs from scratch. Phonetic encoding involves mapping an abstract phonological representation of the word onto a concrete feature specification or specification of its articulatory gestures.

As with the access of lemma information and morphemes, the retrieval of syllable programs from storage should depend on frequency of usage. Levelt and Wheeldon, 1994 indeed observed an effect of syllable frequency that is independent of the word-frequency effect discussed earlier. Furthermore, in producing disyllabic words, the syllable-frequency effect was confined to the second syllable. By assuming that a production rule for a syllable program node is applied faster for a high-frequency syllable than for a low-frequency one, the finding of an independent effect of syllable frequency is readily explained by WEAVER++. Furthermore, during the encoding of disyllables, the encoding of the first syllable will have a head-start as a result of the left-to-right prosodification of segments. Thus, according to the model, the second syllable typically sets the pace of the encoding of the whole word form. Therefore, one expects the syllable-frequency effect to be confined to the second syllable, as is observed by Levelt and Wheeldon. However, the syllable frequency effects in the experiments were very small. Furthermore, in some experiments, syllable and segment frequency were correlated. In recent experiments that controlled for a number of possible confounds, effects of syllable and segment frequency were not obtained (Levelt et al., 1999b). Clearly, the speed of accessing motor programs for syllables does not depend very much, if at all, on their frequency. The validity of the syllabary assumption needs to be tested further.

Underspecification concerns the issue of whether certain features are stored with the underlying segments of morphemes in memory. A number of different views have been advanced (e.g., Archangeli, 1988; Kenstowicz, 1994, for review). In one view, only contrastive features are specified underlyingly (e.g., Halle, 1959; Steriade, 1987). For example, voicing is not contrastive among the sonorant segments of Dutch, whereas it is distinctive among obstruents. Then, voicing would not be specified with sonorant segments in memory. The second, stronger view, is based on the phenomenon that, in certain phonological contexts, contrastive features have marked (i.e., "unexpected") and unmarked (i.e., "expected") values (e.g., Archangeli, 1988; Kiparsky, 1982; Pulleyblank, 1983). On this account, only the marked values are stored and the unmarked values are assigned by rule. For example, in Dutch, the segment following /s/ in syllable onset position is never voiced (e.g., /sp/ occurs, but /sb/ does not). Consequently, voicing does not have to be specified for such segments in these contexts, because the feature value (unvoiced) can be assigned by a rule. In a third view, the mental lexicon contains archiphonemes such as the segment /P/ standing for either /b/ or /p/ (Levelt, 1989). The difference between the second and the third view is that archiphonemes can take both marked as well as unmarked values, whereas segments not specified for unmarked feature values can take the unmarked value of a feature only (their specified counterparts contain the marked value already).

Whereas the justification of underspecification in linguistic theory may be evident (i.e., eliminate as much redundancy in the linguistic representations as possible and capture the redundancy in a rule), the significance of underspecification for a model of speech production is much less clear. Archiphonemes and the elimination of noncontrastive or unmarked features place different demands on the number of memory representations needed to perform the appropriate computations. Whereas the view of unspecified noncontrastive or unmarked features seems to be fully compatible with WEAVER++ as it stands, the view of archiphonemes requires extra representations. For example, in WEAVER++ elimination of noncontrastive or unmarked features may be achieved by having segment nodes point to their contrastive or marked features only. The noncontrastive or unmarked features may then be filled in by rule or by retrieving motor programs from the syllabary. Archiphonemes (as conceived by Levelt, 1989), however, ask for something extra. Consider the memory representation of the Dutch words *speer* (*spear*), *peer* (*pear*), and *beer* (*bear*). Connecting the morpheme nodes <speer>, <peer>, and <beer> to the archiphoneme /P/ will not work, because although the feature value for voicing (here, voiceless) can be assigned by rule to /P/ in case of <speer>, it has to be specified for <peer> and <beer> in order to make explicit the distinction between *peer* and *beer*. Thus, memory has to contain segments such as /b/ and /p/ in addition to an archiphoneme such as /P/ (cf. Spencer, 1991). This raises the question of what is gained by archiphonemes. Why not connecting <speer> to /p/? What is gained by having both segments and their archiphonemes in the network? In short, for a model of speech production, the functional significance of archiphonemes is not so clear.

Of course, the ultimate judgement about underspecification should be based on empirical evidence. Although some evidence from speech errors suggests that there may be archiphonemes involved in speech production (e.g., Stemberger, 1991), I do not think we have the final answer here. Stemberger observed errors such as " ... beer binnen" ("... bear inside"), where " ... speer binnen" was intended. The key observation here is that, after the /s/ has got lost, the /p/ of <speer> is realized as /b/. The error might be explained (as Stemberger does) by assuming that <speer> connects to /P/ in memory. In the production of *speer*, the /P/ surfaces as /p/, because it is preceded by the /s/. However, without the context of /s/, the phonotactic rule fails to apply. Then, the underlying /P/ is free to surface as either /p/ or /b/. This might explain why, after the /s/ got lost in the error, /b/ is produced instead of /p/. WEAVER++ can only accommodate this finding if archiphonemes are included in the model. Then, when the /s/ gets lost, the syllable programs [ber] and [per] would fit the phonological syllable $(\text{Per})_\sigma$. So, there might be a race between [ber] and [per], with the chances of winning being equal. The error *beer* for *speer* might then occur.

9. Conclusions

I have argued that word production can be characterized by a storage versus computation trade-off. The planning of a word calls forth some mixture of retrieval from storage and computation. That mixture not only varies over the ensemble of planning stages but also within stages. I have discussed the distribution of trade-offs in the context of a concrete model of lexical access in spoken word production, the WEAVER++ model. The model falls into the class of hybrid models in that it implements lexical knowledge symbolically as rules and facts but also has an activation process that determines which facts and rules get deployed for particular words. WEAVER++ implements the claim that lemmas are retrieved from stored non-decomposed representations of lexical concepts. Furthermore, morphological and phonological structures are computed on-line, typically followed by the retrieval of stored motor programs for the computed phonological syllables. As concerns phonological feature underspecification, WEAVER++ can handle several theoretical possibilities, so for the model, this is more of an empirical issue rather than a theoretical one.

References

Archangeli, D. (1988). Aspects of underspecification theory. *Phonology*, 5:183–207.

Aronoff, M. (1994). *Morphology by itself.* Cambridge, MA: MIT Press.

Bierwisch, M. and Schreuder, R. (1992). From concepts to lexical items. *Cognition*, 42:23–60.

Booij, G. E. (1995). *The phonology of Dutch.* Oxford: Clarendon Press.

Bowers, J. S. (1999). Grossberg and colleagues solved the hyperonym problem over a decade ago. *Behavioral and Brain Sciences*, 22:38–39.

Browman, C. P. and Goldstein, L. (1986). Towards an articulatory phonology. *Phonology Yearbook*, 3:219–252.

Caramazza, A. (1997). How many levels of processing are there in lexical access? *Cognitive Neuropsychology*, 14:177–208.

Collins, A. M. and Loftus, E. F. (1975). A spreading-activation theory of semantic processing. *Psychological Review*, 82:407–428.

Cutting, C. J. and Ferreira, V. S. (1999). Semantic and phonological information flow in the production lexicon. *Journal of Experimental Psychology: Learning, Memory, and Cognition*, 25:318–344.

Dell, G. S. (1986). A spreading-activation theory of retrieval in sentence production. *Psychological Review*, 93:283–321.

Dell, G. S. (1988). The retrieval of phonological forms in production: Tests of predictions from a connectionist model. *Journal of Memory and Language*, 27:124–142.

Dell, G. S., Juliano, C., and Govindjee, A. (1993). Structure and content in language production: A theory of frame constraints in phonological speech errors. *Cognitive Science*, 17:149–195.

Dell, G. S. and O'Seaghdha, P. G. (1992). Stages of lexical access in language production. *Cognition*, 42:287–314.

Dennett, D. C. (1991). *Consciousness explained.* London: Penguin Books.

Fodor, J. A., Garrett, M. F., Walker, E. C. T., and Parkes, C. H. (1980). Against definitions. *Cognition*, 8:263–367.

Garrett, M. F. (1975). The analysis of sentence production. In Bower, G. H., editor, *The psychology of learning and motivation.* New York: Academic Press.

Garrett, M. F. (1980). Levels of processing in sentence production. In Butterworth, B., editor, *Language production (Vol 1). Speech and talk.* London: Academic Press.

Garrett, M. F. (1988). Processes in language production. In Newmeyer, F. J., editor, *Linguistics: The Cambridge survey*, volume 3. Cambridge, MA: Harvard University Press.

Glaser, W. R. and Düngelhoff, F.-J. (1984). The time course of picture-word interference. *Journal of Experimental Psychology: Human Perception and Performance*, 10:640–654.

Goldsmith, J. (1990). *Autosegmental and metrical phonology.* Cambridge, MA: Basil Blackwell.

Halle, M. (1959). *The sound pattern of Russian.* The Hague: Mouton.

Hankamer, J. (1989). Morphological parsing and the lexicon. In Marslen-Wilson, W., editor, *Lexical representation and process.* Cambridge, MA: MIT Press.

Jackendoff, R. (1990). *Semantic structures.* Cambridge, MA: MIT Press.

Janssen, D. (1999). Producing past and plural inflections. Unpublished doctoral dissertation, University of Nijmegen, The Netherlands.

Janssen, D., Roelofs, A., and Levelt, W. J. M. (2001). The production of inflected verbs. *Language and Cognitive Processes.* In press.

Jescheniak, J.-D. and Levelt, W. J. M. (1994). Word frequency effects in speech production: Retrieval of syntactic information and phonological form. *Journal of Experimental Psychology: Learning, Memory, and Cognition*, 20:824–843.

Kenstowicz, M. (1994). *Phonology in generative grammar.* Oxford: Blackwell.

Kiparsky, P. (1982). Lexical morphology and phonology. In Yang, I. S., editor, *Linguistics in the morning calm.* Seoul: Hanshin.

Koskenniemi, K. (1984). A general computational model for word-form recognition and production. In *Proceedings of the 10th International Conference on Computational Linguistics.*

Levelt, W. J. M. (1989). *Speaking: From intention to articulation.* Cambridge, MA: MIT Press.

Levelt, W. J. M. (1992). Accessing words in speech production: Stages, processes and representations. *Cognition*, 42:1–22.

Levelt, W. J. M., Roelofs, A., and Meyer, A. S. (1999a). Multiple perspectives on word production. *Behavioral and Brain Sciences*, 22:61–75.

Levelt, W. J. M., Roelofs, A., and Meyer, A. S. (1999b). A theory of lexical access in speech production. *Behavioral and Brain Sciences*, 22:1–38.

Levelt, W. J. M. and Wheeldon, L. (1994). Do speakers have access to a mental syllabary? *Cognition*, 50:239–269.

Meyer, A. S. (1990). The time course of phonological encoding in language production: The encoding of successive syllables of a word. *Journal of Memory and Language*, 29:524–545.

Meyer, A. S. (1991). The time course of phonological encoding in language production: The phonological encoding inside a syllable. *Journal of Memory and Language*, 30:69–89.

Meyer, A. S. (1996). Lexical access in phrase and sentence production: Results from picture-word interference experiments. *Journal of Memory and Language*, 35:477–496.

Meyer, A. S. and Schriefers, H. (1991). Phonological facilitation in picture-word interference experiments: Effects of stimulus onset asynchrony and types of interfering stimuli. *Journal of Experimental Psychology: Learning, Memory, and Cognition*, 17:1146–1160.

Miller, G. A. and Johnson-Laird, P. N. (1976). *Language and perception.* Cambridge, MA: Harvard University Press.

Pinker, S. (1994). *The language instinct: The new science of language and mind.* London: The Penguin Press.

Plunkett, K. (1995). Connectionist approaches to language acquisition. In Fletcher, P. and MacWhinney, B., editors, *The handbook of child language.* Oxford: Blackwell.

Pulleyblank, D. (1983). *Tone in lexical phonology.* PhD thesis, MIT.

Roelofs, A. (1992). A spreading-activation theory of lemma retrieval in speaking. *Cognition*, 42:107–142.

Roelofs, A. (1993). Testing a non-decompositional theory of lemma retrieval in speaking: Retrieval of verbs. *Cognition*, 47:59–87.

Roelofs, A. (1994). On-line versus off-line priming of word-form encoding in spoken word production. In Ram, A. and Eiselt, K., editors, *Pro-*

ceedings of the Sixteenth Annual Conference of the Cognitive Science Society. Hillsdale, NJ: LEA.

Roelofs, A. (1996a). Computational models of lemma retrieval. In Dijkstra, T. and De Smedt, K., editors, *Computational psycholinguistics: AI and connectionist models of human language processing*. London: Taylor & Francis.

Roelofs, A. (1996b). Morpheme frequency in speech production: Testing WEAVER. In Booij, G. E. and van Marle, J., editors, *Yearbook of Morphology 1996*. Dordrecht: Kluwer Academic Publishers.

Roelofs, A. (1996c). Serial order in planning the production of successive morphemes of a word. *Journal of Memory and Language*, 35:854–876.

Roelofs, A. (1997a). A case for nondecomposition in conceptually driven word retrieval. *Journal of Psycholinguistic Research*, 26:33–67.

Roelofs, A. (1997b). Syllabification in speech production: Evaluation of WEAVER. *Language and Cognitive Processes*, 12:657–693.

Roelofs, A. (1997c). The WEAVER model of word-form encoding in speech production. *Cognition*, 64:249–284.

Roelofs, A. (1998). Rightward incrementality in encoding simple phrasal forms in speech production: Verb-particle combinations. *Journal of Experimental Psychology: Learning, Memory, and Cognition*, 24:904–921.

Roelofs, A. (1999). Phonological segments and features as planning units in speech production. *Language and Cognitive Processes*, 14:173–200.

Roelofs, A. and Baayen, H. (2001). Morphology by itself in planning the production of spoken words. *Psychonomic Bulletin and Review*. In press.

Roelofs, A., Meyer, A., and Levelt, W. J. M. (1996). Interaction between semantic and orthographic factors in conceptually driven naming: Comment on Starreveld and La Heij (1995). *Journal of Experimental Psychology: Learning, Memory, and Cognition*, 22:246–251.

Roelofs, A. and Meyer, A. S. (1998). Metrical structure in planning the production of spoken words. *Journal of Experimental Psychology: Learning, Memory, and Cognition*, 24:922–939.

Roelofs, A., Meyer, A. S., and Levelt, W. J. M. (1998). A case for the lemma-lexeme distinction in models of speaking: Comment on Caramazza and Miozzo (1997). *Cognition*, 69:219–230.

Rosenbaum, D. A. (1980). Human motor initiation: Specification of arm direction and extent. *Journal of Experimental Psychology: General*, 169:444–474.

Sandra, D. (1994). The morphology of the mental lexicon: Internal word structure viewed from a psycholinguistic perspective. *Language and Cognitive Processes*, 9:227–269.

Shattuck-Hufnagel, S. (1979). Speech errors as evidence for a serial-order mechanism in sentence production. In Cooper, W. E. and Walker, E. C. T., editors, *Sentence processing: Psycholinguistic studies presented to Merrill Garrett.* Hillsdale, NJ: Erlbaum.

Spencer, A. (1991). *Morphological theory.* Cambridge, MA: Blackwell.

Starreveld, P. A. and La Heij, W. (1996). Time-course analysis of semantic and orthographic context effects in picture naming. *Journal of Experimental Psychology: Learning, Memory, and Cognition*, 22:896–918.

Stemberger, J.-P. (1985). An interactive activation model of language production. In Ellis, A. W., editor, *Progress in the psychology of language (Vol. 1).* London: LEA.

Stemberger, J.-P. (1991). Radical underspecification in language production. *Phonology*, 8:73–112.

Steriade, D. (1987). Redundant values. In Bosch, A., Need, B., and Schiller, E., editors, *Papers from the parasession on autosegmental and metrical phonology.* Chicago: Chicago Linguistic Society.

Zorzi, M. and Vigliocco, G. (1999). Compositional semantics and the lemma dilemma. *Behavioral and Brain Sciences*, 22:60–61.

V

BUFFERING AND COMPUTING

Chapter 8

EFFECTS OF SHORT-TERM STORAGE IN PROCESSING RIGHTWARD MOVEMENT

Peter Ackema
and Ad Neeleman

Abstract There is a striking asymmetry between leftward and rightward movement in syntax: whereas leftward movement can in principle be unbounded, rightward movement is subject to very strict locality conditions. There are two possible approaches to explaining this asymmetry. One can either assume that some syntactic principle disfavours rightward movement, or that some mechanism having to do with sentence processing is responsible. In this chapter we will argue that a processing approach to limitations on rightward movement is more fruitful. In particular, we will argue that the human parser cannot process certain instances of rightward movement because the introduction of an antecedent-trace relation leads to a conflict with information about the parse which is already stored in short-term memory before this relation can be established. Similar problems do not occur in cases of leftward movement.

Keywords: Rightward movement, processing, short-term storage, (a)symmetric syntax, Verb Raising, P-incorporation, Heavy NP Shift.

1. Introduction

At least since Ross, 1967 it is known that there is a striking asymmetry between leftward and rightward movement in syntax.[1] Whereas leftward movement can in principle be unbounded, rightward movement

[1]Natural language allows 'displacement': elements may show up in positions they do not usually occupy. For example, in *who did she see*, *who* is interpreted as the direct object of *see*. The analysis of this example involves an unpronounced 'trace' that occupies the object position of *see*. The relation between the fronted category *who* and the trace is called 'movement'.

S. Nooteboom et al. (eds.), Storage and Computation in the Language Faculty, 219–256.

is subject to very strict locality conditions. There are two possible approaches to explaining this asymmetry. One can either assume that some syntactic principle disfavours rightward movement, or that some mechanism having to do with sentence processing is responsible.

A syntactic approach to the problem has been advanced by Kayne, 1994. Kayne proposes a principle which has the effect (for reasons that need not concern us here) that syntactic trees go 'downward' from left to right. If a head Y has two dependents XP_1 and XP_2, the right-branching structure in (8.1a) is the only structure allowed; (8.1b-d) are ruled out.

(8.1)

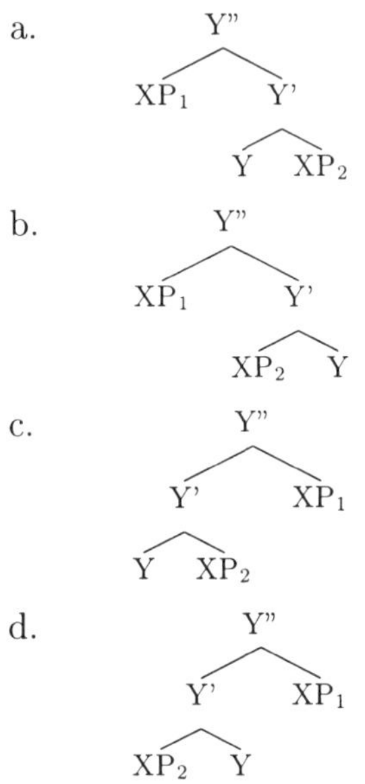

Since there is overwhelming evidence that an element cannot be moved to a position that is lower in the tree than the position it originates in (see for instance Van Riemsdijk and Williams, 1986, p.202), the so-called antisymmetric theory illustrated in (8.1) implies that rightward movement cannot exist, since in this theory 'rightward' implies 'downward in the tree'.

Kayne's theory of antisymmetry faces difficulties in two areas. First, there appears to be pervasive evidence that trees as in (1b-d) exist. (We will discuss this evidence in some detail below). Second, there are in fact instances of rightward movement. Under a Kaynean approach, these are unexpected and hence require an alternative account (see Büring and Hartmann, 1997 for discussion).

In this chapter we will argue that a processing approach to limitations on rightward movement is more fruitful than a syntactic approach.

In sentence processing a syntactic representation is constructed on the basis of an essentially linear (left-to-right) input. As pointed out by Just and Carpenter, 1992; Gibson, 1998, and Kaan and Stowe, 2001 (this volume), this process involves both storage and computation. The parser must compute a syntactic representation of the incoming sentence. Since it cannot do so for the whole sentence at once, short-term storage of partially analyzed substrings is required. We further assume that the parser employs a so-called filler-driven strategy in dealing with movement dependencies, which means that the parser can only postulate a trace (which indicates the base position of a moved element) after it hypothesizes that some element it encounters has been moved. Hence, rightward movement requires the insertion of a trace in an already partially analyzed string. After all, the moved element follows the part of the string in which the trace should be inserted. We will argue that introduction of a trace in an already analyzed string is sometimes incompatible with information stored in short-term memory. If in addition no alternative parse is available, the structure cannot be processed at all. In contrast, in cases of leftward movement the trace can be inserted at the same time that the string in which it should be placed is analyzed. Consequently, leftward movement does not cause this kind of processing difficulty.

The advantage of the approach just sketched is that it reconciles the evidence that syntax equally allows left-branching and right-branching structures with differences in the nature of rightward and leftward movement; the correct locality conditions on rightward movement follow from independently motivated properties of the parser.

This chapter is organised as follows. First, we will discuss some evidence for the existence of the structures in (8.1b-d), and show which difficulties theories based on antisymmetry face in accounting for the relevant data (sections 2 and 3). Then, we will outline the properties of the human parser (section 4). These allow us to explain in which circumstances head movement to the right is impossible (section 5), and in which circumstances it is possible (section 6).[2] Then we will present the empirical evidence that relates to our predictions with respect to rightward head movement (section 7). Finally, we will consider how the parser restricts rightward XP-movement (section 8).

---

[2]X-bar theory assigns constituents the following general three-layered structure, which we will adopt for concreteness: [XP ...[X' ...X ...] ...]. Phrasal movement is movement of the entire constituent, XP. Head movement is movement of its head, X. In a Verb Second language like Dutch, for example, the finite verb that heads the VP is moved to the second position in main clauses: Jan geeft$_i$ Marie een boek t$_i$. 'John gives Mary a book'. (Compare with the embedded clause *dat Jan Marie een boek geeft* 'that John Mary a book gives').

2. Symmetric syntax

Traditional views of syntactic structure allow both left- and right-branching structures (cf. Chomsky, 1986, p.3). Complements, specifiers and adjuncts can in principle either precede or follow the head.[3] Given that each of these constituents in a phrase is attached at a specific level of that phrase, such a theory of syntactic structure predicts mirror image effects: the order in which two base-generated (unmoved) elements appear to the left of the head is the reverse of the order of those elements if they are generated to the right of the head:[4]

(8.2) a. $[_{Y''}\ XP_1\ [_{Y'}\ XP_2\ Y]]$ (= (1b))
b. $[_{Y''}\ [_{Y'}\ Y\ XP_2]\ XP_1]$ (= (1c))

We will refer to this as the symmetric theory.

For independent reasons, it is not always possible to generate a specific constituent on either side of the head. In particular, nominal arguments are assigned case by the verb, which, for reasons we cannot discuss here, can have the effect that they must be in a fixed position with respect to the verb (see Neeleman and Weerman, 1999 for discussion).[5] For elements within VP that *can* be generated on both sides of the head V, however, mirror image effects can indeed be observed. Their distribution therefore confirms the view that base-generated structure to the right of the head is left-branching.

One such mirror image effect occurs with prepositional phrases in Dutch. In Dutch it is possible to have (nonpredicational) PPs on both sides of V. Koster, 1974 observed that the order in which the PPs stand when they occur in preverbal position is the reverse of their order in postverbal position. This is illustrated in (8.3).

---

[3]In X-bar theory, a complement is the sister of a head X and the daughter of an X'. A specifier is the daughter of an XP and the sister of an X'. Adjuncts are elements attached to a recursive category: they are either the sister of an XP and the daughter of an XP, or the sister of an X' and the daughter of an X'. The former option gives rise to the following structure: [XP adjunct [XP ...] ...].

[4]For ease of presentation, we will represent the dependents of the head as being generated within the head's projection, abstracting away from possible functional structure. However, the predictions that a symmetric X-bar theory makes with respect to mirror image effects do not change if functional structure is added to (8.2).

[5]With double object constructions, a cross-linguistic anti-mirror image effect can be observed. The order in which the objects show up in English is identical to that in Dutch: V-IO-DO and IO-DO-V, respectively. It is argued in Neeleman and Weerman, 1999 that these data follow from the way the case systems of OV and VO languages are organised.

(8.3) a. dat Jan [[tijdens de pauze]$_1$ [[aan zijn vader]$_2$
that John during the break of his father
dacht]].
thought.
'that John thought of his father during the break'.

a'. ?? dat Jan [[aan zijn vader]$_2$ [[tijdens de pauze]$_1$ dacht]].

b. dat Jan [[dacht [aan zijn vader]$_2$] [tijdens de pauze]$_1$].

b'. ?? dat Jan [[dacht [tijdens de pauze]$_1$] [aan zijn vader]$_2$]].

An argument for the claim that PP_1 is attached higher than PP_2 in (8.3b) as well as in (8.3a) can be given on the basis of the examples below. When the VP is moved to the front of the clause ('VP-topicalization'), it is possible to include PP_2 in the moved VP and leave PP_1 behind. The reverse, however, is impossible. This shows that the verb and PP_2 form a constituent which excludes PP_1. In (8.4) both PPs are generated to the left of the basic V-position, but in (8.5) they are both generated to the right. The contrast remains the same.

(8.4) a. ?Aan zijn vader denken heeft Jan alleen tijdens
of his father think has John only during
de pauze gedaan.
the break done.
'Thought of his father, John only has during the break.'

b. *Tijdens de pauze denken heeft Jan alleen aan zijn vader gedaan.

(8.5) a. ?Denken aan zijn vader heeft Jan alleen gedaan
think of his father has John only done
tijdens de pauze.
during the break.
'Thought of his father, John only has during the break.'

b. *Denken tijdens de pauze heeft Jan alleen gedaan aan zijn vader.

Scope relations, too, can be used to illustrate the symmetry of base-generated structures. Since projections are right-branching before and left-branching after the head in the symmetric theory (see (8.2)), the prediction is that in case two adverbials precede the head, the left one takes scope over the right one, whereas the reverse should be true of two adverbials that follow the head. The data in (8.6) bear out this prediction. Both (8.6a) and (8.6b) receive an interpretation such that *in die dagen* 'in those days' takes scope over *volgens Marleens plan* 'according to Marleen's plan': the sentences mean that, in those days, we followed Marleen's ideas about where to spend the holidays. In both (8.6a') and (8.6b') the scope relations are reversed: these sentences mean that, in accordance with Marleen's plan, we went on holiday at a particular time.[6]

(8.6) a.

dat	we	[in	die	dagen	[volgens	Marleens
that	we	in	those	days	according to	Marleen's
plan	op	vakantie	gingen]].			
plan	on	holiday	went.			

'that we used to go on holiday in accordance with Marleen's plan in those days'.

a'.

dat	we	[volgens	Marleens	plan	[in	die
that	we	according to	Marleen's	plan	in	those
dagen	op	vakantie	gingen]].			
days	on	holiday	went.			

'that, in accordance with Marleen's plan, we went on holiday in that period'.

b. dat we [[op vakantie gingen volgens Marleens plan] in die dagen].
'as in (a)'

b'. dat we [[op vakantie gingen in die dagen] volgens Marleens plan].
'as in (a')'

It is further predicted that the sentence will be ambiguous in case one adverbial appears to the left of the head and the other to its right. This is confirmed as well. As indicated, the sentences in (8.7a, a') and (8.7b, b') are ambiguous in that they can be associated with both scope relations discussed above.

---

[6]Of course, the sentences in (8.6b,b') can be read in such a way that the second PP is an afterthought. This leads to scope ambiguity. However, the sentences are unambiguous when pronounced without a prosodic break.

(8.7) a. dat we [in die dagen [op vakantie gingen
that we in those days on holiday went
volgens Marleens plan]].
according to Marleen's plan.

a'. dat we [[in die dagen op vakantie gingen] volgens Marleens plan].

b. dat we [volgens Marleens plan [op vakantie gingen in die dagen]].

b'. dat we [[volgens Marleens plan op vakantie gingen] in die dagen].

Note that, without further qualification, the antisymmetry theory predicts that in (8.6) and (8.7) the left-hand adverbial must always have scope over the right-hand one, since the tree goes 'downward' from left to right.

Mirror image effects can not only be observed within one language, but also cross-linguistically. The order of preverbal adverbials in Dutch, for instance, turns out to be the mirror image of the order of postverbal adverbials in English, see (8.8). The assumption that in (8.8b) *yesterday* is attached higher than *passionately*, which occurs to its left, is corroborated by the fact that under VP-preposing *yesterday* can, but *passionately* cannot be stranded, as illustrated in (8.9) (see Roberts, 1985).

(8.8) a. dat Jan [[gisteren]$_1$ [[vurig]$_2$ [een meisje
that Jan yesterday passionately a girl
kuste]]].
kissed.
'that Jan kissed a girl passionately yesterday'.

a'. ?*dat Jan [[vurig]$_2$ [[gisteren]$_1$ [een meisje kuste]]].

b. John [[[kissed a girl] [passionately]$_2$] [yesterday]$_1$].

b'. ?*John [[[kissed a girl] [yesterday]$_1$] [passionately]$_2$].

(8.9) a. John wanted to kiss a girl passionately and [kiss a girl passionately]i he did ti (yesterday).

b. John wanted to kiss a girl yesterday and [kiss a girl yesterday]$_i$ he did t$_i$ (*passionately).

Some further evidence for posthead left-branching structures in English can be based, as in Dutch (cf. (8.6) and (8.7)), on scopal relations. Ernst, 1994 observes that the examples in (8.10) differ in interpretation.

(8.10) a. She kissed him willingly many times.
a'. She kissed him many times willingly.
b. Joe hit him on purpose frequently.
b'. Joe hit him frequently on purpose.

In the sentences (8.10a,b) the rightmost adverbial unambiguously takes widest scope, as predicted by the symmetric theory. The sentences in (8.10a',b') are ambiguous. In one reading it is again the rightmost adverbial that takes widest scope, but a reading with reversed scope is possible as well. However, this latter reading may be the result of an alternative structural analysis in which the frequency adverbial is a modifier of the adverb of intention. One argument for this analysis is that, when a PP is inserted between the frequency adverbial and the adverb of intention, the scope relations are unambiguous again, with the rightmost adverbial taking wide scope:

(8.11) a. She kissed him many times in the bathroom willingly.
b. Joe hit him frequently with a baseball bat on purpose.

In short, when two constituents occur before the head they are dependents of, scope relations go from left to right, but when they occur after the head, scope relations go from right to left; this is exactly what the symmetric theory in (8.2) predicts.

Mirror image effects do not only occur in the verbal, but also in the nominal domain. One example of this is the order of prenominal adjectives in English in comparison with that of postnominal adjectives in French (see Lamarche, 1991):

(8.12) a. A [[rusty]$_1$ [[white]$_2$ car]]
b. Une [[voiture [blanche]$_2$] [rouillé]$_1$]
a car white rusty
'a rusty white car'

A language-internal example of the same phenomenon can be found in Tagalog, as pointed out to us by Norvin Richards. Tagalog adjectives can appear on either side of the noun. (A morpheme referred to as the 'linker' must appear between them; this takes the form of a velar nasal attached to the first word when this is phonologically feasible and *na* otherwise.) In those cases where two nonconjoined adjectives are generated on the same side of the noun, their order shows the by now familiar mirror image effect:

(8.13) a. pinakamalapit na pulang bahay
nearest red house
'the nearest red house'

a'. *pulang pinakamalapit na bahay

b. bahay na pulang pinakamalapit

b'. *bahay na pinakamalapit na pula

In fact, the argument holds more generally. Greenberg, 1966 observes that in the majority of cases the order of determiners, numerals and adjectives in languages in which these elements follow the noun is the mirror image of the order found in languages in which they precede the noun, as in (8.14). (See below for a fuller discussion of the cross-linguistic possibilities of the order in a DP, incorporating the possibility of N-movement.)

(8.14) a. determiner - numeral - adjective - noun

b. noun - adjective - numeral - determiner

In conclusion, the symmetric theory of phrase-structure predicts that elements generated to the right of the head appear in the reverse order of elements generated to its left, if no movement occurs. The data discussed in this section appear to confirm this prediction.

3. Mirror image effects in an antisymmetric theory

It is, of course, not impossible to account for mirror image effects in a theory such as that of Kayne, 1994, which does not allow the structures in (8.1b-d). However, as we will argue in this section, this can only be done at the cost of some ad hoc assumptions.[7] Kayne proposes that the linear order of terminal nodes in a tree reflects the hierarchical structure of the nonterminal nodes dominating the terminals. In particular, the c-command relations between the nonterminal nodes are crucial. A category α c-commands a category β if every category that dominates α also dominates β. (Roughly speaking, α is at least as high in the tree as β.) For example, in (8.15a) α c-commands β, but in (8.15b) it does not (because here γ dominates α but not β).

[7]This section by necessity contains a few syntactic technicalities, which a general readership might not be familar with. It briefly reviews an alternative account of the data discussed so far. Readers mainly interested in the nonsyntactic account of movement asymmetries may therefore wish to skip it. This can be done without losing the thread of the argument.

(8.15) a.

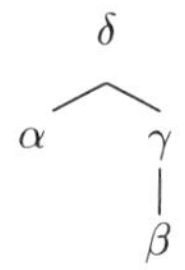

b.

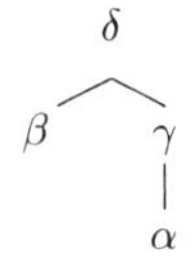

What Kayne hypothesizes is that, if α c-commands β, the terminal nodes dominated by α precede the terminal nodes dominated by β. One of the consequences of this is that there must be a universal specifier-head-complement order, as in (8.1a), and, as already discussed, rightward movement cannot exist.

The question of how to derive mirror image effects in such an antisymmetric syntax is addressed by Cinque, 1996, in connection with such effects within DPs (Determiner Phrases, i.e. nominal constituents). His proposal straightforwardly carries over to mirror image effects in the verbal domain. Below, we will therefore abstract away from the labels of the particular projection involved (as Cinque in fact does himself).

Suppose that the observed order of three modifiers to the left of a lexical head L is the reverse of those elements to the right of L:

(8.16) a. XP YP ZP L
b. L ZP YP XP

From Kayne's theory it follows that there is only one specifier or adjunct per head, generated to the left of this head. Modifiers must therefore each be generated in a distinct functional projection.[8] In the structure below, 2P, 4P and 6P accommodate XP, YP and ZP respectively. The problem, then, is how to derive (8.16b) from (8.16a). To this end, extra functional projections must be introduced, providing the landing sites for the necessary movements. These are 1P, 3P and 5P in the structure below:

[8] A functional projection is the projection of a functional head like Tense (projecting a TP), Aspect (projecting an AspP), Agreement (projecting an AgrP) and so on. The projection of a lexical head is dominated by functional projections pertaining to that lexical category only (e.g. a verb phrase but not a noun phrase is dominated by a Tense Phrase, whereas a noun phrase but not a verb phrase is dominated by a Determiner Phrase), so functional projections are in some sense parasitic on, or an extension of, a lexical projection. Since the precise content of the functional projections is not relevant for our argument, we have simply numbered them in the example structures.

(8.17)

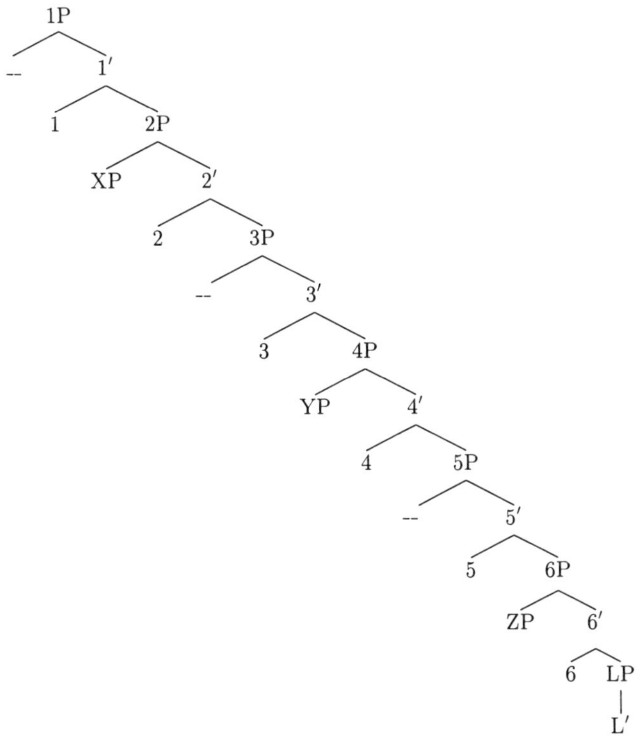

The pattern in (8.16b) can now be derived by movement of LP to the specifier position of 5P, followed by movement of 5P to spec-3P, followed by movement of 3P to spec-1P (the structure is 'rolled up' as it were).

However, if mirror image effects are to be accounted for along these lines, motivation must be given for some crucial assumptions. First, the analysis presupposes that LP is dominated by an extensive functional structure, which provides the landing sites for movement. In particular, every functional projection hosting a modifier must be dominated by a functional projection to whose specifier movement is possible. Apart from the conceptual consideration that such a theory is rather far removed from the ideal of structural economy (cf. Chomsky, 1995), it must be noted that independent syntactic evidence for 3P and 5P in (8.17) cannot be given. That is to say, distributional data can never distinguish movement of L to 2 from movement to 3, or movement of L to 4 from movement to 5. The reason is that no adverbials or other material can be generated in between these positions, given that spec-3P and spec-5P must be empty in order to function as landing sites for movement.

Second, the movements needed to derive (8.16b) should all be motivated. In the minimalist program (Chomsky, 1995) it is assumed that movement occurs to 'check' a 'strong' feature of a functional head. For (8.17) this implies some feature that triggers movement must be present on the heads of the odd-numbered projections, and these features must be 'checked' by movement of LP, 5P and 3P to the relevant specifier positions. Again, such triggering features cannot be introduced without further argumentation. The content of the odd-numbered projections must motivate their presence. However, as we have seen above, it is impossible to find independent evidence for the existence of these projections, and consequently for their content. Moreover, if the odd-numbered projections are assigned such features, these should not attract the even-numbered projections. Given that the even-numbered projections are closer to the relevant specifier positions, they would otherwise block the movements necessary to derive (8.16b). Finally, the problem of finding triggers is complicated by the fact that many mirror image effects occur language-internally (compare the Dutch and Tagalog data in (8.3)-(8.6) and (8.13) discussed above). In order to account for this, the various movements would have to be optional, which would imply that the attracting features have a variable strength.

Third, even if the analysis is adopted as it stands, orders can be derived which the analysis is intended to exclude. One would expect that the lexical head in (8.17) can undergo successive head-to-head movement (from L to 6 to 5 and so on) — both in verbal and nominal contexts such movements are well-attested. Suppose that phrasal movement of the type under discussion is combined with head movement. Suppose, more specifically, that head movement of L to 3 is followed by phrasal movement of 3P to spec-1P. The resulting order would be L-YP-ZP-XP. If this order is to be excluded, as in the case at hand, there must be a condition that forbids phrasal movement if head movement has taken place — a condition for which there seems to be no independent motivation.

Finally, note that the structure assigned to (8.16b) in the analysis under discussion is, in fact, a left-branching structure as far as the lexical elements in it are concerned. This structure is the following:

(8.18)

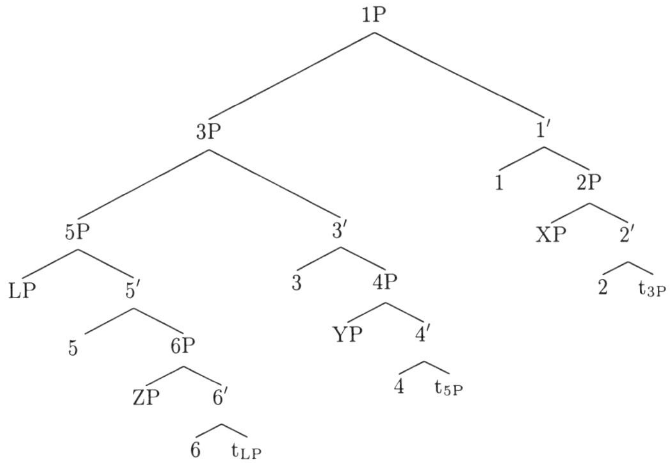

The structural relations between the lexical material in this tree become apparent when we remove all nodes that do not branch into nodes that each dominate lexical material (that is, when we remove all structure assumed for theory-internal reasons). The result is the tree in (8.19).

(8.19)

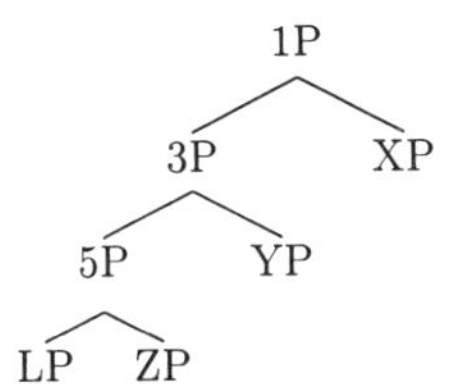

The structural configuration in (8.19) is identical to the one in a base-generated left-branching structure. In other words, the antisymmetric theory imitates, at the cost of introducing potentially problematic movements, the structure directly derived in the symmetric phrase-structure theory. We conclude that the mirror image phenomena are captured more satisfactorily in the symmetric theory than in the antisymmetric one. This means we have to look for an alternative explanation of the different properties of leftward and rightward movement than the one the antisymmetric theory offers. We now turn to this issue.

4. Asymmetric parsing

In addition to the mirror image effects discussed in section 2, some specific anti-mirror image effects are attested. In a number of noun-initial languages, for instance, the dependent elements show up in the same order as in noun-final languages, see (8.20c). This can be explained by head movement of the noun to the left, starting with the basic structure in (8.20a) (= (8.14a)). (As noted, such head movement is well-motivated in both the verbal and the nominal domain). However, a fundamental asymmetry can now be observed. Head movement of the noun to the right appears to be impossible. Alongside (8.20b) (= (8.14b)), no languages exist in which the order in (8.20d) is found (Greenberg, 1966).[9]

(8.20)
a. determiner - numeral - adjective - noun
b. noun - adjective - numeral - determiner
c. noun - determiner - numeral - adjective
d. *adjective - numeral - determiner - noun

The asymmetry of head movement, as opposed to the symmetry of base generation, is also attested in the verbal domain. The assumption that subjects can be generated on either side of V' and objects on either side of V gives rise to an acceptable language typology. In addition to this, some languages display head movement of V to the left. Examples are VSO languages and languages with Verb Second. There are no languages, however, in which there is straightforward distributional evidence that the verb moves to the last or one but last position in the clause.

In view of the discussion in sections 2-3, we take it that syntax is not fundamentally asymmetric. This implies that we must either assume a principle of asymmetry specific to movement processes, or look for the explanation of the observed asymmetries elsewhere. We will pursue the latter option, because we think that the grammar as a whole can be simplified if a nonsyntactic explanation is sought. In particular, we would like to suggest an explanation in terms of universal parsing strategies.

The parser is generally assumed to be a mechanism that assembles structures, whereas the grammar is the knowledge base which the parser uses to do this processing. It is likely that certain structures are grammatical but cause difficulties for the processing mechanism (cf. Kimball, 1973). Such difficulties may lead to so-called garden path effects, in which a hearer is forced to abandon his initial analysis of a string and pursue an alternative. Below we will argue that some instances of rightward movement lead to a more serious processing problem: the hearer's initial analysis again turns out to be incorrect, but this time there is

[9] There are also languages in which the order determiner - numeral - adjective is attested and in which the noun occurs between two of these elements, instead of at the beginning or end of the sequence. This can of course also be explained by noun movement to the left, starting from the basic structure in (8.20a). As far as we know, however, there are no languages with the order adjective - numeral - determiner with the noun in between, showing again that noun movement to the right, starting from the structure in (8.20b), is impossible.

no alternative. The result is that the sentence in question is not just difficult to process, but ruled out altogether.

As explained in the introduction, leftward movement and rightward movement differ in that rightward movement requires the introduction of a trace in a partially analyzed string, whereas leftward movement allows the trace to be introduced at the same time that the string is analyzed (provided that first the moved element is recognized as such, of course). Hence, rightward movement may lead to difficulties if further computation involving insertion of the trace is incompatible with information stored in short-term memory. Before discussing the details of our proposal, let us briefly consider some basic properties of the human parser.

First, it is obvious that, due to the temporal order in which the input is received, the parser scans this string from left to right, computing a representation of the sentence as it goes along. During this process, it can store information concerning already analyzed parts of the string in short-term memory (see Kaan & Stowe, this volume, on the distinction between the computational and storage functions of the parser).

Second, we assume that there are severe limitations on holding unstructured linguistic material in short-term memory (Just and Carpenter, 1992). The consequence of this is that the parser must have limited look-ahead capacity. The most strict assumption is that it has no look-ahead at all, as has been argued by Frazier and Rayner, 1982, Gorrell, 1995, and others. This means that at any stage, the parser can only consider the current input symbol and (a limited amount of) the already parsed material when it is deciding what to do next. Crucially, information from its right context is not available.

Third, the parser builds a syntactic tree. Of course, a syntactic tree is nothing more than a set of dominance and precedence relations between nodes. What the parser does, then, is hypothesize such relations for a particular input string. For our purposes, precedence relations will be crucial. In order to maintain a maximally economical use of its storage function, the relations that the parser hypothesizes will be kept to the minimum that is necessary to construct a full, coherent, tree. For instance, if A dominates B and B dominates C, the parser will not also notate that A dominates C, as this is superfluous. For precedence relations between XPs and heads this implies that these are only notated with respect to the head that the XP is a dependent of, since, combined with the precedence relations between heads, this is the minimal information that is needed to describe the order in a tree. (This way of notating information about the structure that is being parsed will be amply illustrated below.)

Fourth, we assume that the parser handles antecedent-gap relations by applying a so-called filler-driven strategy (cf. Frazier, 1987; 1993; Frazier and Flores d'Arcais, 1989; Gibson, 1998). This means that the postulation of a gap depends on the presence of an antecedent. Once an antecedent is identified as a moved element (on the basis of the grammar of the language in question, which the parser uses as a knowledge base), a position to insert a gap in is looked for. This is done by considering selectional information of heads as well as by applying 'gap-finding' strategies such as the Active Filler Strategy of Frazier, 1987 (which says that the gap should be inserted as soon as is possible). The filler-driven strategy differs from so-called gap-driven strategies, which assume that postulation of a gap depends on lexical (for instance selectional) information and then look for the antecedent in the left context. Experimental evidence (Frazier and Flores d'Arcais, 1989) as well as the possibility of adjunct movement (i.e. movement of unselected elements) seem to support the first assumption.[10]

The above assumptions are more or less standard (see also Davis and Alphonce, 1992, p.88). More controversy arises in connection with the issue of locally ambiguous inputs. What does the parser do when it encounters material that can be integrated into the existing parse in more than one way? Various answers have been proposed. Some authors have argued that analysis is delayed until disambiguating information becomes available (Berwick and Weinberg, 1985; Weinberg, 1988). Others have argued that the parser pursues one analysis (preferred on grounds that need not concern us here) and only returns to the second if it fails (Frazier and Clifton, 1996). Yet others claim that the parser computes all possible analyses in parallel, ranking them according to some preference principle(s) (Gibson, 1991).

All these approaches appear to share a basic assumption, namely that it is impossible to alter established structural relations *within a single parse*. The point of delaying analysis is exactly to guarantee that no established information is destroyed ('informational monotonicity', cf. Marcus et al., 1983). In both ranked parallel and serial parsers the preferred parse is abandoned when new input is incompatible with it. The next best alternative is pursued. Crucially, what does not happen in any of these models is that the parser changes structure it has already postulated.[11] We assume that this is indeed impossible. So, if at some

[10] For example, there is nothing in *Do you think Mary fixed the bike* which suggests that it contains a gap. Therefore, in *How do you think Mary fixed the bike*, postulation of a gap (a trace) is dependent on the presence of the fronted element *how*.

[11] One exception is Pritchett, 1992, where it is argued that under restricted circumstances altering syntactic relations in a parse is possible, namely in case the new position of an

point P the parser cannot decide between analyses, it may first try one of the analyses and then (in case of failure) shift to another. But if at P the input string allows only one analysis, each continuation of the parse after P (i.e. each parse that can be pursued) must comply with this analysis. If material encountered later is incompatible with it, the sentence is not parsable.

Summarizing, the parser has the following properties:

(8.21)
a. It scans the input string from left to right.
b. It constructs a tree, that is, a set of dominance and precedence relations.
c. It has no look-ahead.
d. It can only postulate a trace after having encountered an antecedent.
e. It cannot alter information (dominance and precedence relations) stored in short-term memory for a given parse.

As said, we will argue that the problem with most instances of head movement to the right concerns (8.21e). Moreover, we will show that, exactly when it does not lead to problems with respect to (8.21e), head movement to the right is in fact possible. XP-movement to the right does not violate (8.21e) and is therefore possible, at least in principle. We will suggest that the fact that it is more restricted than XP-movement to the left follows from (8.21d) in combination with closure of already parsed material.

5. Infelicitous rightward head movement

Let us now consider the effects of (8.21). Suppose that the first part of an input string has been analyzed as an XP.[12] The parser then postulates that this maximal projection precedes the head that it is a dependent of. Formally, this means that the parser hypothesizes the following syntactic relations: the XP is immediately dominated by a projection H^i of some head H, XP precedes H and, trivially, H^i is projected from H. Crucially, the parser cannot assume that XP follows H, since it has not encountered

element is dominated or governed by its original position. This condition, however, can easily be adapted so as to apply between parses (whether parallel or serial) rather than within a parse.

[12] For the moment, we abstract away from the internal structure of XP. The maximal projections we will talk about are specifiers, complements or adjuncts of the heads under discussion. (We will use the general term 'dependent' of a head to refer to such elements.) We also abstract away from the option that such a projection has moved. We turn to movement of maximal projections in section 8.

a head yet. It cannot assume that H is the trace of a moved head either, with XP following this trace, because traces cannot be inserted unless an antecedent has been identified (cf. (8.21d)). Thus, if (8.22a) represents the current stage of the parse, the additional information in (8.22b) becomes available (where P means 'precede', ID means 'immediately dominate' and Proj means 'project'). The minimal tree compatible with this information is given in (8.22c).

(8.22) a. XP

b. P(XP,H); ID(H^i,XP); Proj(H,H^i)

c. 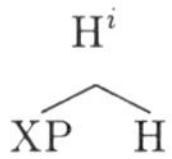

As will be obvious, H is an abstract head at this point, which can only be given content when an actual head is encountered or when the trace of a moved head is inserted. The parser will continue to build a right-branching tree. That is, if it again has analyzed a substring as a constituent, it will assume that this constituent precedes H and is immediately dominated by a projection of H.[13] This continues until the parser encounters that head which it hypothetises (e.g. on the basis of selectional information) to be the head of which the XPs analyzed thus far are dependents. In other words, if the parser identifies two maximal projections XP and YP before it encounters this head, the relations in (8.23b) are postulated (where D means 'dominate'). These are compatible with the minimal tree in (8.23c).

(8.23) a. XP YP

b. P(XP,H); ID(H^i,XP); Proj(H,H^i)
P(YP,H); ID(H^j,YP); D(H^i,H^j); Proj(H,H^j)

c. 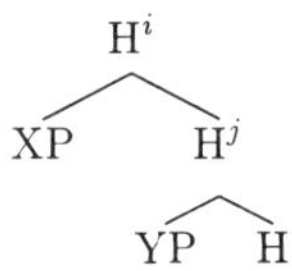

Note that the extension in (8.23b) of the parse in (8.22b) does not involve alteration of relations already stored in short-term memory (cf. (8.21e)), it only involves adding new relations. Note also that the parser need not lay down precedence relations between maximal projections, as these

[13]Strictly speaking, the heads of which the first and the second constituent are dependents need not be the same. We abstract away from this matter here, as it does not affect the argument we are about to present. See below for discussion.

follow from the dominance relations given in (8.23b) in combination with the information that XP and YP precede H.

When the parser encounters a head, there are two options. It can assume that this head has moved or is in its base position. The latter case is by far the simplest: the parser simply assumes that this head is H. So, if the input contains a verb, the parse can be extended as in (8.24).

(8.24) a. XP YP V

b. P(XP,H); ID(H^i,XP); Proj(H,H^i)
P(YP,H); ID(H^j,YP); D(H^i,H^j); Proj(H,H^j)
H = V

c.

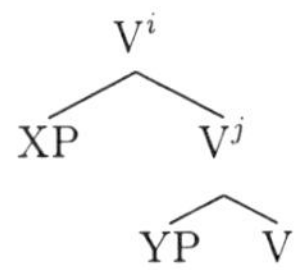

For any further maximal projection the parser identifies, it will now notate that it follows V and is immediately dominated by a projection of V.[14] Suppose that the parser identifies two more maximal projections. Then the parse is extended to (8.25).

(8.25) a. XP YP V ZP WP

b. P(XP,H); ID(H^i,XP); Proj(H,H^i)
P(YP,H); ID(H^j,YP); D(H^i,H^j); Proj(H,H^j)
H = V
P(H,ZP); ID(H^k,ZP); Proj(H,H^k)
P(H,WP); ID(H^l,WP); D(H^l,H^k); Proj(H,H^l)

These relations do not define a complete tree yet, since the dominance relations between H^i and H^j on the one hand and H^k and H^l on the other are not specified yet. This leads to local ambiguities which will partly be resolved on the basis of the grammar and partly on the basis of pragmatic considerations (for instance if the context favours certain scopal relations between preverbal and postverbal material, compare section 2). Consider, for instance, the example in (8.6b'), repeated here as (8.26).

[14]There is another option: the constituent can be parsed as part of the projection of a not yet identified following head. Such structures are similar to those involving leftward head movement, which are discussed below.

(8.26) dat we op vakantie gingen in die dagen
that we on holiday went in those days
volgens Marleens plan.
according to Marleen's plan.
'that, in accordance with Marleen's plan, we went on holiday in that period'.

In this example, the string following the complementizer can be parsed along the lines sketched above, where *we* is XP, *op vakantie* 'on holiday' is YP, *in die dagen* 'in those days' is ZP and *volgens Marleens plan* 'according to Marleen's plan' is WP. The scopal relations between the PPs suggest that both postverbal PP adverbials are attached higher than the preverbal selected PP (see section 2). Suppose that the grammar tells the parser that the subject must be attached higher than the PP adverbials. Then, in addition to the relations in (8.25), the ones in (8.27a) are added to the parse, giving the complete tree in (8.27b).

(8.27) a. $D(H^i,H^l)$; $D(H^k,H^j)$

b.

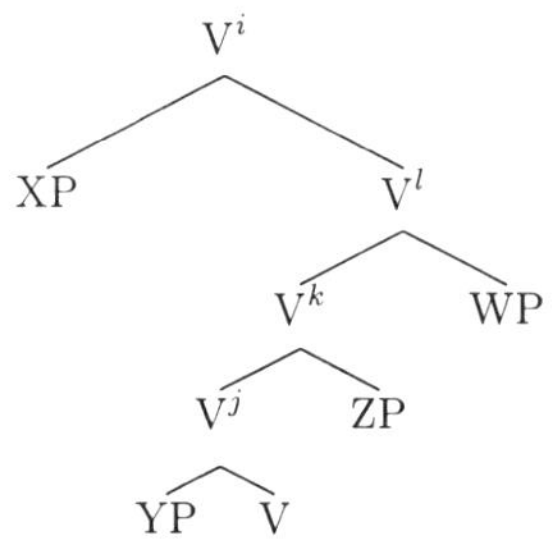

When the parser encounters the verb, there is a second option. It may again assume that the verb equals H, but that it has been moved (leftward). Which option it chooses - movement or not - depends on the grammar of the pertinent language. For instance, in a verb second language like Dutch, the parser will choose this option in a main clause like (8.28).

(8.28) Overigens gingen we op vakantie *t* in die dagen
By-the-way went we on holiday in those days
volgens Marleens plan.
according to Marleen's plan.
'By the way, in accordance with Marleen's plan, we went on holiday in that period'.

If the verb has moved, the tree must remain right-branching until the parser introduces the verb's trace. Otherwise this trace would fail to be c-commanded by the moved verb. Subsequent maximal projections identified before the verb's trace is inserted can therefore not be attached to H's projection. Instead, they must be part of the projection of a lower head, say H2, which hosts the verb's trace. The parser will notate that a projection of H immediately dominates $H2^{max}$ and that $H2^{max}$ follows H. Internal to $H2^{max}$, precedence relations are notated in the usual way. Consider once more the string in (8.25a), repeated here as (8.29a), and suppose that this time the parser hypothesizes that the verb has moved (this is indicated by M(V) below). Assuming the trace is inserted in final position, the parse is extended as in (8.29b); (8.29c) is the resulting minimal tree.

(8.29) a. XP YP V ZP WP

b. $P(XP,H); ID(H^i,XP); Proj(H,H^i); P(YP,H); ID(H^j,YP);$
$D(H^i,H^j); Proj(H,H^j)$
$H = V; M(V)$
$P(H,H2^{max}); ID(H^k,H2^{max}); ID(H^k,H); Proj(H2,H2^{max})$
$P(ZP,H2); ID(H2^l,ZP); Proj(H2,H2^l)$
$P(WP,H2); ID(H2^k,WP); D(H2^l,H2^k); Proj(H2,H2^k)$
$H2 = t$

c.

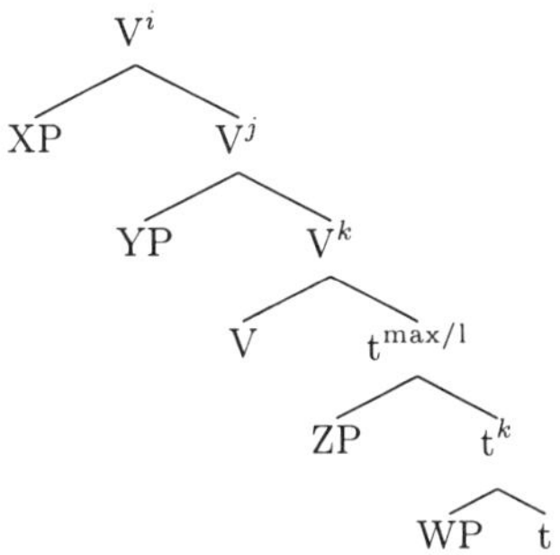

For any maximal projections the parser identifies after having inserted the verb's trace, local ambiguities arise again. If they are attached to the projection of H2 (the verb's trace), c-command relations with respect to ZP and WP must be determined. If they are attached to the projection of H (the verb), c-command relations with respect to XP and YP. Which analysis is chosen is again determined by grammatical and pragmatic factors, but we will not pursue this here.

So, the parser can analyze the string under discussion either as a basic structure or as a structure involving head movement of the verb to the left. However, an analysis in which the verb has been moved rightward across one of its dependents (that is, a maximal projection contained in the projection of its trace) cannot be pursued successfully. In other words, a tree like (8.30) is ruled out.

(8.30) *

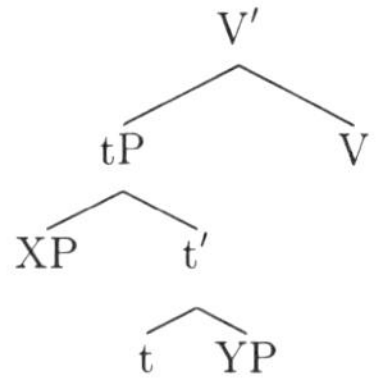

Consider why. According to (8.21d), a trace can only be inserted after the parser has encountered a moved element, an antecedent. This implies that if the parser hypothesizes rightward verb movement, insertion of the trace must be in accordance with the information in (8.23b), repeated in (8.31). The reason is that, at the time the parser encounters the verb, this information has already been stored (see the discussion above).

(8.31) P(XP,H); ID(H^i,XP); Proj(H,H^i)
P(YP,H); ID(H^j,YP); D(H^i,H^j); Proj(H,H^j)

Suppose that the parser tries out the analysis in (8.30) and inserts the verb's trace between XP and YP. In (8.30), YP is immediately dominated by a projection of the trace. This is only in accordance with the statements in (8.31) if the projection in question is H^j. (8.31) states ID(H^j,YP), and a node cannot be immediately dominated by two different nodes. If H^j is a projection of the trace, the trace must be H. However, if the trace is H, a conflict arises with another statement in (8.31), namely P(YP,H): YP does not precede the trace in the attempted analysis. Hence, this analysis is incompatible with already established information. Since such information may not be destroyed according to (8.21e), this analysis is in fact impossible. Hence, rightward head movement across one of the dependents of the moving head cannot be parsed. Put informally, the problem that can arise with rightward head movement is this: for all XPs the parser encounters before it encounters a head, it notates that they precede the head they are a dependent of. It is then impossible to insert a trace of the moved head before any such XP, because that would mean the XP in fact follows the head it is a dependent of, which conflicts with the previously established information about this XP.

Note that the impossibility of parsing this type of rightward head movement is very different from difficulties that may originate in local ambiguities. In the case of local ambiguities the parser can at some point pursue two possible analyses (which are computed either in parallel or serially, an issue on which we remain agnostic). However, because of the filler-driven strategy to gap postulation, the parser does not face a local ambiguity at the point where the trace of the rightward-moved head should be inserted. Hence, before it encounters the moved verb, the parser must notate that the XPs it identifies precede the head of their projection. As just discussed, this leads to unparsability in case one or more of these XPs in fact follow the trace.

The situation that arises under rightward head movement differs, therefore, from situations in which an XP can be put on a right branch of the projection of a preceding head, as well as on a left branch of the projection of a head that is still to follow. Such cases do involve a local ambiguity. Consider, for instance, the following Dutch examples (cf. Frazier, 1987):

(8.32) a. dat $[_{VP}[_{NP}$ het meisje] $[_{V'}[_{PP}$ van de buren] houdt]]
that the girl from the neighbours likes
'that the girl likes the neighbours'

b. dat $[_{VP}[_{NP}$ het meisje $[_{PP}$ van de buren]] $[_{V'}$ glimlacht]]
that the girl from the neighbours smiles
'that the girl next door smiles'

In (8.32a), the PP *van de buren* is on a left-branch of the verbal projection, since it is a PP-complement selected by the verb. In (8.32b) the same PP is on a right branch of the projection of the noun *meisje*, it being a modifier of this noun here. In this case, the string is locally ambiguous when the parser postulates the PP. Consequently, two possibilities arise. If the PP is analyzed as a dependent of the noun, the parser notates the relations ID(N^i,PP) and P(N,PP). If the PP is analyzed as a dependent of the following verb, the parser notates the relations ID(H^i,PP) and P(PP,H) (where H will later be identified with the verb). This ambiguity is resolved in whatever way ambiguities are resolved in general. But in the case of (attempted) head movement to the right, the parser has already fixed the structure of the string for which it should have pursued a different analysis.

6. Felicitous rightward head movement

The result that a head cannot move rightward across one of its dependents explains the problem that we started out with. As we have seen in section 2, basic syntactic structures are symmetric, but typologically head movement is not. N-to-D and V-to-C (verb second) movement are systematically leftward. They can, indeed, not be rightward since that would lead to unparsable structures. For example, the absence of languages with the order in (8.20d) (*adjective - numeral - determiner - noun) follows. The order of adjective, numeral and determiner indicates that the NP is head-initial underlyingly (as in (8.20b)). The illegitimate order must hence have been derived by rightward movement of the noun across its dependents, which we have just shown to be impossible.

The argumentation in section 5 implies that head movement to the right should be possible if the syntactic relations already established do not have to be altered when the trace is inserted. In this section we will spell out under what circumstances this is possible. In the next section we present empirical evidence that bears out this prediction.

The simplest case involves rightward head movement in which the head does not cross any maximal projection. Consider once more the situation in which the parser has identified two maximal projections, XP and YP, but has not yet encountered the head. As noted in section 5, the information already stored at that point consists of the statements in (8.23b), repeated here in (8.33).

(8.33) P(XP,H); ID(H^i,XP); Proj(H,H^i)
P(YP,H); ID(H^j,YP); D(H^i,H^j); Proj(H,H^j)

If the parser now encounters the verb and hypothesizes that this element has moved rightward, it can insert a trace without violating the statements in (8.33) by inserting it to the right of both XP and YP and identifying it with H. Thus, string-vacuous rightward head movement is possible: the tree in (8.34) is in accordance with (8.33) if *t* is H.

(8.34)

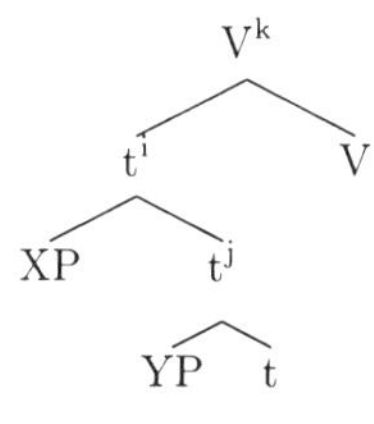

Indeed, string-vacuous rightward head movement (namely movement of the verb to a sentence-final C(omplementizer) position in the strictly head-final languages Japanese and Korean) is argued for by Whitman, 1991. Whitman shows that certain properties shared by Verb Second languages (like Dutch) and Japanese/Korean can be explained by assuming that there is V-to-C movement in both.

Interestingly, there is a type of structure in which rightward head movement can be parsed in which it is not string-vacuous. Let us once more consider the situation in which the parser has identified two maximal projections but has not yet encountered a head. Thus far we have assumed that these projections are dependents of the same head H. However, it is possible that they belong to different projections, which are projected from two distinct heads, H1 and H2. In that case, the following information will be notated (compare with (8.33)):

(8.35) $P(XP,H1); ID(H1^i,XP); Proj(H1,H1^i)$
$P(YP,H2); ID(H2^j,YP); Proj(H2,H2^j)$

Suppose that at this stage the parser encounters a verb, which it identifies as H2, plus another head, say Z, which occurs in an adjoined position to the verb. In that case no problems arise if the parser assumes that this adjoined head has undergone rightward movement across YP. The trace of this rightward moved head can be identified with H1 without leading to conflicts with the information already stored (given in (8.35)). This is so because the statement that YP precedes the head of its projection is with respect to H2 (the verb), not H1 (the trace of the adjoined Z head). The complete set of relations the parser establishes is given in (8.36a), with the corresponding minimal tree in (8.36b).

(8.36) a. $P(XP,H1); ID(H1^i,XP); Proj(H1,H1^i)$
$P(YP,H2); ID(H2^j,YP); Proj(H2,H2^j)$
$ID(H2^k,H1^{max}); D(H2^k,H2^j); Proj(H2,H2^k);$
$Proj(H1,H1^{max})$
$ID(V^l,Z); D(V^j,V^l); Proj(V,V^l); M(Z)$
$H1 = t_z; H2 = V$

b.

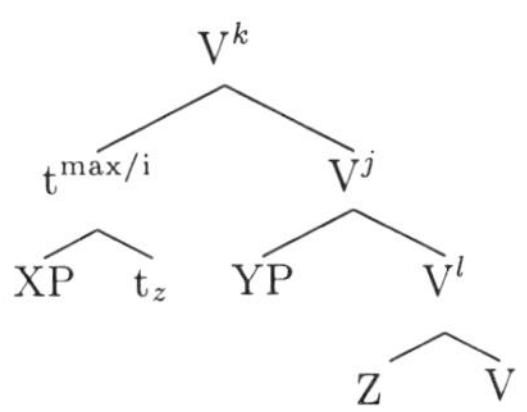

Thus it should be possible to have non-string-vacuous rightward head movement as long as the elements crossed are not dependents of the moved head, but of another head. In many cases, the requirement that movement be to a c-commanding position (a 'higher' position in the tree, see section 3) will make it impossible to identify H1 in (8.36) with the trace of a head adjoined to H2. (Z in (8.36b) may not be 'lower' than its trace). We will show in the next section, however, that there is a limited set of structures which allow such identification without violating the ban on downward movement.

Note that the parser must be allowed to hypothesize that XP and YP belong to the projections of different heads for independent reasons.

Consider the case of parsing embedded clauses in strictly head-final languages like Japanese. In that case, too, the maximal projections the parser identifies before encountering a head do not all belong to the projection of the same head. The difference with the case discussed above is that in these cases the head of which XP is a dependent is the higher head (i.e. the projection of H1 contains the projection of H2). So, if the embedded clause is an infinitival for example, the parser does not extend the set of statements in (8.35) to (8.36a) in this case, but to (8.37a). These are compatible with the minimal tree in (8.37b).

(8.37) a. P(XP,H1); ID($H1^i$,XP); Proj(H1,$H1^i$)
P(YP,H2); ID($H2^j$,YP); Proj(H2,$H2^j$)
ID($H1^k$,$H2^{max}$); D($H1^i$,$H1^k$); Proj(H1,$H1^k$);
Proj(H2,$H2^{max}$)
H1 = V_{fin}; H2 = V_{inf}

b.

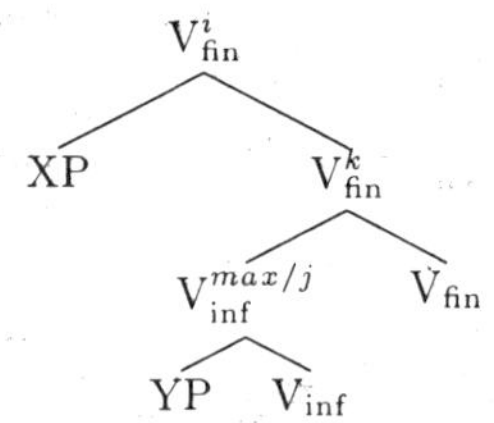

Thus, independently of rightward movement structures, the parser must be able to adopt the statements in (8.35) when it identifies two maximal projections before having encountered a head.

7. Rightward P-incorporation and V-to-V raising in Dutch

In the previous section we have derived the following theorem:

(8.38) *Rightward Head Movement Theorem* (RHMT)
Rightward head movement is possible as long as no dependent of the moving head is crossed.

In this section we will provide empirical evidence that confirms (8.38). The first type of rightward head movement we will discuss concerns stranded prepositions in Dutch. Prepositions are said to be stranded when the NP complement of the P undergoes movement on its own, leaving the P behind. It can be argued that such stranded prepositions must incorporate into the verb in Dutch (see Sturm and Kerstens, 1978 and Hoeksema, 1991). The observation on which this claim is based is that they must be adjacent to the verb:[15]

(8.39) a. Daar$_i$ wil ik tijdens de lunch [t$_i$ t$_j$] [over$_j$
that want I during the lunch about
praten].
speak.
'I want to speak about that during lunch'.

b. *Daar$_i$ wil ik [t$_i$ over] tijdens de lunch
that want I about during the lunch
praten.
speak.

This restriction cannot be reduced to the distribution of PPs in general, since PPs do occur in positions preceding adverbials (so nonadjacent to the verb), see (8.40a). It can also not be reduced to some prohibition on moving elements out of constituents that are not adjacent to the verb, since this is allowed in constructions like (8.40b).

(8.40) a. Ik wil daarover tijdens de lunch praten.
I want that-about during the lunch speak.

b. Wat$_i$ heb je [t$_i$ voor mensen] tijdens de
what have you for people during the
lunch gesproken?
lunch spoken.
'What kind of people did you talk to during lunch?'

(Presumably, the trigger for P-incorporation into the verb is that the trace of the element that is extracted out of PP must be properly governed; this is a general demand on traces, see for instance Chomsky, 1986 and Rizzi, 1990. P is not itself a proper governor for elements to its left. However, after incorporation of P into V, V governs the trace; see Baker, 1988).

The example of P-incorporation in (8.39a) is a case of string-vacuous rightward head movement, parsable on a par with (8.34). It is remarkable, however, that in other cases the movement may be non-string-vacuous: the preposition may cross a dependent of the verb. The relevant examples are given in (8.41).

[15] There are a few exceptions to this generalisation: locational PPs can intervene between the verb and a very small group of stranded prepositions. For other prepositions the generalisation is robust. Whether or not P-incorporation is obligatory or optional is irrelevant to the argumentation in this section, since the fact remains that it can be non-string-vacuous, as we will show below.

(8.41) a. dat ik de deur daarmee groen verf.
that I the door that-with green paint.
'that I paint the door green with that.'

b. *dat ik de deur groen daarmee verf.
that I the door green that-with paint.

c. de verf waar$_i$ ik de deur [t$_i$ t$_j$] [$_V$ mee$_j$ [$_V$ groen verf]]
the paint that I the door with green paint.
'the paint with which I paint the door green'.

d. de verf waar$_i$ ik de deur [t$_i$ t$_j$] [$_V$ groen [$_V$ mee$_j$ verf]]
the paint that I the door green with paint.
'idem'

There is reason to believe that *groen verven* 'green paint' (i.e. 'paint green') is a complex predicate, that is, a complex V^0 category, generated by adjunction of the resultative to the verb, as in (8.42) (see Neeleman, 1994 for motivation).

(8.42)

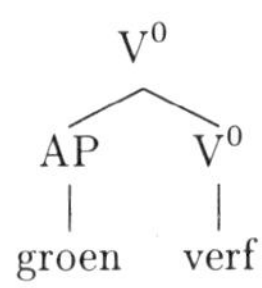

This immediately accounts for the possibility of (8.41c): although the stranded preposition is not adjacent to the verb, it is adjacent to the verbal complex. It has incorporated into the higher V^0 node of the complex predicate. Crucially, the lower V^0 segment is also a target for P-incorporation. This accounts for (8.41d). Note that the P-incorporation in (8.41d) does not involve lowering, since the incorporated preposition still c-commands its trace according to the definitions of c-command and domination of Chomsky, 1986, given in (8.43).

(8.43) a. α c-commands β iff α does not dominate β and every γ that category-dominates α category-dominates β.

b. α is category-dominated by β iff α is dominated by every segment of β.

In (8.41d), the incorporated preposition is not category-dominated by V^0, since it is not dominated by every segment of V^0. This means there is no category that category-dominates the preposition but not its trace. Hence, the preposition c-commands its trace, as required.

What (8.41d) shows, then, is that rightward head movement may cross a dependent of the head into which incorporation takes place, in accordance with the RHMT in (8.38). The case in (8.41d) can be parsed as in (8.36) (Z is *mee*, YP is *groen*, V is *verf*, and XP is (the trace of) *waar*).

There is, in other words, no absolute adjacency condition on rightward incorporation. Given this, it is remarkable that rightward incorporation may not cross dependents of the incorporating head itself. Yet, this is what the RHMT states, and indeed it can be shown that movement of this type is impossible. In order to do so, we use a construction that involves non-string-vacuous V-movement to the right, namely Dutch V-to-V raising (see Evers, 1975). V-to-V raising involves adjoining the head verb of an embedded infinitival clause to the right of the matrix verb. An example is given in (8.44).

(8.44)	dat	Jan	[Marie	de	samba	t_i]	[zag	$dansen_i$]
	that	Jan	Marie	the	samba		saw	dance
	'that Jan saw Marie dance the samba'							

From the perspective of the parser, (8.44) involves a number of substrings to be analyzed as XPs, followed by two verbs. This string can be analyzed by the parser on a par with (8.37b), except that the infinitive is moved and H2 is identified with its trace. The movement of the infinitive does not cross any maximal projections, and hence it can be parsed without problems (compare the discussion of (8.33) and (8.34)).

Although we have shown that there is no absolute adjacency condition on rightward head movement, the embedded verb in a V-to-V raising construction cannot move across any of its own dependents. Evidence for this claim can be based on an observation by Reuland, 1990. In Dutch, a postverbal PP can take scope over a preverbal adverbial (as expected given the symmetry of basic structures). The example in (8.45) can mean both that it was the case for some time that Jan frequently hampered the project or that it was frequently the case that Jan hampered the project for some time (see also section 2).

(8.45)	dat	Jan	het	project	regelmatig	hinderde	gedurende
	that	Jan	the	project	frequently	hampered	for
	een	tijdje					
	some	time					

Consider now an infinitival version of (8.45) and suppose the infinitive heading it adjoins to a higher verb, across the postverbal PP. We would then still expect the same ambiguity. However, in a V-to-V raising construction like (8.46) only one reading is available, namely the reading in which the adverbial takes scope over the PP.

(8.46) dat ik Jan het project regelmatig gedurende een
that I Jan the project frequently for some
tijdje zag hinderen.
time saw hamper.

This means that, apparently, the trace of the raised verb in (8.46) cannot precede the PP, as in (8.47a). The interpretation of (8.46) is only compatible with the analysis in (8.47b), with the trace following both the adverbial and the PP. As noted in section 2, in case of two prehead modifiers, scope relations go from left to right. Hence the unambiguous scopal relation in (8.46). (For more evidence for the adjacency requirement between the two verbs in cases of V-to-V raising see Van Riemsdijk, 1998).

(8.47) a. *dat ik [Jan het project regelmatig t_i gedurende een tijdje] [zag $hinderen_i$]
b. dat ik [Jan het project regelmatig gedurende een tijdje t_i] [zag $hinderen_i$]

So, while there is no adjacency condition as such on rightward incorporation, as shown above (see (41d)), adjacency is required in (8.47). It seems fairly problematic to derive this difference from syntactic principles, but it follows directly from the parsing strategies we have assumed. From these strategies we have derived the theorem in (8.38): a head cannot move rightward across one or more of its own dependents. This, however, is precisely what has happened in (8.47a). Hence, (8.47a) is unparsable. No such problems arise in (8.47b), where no maximal projections are crossed, or in (8.41d), where the maximal projection crossed is not a dependent of the moving head.

8. Rightward XP-movement

The kind of parsing problems that make rightward head movement impossible under some circumstances do not arise in the case of rightward XP-movement. The reason for this is that precedence relations which mention a particular XP are not notated until that XP has been identified. This implies that in the case of rightward XP-movement statements must be added, but no already stored statements ever would have to be revised. In contrast, abstract heads are mentioned in precedence relations before an actual head is encountered (in head final constructions at least), which may lead to the problems discussed above.

Consider for example a situation in which the parser has identified two maximal projections and a head. As explained in section 5, the parse at that stage contains the information in (8.24b), repeated in (8.48).

(8.48) P(XP,H); ID(H^i,XP); Proj(H,H^i)
P(YP,H); ID(H^j,YP); D(H^i,H^j); Proj(H,H^j)
H = V

If the parser now identifies a third maximal projection, ZP, it may hypothesize that ZP has moved from a position between XP and YP and insert a trace there without contradicting any of the statements in (8.48). After all, these statements do not mention ZP or its trace. One of the possible resulting parses is that in (8.49).

(8.49) a. P(XP,H); ID(H^i,XP); Proj(H,H^i)
P(YP,H); ID(H^j,YP); D(H^i,H^j); Proj(H,H^j)
H = V
P(H,ZP); ID(H^l,ZP); D(H^l,H^i); Proj(H,H^l); M(ZP)
P(t_{ZP},H); ID(H^k,t_{ZP}); D(H^i,H^k); D(H^k,H^j)

b.

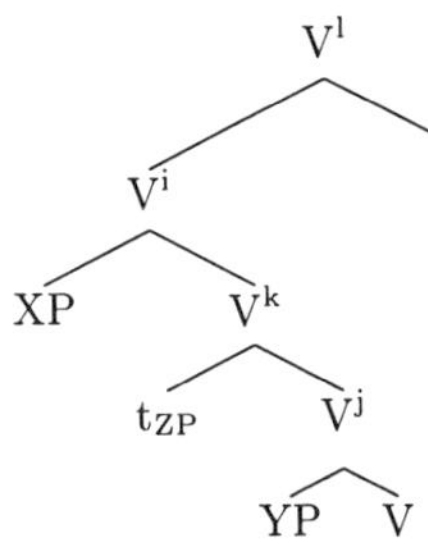

In conclusion, rightward XP-movement across a maximal projection need not lead to parsing difficulties. Following Rochemont and Culicover, 1990, we assume that such movement indeed exists. Rochemont & Culicover argue that, whereas extraposition of PPs and CPs should be analyzed in terms of base generation and an interpretational rule, heavy NP shift is an instance of rightward adjunction.[16]

---

[16]Extraposition is the phenomenon that a complement PP or CP, or a relative CP, occurs further to the right instead of directly after the noun it is a dependent of; examples are given in (i)-(ii). Heavy NP shift involves movement to the right of a 'heavy', focused, nominal constituent; an example is given in (iii).

(i) John saw the girl yesterday with the red umbrella

(ii) John saw the girl yesterday that has a red umbrella

(iii) (Who did John see yesterday?)
John saw yesterday THE GIRL WITH THE RED UMBRELLA

If rightward movement indeed exists, it is unexpected that, as already shown by Ross, 1967, it is much more local than leftward movement. Culicover and Rochemont, 1990 show that (once extraposition of PPs and CPs is discarded as an instance of movement) the proper locality condition on rightward movement is that it is phrase-bound. For example, heavy NP shift is not possible out of clauses, as shown by the data in (8.50), and it is not possible out of PPs, as shown by (8.51) (from Rochemont, 1992, p.387).

(8.50) a. John wanted [S PRO [VP to study t_i carefully [the entire book of Revelation]$_i$]]

b. *John wanted [S PRO [VP to study t_i]] dearly [the entire book of Revelation]$_i$

(8.51) a. *Mary put the money [on t_i] yesterday [a table that was standing at the entrance to the hall]$_i$

b. *John threw a look [at t_i] as he was walking by [a man who was standing outside his office]

An advantage of the antisymmetry framework (see sections 1-3) is that this contrast between leftward and rightward XP-movement can be made to follow from the assumption that the apparent cases of rightward movement do not, in fact, involve such movement at all (but rather leftward movement of other material, see Kayne, 1994, p.72-73). However, the contrast can be made to follow from the design of the human parser as well, as suggested before by Fodor, 1978; Rochemont, 1992 and Davis and Alphonce, 1992. Consider how.

It is generally assumed that in analyzing an input string, the parser closes off certain units of already parsed structure and removes them from short term memory (see Kimball, 1973). What this means is that once the internal structure of a syntactic unit has been determined, and its semantics has been calculated, the parser treats that unit as an atom. It removes all statements that describe the internal structure of the unit in question from the set of statements in its storage component. It replaces all this information with a single symbol with the appropriate semantics. As will be clear, this procedure reduces the pressure on short-term memory.

Closure implies that the restriction on inserting traces in already parsed structure is even stricter than we already argued it to be. It is not only impossible to introduce traces if this would require alteration of already established information about the structure, but it is also impossible to introduce traces into those syntactic units that have been closed. If the unit of closure is the phrase, as Kimball, 1973 and

Rochemont, 1992 suggest, the locality of rightward XP-movement follows straightforwardly from the filler-driven strategy the parser applies in dealing with filler-gap dependencies.

The ban on reopening phrases that have been closed discriminates sharply between rightward XP-movement and leftward XP-movement. Recall that the parser can only insert traces after it has hypothesized that some constituent is an antecedent. If the trace follows its antecedent, in principle it can be inserted in any phrase, since insertion will coincide with the building up of that particular phrase. If the trace is to precede its antecedent, however, the antecedent and its trace must be in the same phrase, or else a closed phrase would have to be reopened, which is impossible.

Consider the structures in (8.52), which correspond to the examples in (8.50a) and (8.50b) respectively.

(8.52) a. $[_S$ NP V $[_S$ $[_{VP}$ V t_i AdvP $NP_i]]]$
b. *$[_S$ NP V $[_S$ $[_{VP}$ V $t_i]]$ AdvP $NP_i]$

If the parser hypothesizes that the sentence-final NP is an antecedent, it may insert a trace in the phrase that it puts the NP in, but not in an already parsed, and therefore closed, phrase. The parser treats closed phrases as atoms, and can therefore not modify their internal structure. However, this is exactly what would be necessary if a trace is to be inserted in a closed phrase.

So, the parser can handle a structure like (8.52a), since the embedded VP has not been closed at the moment the shifted NP is encountered. A trace may consequently be inserted in this VP. In (8.52b), however, the moved NP follows a constituent that must be part of the matrix VP. The adverb separating the heavy NP and its trace, *dearly* in (8.50b), must be a modifier of the matrix verb *want* for semantic reasons. This implies that the parser must already have closed the embedded VP when it reaches the heavy NP. This in turn implies that it can only insert the trace of the heavy NP in the matrix VP, which will not result in a grammatical structure (since the shifted NP is not thematically related to the matrix verb).

The same line of reasoning applies to the examples of heavy NP shift out of PPs in (8.51). The parser has only one option when it encounters the adverbial following the preposition in these examples. The grammar determines that the adverbial cannot be a complement of the preposition. It must go with the matrix verb. Again, this means that the parser must have closed the PP when it encounters the heavy NP. It cannot reopen this PP, and therefore the trace of the heavy NP must be inserted in the matrix clause. Hence, heavy NP shift out of PPs is impossible.

As noted, leftward XP-movement is not restricted in this way. Consider, for example, a string that should be assigned the structure in (8.53).

(8.53) $[_S$ XP_i YP V $[_S$ ZP V $[_S$ WP V $t_i]]]$

Once the parser hypothesizes that XP has been moved, it must introduce a trace somewhere. It can do so in any of the phrases, however deeply embedded, that it is working on. The introduction of the trace finds place at the moment the structure of that particular phrase is determined, and so it does not require the reopening of closed material.

Note that from this proposal it follows that a type of movement that necessarily crosses a phrasal boundary can only take place to the left. This type of movement, when taking place to the right, would be unparsable. Hence, it follows that movement to the specifier position of CP, for example, must be leftward because such movement necessarily crosses the VP boundary. As far as we know, operator movement to spec-CP (like wh-movement in questions) is indeed invariably leftward.

So, certain instances of rightward movement cannot be parsed, and are therefore impossible. This phenomenon must be differentiated from the phenomenon of garden paths, which involves constructions that are difficult but not impossible to parse. Garden paths can occur when there is a local ambiguity in the analysis of a string. As noted in sections 4 and 5, the parser postulates two possible analyses in such cases, which are either pursued in parallel or serially. One might think this option affects the explanation of the boundedness of rightward XP-movement just given. Suppose that in an example parallel to (8.50) heavy NP shift crosses material that induces a local ambiguity. For example, suppose that the adverbial it crosses can either be attached in the matrix or in the embedded clause, as in (8.54).

(8.54) John expected Bill to meet his favorite uncle from Cleveland yesterday
(i) expect yesterday; (ii) meet yesterday

If heavy NP shift takes place, the adverbial must be construed as part of the embedded clause, indicating that even in cases like this rightward XP-movement is phrase-bound:

(8.55) John expected Bill to meet yesterday his favorite uncle from Cleveland
(i) *expect yesterday; (ii) meet yesterday

Data like (8.55) do not really form a problem for the analysis above, however. The point is that the local ambiguity induced by *yesterday* gives rise to two possible parses, neither of which can accommodate heavy NP shift into the matrix clause. In the first parse, *yesterday* is a matrix adverbial. This implies that the embedded clause will have been closed when the parser identifies the shifted NP. Consequently, in this parse the NP must have been shifted from within the matrix clause (which, as noted, is impossible since this NP is not selected by the matrix verb). In the second parse, *yesterday* is attached to the embedded clause. This means that when the parser identifies the shifted NP the embedded clause need not have been closed yet, and hence a trace can be inserted in it. (Of course, if the embedded clause *has* been closed at that time, the trace must again be inserted in the matrix clause, which leads to the problem just mentioned.)

9. Conclusion

We have argued that base-generated structures are in principle symmetrical. With respect to movement, however, two asymmetries can be observed. First, head movement to the right seems to be impossible when the head crosses its own dependents, while for head movement to the left (for instance in cases of Verb Second) this is not a problem. Second, XP-movement to the right is extremely local (namely phrase-bound), while for XP-movement to the left this is not necessarily the case. We have argued that both these asymmetries do not impede the basic symmetry of syntax, but are consequences of parsing strategies. In particular, both types of asymmetry can be traced back to the parser's inability to adapt already stored information to the consequences that the introduction of a trace would have in computing certain cases of rightward movement.

Our analysis implies that the apparent ungrammaticality of certain syntactic structures should not be accounted for by syntax proper (that is, by the theory of competence), but rather by the theory of performance. The latter acts as a filter on possible linguistic representations. It might seem that an explanation in these terms is less desirable than an explanation that invokes syntactic principles only. However, the assumption that there is a system of performance which renders part of the output of the system of competence unacceptable allows for an overall simplification of the theory (see Kluender, 1998 for a similar argument in connection with other restrictions on movement). The general rationale for such a modular approach is that it is better to have two simple modules than it is to have a single complicated one. In the case at hand, we believe that the theory of syntax is simplified by transferring some of its load to the parser.

Acknowledgments

For useful comments we are indebted to Carl Alphonce, Arthur Dirksen, Lyn Frazier, Edward Gibson, Hans van de Koot, Jan Odijk, Colin Phillips, Tanya Reinhart, Eddy Ruys, Fred Weerman, and audiences at Utrecht University (Linguistics in the Netherlands), University of California at Santa Cruz (WECOL) and University of Cologne (Linguistisches Arbeitskreis).

References

Baker, M. (1988). *Incorporation.* Chicago: University of Chicago Press.

Berwick, R. and Weinberg, A. (1985). Deterministic parsing: a modern view. In Berman, S., Choe, J.-W., and McDonough, J., editors, *Proceedings of NELS 18*, pages 15–33, Amherst: GLSA.

Büring, D. and Hartmann, K. (1997). The Kayne mutiny. In Beerman, D., LeBlanc, D., and van Riemsdijk, H., editors, *Rightward movement*, pages 59–80. Amsterdam: Benjamins.

Chomsky, N. (1986). *Barriers.* Cambridge, MA: MIT Pres.

Chomsky, N. (1995). *The minimalist program.* Cambridge, MA: MIT Press.

Cinque, G. (1996). The 'antisymmetric' programme: theoretical and typological implications. *Journal of Linguistics*, 32:447–464.

Culicover, P. and Rochemont, M. (1990). Extraposition and the complement principle. *Linguistic Inquiry*, 21:23–47.

Davis, H. and Alphonce, C. (1992). Parsing, linear asymmetry, and wh-movement. In *Proceedings of NELS 22*, pages 87–100, Amherst: GLSA.

Ernst, T. (1994). M-command and precedence. *Linguistic Inquiry*, 25:327–335.

Evers, A. (1975). *The transformational cycle in Dutch and German.* PhD thesis, Utrecht University.

Fodor, J. (1978). Parsing strategies and constraints on transformations. *Linguistic Inquiry*, 9:427–473.

Frazier, L. (1987). Syntactic processing: evidence from Dutch. *Natural Language and Linguistic Theory*, 5:519–559.

Frazier, L. (1993). Processing Dutch sentence structures. *Journal of Psycholinguistic Research*, 22:83–108.

Frazier, L. and Clifton, C. (1996). *Construal.* MIT Press.

Frazier, L. and Flores d'Arcais, G. (1989). Filler driven parsing: a study of gap filling in Dutch. *Journal of Memory and Language*, 28:331–344.

Frazier, L. and Rayner, K. (1982). Making and correcting errors during sentence comprehension: eye movements and the analysis of structurally ambiguous sentences. *Cognitive Psychology*, 14:178–210.

Gibson, E. (1991). *A computational theory of human linguistic processing: memory limitations and processing breakdown.* PhD thesis, Carnegie Mellon University, Pittsburgh.

Gibson, E. (1998). Linguistic complexity: locality of syntactic dependencies. *Cognition*, 68:1–76.

Gorrell, P. (1995). *Syntax and parsing.* Cambridge, MA: Cambridge University Press.

Greenberg, J. (1966). Some universals of grammar with particular reference to the order of meaningful elements. In Greenberg, J., editor, *Universals of Language (2nd edition)*, pages 73–113. Cambridge, MA: MIT Press.

Hoeksema, J. (1991). Complex predicates and liberation in Dutch and English. *Linguistics and Philosophy*, 14:661–710.

Just, M. and Carpenter, P. (1992). A capacity theory of comprehension: Individual differences in working memory. *Psychological Review*, 99:122–149.

Kaan, E. and Stowe, L. (2001). Storage and computation in sentence processing: a neuroimaging perspective. This volume.

Kayne, R. (1994). *The antisymmetry of syntax.* Cambridge, MA: MIT Press.

Kimball, J. (1973). Seven principles of surface structure parsing in natural language. *Cognition*, 2:15–47.

Kluender, R. (1998). On the distinction between strong and weak islands: a processing perspective. In Culicover, P. and McNally, L., editors, *Syntax and semantics 29: The limits of syntax*, pages 241–279. San Diego: Academic Press.

Koster, J. (1974). Het werkwoord als spiegelcentrum. *Spektator*, 3:601–618.

Lamarche, J. (1991). Problems for N^0-movement to NumP. *Probus*, 3:215–236.

Marcus, M., Hindle, D., and Fleck, M. (1983). D-theory: talking about talking about trees. In *Proceedings of the 21st annual meeting of the Association for Computational Linguistics*, pages 129–136. Cambridge, MA: MIT Press.

Neeleman, A. (1994). *Complex predicates.* PhD thesis, Utrecht University.

Neeleman, A. and Weerman, F. (1999). *Flexible syntax.* Dordrecht: Kluwer.

Pritchett, B. (1992). *Grammatical competence and parsing performance.* Chicago: University of Chicago Press.

Reuland, E. (1990). Head movement and the relation between morphology and syntax. In Booij, G. and Van Marle, J., editors, *Yearbook of morphology 1990*, pages 129–161. Dordrecht: Foris.

Rizzi, L. (1990). *Relativized minimality*. Cambridge, MA: MIT Press.

Roberts, I. (1985). *The representation of implicit and dethematized subjects*. PhD thesis, University of Southern California, Los Angeles.

Rochemont, M. (1992). Bounding rightward A'-dependencies. In Goodluck, H. and Rochemont, M., editors, *Island constraints*, pages 373–397. Dordrecht: Kluwer.

Rochemont, M. and Culicover, P. (1990). *English focus constructions and the theory of grammar*. Cambridge, MA: Cambridge University Press.

Ross, J. (1967). *Constraints on variables in syntax*. PhD thesis, MIT.

Sturm, A. and Kerstens, J. (1978). Over verklaren in de taalkunde. In van Putte, P. and Verkuyl, H., editors, *Nieuwe tegenstellingen op Nederlands taalgebied*, pages 130–172. Instituut de Vooys, Utrecht.

Van Riemsdijk, H. (1998). Head movement and adjacency. *Natural Language and Linguistic Theory*, 16:633–678.

Van Riemsdijk, H. and Williams, E. (1986). *Introduction to the theory of grammar*. Cambridge, MA: MIT Press.

Weinberg, A. (1988). *Locality principles in syntax and in parsing*. PhD thesis, MIT.

Whitman, J. (1991). String vacuous V to COMP. *GLOW Newsletter*, 26:62–63.

Chapter 9

STORAGE AND COMPUTATION IN SENTENCE PROCESSING

A Neuroimaging Perspective

Edith Kaan
and Laurie Stowe

Abstract In this article we review research relating to computation and to storage in working memory during sentence comprehension from two forms of neuroimaging. We relate this evidence to recent sentence processing models that suggest that these two are conceptually distinct. We show that research using neuroimaging methods that localize language functions and methods which track neuronal activity on-line suggest that computation and storage are supported by separate neuronal substrates.

Keywords: Language comprehension, working memory, positron emission tomography, event-related potentials, blood flow change.

1. Storage and computation in sentence processing

1.1. Introduction

When you hear or read a sentence, you construct syntactic and semantic representations on the basis of (roughly) word-by-word input. This process involves both storage and computation (Just and Carpenter, 1992; Gibson, 1998): computation, because in most cases, the sentence will not have been heard before, and corresponding syntactic and semantic representations need to be constructed; storage, because new input cannot always be directly combined into a complete representation, and partial representations have to be stored in working memory while new input is being processed.

S. Nooteboom et al. (eds.), Storage and Computation in the Language Faculty, 257–295.

In this paper we will deal with the conceptual distinction between storage and computation, and relate this distinction to brain imaging data that suggest that storage and computation are physiologically distinct processes. We will discuss data from two techniques investigating differences in blood flow (positron emission tomography (PET) and functional magnetic resonance imaging (fMRI)), and one technique which measures differences in electrical activity in the brain (event-related brain potentials, ERPs). Ideally the two techniques complement each other: event-related brain potentials can track brain activity on a millisecond by millisecond basis. Localization of the activity is, however, relatively inaccurate. On the other hand, techniques based on blood flow differences yield a rather precise localization, but do not provide any fine-grained data concerning the time course of the activity.

Localization techniques show that both the left inferior frontal gyrus (Broca's area) and an area within the posterior temporal lobe (part of classical Wernicke's area) support sentence comprehension. This confirms observations from aphasia data, which have implicated both these areas in sentence comprehension. However, neuroimaging data provide additional evidence on the cognitive functions of these areas, which suggests a radical reinterpretation of the functions generally assumed in models based on aphasia. We will argue that Broca's area is primarily involved in storage, whereas part of Wernicke's area is a better candidate for carrying out (aspects of) computation, although it is not clear whether this computation involves semantics or syntax. Electrophysiological responses also support a distinction between storage and computation. Storage is probably reflected in a slow negative wave, whereas computational difficulty is reflected in faster responses, which are distinct for semantic and syntactic computational difficulty.

1.2. Modelling sentence comprehension: computation and storage

First, let us be more concrete about what we understand by storage and computation in this paper. We will take a processing model along the lines of Gibson, 1998 as a basis for our discussion. In this model, when a word is read or heard, all syntactic and semantic features associated with it in the mental lexicon are activated. In addition, predictions are made concerning which syntactic categories are minimally needed to create a complete, grammatical sentence. For instance, when the first word of the sentence in (9.1), *a*, is recognized, the following information is activated: the word is a determiner; at least a noun and a finite verb are required in order to form a complete clause; the upcoming noun must be singular; the resulting NP is indefinite and probably denotes an entity that has not been mentioned previously in the discourse.

(9.1) A kitten sneezed.

What we will refer to as *storage* in the rest of this paper is the retention in working memory of incomplete representations, i.e. representations with a number of unsatisfied syntactic predictions. Note that in addition to category information, at least also case, number, and semantic information associated with the incomplete representation is maintained.

We use the term *computation* to refer to the integration of the current input with the syntactic and semantic representations that have already been constructed. For instance, in (9.1), integration takes place at the noun *kitten*: the noun meets the syntactic category prediction of, and hence is integrated with the article *a*. Another integration takes place at the verb *sneezed*, which must be integrated with the NP *a kitten*. Integration concerns the combination of the current input with a number of aspects of the preceding structure, including at least categorical, thematic and semantic features. When integration takes place, any syntactic category predictions that it fulfills are removed from working memory.

A sentence may be more or less complex depending on storage and computational demands. Following Gibson, 1998 we assume that storing syntactic category predictions becomes more demanding when more intervening material has to be processed before the predictions are met. Computation also becomes more difficult with increasing distance between the point at which the predictions were first made, and the point at which integration can take place.[1] To be more concrete, consider the subject relative in (9.2a) and the object relative in (9.2b).

(9.2) a. The senator who attacked the reporter admitted the error.

b. The senator who the reporter attacked admitted the error.

Numerous studies have shown that object relatives are harder to comprehend than subject relatives (cf. e.g. Holmes, 1973; Wanner and Maratsos, 1978; King and Just, 1991). In the model proposed by Gibson, the difficulty for object vs. subject-relatives is accounted for in the following way. When the relative pronoun *who* is encountered, the prediction is made that (i) a finite verb is needed to make a complete relative

[1]We are not concerned with an exact definition of distance here. For the remainder of this paper, the number of intervening words will serve our purposes. However cf. Gibson, 1998 for a more detailed proposal.

clause, and (ii) a trace is needed, by means of which the wh-phrase can receive a thematic role and be semantically and syntactically integrated into the representation. In the subject relative in (9.2a), these predictions are satisfied immediately at the next word: *attacked* is a finite verb, and a trace can be postulated in subject position. Both storage demands and integration costs are relatively low. In (9.2b), on the other hand, the predictions are met only after another noun phrase, *the reporter*, has been processed. This means, first, that storage is more demanding in (9.2b) compared to (9.2a), because the predictions have to be retained across a longer distance. In addition, the integration of the verb and trace with the wh-phrase is more difficult in (9.2b) than in (9.2a). This may be because the information associated with the wh-phrase has decayed while the intervening words were being processed. At the verb, then, extra resources are needed to reactivate these features in order to successfully integrate the verb and the wh-phrase. The processing difficulty of object versus subject relatives, according to the theory, therefore is due to an increase in both storage and computational demands.

1.3. Relating storage and computation to the brain

A model like Gibson's raises many issues about how various aspects of sentence processing are carried out in the brain. The conceptual distinction between computation and storage is clear, but it is not clear whether these two aspects of processing make use of the same resources, as suggested by Just and Carpenter, 1992 for example, or are separate. Further it is not clear whether different aspects of linguistic structure, such as syntactic and semantic structure, are computed and stored using the same resources, as claimed by Just and Carpenter, 1992 or by separate resources, as suggested by Waters et al., 1987 and Martin and Romani, 1994.

The correlation between storage demands and computational difficulty which we have just described makes it particularly hard to determine whether storage and computation share resources solely on the basis of behavioral data, e.g. reading times or off-line judgments. Longer reading times may reflect a relative increase in storage demands, computational demands, or both. Even word by word reading times remain ambiguous: suppose that one finds increased reading times at word positions following *who* in (9.2b) relative to (9.2a). One could argue that this increase is primarily caused by increased storage demands. However, one cannot tell whether the increase in reading times is caused by processes involved in retaining syntactic predictions in working memory, or by an increased computational difficulty when *the reporter* and following words are integrated under a concurrent memory load. So, although the distinction between storage and computation is conceptually clear, it is hard to distinguish the corresponding cognitive processes on the basis of behavioral data.

However, one way to try to distinguish the two is to see how storage and computational processes are instantiated in the brain. Are different parts of the brain differently affected by storage and computational manipulations? If so, this physiological distinction supports the view that the cognitive processes involved are different as well, at least at some level of description (cf. Rugg and Coles, 1995). In section 2 we will present evidence from blood flow change studies; in section 3 evidence from ERPs will be discussed. Both of these sources of evidence support the hypothesis that storage and computation make use of different neuronal resources.

2. Localization of sentence processing functions using regional cerebral bloodflow

2.1. Introduction

According to one very generally accepted model of localization of language functions in the brain, Broca's area (in the left inferior frontal gyrus) is responsible for syntactic processing. Wernicke's area (in the left posterior temporal lobe), on the other hand, is responsible for (lexical) semantic processing (Zurif et al., 1972; Caplan, 1986). We will now discuss evidence that suggests that Broca's area is responsible for storage during processing, while Wernicke's is responsible for (some aspects of) computation.

First we will show that both Broca's and Wernicke's area become more activated as sentential complexity increases.[2] Next, we will discuss evidence which (i) suggests that Broca's is not necessarily activated during the computation of a syntactic structure; (ii) shows that it is activated in storage tasks which are non-syntactic in nature; and (iii) that non-syntactic storage load affects syntactic storage demands. We will also show that Wernicke's area does not show any evidence of responding to

[2] We will use the terms *Wernicke's area* and *Broca's area* throughout the rest of the article to indicate the posterior left temporal lobe quite generally, and the ventral portion of the left inferior frontal gyrus, respectively. The locations of the (centers of the) activations reported in the various studies vary to some extent, but this variation is within reasonable limits given the techniques. Broca's area in our usage includes locations deeper than normally assumed in classical descriptions; the Wernicke's activations are in the lower and posterior part of what is normally sketched as Wernicke's area in textbooks.

storage demands. On the basis of these four types of evidence, we conclude that the distinction between storage and computation is supported by the existing evidence in the localization literature. At the end of this section we will discuss some of the limitations of this sort of data.

2.2. Techniques

In the studies which we will discuss below, positron emission tomography (PET) and functional magnetic resonance imaging (fMRI) were used to measure changes in regional cerebral blood flow. Both techniques make use of the fact that when an area of the brain is involved in a certain task, its metabolic activity increases, which leads to additional blood flow within this area. This change can be seen when regional blood flow in one condition is compared with the blood flow during a control condition in which less or no processing of a particular sort is necessary.

In PET, blood flow is measured by introducing a radioactive tracer into the body. The tracer most often used for cognitive brain imaging studies is radioactively labeled water, $H_2{}^{15}O$. This tracer is injected into the blood; therefore the image indicates how much blood flows through various regions of the brain. In functional MRI, regional differences in blood flow are detected by looking at differences in the amount of deoxygenated hemoglobin in the blood. Activated regions of the brain will contain blood with less deoxygenated hemoglobin than unactivated regions. These differences can be traced by placing the subject in a rapidly changing magnetic field, and looking at changes in the radio magnetic responses of the brain. Since deoxygenated hemoglobin affects the magnetic properties of the brain tissue, changes between two conditions can be clearly visualized with this technique.

2.3. Sentential complexity activates Broca's and Wernicke's areas

A number of studies have been carried out in which syntactically relatively simple structures are compared with more complicated sentences. Two areas of activation have quite consistently been found across these studies: Broca's area and Wernicke's area. Activations in these two areas are illustrated in Figure 9.1, below. Figure 9.2 illustrates the pattern of increasing blood flow seen in Broca's area as sentence complexity increases across three sentence conditions.

One of the earliest studies of this sort was carried out by Stromswold et al., 1996, using PET. They compared sentences containing center-embedded object relative clauses (9.3a) to sentences containing right-branching subject relative clauses, cf. (9.3b).

(9.3) a. The limerick that the boy recited appalled the priest.
b. The biographer omitted the story that insulted the queen.

In half of the sentences in the Stromswold et al. study, the first animate and inanimate NP were reversed, creating an anomalous sentence. Participants in the experiment were asked to read each sentence and give a plausibility judgment. The object relative clause condition showed activation of Broca's area relative to subject relative sentences.

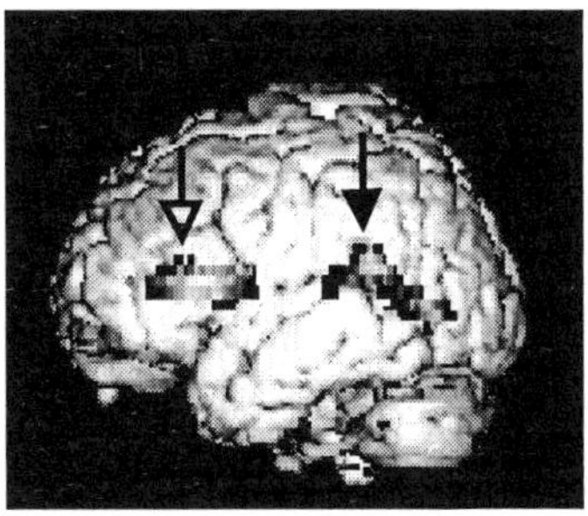

Figure 9.1. The location of temporal and frontal activations projected onto a view of the left hemisphere. The significant activation in Wernicke's area is indicated with a closed arrow; the significant activation in Broca's area is shown with an open arrow.

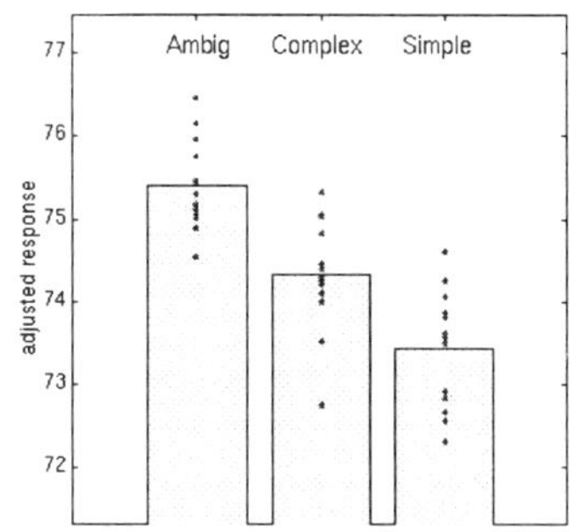

Figure 9.2. Plot of the regional blood flow in Broca's area under three sentence processing conditions, in ml blood flow per dl brain volume per minute, adjusted for global blood flow (data from Stowe et al., 1998).

Activation around Broca's area for object versus subject relatives has been replicated in a number of other studies. Stowe et al., 1995 also found a left frontal activation using PET. Caplan et al., 1998, experiment 1 replicated the frontal activation reported by Stromswold et al., 1996 using fMRI. In an additional PET study, Caplan et al., 1999 showed that clefts containing object relatives also cause left inferior frontal activation relative to clefts with subject relatives.

Activation in both Broca's and Wernicke's area has been reported by Just et al., 1996 using fMRI. They tested object relatives, subject relatives, and a third condition with conjoined VPs (cf. (9.4)).

(9.4) The boy recited the limerick and appalled the priest.

This sort of sentence is less complex than sentences containing an object relative clause as in (9.3a): no predictions have to be maintained across more than one word, although some computational difficulty may occur at *appalled*, since the matrix subject may need to be reactivated. Just et al., 1996 report an activation in Broca's area, in which blood flow increased from the simplest (conjoined VPs) to the most difficult condition (object relatives). In addition, a Wernicke's area activation was found for the same three level comparison.

A PET activation in Wernicke's area has also been reported by Broere et al., 1997 for center-embedded clauses (cf. (9.5a)) relative to right-adjoined clauses (cf. (9.5b)).[3]

(9.5) a. De stoere held heeft de kleine drenkeling,
The brave hero has the small drowning-child,
hoewel de gasten niets hebben gezien, gered.
although the guests nothing have seen, saved.

b. De stoere held heeft de kleine drenkeling
The brave hero has the small drowning-child
gered, hoewel de gasten niets hebben gezien.
saved, although the guests nothing have seen.

These sentences are comparable to the English object and subject relatives in that the (a) and (b) sentences differ in both computational and storage demands. At the position of *drenkeling* in both sentences, a lexical verb is needed to assign a thematic role to both the subject and the object. In (9.5b) this verb, *gered*, follows the NPs immediately; in (9.5a), on the other hand, an intervening adjunct clause has to be processed first. Storage demands are therefore much higher in (9.5a) than in (9.5b). In addition, (9.5a) is more costly in terms of computation: integration of the verb should be harder in (9.5a), because information associated with the main clause nouns is likely to have decayed before the lexical verb is processed, and must be reactivated.

We conclude with an example from our own research, showing activation in both Broca's and Wernicke's areas (data shown in Figure 9.1). Stowe et al., 1998 used PET to compare simple sentences (9.6a), complex sentences containing center-embedded clauses (9.6b), and a third condition containing syntactically ambiguous sentences, as in (9.6c).

[3]Several kinds of center-embedded constructions were employed in this study, including adverbial clauses as in the example, relative clauses, and embedded subject clauses. Each was contrasted with a right-embedded control. The most important point here is that the embedded clauses were identical across the two conditions except for their position; they did not differ in internal structure.

(9.6)

a.

Ze	wilden	interviews	met	de	journalisten	niet
They	wanted	interviews	with	the	journalists	not

uitzenden.
to-broadcast.

b.

Of	hogere	straffen,	waartegen
Whether	more-severe	punishments,	against-which

rechters	protesteren,	dergelijke	gevallen	voorkomen,
judges	protest,	similar	cases	prevent

kan	betwijfeld	worden.
can	doubted	be.

c.

Ze	kunnen	bakken	met
They	can	bake(verb)/containers(noun)	with

zulk	deeg	niet	verplaatsen.
such	dough	not	move.

The sentences in the simple condition contained only one clause, and did not require heavy storage or computation. Sentences in the complex condition generally consisted of several clauses, and were rather demanding in terms of storage and computation.[4] In the example in (9.6b) *of* signals the beginning of a clausal subject. At this position, at least two verbs are predicted in order to form a complete sentence: the verb in the embedded clause (satisfied by *voorkomen*), and the main clause verb (satisfied by *kan* or the lexical verb *betwijfeld*). Furthermore, the main clause predicate is passive, which requires the postulation and binding of syntactic traces. While these syntactic category predictions are being stored, a relative clause (introduced at *waartegen*) must be processed, with its own storage and computational demands.

The third condition consisted of sentences containing syntactically ambiguous words (*bakken* in (9.6c), which can either be a verb or a noun). The sentences were disambiguated only several words later. In all cases, the disambiguation was towards the less frequent reading of the ambiguous word. This type of sentence is demanding in terms of storage and computation: either two different syntactic and semantic representations are pursued from the point of ambiguity and must be retained in working memory, or only one reading is pursued, which has to be revised when disambiguating information comes in. During this revision, parts of the representation that are internally unaffected by the

[4]The complex sentences contained embeddings and list-like constructions: four sentences containing center-embedded clauses or adjectival verb phrases, one center-embedded gapping construction, two right-branching embedded clauses plus non-canonical order (passive and object relative), and one noun phrase in which the noun was preceded by three adjectives.

ambiguity (e.g. the PP *met zulk deeg*) need to be stored in order to be reattached to the new syntactic tree. In this study activity was shown to increase in both Broca's and Wernicke's areas as complexity increased from simple (9.6a) to complex (9.6b) to ambiguous sentences (9.6c), just as in the Just et al., 1996 study. This pattern of increasing activation is shown graphically in Figure 9.2.

In sum, a number of studies report increased activity with increasing syntactic complexity in Broca's and/or Wernicke's area, using a range of syntactic constructions and complexity manipulations. However, on the basis of these data alone, one cannot readily distinguish between areas involved in storage, and areas involved in computation. In the complex conditions, both storage and computation become more demanding relative to the sentences in the simple conditions. Below, however, we will argue that Broca's area is responsible for storage, whereas Wernicke's seems more likely to be involved in computation.

2.4. Evidence against computation in Broca's area: Broca's area does not carry out most aspects of syntactic processing

According to a common view of the neurological basis of language Broca's area is involved in syntactic processing, while Wernicke's area carries out word recognition and semantic processing. This model is based on studies of aphasics who have suffered damage to the posterior temporal lobe (Wernicke's area) and have severe comprehension deficits as a result, with relatively intact production. Damage to the inferior frontal gyrus (Broca's area) results in the inability to construct a syntactic structure in production.[5] Patients who exhibit a pattern of agrammatic production generally also have problems with sentence comprehension. A deficit in the ability to compute a syntactic structure could explain both deficits. However, evidence from both neuroimaging and aphasia suggests that Broca's area is not involved in all aspects of syntactic processing.

Brain imaging studies immediately raise some issues for the hypothesis that Broca's area supports *all* aspects of syntactic processing. Broca's area frequently shows no or very little activation when simple sentences are compared to a neutral baseline condition. This was first observed by Mazoyer et al., 1993 who found a PET activation in Broca's area for complete texts, but not for individual sentences, although these clearly

[5]There are a number of issues about the association between deficit and location of lesion which we will not discuss here; the evidence is certainly not as clear cut as we present it here.

involve processing of syntactic structure. Stowe et al., 1994 and Stowe et al., 1998 also failed to find activation in Broca's area for simple sentences relative to passive fixation, using PET. Areas activated during the reading of simple sentences containing no embedded clauses are shown in Figure 9.3A. There is no significant activation in Broca's area (area indicated by the arrow), although even simple sentences would be expected to cause significant activation in an area which is responsible for syntactic processing. In Figure 9.3B, areas activated during the reading of syntactically ambiguous sentences are shown. Broca's area is clearly activated in this comparison (area indicated by the arrow). Both sentence types show extensive activation in the left temporal lobe, including Wernicke's area, however.[6]

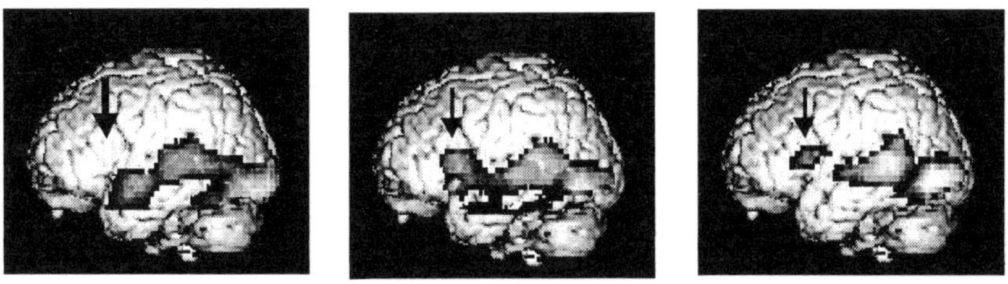

A: Simple Sentences B: Ambiguous Sentences C: Word Lists

Figure 9.3. Activation in Broca's area relative to passive fixation for simple sentences (9.3A), ambiguous sentences (9.3B) and word lists (9.3C). Broca's area is marked in each panel with an arrow. Activation is also seen in left motor cortex for complex sentences and word lists.

Evidence from aphasia also suggests that Broca's area does not support syntactic processing in general. Grodzinsky, 2000 reviews evidence that shows that in general, agrammatic (Broca's) aphasics are able to recognize ungrammaticality (Haarmann and Kolk, 1994). Further, it has been shown that agrammatics produce phrase types that are locally grammatical, although they do not form a grammatically complete sentence (Bastiaanse and Van Zonneveld, 1998). Agrammatics' prob-

[6]One may object that the lack of activation in Broca's area is due to the baseline condition. When subjects are asked to fixate on a point on the screen, their attention is not fully engaged and they are likely to think about other matters. For this reason, regional blood flow in this condition tends to be relatively variable, which could make it difficult to detect statistically a real difference between the simple sentence condition and the baseline. However, this cannot be the entire explanation for the lack of activation: more complex sentences did show clear activation relative to this baseline, which suggests that the variability of the baseline cannot be too extreme.

lems with structure are thus more limited than would be expected if the "syntax" area had been destroyed or damaged to any great extent.

The constructions that are the most difficult for aphasics are those which contain a syntactic dependency between a moved XP and a trace (as in wh-questions, relative clauses and passives). Grodzinsky therefore hypothesizes that agrammatic aphasics have a deficit in a specific type of syntactic computation, establishing an XP-trace dependency. We agree with Grodzinsky that the hypothesis that syntactic computation resides in Broca's area is too strong. However the function of Broca's area in comprehension extends beyond the processing of XP-trace dependencies. Recall from section 2.3 that syntactically ambiguous sentences such as in (9.6c) caused a clear increase in blood flow, even though they contained no more XP-trace dependencies than the simple condition (9.6a) and definitely less than the unambiguous, complex conditions (9.6b). In Figure 9.2, the relative blood flow over the three sentence conditions was shown. These data suggest that the function of Broca's area in sentence comprehension is not limited to establishing XP-trace dependencies.

We propose that Broca's area is not responsible for computation, but rather for storage of incomplete syntactic representations. Maintenance of XP's in an XP-trace dependency is the paradigmatic case of storage, which explains the activation of this area by wh-constructions (object relatives) in neuroimaging studies. If the storage function is damaged, aphasics will also have difficulty in understanding these constructions. The same function is also necessary for producing complete or complex syntactic structures, which explains why this patient population has difficulty producing grammatical sentences.

2.5. Evidence for storage in Broca's area

We will now turn to two sorts of evidence about the function of Broca's area that suggest that it is involved in the storage of verbal information. The first is evidence that shows that the same area of the brain that is activated for complex sentences is also activated by non-syntactic verbal input. Next, we will discuss evidence that this area is involved in the storage of both lexical and phrasal information.

2.5.1 Word lists. Broca's area is also activated during reading or storage of unstructured word lists. Word lists do not require computation of sentence structure, although they require storage. This observation was originally made by Mazoyer et al., 1993, who reported that word lists activated Broca's area, although their individual sentences did not do so. A similar result was found by Stowe et al., 1998.

Figure 9.3C shows the comparison between word lists like those in (9.7) and a condition in which participants were fixating on an asterisk.

(9.7)	koning	graag	onmogelijk	zouden	ontbijt	vrijwel
	king	gladly	impossible	shall	breakfast	nearly
	taaltje	rechters	Joost			
	language	judges	Joost(name)			

As can be seen, there is significant activation for word lists in Broca's area. These data are from the same volunteers as those in Figure 9.3A and B. The activation is comparable to that evoked by complex (ambiguous) sentences (Figure 9.3B), and stronger than that seen in the same subjects for simple sentences relative to passive fixation (cf. 9.3A). If Broca's area is primarily responsible for syntactic processing, this result is unexpected. These findings, however, support our hypothesis that Broca's area is responsible for storage.

In both the Mazoyer et al. and the Stowe et al. study, participants were asked to passively read or listen to the word lists rather than actively remembering them. However, results from a number of working memory studies suggest that Broca's area is consistently activated by storage of words. Activation is found whether (i) participants are asked to memorize a list presented during the scan (e.g. Grasby et al., 1994); (ii) participants are asked to maintain a short list presented before the beginning of the scan until after the scan is finished (e.g. Fiez et al., 1996); (iii) participants are asked to continuously update a short list for comparison with new input (n-back task; e.g. Awh et al., 1996); or, (iv) participants are asked to recall or to recognize words out of a short study list presented before the beginning of the scan (e.g. Buckner et al., 1996). This is compatible with an interpretation of the word list activation as a memory effect.

Furthermore, the activations found in these latter experiments cannot be explained in most of these experiments as resulting from implicit, although unsuccessful, syntactic processing. This explanation might have accounted for the activation found in the Stowe et al., 1998 experiment. However, the force of this suggestion is considerably diminished by the consistent activation found in memory tasks, which it cannot explain. It should be noted that the location of the left frontal activations found in these memory tasks is nearly identical to that of those found during sentence processing. This set of results is compatible with the hypothesis that Broca's area supports a storage function that may be employed in both sentence processing and short-term memory tasks.

Wernicke's area, on the other hand, is not typically activated during verbal memory tasks. Note that the left temporal lobe, including Wernicke's area, is activated less extensively for word lists than for either of the two sentence conditions in Figure 9.3. Thus these experiments do not provide any evidence that Wernicke's area supports storage.

2.5.2 Storage of phrasal information. In the previous section we showed that Broca's area supports a cognitive function which is consistently invoked when subjects must store words for short periods of time. On the basis of these data one might conclude that Broca's area stores only lexical information. However, during sentence processing, it is also necessary to store predictions and other information about incomplete phrases. The question is thus whether both types of information are stored in the same area.

Stowe et al., 1998 pointed out that words are clearly stored in Broca's area only until a syntactic representation, e.g. a phrase, is produced, otherwise there would be no explanation for the sentential complexity effects observed in Broca's area which we discussed in section 2.3. So, if only lexical information is stored in Broca's area, and if lexical items are stored until a phrase is constructed, unstructured word lists should activate Broca's area more than the most complex sentences. This is because no phrase is produced and thus the words cannot be dismissed from working memory. On the other hand, if both lexical items and incomplete syntactic structure are stored in Broca's area, then the most complex sentences should activate Broca's area more than unstructured word lists. Both lexical and structural information are stored in the complex condition, whereas the word list condition only involves storage of lexical items.

These predictions were tested by Stowe et al., 1998. The pattern of blood flow is shown in Figure 9.4. More activation was found in Broca's area for syntactically ambiguous sentences, their most complex condition, than for word lists, although word lists showed more activation than simple sentences, which do not require extensive storage of either words or phrases. This supports the hypothesis that both lexical and structural information is stored in Broca's area during sentence comprehension.

This experiment suggests at least that both lexical and structural information is stored in Broca's area. It leaves open the possibility that two separate neuronal networks in this area support two separate storage functions. A way to investigate this issue is to test whether activation due to syntactic complexity is affected by word list retention (or vice versa). If two processes are subserved by the same neuronal structures, they must share the available resources. As storage demands increase during sentence processing, the amount of resources available

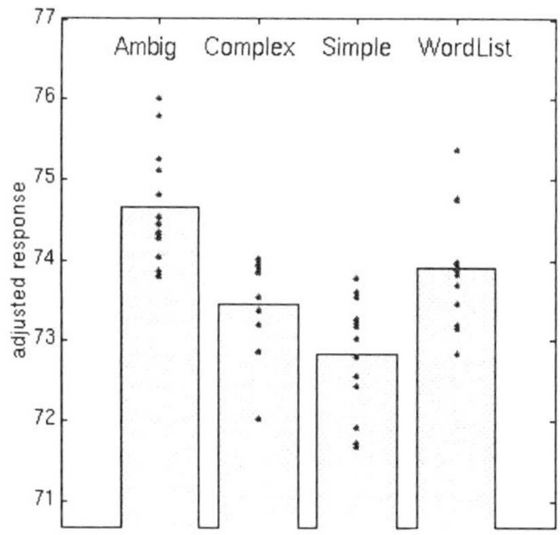

Figure 9.4. Storage demands and blood flow in Broca's area: Word lists are compared with simple sentences, more complex sentences and with ambiguous sentences, which were most complex. Activation level is given in ml blood flow per dl brain volume per minute, adjusted for global blood flow (data from Stowe et al., 1998).

to carry out a verbal memory task will decrease. A PET study which investigated this prediction was reported by Stowe et al., in press. They asked participants in the experiment to read one and two clause sentences like those in (9.8).

(9.8) a. De stoere held heeft de kleine drenkeling
The brave hero has the small drowning-person
gered. De gasten hadden niets gezien.
saved. The guests have nothing seen.

b. De stoere held heeft de kleine drenkeling,
The brave hero has the small drowning-person,
hoewel de gasten niets hebben gezien, gered.
although the guests nothing have seen, saved.

The two-clause sentence in (9.8b) is more demanding than (9.8a) in terms of storage, as the predictions of the incomplete first clause have to be retained while the adjunct clause is processed. To manipulate lexical memory load, the participants were asked to monitor for words out of a short list containing one word or a longer list containing five words which had been presented at the beginning of the scan (cf. Vos et al., 2001) and to respond as soon as they saw one of the words during the scan. The activation in Broca's area in response to the length of the word list was quite different for the complex sentences than for the simple sentences, see Figures 9.5A and 9.5B.

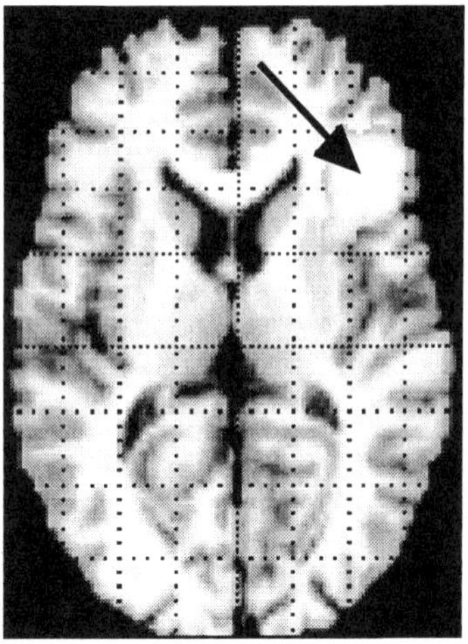

Figure 9.5A. Area which showed a significant interaction between verbal memory load and syntactic complexity. The activated area is projected on a standard MRI slice viewed from below so that the left hemisphere appears on the right. The front of the head is at the top, back at the bottom.

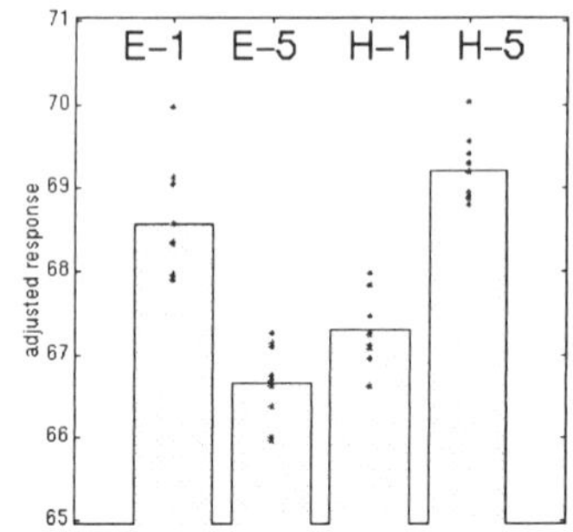

Figure 9.5B. The form of the interaction, E = easy sentences; H = complex sentences; 1 = one word list; 5 = five word list.

This pattern of results suggests strongly that any account of the function of Broca's area which assumes that there are two separate functions must be incorrect, since this hypothesis predicts that the use of one function will occur quite independently of the other and thus that the pattern of blood flow changes will not depend on the combination of the two loads.

However, the form of the interaction which is seen here is unexpected. When sentence complexity was low and the amount of verbal information to be retained was limited (E1: easy sentences with low memory load), subjects used Broca's area more extensively than when either one or the other of the factors had a heavier load. Presumably this is because this combination of the two factors taxed this area more in some way. Although a full discussion of this result is beyond the scope of this paper, we will consider one possibility why this pattern was found.

There was also a main effect of memory load in a completely separate area located in the left occipital lobe. This area supports visual processing in general and has been reported for visual working memory tasks (Fiez et al., 1996). We thus interpret this activation as a visual memory store which is used to carry out the memory task, similar to Baddeley's visuospatial sketch pad (Baddeley, 1986). Thus, not only verbal memory, but also visual memory was used to carry out the explicit memory task. An additional point is that this area showed a tendency to become more extensive when the sentential complexity or the word load was increased (in conditions E5 and H1). Taken together, these results suggest that as verbal memory load increased either due to additional words in memory (E5) or to additional sentential complexity (H), resources became less available to subjects, so that they attempted to carry out the explicit verbal memory task using this visual memory store rather than the verbal storage system insofar as that was possible. The result of such a switch in strategy for the E5 and H1 conditions could be a decrease in activation relative to the simplest condition (E1). Under the assumption that it is not possible to entirely block use of the verbal storage system in this task, however, the H5 condition with combined load would still be expected to lead to increased verbal storage demands. This explanation suggests that the use of Broca's area to carry out an explicit verbal memory task is at least partially under control and can to some extent be avoided if there are insufficient resources to carry out the task.

Clearly further research is necessary to verify this hypothesis; nevertheless, the fact that the blood flow response to the size of the word lists is affected by the demand being made on the area by complex vs. simple sentences supports the hypothesis that a single neuronal mechanism in Broca's area subserves storage of both lexical and structural information.[7]

Both of the experiments just discussed suggest that Broca's area is involved in storage of verbal information, including syntactic structural information, during sentence processing. Neither experiment suggests that Wernicke's area is involved in a comparable process, since the activation patterns predicted for storage were not found in this area. We will now turn to evidence for the function of Wernicke's area during the processing of sentences.

[7]We should point out that the evidence provided by the two experiments just discussed argue not only against a purely lexical interpretation of the storage function of this area but also against an "articulatory" interpretation. It has frequently been assumed in discussions of verbal working memory activations that the representation maintained in this area is articulatory (Paulesu et al., 1993; Smith et al., 1996), but an incomplete phrase is clearly represented in some more abstract way. In this sense, the current results are consistent with the claim of the theory based on aphasic data that Broca's area does not simply provide an articulatory motor plan for an intended utterance.

2.6. Evidence for computation in Wernicke's area

If computation does not occur in Broca's area, then where does it occur? We would like to suggest that Wernicke's area, or more probably an even more extensive part of the left temporal lobe, is a good candidate for this function as concluded by Grodzinsky, 2000. As we have already seen, sentence conditions lead to a more extensive activation of the temporal lobe than word lists (cf. Figure 9.3). Moreover, the posterior temporal lobe was the only other location in which blood flow increased as sentential complexity increased. Finally, as pointed out in section 2.5, there is no evidence that this area is involved in storage. The left temporal lobe including Wernicke's area is thus the most likely candidate for subserving computation of sentence structure.

This hypothesis makes specific predictions about blood flow in this area. If Wernicke's area is involved in sentential computation, this area should be more highly activated during the processing of simple sentences than word lists: in the former a structure needs to be computed, but not in the latter. Results from the study conducted by Stowe et al., 1998 confirm this prediction: the word list condition produced less regional blood flow in Wernicke's area than simple sentences and still less than other more complex sentence types, cf. Figure 9.6). Thus, the results that are currently available support the claim that Wernicke's area is not involved in storage, but rather supports some aspect of computation during sentence comprehension.

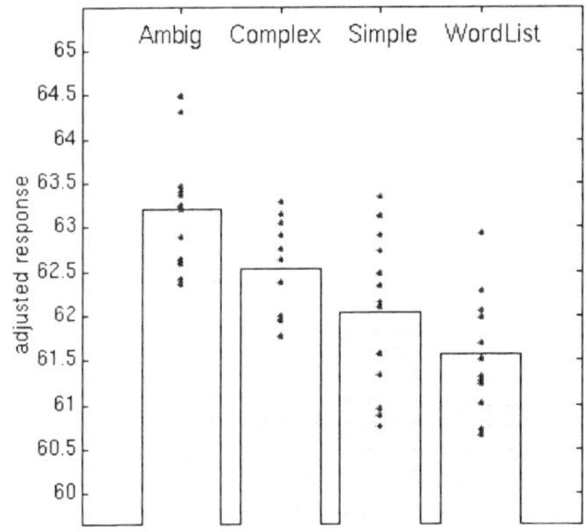

Figure 9.6. Blood flow in Wernicke's area across four processing conditions: Activation increases with computational load (activation given in in ml blood flow per dl brain volume per minute, adjusted for global blood flow; data from Stowe et al., 1998.

Up to this point we have not considered the kind of computation that is carried out in Wernicke's area. Is it syntactic or semantic, or both? Are semantic and syntactic computation subserved by different areas of the brain? Although we raised these issues in the introduction, in the discussion up to this point we have assumed that the sentential complexity manipulations which have produced activation in Broca's and Wernicke's areas are primarily syntactic in nature: that is, that the representations being stored, and the computations being carried out are primarily syntactic. The assumption that manipulation of syntactic complexity tests only aspects of syntactic processing is, however, problematic. When syntactic complexity is manipulated, semantic computational complexity may also increase, since the combination of lexical semantics via the syntactic instructions becomes more complex. Therefore, we cannot argue on the basis of these studies that the activation in Wernicke's area is caused solely or primarily by syntactic processing. The function of the left posterior temporal lobe may combine syntactic and semantic computation, or even represent solely semantic computation. Equally, the frontal activation may represent storage of semantic information as well as syntactic information. We will return to the issue of whether semantic and syntactic processing can be distinguished in the section on ERP research.

The suggestion that Wernicke's area may be primarily involved in semantic computation is compatible with the observation that aphasics with lesions in Wernicke's area have noticeable semantic deficits, whereas their syntax is relatively intact, at least, in mild Wernicke's aphasics. However, it would leave open the question of where syntactic computation takes place. No other areas are obvious candidates for this function, but that may be explained by one of the limitations of the technique discussed in the next section.

2.7. Conclusions and caveats

To conclude, the evidence from blood flow change studies is consistent with the hypothesis that at least two areas in the brain are involved in sentence comprehension. On the evidence available, Broca's area is not responsible for syntactic computation. Rather it appears to be responsible for the storage of lexical and structural information during sentence processing for use by later computational processes. Wernicke's area, on the other hand, appears to be involved in some form of computation.

One disadvantage of looking at blood flow changes, however, is that the blood flow response is rather slow. In general, it takes about 2-6 seconds after onset of a stimulus before the blood flow response measured with fMRI becomes maximal. In PET, one scan must span about 40 seconds in order to obtain a reasonably clear map of regional cerebral blood flow. Blood flow techniques therefore only track the brain's reaction to an entire sentence (event-related fMRI) or a block of sentences of a certain type (PET). Since the complexity of a sentence as a whole is a combination of storage and computational demands, it is difficult to tease apart storage and computation using these techniques, although as we have shown, they provide data which forms an important source of evidence for this issue. Further, due to the time necessary for the measurement the technique may be more sensitive to long-lasting effects, such as storage demands, than it is to short-lived effects, such as a difference in computational complexity which occurs at a single word. This may account for the lack of a plausible candidate for an area supporting syntactic computation.

If brain activity can be tracked word by word, one may be able to distinguish storage from computation more easily. In an object relative like (9.9), activation reflecting the maintenance of syntactic predictions in working memory should begin at the word *who* and continue over the intervening words, until the predictions are satisfied at the verb *attacked.*

(9.9) The senator who the reporter attacked admitted the error.

Effects of computational difficulty are expected primarily at the verb *attacked* where integration takes place between who and the verb. Due to its temporal characteristics, however, blood flow imaging is not suitable to investigate these issues.

3. Event-related potentials

3.1. Introduction

One technique that has the time resolution necessary to look at language processing on line is to record changes in electrical activity in the brain. With this technique of event-related brain potentials (ERPs) it is possible to track brain activity on a millisecond by millisecond basis. Below we will first briefly introduce the ERP technique. Next we will discuss ERP components that may be associated with storage and computation.

3.2. Technique

ERPs are obtained by recording an electroencephalogram (EEG) from scalp electrodes, while a person is presented with stimuli (e.g. words which form a sentence). Next, the EEG is averaged for various categories of stimuli (e.g. words which make a sentence grammatical or ungrammatical). Random brain activity is thus averaged out, leaving a clearer view of the actual response to the stimulus. The resulting event-related potentials (ERP) are commonly presented as a graph of the mean voltages at a particular electrode site, starting from the time at which the stimulus is presented. Usually two or more conditions are plotted against each other. For example, in Figure 9.7 ERPs are plotted for the responses to verbs that agreed with the subject in number (grammatical, solid line) or did not agree (ungrammatical, dotted line) at the midline parietal electrode. The intercept on the x-axis represents the time point at which the verb was presented; the y-axis is the voltage in microVolts, relative to a 100 ms prestimulus baseline.

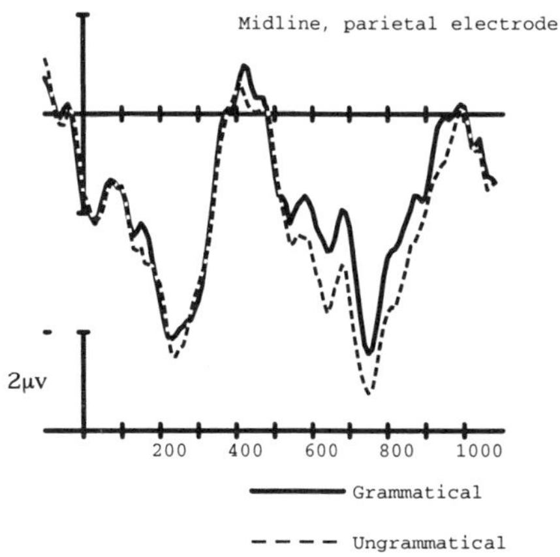

Figure 9.7. ERPs to a grammatical verb (solid line) vs. an ungrammatical verb (dotted line) at the midline parietal electrode. X-axis: time in milliseconds from the onset of the verb; Y-axis: voltage in microVolts. Data from Kaan et al., 2000, Exp. 2.

Several components of an ERP wave can be distinguished on the basis of (i) their polarity (positive or negative), (ii) time of onset, (iii) amplitude difference, and (iv) the distribution of the size of the response across electrode positions at the scalp. Although the polarity and scalp distribution of a particular response do not directly indicate the location of the source, a difference in polarity and distribution between two components shows that the neural sources generating the scalp potentials are different.[8] ERPs therefore potentially allow us to distinguish storage from computational processes. If different ERP components are affected by an increase in storage demands compared to computational demands,

[8]Note that the ERP response is not necessarily largest over the generator. However, the same generator always produces the same distribution.

storage and computation are supported by different groups of neurons. This argues that storage must be distinguished from computation at the cognitive level as well.

Furthermore, since EEG is measured continuously across the sentence, a response that is associated with storage demands can be distinguished from a response that is caused by local computational load in the time domain. As we saw in section 1.1, storage comes into play when e.g. syntactic category predictions have to be maintained in working memory across several words and phrases; computation, on the other hand, occurs immediately when a particular word can be integrated into the current structure. Slow ERP waves which can continue over whole phrases are therefore likely to reflect storage demands, while short term ERP responses in the order of 50-500 milliseconds are more likely to reflect immediate computational processes. Below we will discuss components that have been found to be associated with storage during sentence processing, and components that may reflect computational difficulty.

3.3. Storage: slow anterior negative wave

Difficulty due to storage of partial representations is likely to be reflected in a long-term deflection of the ERP signal that starts at a point where syntactic predictions are generated, and ends when the predictions are satisfied by new input. A slow component that has repeatedly been found for sentences involving retention of syntactic predictions is a slow negative wave with a (left) frontal distribution, i.e. the response is strongest at frontal electrodes, and sometimes, but not always, the response is stronger over the left hemisphere than the right.[9]

3.3.1 Storage during sentence processing. The first study to report this slow wave for sentence processing is King and Kutas, 1995. They compared center-embedded subject and object relatives in English as in (9.10):

(9.10) a. The fireman who speedily rescued the cop sued the city.
b. The fireman who the cop speedily rescued sued the city.

As already mentioned, the object relative in (9.10b) is more demanding than the subject relative in (9.10a). One account for this difficulty

[9]Another component that sometimes is thought to be associated with the use of storage is a short term left anterior negativity (LAN), occurring around 300-500 msec after onset (Kluender and Kutas, 1993). This component has been reported for positions at which a wh-phrase can be assumed to be shunted to or retrieved from working memory. However, the studies reporting this component suffer from baseline and lexical differences at the critical positions, hence the effects are not easy to interpret, and will not be discussed further here.

is that the syntactic category predictions associated with *who*, namely a verb and a trace, have to be stored over a longer distance in (9.10b) than in (9.10a). King and Kutas report a slow negative wave for the object relative vs. the subject relative, cf. Figure 9.8. This waveform was especially prominent at left frontal sites. The deflection started at the point where the two conditions begin to differ in memory load, namely at the first article and noun in the object-relative (*the cop*) compared to the adverb and the verb (*speedily rescued*) in the subject relative conditions. This suggests that the slow frontal negative wave reflects memory load. This component also correlated with success in comprehension: King & Kutas report that the component was larger for participants in the experiment who performed well on subsequent comprehension questions, compared to participants who performed less well.

A slow negative shift is also reported by Kluender and Münte, 1998 for object vs. subject initial wh-questions in German:

(9.11) a. Wer meinst du, soll den sympathischen
who-nom think you should the-acc nice
Probanden nach der Studie für die Teilnahme
subject after the study for the participation
entlohnen?
compensate?

Who do you think should compensate the subject for participation after the study?

b. Wen meinst du, soll der eifrige
who-acc think you should the-nom eager
Wissenschaftler nach der Studie für die
scientist after the study for the
Teilnahme entlohnen?
participation compensate?

Who do you think the eager scientist should compensate for participation after the study?

In (9.11a) the wh-phrase is marked as a nominative and can be linked to its subject position at the verb *soll*. In (9.11b), on the other hand, the sentence initial element, *wen*, is marked as the object. The verb which *wen* is an object of only comes at the end of the clause. Hence, (9.11b) differs from (9.11a) in that the sentence initial element must be stored across several word positions. Kluender & Münte report a fronto-central slow negative wave for (9.11b) versus (9.11a), which started at the matrix verb and continued for at least seven words after the wh-phrase.

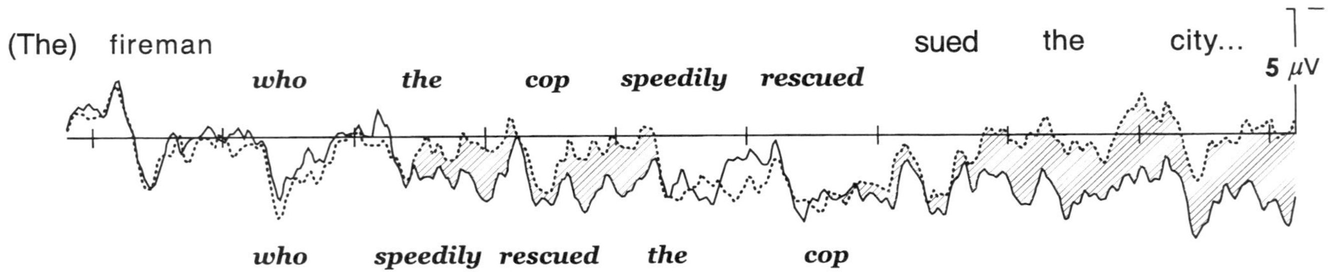

Figure 9.8. Comparison of the grand-average cross-sentence ERPs elicited by subject relative (solid line) and object relative sentences (dotted line) recorded over a left anterior location. The two sentence types are equivalent both before and after the relative clause. The relative clause above the baseline is an example of an object relative and that below the baseline is an example of a subject relative. Words were presented one at a time every 0.5s for a duration of 200 ms. The shading represents the area within which object relative sentences are reliably more negative than the subject relative sentences. Reprinted with permission from Kutas, 1997.

This slow frontal negative wave is not restricted to the processing of wh-constructions, or retention of syntactic representations. A similar response is also elicited when semantic representations must be retained. Münte et al., 1998 compared ERPs measured across two clause sentences starting with *before* vs. *after*:

(9.12) a. After the scientist submitted the paper, the journal changed its policy.

b. Before the scientist submitted the paper, the journal changed its policy.

Before clauses have been argued to be more taxing in terms of memory and processing load because the temporal relation between the propositions expressed by the two clauses is the reverse of the linear order in which the clauses appear. Münte et al. report a slow negative wave, with a left anterior focus for *before* compared to *after* sentences. This negativity started at *before* and continued to increase over the course of the sentence. The magnitude of this effect correlated with working memory span as defined by an independent working memory task (cf. Daneman and Carpenter, 1980): participants with a high working memory score showed a larger negativity for *before* vs. *after* clauses.

There is therefore reason to think that the slow negative wave may be an index of difficulty due to storage of partial semantic and syntactic representations. However, an alternative view is that it reflects increased computational demands in integrating incoming words. Additional evidence is necessary to decide between these two interpretations. The storage interpretation of the slow negative wave predicts (i) that a similar slow wave is obtained in memory tasks that do not involve sentence processing, and (ii) that since storage of lexical information and of syntactic predictions both share neuronal resources, the slow wave found for syntactic complexity will be affected by concurrent lexical memory load. These two predictions are analogous to those that were made with respect to the blood flow activation in Broca's area (section 2.5). Additionally, in order to claim that the slow wave component reflects storage rather than computation, one must show that integration difficulty elicits an ERP response with a completely different morphology. We will return to this latter point in section 3.4. Let us first discuss the two hypotheses made by the storage hypothesis.

3.3.2 Storage of word lists. With respect to the first prediction, a frontal slow negative wave has also been reported for tasks involving retention of verbal material, without sentence processing. For example, Ruchkin et al., 1990 had their subjects retain a string of six consonants, which could consist of one, three or six different letters.[10] After a delay of 2.5 seconds, a target letter was presented, and the subjects had to decide whether it was a member of the string presented earlier. During the delay period, ERPs for the six letter condition showed a frontal slow wave relative to the one and three letter conditions.

Ruchkin et al., 1992 replicated this left frontal negativity in a study in which people were requested to retain pseudoword strings which were 3, 4 or 5 CV syllables in length. The syllables within a pseudoword were all different. The left frontal slow wave was more negative with larger loads (longer strings). Ruchkin et al., 1992 contrasted memory load in this task with the load caused by a similar spatial memory task in which subjects had to remember the locations of the stimuli. The verbal and spatial slow waves differed in scalp distribution, which suggests that the frontal wave reflects a verbal representation of the input.

To sum up, tasks that require the short-term retention of verbal material elicit a slow anterior negative wave, resembling the slow negativity seen for retention of unintegrated material during sentence processing. This correspondence is in line with our view that the slow wave is an index of storage rather than computational demands.

3.3.3 Interaction between word list storage and storage for sentence processing. The studies cited in the previous two sections do not directly compare list retention with storage of partial representations during sentence processing, unfortunately. Although the negative waves look similar, it is difficult to compare scalp distribution from two subject populations, since small variations in brain morphology affect ERP morphology quite strongly (Kutas et al., 1988). One can therefore not conclude that these slow waves index cognitive processes supported by the same neuronal source.

If storage of lists and of unintegrated syntactic representations is supported by the same neuronal mechanisms, one would expect the slow wave found in sentence processing to be affected by the additional load of retaining a list and vice versa. The only ERP study that we are aware of that investigated sentence processing with a concurrent memory load is Vos et al., 2001. Vos et al. had participants remember lists of 1 (low load) or 3 words (high load). Each list was followed by a rather long sentence, containing either a subject relative clause, or a conjoined verb phrase. The task was a word monitoring task: participants had to press a button when one of the words in the sentence was a member of the

[10] A very similar task has been shown to activate Broca's area using PET (e.g. Paulesu et al., 1993; Awh et al., 1996).

word list that had previously been presented. Starting from the first word of the sentence, high load conditions showed a slow negative wave relative to the low load condition, with a maximum at frontal sites. The negativity was stronger for those subjects in the experiment who had a smaller working memory span as determined by an independent test. This replicates the findings reported above that verbal memory load is reflected in a slow negative wave.

However, Vos et al. did not find any modification of the slow wave due to the effect of syntactic structure. This however does not prove that external load and syntactic load elicit different wave forms, since there was no main effect of type of syntactic structure either. It may be that the two structures used in the experiment (subject relatives vs. conjoined VPs) did not differ enough in terms of storage demands to produce such an effect. This study is therefore inconclusive with respect to the questions we are concerned with here, of whether the two slow negative effects interact with each other and of the scalp distribution of the two effects within a single subject group. It would be more suitable to use syntactic structures that are known to elicit a slow negative wave (e.g. object vs. subject relatives in English, or *wen* vs. *wer* questions in German) to investigate the effect of concurrent list retention on the sentential slow wave. If the slow wave is an index of storage demands for unintegrated verbal materials, the size of the slow wave negativity related to retention of partial representations in sentence processing should differ depending on the length of the word list which must be retained simultaneously. As far as we know, no such experiments have been carried out to date.

3.4. Components reflecting computation

In the section above we discussed a slow anterior negative wave that may be an index of storage demands. We will now deal with shorter ERP responses that appear to index computational difficulty when integrating new input. As we mentioned in the introduction, sentence processing involves storage and integration of several kinds of information: syntactic categories, semantic features, and thematic information, among others. Different ERP components have been found for semantic and syntactic integration difficulty. We will discuss these in turn below. As we will see, these components are very different from the slow wave associated with storage.

3.4.1 Semantic integration difficulty: N400. The first ERP studies on sentence processing investigated the effects of semantic anomalies (Kutas and Hillyard, 1980). For instance, the word dog in (9.13) is semantically anomalous:

(9.13) I take my coffee with cream and dog.

Semantic anomalies such as the last word in (9.13) have been found to elicit a larger N400 component relative to neutral control sentences. The N400 is a negative component, which occurs about 300-500 msec after the onset of the critical word; its largest amplitude is usually seen at central positions on the scalp. The amplitude of the N400 has been shown to vary depending on how reliably the word can be predicted: the stronger the expectation for the particular word is, the smaller its N400 component (Kutas and Hillyard, 1984). For instance, in (9.14a) *stamp* is highly predictable given the preceding context, and elicits a small N400 component. In (9.14b) *hour* is rather unexpected, though not actually anomalous, and elicits a larger N400 than *stamp* in (9.14a).

(9.14) a. He mailed the letter without a stamp.
b. The bill was due at the end of the hour.

The N400 can be seen as an index of semantic integration difficulty. The semantic features of the word are matched against the semantic representation stored in working memory. When there is a mismatch, or when the semantic features are somewhat unexpected, effort has to be made to elaborate or modify the current semantic representation and accommodate the new input.[11]

3.4.2 Syntactic integration: P600. We have shown in the previous section that semantic integration difficulty is reflected by an N400 component. A totally different response has been reported when syntactic integration becomes more difficult, e.g. in response to syntactic violations such as the agreement violation at the verb in (9.15a) vs. (9.15b) (cf. e.g. Hagoort et al., 1993; Coulson et al., 1998) or in response to apparent violations such as the occurrence of *to* in (9.16a) vs. (9.16c) (cf. Osterhout and Holcomb, 1992):

(9.15) a. Every Monday he ***mow** the lawn.
b. Every Monday he **mows** the lawn.

[11] Although the N400 is typically seen as a response to semantic violations, it is also sometimes observed at or following words that are syntactically anomalous (e.g. Osterhout and Holcomb, 1992; Hagoort et al., 1993; Osterhout, 1994; Gunter and Friederici, 1999). This may be because difficulties in semantic integration are sometimes caused by syntactically ill-formed sequences.

(9.16) a. The broker persuaded **to** sell the stock...
b. The broker who was persuaded **to** sell the stock...
c. The broker hoped **to** sell the stock...

Both (9.15a) and (9.16a) involve computational difficulty at the position printed in bold. In (9.15a) a singular verb is expected, but the verb is plural instead. Hence, some effort has to be made to repair the structure and construct an interpretable representation. The sentence fragment in (9.16a) is grammatical but is a garden path sentence. Initially the verb *persuaded* is read as a main clause verb, which leads to the prediction of a direct object NP followed by a sentential complement. The next word, *to*, however, is not compatible with these predictions. This incompatibility triggers revision of the structure into a reduced relative clause, with a meaning corresponding to the sentence in (9.16b).

Roughly, two types of ERP component have been found for syntactic anomalies. The first is a left anterior negativity (LAN). This is a negative component, occurring 300-500 msec after onset of the anomalous word, with a frontal, typically left, distribution (cf. Friederici et al., 1993; Münte et al., 1993; Coulson et al., 1998, among others). The second component is a P600: a positive deflection, starting about 500 msec after onset of the violating word, typically largest at posterior electrode positions (cf. among others, Neville et al., 1991; Osterhout and Holcomb, 1992; Friederici et al., 1993; Hagoort et al., 1993; Osterhout et al., 1996). An example of a P600 is shown in figure 9.7: the ungrammatical condition becomes more positive than the grammatical condition around 500 msec after onset of the verb.

A P600 component has been observed for both ungrammatical and garden-path sentences, whereas the LAN effect typically occurs in genuine ungrammaticalities (but cf. Kluender and Kutas, 1993; Rösler et al., 1998). Furthermore, the LAN appears to be relatively insensitive to task manipulations such as the proportion of incorrect sentences in the experiment or the instructions to the subject, whereas the P600 is highly affected by these factors (Gunter et al., 1997; Coulson et al., 1998; Gunter and Friederici, 1999). We therefore consider it likely that the LAN reflects the detection of a feature mismatch, rather than indexing the computational difficulty involved in integrating the input word into the preceding structure.

The P600, in contrast, is more likely to be an index of computational difficulty. First, the P600 amplitude has been shown to vary with the ease of obtaining the correct structure. Osterhout et al., 1994 tested direct object/complement subject ambiguities in English, cf. (9.17).

(9.17) a. The doctor hoped the patient was lying.

b. The doctor believed the patient was lying.

c. The doctor charged the patient was lying.

d. The doctor forced the patient *was lying.

When the sentences in (9.17b) and (9.17c) are read from left to right, *the patient* is structurally ambiguous: it can either be the direct object of the preceding verb, or the subject of the sentential complement of the verb. Osterhout et al. used four different types of main clause verbs: (i) verbs that obligatorily take a complement clause, such as *hoped* in (9.17a); (ii) verbs that preferably take a sentential complement, such as *believed* in (9.17b) (iii) verbs that preferably take a direct object, cf. *charged* (9.17c); and (iv) verbs that obligatorily take a direct object, rendering the sentential complement clause ungrammatical, such as *forced* in (9.17d). The first two classes of verbs should bias toward (or require) a subject reading of *the patient*, while the second two should bias toward the direct object reading. The sentences were disambiguated at the embedded verb *was*, which is only compatible with a sentential complement with *the patient* being the subject. At this verb, Osterhout et al. found a P600 component for ungrammatical clauses like (9.17d) relative to the conditions in which the sentential complement was either obligatory or preferred, like (9.17a) and (9.17b). For the cases in which a sentential complement was grammatical but not preferred, (9.17c), a P600 was also found relative to (9.17a) and (9.17b). However the amplitude was smaller than for the ungrammatical cases like (9.17d). These results suggest that the P600 is sensitive to the difficulty with which the correct reading can be obtained.

A second argument that the P600 component is an index of computational difficulty is that this component has also been found for sentences that are completely grammatical and in which there is no garden path. The only difference relative to their control condition is that integration is more difficult at a certain point in the sentence. Kaan et al., 2000 compared *who* vs. *whether* questions, cf.

(9.18) a. Emily wondered who the performer in the concert imitates for the audience's amusement.

b. Emily wondered whether the performer in the concert imitates a pop star for the audience's amusement.

When the embedded verb, *imitates*, is encountered integration takes place between the subject and the verb in both (9.18a) and (9.18b).

In addition, in (9.18a) a trace is postulated and the clause initial *who*-phrase integrated with the verb. In terms of integration then, (9.18a) requires more effort at the verb than (9.18b). Kaan et al. found a P600 component at the verb for (9.18a) vs. (9.18b). Note that, in contrast to the conditions that elicited the P600 in the Osterhout et al. study, no structural revisions need to take place in (9.18a). The embedded verb is preferably transitive for both sentences. Previous studies have shown that in sentences like (9.18a) the wh-phrase is interpreted as the object as soon as a transitive verb is encountered (Stowe, 1986; Boland et al., 1990; Boland et al., 1995). The results from the Kaan et al. study therefore suggest that the P600 does not necessarily reflect repair and reanalysis processes following detection of (apparent) anomalies, (cf. Friederici and Mecklinger, 1996; Münte et al., 1997) but that it indexes syntactic integration difficulty in general.

Another study reporting a P600 in grammatical, non-garden path sentences is Featherston et al., 2000. They compared the following German sentence constructions, among others:

(9.19) a. Der Sheriff erkannte, als..., den Täter
The sheriff recognized, when..., the-acc offender
endlich im Scheinwerferlicht.
at last in the spot light.
The sheriff recognized, when..., the offender at last in the spot light.

b. Der Sheriff schien, als..., den Täter
The sheriff seemed, when..., the-acc offender
endlich verurteilen zu können.
at last to-sentence to can.
The sheriff seemed, when..., to be able to sentence the offender at last.

The sentences all contained a main clause verb which was separated from an accusative NP (*den Täter*) by an adjunct clause (denoted by *als...* in (9.19)). The conditions differ with respect to the integration of the accusative NP. The accusative NP in (9.19a) is the direct object of the main clause verb and must be integrated with it across the adjunct phrase; in (9.19b) the accusative NP is the object of an infinitival clause. Under general syntactic assumptions, the subject position of the infinitival complement of a raising verb is a trace, which is coindexed with the matrix subject. At the accusative NP, then, a trace must be postulated and linked with the matrix subject. Hence, in terms of syntactic computation, (9.19b) is more difficult than (9.19a).

A P600 component was found at the accusative determiner for (9.19b) vs. (9.19a). Under the assumptions mentioned above, these data suggest that the P600 may be a reflection of computational difficulty. Most important, though, all sentences in (9.19) are grammatical and are not garden paths. This supports our hypothesis that the P600 is not restricted to repair or revision of syntactic anomalies, but may be an index of computational difficulty in general.

Briefly put, the three studies cited above suggest that the P600 component in ERPs may be a reflection of computational difficulty involved in syntactic integration. The N400, on the other hand, is modulated by the difficulty of integrating semantic information.

3.5. Summary

In this section we have discussed evidence that distinct ERP components are associated with storage and computation, respectively: storage is reflected in a slow negative wave; computational difficulty is indexed by the N400 for semantic integration, and a P600 for syntactic integration difficulty. These two short components are completely different from the slow wave component: both the N400 and the P600 are largest at central and posterior sites on the scalp, respectively, whereas the slow negative wave has its focus over (left) anterior sites. These differences therefore suggest that storage and computation in sentence processing are physiologically distinct.

In the conclusion to the section on blood flow change studies, we pointed out that the results of the studies discussed there did not obviously support the standard distinction between syntactic and semantic processing. The differences in scalp distribution and polarity associated with the two computational ERP responses which we have discussed shows that structural processes are indeed dissociable from some aspects of semantic computation, at least those which respond to lexical-semantic and pragmatic expectations. The extent to which those processes are related to the sort of sentential semantics which depend on syntactic structure is a point for further research.

4. Comparing blood flow and electrophysiology: some caveats

In the previous two sections we have shown that both blood flow change studies and ERPs suggest that computation and storage are neurologically dissociable. It is very tempting to directly combine the ERP results with the results obtained in the blood flow studies. However, one should be extremely careful about concluding that the slow negative wave indexing storage is generated in Broca's, and the P600 or N400 in Wernicke's area. The problem is that the two methods do not measure the same thing: ERP measures the electrical activity generated within the brain while PET and fMRI measure the changes in blood flow which result from changes in neuronal activity. The two sorts of measurements are each potentially insensitive to certain sorts of brain activity, and these are not necessarily the same sorts of insensitivity.

On the one hand, not all active sources can be measured with ERPs. Some sources may be too small to be recorded at the scalp, since large numbers of neurons must be active at the same time to produce a response. Moreover, some active neurons may be arranged so that their electrical activity cancels out (closed field configuration). This is particularly likely to be true for subcortical structures, but is also true for cortical areas which can have highly variable configurations of folds (gyri and sulci; cf. Roland and Zilles, 1998). On the other hand, not all sources of brain activity necessarily lead to increased blood flow: some sources may be active too briefly to have an effect on the blood flow differences recorded with the current techniques. So, although the correspondence between the blood flow and ERP data is very suggestive, we cannot, nor do we wish to, designate Broca's as the source of the slow negativity and the posterior temporal lobe as the location of the P600 or N400 generators. The possibility that this is the case can, however, form a background for further research.

5. What does neuroimaging tell us about storage and computation during sentence comprehension?

We began this paper by distinguishing storage of partial representations during sentence processing from computation of sentential representations as such. The issue that we wished to address was whether it is possible to distinguish these two functions from each other. Evidence from both blood flow studies and ERPs suggest that this distinction has a neurological basis.

We saw in section 2 that blood flow studies suggest that two separate areas are involved in sentence processing. One of these areas can be equated with Broca's area, while another can be equated with Wernicke's. We summarized evidence from neuroimaging and aphasia which shows that Broca's area is not the site in which syntactic computation takes place, as posited by some theories of the neurological basis of language. Additionally we discussed evidence that Broca's area is active during non-sentential verbal working memory tasks. The overlap between these activations suggests that Broca's area is responsible for storage of verbal information. Further neuroimaging results suggested that sentential structural information is maintained in this area as well as purely lexical information. The fact that extremely complex sentences lead to more activation than word lists, and the interaction between sentential complexity and a verbal maintenance task were both used to argue for this claim.

Furthermore, we argued that some aspect of sentential computation takes place in Wernicke's area: in contrast to Broca's area, Wernicke's area is more activated during processing of even simple sentences than during passive fixation or the reading of word lists. Furthermore, it is not activated in memory tasks. Both of these differences between the conditions under which these two areas are active during language processing support the distinction between storage and computation that we introduced in the introduction.

ERPs also provide evidence for a dissociation between storage and computation. Long-lasting frontal negative waves are typically seen for complex sentential structures, starting at the point at which storage is assumed to begin. Interestingly, a very similar response was seen for storage of words and for storage of unintegrated material within sentences, parallel to the activations seen for both word storage and syntactic storage in the blood flow change studies.

The long-lasting ERP waves that are seen in response to increased storage load contrast with responses found at precisely those points where a more difficult computation is thought to be necessary. Two time-limited responses were discussed in some detail: (i) the N400, which has been argued to reflect semantic integration of a single word into its context and which has a more central-parietal distribution than the long lasting negative waves found for storage, and (ii) the P600, a positivity which is largest at posterior sites, in response to syntactic complexity. The different polarities and scalp distributions seen for storage and computation responses suggest that they are generated by different areas within the cortex and thus that the functions are physiologically dissociated.

We have shown that neuroimaging studies, both blood flow studies and electrophysiological measurements, support a distinction between storage and computation during sentence comprehension. This evidence allows us to argue that computation and storage are neurologically, and thus functionally, distinct. Although it is true that at a more global level Broca's and Wernicke's area form part of a functional network with one single function, the dissociation makes it clear that at a finer-grained level of description, the functions are physiologically distinguishable.

This is an important point, which would have been difficult to establish without the use of neuroimaging techniques, since most behavioral techniques cannot provide the relevant data in any direct way, while data from aphasia tends to be subject to too many interpretations.

References

Awh, E., Jonides, J., Smith, E., Schumacher, E., Koeppe, R., and Katz, S. (1996). Dissociation of storage and rehearsal in verbal working memory: Evidence from positron emission tomography. *Psychological Science*, 7:25–31.

Baddeley, A. (1986). *Working memory.* Oxford: Clarendon Press.

Bastiaanse, R. and Van Zonneveld, R. (1998). On the relation between verb inflection and verb position in Dutch agrammatic aphasics. *Brain and Language*, 64:165–181.

Boland, J., Tanenhaus, M., and Garnsey, S. (1990). Evidence for the immediate use of verb control information in sentence processing. *Journal of Memory and Language*, 29:413–432.

Boland, J., Tanenhaus, M., Garnsey, S., and Carlson, G. (1995). Verb argument structure in parsing and interpretation: Evidence from wh-questions. *Journal of Memory and Language*, 34:774–806.

Broere, C., Stowe, L., Wijers, A., Mulder, G., Koster, J., and Vaalburg, W. (1997). A complex syntax processing area in the temporal cortex. *Journal of Cerebral Blood Flow and Metabolism*, 17 (Supplement 1):S265.

Buckner, R., Raichle, M., Miezin, F., and Peterson, S. (1996). Functional anatomic studies of memory retrieval for auditory words and visual pictures. *Journal of Neuroscience*, 16:6219–6235.

Caplan, D. (1986). In defense of agrammatism. *Cognition*, 24:263–276.

Caplan, D., Alpert, N., and Waters, G. (1998). Effects of syntactic structure and propositional number on patterns of regional cerebral blood flow. *Journal of Cognitive Neuroscience*, 10:541–552.

Caplan, D., Alpert, N., and Waters, G. (1999). PET studies of syntactic processing with auditory sentence presentation. *NeuroImage*, 9:343–351.

Coulson, S., King, J., and Kutas, M. (1998). Expect the unexpected: Event-related brain response to morphosyntactic violations. *Language and Cognitive Processes*, 13:21–58.

Daneman, M. and Carpenter, P. (1980). Individual differences in working memory and reading. *Journal of Verbal Learning and Verbal Behavior*, 19:450–466.

Featherston, S., Gross, M., Münte, T., and Clahsen, H. (2000). Brain potentials in the processing of complex sentences: An ERP study of control and raising constructions. *Journal of Psycholinguistic Research*, 29(2):141–154.

Fiez, J., Raife, E., Balota, D., Schwarz, J., and Raichle, M. (1996). A positron emission tomography study of the short-term maintenance of verbal information. *Journal of Neuroscience*, 16:808–822.

Friederici, A. and Mecklinger, A. (1996). Syntactic parsing as revealed by brain responses: First pass and second pass parsing processes. *Journal of Psycholinguistic Research*, 25:157–176.

Friederici, A., Pfeifer, E., and Hahne, A. (1993). Event-related brain potentials during natural speech processing: Effects of semantic, morphological and syntactic violations. *Cognitive Brain Research*, 1:183–192.

Gibson, E. (1998). Linguistic complexity: Locality of syntactic dependencies. *Cognition*, 68:1–76.

Grasby, P., Frith, C., Friston, K., Simpson, J., Fletcher, P., and Frackowiak, R. (1994). A graded approach to the functional mapping of brain areas implicated in auditory-verbal memory. *Brain*, 117:1271–1282.

Grodzinsky, Y. (2000). The neurology of syntax: Language use without Broca's area. *Behavioral and Brain Sciences*, 23:1–21.

Gunter, T. and Friederici, A. (1999). Concerning the automaticity of syntactic processing. *Psychophysiology*, 36:126–137.

Gunter, T., Stowe, L., and Mulder, G. (1997). When syntax meets semantics. *Psychophysiology*, 34:660–676.

Gunter, T. C., Jackson, J. L., and Mulder, G. (1995). Language, memory and aging: An electrophysiological exploration of the N400 during reading of memory-demanding sentences. *Psychophysiology*, 32:215–229.

Haarmann, H. and Kolk, H. (1994). On-line sensitivity to subject-verb agreement violations in Broca's aphasics: The role of syntactic complexity and time. *Brain and Language*, 46:493–516.

Hagoort, P., Brown, C., and Groothusen, J. (1993). The syntactic positive shift (SPS) as an ERP-measure of syntactic processing. *Language and Cognitive Processes*, 8:439–484.

Holmes, V. (1973). Order of main and subordinate clauses in sentence perception. *Journal of Verbal Learning and Verbal Behavior*, 12:285–293.

Just, M. and Carpenter, P. (1992). A capacity theory of comprehension: Individual differences in working memory. *Psychological Review*, 99:122–149.

Just, M., Carpenter, P., Keller, T., Eddy, W., and Thulborn, K. (1996). Brain activation modulated by sentence comprehension. *Science*, 274:114–116.

Kaan, E., Harris, A., Gibson, E., and Holcomb, P. (2000). The P600 as an index of syntactic integration difficulty. *Language and Cognitive Processes*, 15:159–202.

King, J. and Just, M. (1991). Individual differences in syntactic processing: The role of working memory. *Journal of Memory and Language*, 30:580–602.

King, J. and Kutas, M. (1995). Who did what and when? Using word- and clause level ERPs to monitor working memory usage in reading. *Journal of Cognitive Neuroscience*, 7:376–395.

Kluender, R. and Kutas, M. (1993). Bridging the gap: Evidence from ERPs on the processing of unbounded dependencies. *Journal of Cognitive Neuroscience*, 5:196–214.

Kluender, R. and Münte, T. (1998). ERPs to grammatical and ungrammatical subject/object asymmetries in German Wh-questions. Poster presented at the 11th CUNY conference on Human Sentence Processing, New Brunswick.

Kutas, M. (1997). Views on how the electrical activity that the brain generates reflects the functions of different language structures. *Psychophysiology*, 34:383–398.

Kutas, M. and Hillyard, S. (1980). Reading senseless sentences: Brain potentials reflect semantic incongruity. *Science*, 207:203–205.

Kutas, M. and Hillyard, S. (1984). Brain potentials during reading reflect word expectancy and semantic association. *Nature*, 307:161–163.

Kutas, M., Van Petten, C., and Besson, M. (1988). Event-related potential asymmetries during the reading of sentences. *Electroencephalography and Clinical Neurophysiology*, 69:218–233.

Martin, R. and Romani, C. (1994). Verbal working memory and sentence comprehension: A multiple components view. *Neuropsychology*, 4:506–523.

Mazoyer, B., Tzourio, N., Frak, V., Syrota, A., Murayama, N., Levrier, O., Salamon, G., Dehaene, S., Cohen, L., and Mehler, J. (1993). The cortical representation of speech. *Journal of Cognitive Neuroscience*, 5:467–479.

Münte, T., Heinze, H., and Mangun, G. (1993). Dissociation of brain activity related to syntactic and semantic aspects of language. *Journal of Cognitive Neuroscience*, 5:335–344.

Münte, T., Schiltz, K., and Kutas, M. (1998). When temporal terms belie conceptual order. *Nature*, 396:71–73.

Münte, T., Szentkuti, A., Wieringa, B., Matzke, M., and Johannes, S. (1997). Human brain potentials to reading syntactic errors in sentences of different complexity. *Neuroscience Letters*, 235:105–108.

Neville, H., Nicol, J., Barss, A., Forster, K., and Garrett, M. (1991). Syntactically based sentence processing classes: Evidence from event related brain potentials. *Journal of Cognitive Neuroscience*, 3:151–165.

Osterhout, L. (1994). Event-related brain potentials as tools for comprehending language comprehension. In Clifton, C., Frazier, L., and Rayner, K., editors, *Perspectives on Sentence Processing.* Hillsdale, NJ: Lawrence Erlbaum Ass.

Osterhout, L. and Holcomb, P. (1992). Event-related brain potentials elicited by syntactic anomaly. *Journal of Memory and Language*, 31:785–806.

Osterhout, L., Holcomb, P., and Swinney, D. (1994). Brain potentials elicited by garden-path sentences: Evidence of the application of verb information during parsing. *Journal of Experimental Psychology. Learning, Memory and Cognition*, 28:786–803.

Osterhout, L., McKinnon, R., Bersick, M., and Corey, V. (1996). On the language specificity of the brain response to syntactic anomalies: Is the syntactic positive shift a member of the P300 family? *Journal of Cognitive Neuroscience*, 8:507–526.

Paulesu, E., Frith, C., and Frackowiak, R. (1993). The neural components of the verbal component of working memory. *Nature*, 362:342–344.

Roland, P. and Zilles, K. (1998). Structural divisions and functional fields in the human cerebral cortex. *Brain Research and Brain Research Review*, 26:87–105.

Rösler, F., Pechmann, T., Streb, J., Röder, B., and Henninghausen, E. (1998). Parsing of sentences in a language with varying word order: Word-by-word variations of processing demands are revealed by event-related potentials. *Journal of Memory and Language*, 38:150–176.

Ruchkin, D., Johnson, R., Canoune, H., and Ritter, W. (1990). Short-term memory storage and retention: An event-related brain potential study. *Electroencephalography and Clinical Neurophysiology*, 76:419–439.

Ruchkin, D., Johnson, R., Grafman, J., Canoune, H., and Ritter, W. (1992). Distinctions and similarities among working memory processes: An event-related potential study. *Cognitive Brain Research*, 1:53–66.

Rugg, M. and Coles, M. (1995). The ERP and cognitive psychology: Conceptual issues. In Rugg, M. and Coles, M., editors, *Electrophysi-*

ology of Mind. Event-related Brain Potentials and Cognition. Oxford: Oxford University Press.

Smith, E., Jonides, J., and Koeppe, R. (1996). Dissociation of verbal and spatial working memory. *Cerebral Cortex*, 6:11–20.

Stowe, L. (1986). Parsing WH-constructions: Evidence for on-line gap location. *Language and Cognitive Processes*, 1:227–245.

Stowe, L., Broere, C., Paans, A., Wijers, A., Mulder, G., Vaalburg, W., and Zwarts, F. (1998). Localizing cognitive components of a complex task: Sentence processing and working memory. *NeuroReport*, 9:2995–2999.

Stowe, L., Wijers, A., Willemsen, A., Reuland, E., Paans, A., and Vaalburg, W. (1994). PET studies of language: An assessment of the reliability of the technique. *Journal of Psycholinguistic Research*, 23:499–527.

Stowe, L., Willemsen, A., Wijers, A., Zwarts, F., Mulder, G., and Vaalburg, W. (1995). Effects of sentence complexity on rCBF: A PET study. Poster presented at the Meeting of the Cognitive Neuroscience Society, San Francisco, 1995.

Stowe, L., Withaar, R., Wijers, A., Broere, C., and Paans, A. Encoding and storage in working memory during sentence comprehension. In Merlo, P. and Stevenson, S., editors, *Sentence Processing and the Lexicon: Formal, Computational and Experimental Perspectives*, Research In Computational Psycholinguistics Series. Philadelphia: Benjamins. In press.

Stromswold, K., Caplan, D., Alpert, N., and Rauch, S. (1996). Localization of syntactic comprehension by positron emission tomography. *Brain and Language*, 52:452–473.

Vos, S., Gunter, T., Kolk, H., and Mulder, G. (2001). Working memory constraints on syntactic processing: An electrophysiological investigation. *Psychophysiology*, 38:41–63.

Wanner, E. and Maratsos, M. (1978). An ATN approach in comprehension. In M. Halle, J. B. and Miller, G., editors, *Linguistic Theory and Psychological Reality*. Cambrige, MA: MIT Press.

Waters, G., Caplan, D., and Hildebrandt, N. (1987). Working memory and written sentence comprehension. In Coltheart, M., editor, *Attention and Performance*, volume 12: The psychology of reading, pages 531–555. Hove, England UK: Lawrence Erlbaum Press.

Zurif, E., Caramazza, A., and Myerson, R. (1972). Grammatical judgments of agrammatic aphasics. *Neuropsychologia*, 10:405–417.

VI

COMPUTING AND STORING ASPECTS OF DISCOURSE

Chapter 10

COMPUTATION AND STORAGE IN DISCOURSE INTERPRETATION

Nicholas Asher

Abstract In this paper I discuss why computation has come to have an increasingly important place in the theory of discourse interpretation. I argue that essential to discourse interpretation is the idea of computing a discourse structure for a discourse; from this structure the interpretation follows. This structure is part of the logical form for a discourse. After examining several ways in which one might compute such structures, I argue that the preferred method is a local and opportunistic strategy that makes defeasible guesses. I end by suggesting that once we have constructed a decent model of computing discourse structure, we are in a better position to evaluate what role storage can play.

Keywords: Discourse, interpretation, logical form, defeasible guesses.

1. Introduction: What's at issue

Computation and storage are two essential parameters in many branches of linguistics and semantics, and the theory of discourse interpretation is no exception. Nevertheless, in analyzing the meaning of discourses, the emphasis has recently been on computation. In this paper, I will detail why computation came to the fore in this branch of linguistics and give several models of computation in discourse interpretation. I'll suggest at the end where storage might play an important role in discourse interpretation.

Why has computation been the focus of study in discourse interpretation? One reason is that discourse interpretation builds on a theory of sentential meaning, and the most successful theory of sentential meaning has been truth-conditional semantics, in which the meaning of the sentence or discourse is calculated from the meanings of its constituents. For a long time in these theories the focus has been on the effects of com-

S. Nooteboom et al. (eds.), Storage and Computation in the Language Faculty, 299–328.

posing lexically given elements together in a recursive manner.[1] The recursive computation of meaning is generally acknowledged to be essential because of the potentially infinite number of meanings generated from a finite vocabulary and the recursive rules of syntax that generate an infinite number of well-formed expressions. Once one accepts the idea that there are an infinite number of meaningful sentences in the language, the recovery of the meaning of an arbitrary sentence cannot be a matter of retrieving that meaning from a memory in which the meaning of each sentence is explicitly stored.

2. A storage-intensive approach to discourse interpretation

Given this emphasis on compositional semantics, it is nevertheless noteworthy that one of the first computational approaches to discourse interpretation, or what was called then "story understanding," emphasized storage over computation. This was the approach pioneered by Schank and Abelson, 1977 and also Minsky, 1975 that used scripts or frames. The idea was that certain words like *restaurant* would introduce a data structure involving predicates about actions, events and other related objects, many of whose arguments or "slots" would be unfilled. Discourse interpretation then proceeded by recovering from the rest of the discourse elements that could fill in the slots. In current terminology, we could think of the slots as variables and the filling in procedure as one of unification. Another set of operations conjoined or combined scripts into higher level data structures. For instance, Schank's restaurant script had a number of slots for events and actors; there would be a slot for the ordering of a meal event, the eating of the meal, the paying of the check and the leaving.

This approach was extremely top down and storage intensive. The meaning of a discourse was stored basically in a large structure, and interpretation merely consisted in assigning values to variables. The nice part of this picture was that there was a uniform and simple computation method for interpretation from the clausal to discourse level (unification).

The fatal drawback of the script approach was its extremely strong top down assumptions—that discourse meaning consisted mainly in the recovery of a large data structure from memory within which variables

[1] In philosophy, the meanings of individual words have traditionally been taken to be atoms (a view still forcefully defended by, for instance, Fodor and Lepore, 1998). But one can eschew this position, as most people working in lexical semantics have, and still adhere to a view that meaning is compositional.

would then be assigned particular values based on the discourse context. Scripts or frames proved unwieldy to modify and extend in a particular discourse context and any general story understander would thus have to have a huge, perhaps unbounded, number of scripts with which to process arbitrary texts. For example, consider a discourse about restaurants, where new elements like *nursing a cocktail* or *rehearsing in one's mind the events of the day* could easily be introduced:

(10.1) John entered the restaurant. He sat down. While nursing a cocktail, he rehearsed in his mind the events of the day.

This discourse could plausibly continue elaborating what had happened to John. To integrate all the information in such a story, the restaurant script would have to have slots for cocktail drinking and mental events transpiring during the agent's stay at the restaurant. It's unclear how one or even some reasonable number of scripts could handle all such possible stories about restaurants.

Undoubtedly interpreters access large amounts of information in processing discourse. So the idea behind scripts is not entirely wrong. But the script/frame paradigm and the simple mechanisms for modifying them in a given discourse context can't be the right model for discourse interpretation; they can't handle the infinite productivity of discourse meaning—viz. that infinitely many meaningful discourses can arise from a finite vocabulary. Over the past twenty years, we have learned that discourse contexts have complex and subtle effects on semantic and pragmatic phenomena; and many linguists, computer scientists and philosophers have devoted considerable effort to modelling discourse contexts and their effects on interpretation. Very different, computationally oriented approaches have evolved, each incorporating a recursive element enabling them to compute interpretations for arbitrary discourses. Semanticists, for instance, have given algorithms or procedures for how the meaning of one sentence or a clause, which itself is built up recursively from the meanings of the constituent words, changes the discourse context and interpretation. These authors have recast the traditional, static truth-conditional notion of meaning for sentences in terms of a dynamic picture, in which the meaning of a sentence in a given discourse context is a transition from the given context to a new context. This new context in turn can serve to interpret new sentences. To put the new view in a slogan: the meaning of a sentence, clause or even discourse is its context change potential. This view of interpretation has come to be known as *dynamic semantics.*[2]

But while dynamic semantics has become an established approach amongst semanticists, many questions still remain as how to best model the interpretation of discourse. In a number of recent papers, several authors have claimed that discourse structure is an essential component in discourse interpretation. Information about discourse structure is needed to compute a variety of semantic effects of interpretation: temporal and pronominal anaphora (Asher, 1993; Lascarides and Asher, 1993), VP ellipsis (Gardent, 1991; Prüst and Scha, 1990; Asher, 1993; Asher et al., 1997), lexical ambiguity (Asher and Lascarides, 1995), presupposition and implicature (Beaver, 1997; Asher and Lascarides, 1998b). Many more people have voiced and argued for the claim that discourse comes in chunks, and these chunks are relevant to interpretation. Dynamic semantics trivializes the notion of discourse structure; distinctions between clauses, paragraphs all largely disappear within the dynamic semantic notion of context, a notion that many including myself have argued is too impoverished to do full justice to the contextual effects on discourse interpretation (Asher, 1993; Lascarides and Asher, 1993; Bras and Asher, 1994; Asher and Lascarides, 1995; Txurruka, 1997; Asher and Lascarides, 1998a; 1998b; Asher and Fernando, 1999).

3. Discourse structure as logical form

Suppose that we accept the conclusion that discourse structure is essential to interpretation and that it is not captured by standard dynamic semantic theories. There remains the question, how should discourse structure be computed, if it's not stored in something like the script paradigm? To answer such a question, we need to decide what level of linguistic analysis discourse structure is part of; is it a syntactic structure, a semantic logical form, or a model-theoretic construct? Different types of computation are appropriate to each of these domains.

Model-theoretic constructs are supposed to determine truth conditions, the circumstances in which a given discourse is true. They are set theoretic objects, and so we can use the tools of set-theory for computing them. But typically these set theoretic objects are not themselves computable (certainly not Turing computable for instance). Furthermore, while truth conditions will reflect truth-conditional *effects* of discourse structure, it is hard to imagine that they *encode* or mirror the discourse

[2] There are now quite a few ways of fleshing out the picture, and there are many technical details which I will pass over here. For a survey of some dynamic systems, see Van Eijck and Kamp, 1997; the most prevalent approach is developed in Kamp and Reyle, 1993.

structure itself. Many discourses will have the same truth conditions even though they differ in structure and in how those truth conditions are determined. So it appears very implausible that discourse structure is itself a model-theoretic construct.

On the other hand, some people (e.g. Polanyi, 1985, Scha and Polanyi, 1988) have thought that discourse structure was a syntactic construct. Discourse structures are acknowledged to have features in common with syntactic structures—for example, subordinate and coordinate elements. For Polanyi discourse structures in the form of trees (D trees) are constructed out of discourse constituent units or dcu's and discourse relations using an extremely simple set of context free rewrite rules. Webber et al., 1999 have argued that such syntactic discourse structures are best computed using some sort of a rewriting system, like tree adjunction. This is a very efficient, recursive procedure that could compute discourse structure, *provided* all the building blocks are given and the construction depends only on syntactic categories. The procedure looks something like this, where b is the new information:

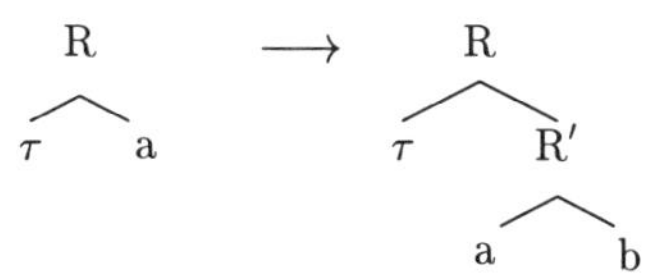

This operation of adjunction encodes a right frontier constraint—namely that information may be added only to constituents on the right of the tree. Now this indeed looks like a syntactic constraint, although it's hard to see what this constraint does in either Polanyi's or Webber's theory. If we couple this or something similar to a theory of anaphoric accessibility in discourse (Asher, 1993), we do get a constraint on where an anaphoric expression can find an antecedent. However, as Webber et al., 1999) themselves point out (and is also noted in Asher, 1993), there are counterexamples to this right frontier constraint applied to anaphora.[3]

There are much deeper problems with this view of discourse structure. First of all, discourse structures have a trivial categorical structure. The

[3]In Asher, 1993 there are examples of so called "discourse subordination," where repetitions of verbal content from normally inaccessible constituents allows attachment of new information to sites other than on the right frontier. The examples of Webber et al. concerning violations of the predictions of right frontier accessibility occur in contexts where structurally sensitive relations like Parallel and Contrast are present; in Asher, 1993 these sorts of relations allow additions to elements not on the right frontier of the contextually given discourse structure.

consensus from many years of research is that discourse structure is built up from discourse units linked together by different sorts of discourse relations. So from an abstract syntactic point of view, the structure of a discourse appears to involve just one basic category, the discourse unit (be it a proposition, event, fact, dcu, discourse segment, or whatever) and then relations on semantic units. But this isn't a complete description of the syntactic system. What is the category of the structure that results from applying a discourse relation to its arguments? Either it's a discourse unit of the same category as the arguments to the relation or it's not. If it is a dcu, then we have only one saturated category—dcu—in these structures; discourse structures are no more interesting syntactically than formulas of sentential logic. If such structures don't form discourse units of the same type as basic clauses, then it's mysterious as to what they are and how they are to be interpreted.

Because the categorial structure is trivial, discourse structures can't be constructed simply on the basis of categorical information. The Tree Grammar of Scha and Polanyi at best describes the set of possible discourse trees, but it does little if anything to tell us how to *parse* or to construct them. Consider, for instance, the problem of attachment. A crucial question in building a discourse structure is where to attach new information. But this is itself dependent on particular semantic cues and on the presence of particular discourse relations present in the context. Consider for instance the simple example studied in Lascarides and Asher, 1993:

(10.2) a. Guy experienced a lovely evening last night.
b. He had a fantastic meal.
c. He ate salmon.
d. He devoured lots of cheese.
e. He won a dancing competition.

(10.2e) intuitively attaches to (10.2b) and continues to elaborate with (10.2b) Guy's lovely evening. Since it also moves the story along with respect to the events in (10.2b), it attaches to that constituent with Narration. But it doesn't have much to do with his meal and so wouldn't attach to the description of the meal (10.2c-d) which narrate the meal, even though (10.2d) is the last introduced information. In terms of discourse trees, the context would look like this:

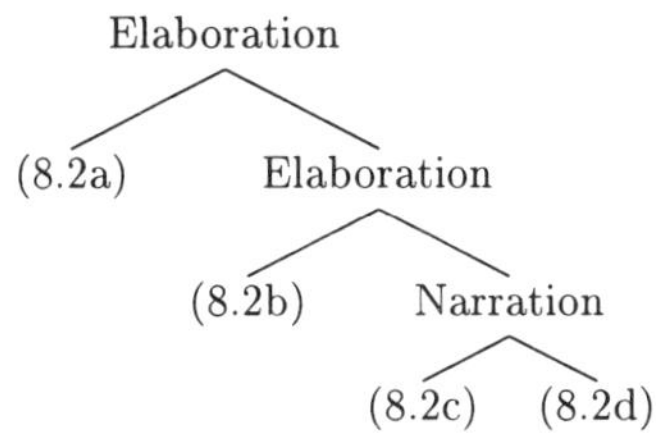

To represent the discourse (10.2), we would adjoin the last sentence's dcu via Narration to the Elaboration subtree underneath the first Elaboration above. But this is only one of many possibilities; clearly we would need to access semantic information in order to locate the appropriate attachment point. Semantic information also decides whether the right frontier constraint holds or not.[4] Attachment facts supervene upon semantic information.

Further, whatever types of discourse relations we choose, they seem to be individuated in terms of their semantic properties and sensitive to the meanings of their constituents. Consider, for instance, the types of discourse relations in SDRT (Asher, 1993), RST (Thompson and Mann, 1987; Mann and Thompson, 1987) or Hobbs's theory (Hobbs et al., 1993). These are sensitive to truth-functional operators—once again an indication that discourse structure is not freely generated from syntactic categories.

(10.3) a. John fell down. He hurt himself.

b. John fell down. He didn't hurt himself.

The presence of the negation changes the nature of the rhetorical function or connection between the two units in the discourse structure that come from the two sentences. They change what sort of discourse structure we have. In (10.3a), the second sentence serves to tell us about a result of John's falling down or it elaborates on the episode of falling down, whereas in (10.3b), there is some sort of contrast indicated—we'd like to add a 'though' at the end of (10.3b). These examples indicate that discourse units are *semantic units*, and that the relations that hold between them do so in virtue of their content.

The fact that discourse relations hold between constituents in virtue of their context explains why a syntactic account of discourse cannot say anything about the ill-formedness and well-formedness of discourses. There are well-formed and ill-formed discourses, and discourse structure ought to be able to explain this. But to give such an explanation, we

[4]See footnote 2.

need information about the semantic interpretation and pragmatic effects of the structure's discourse relations, as well as the content of the propositional constituents. A discourse like the following is incoherent

(10.4) My car broke down. Mary dyed her hair.

because of the contents of the propositional constituents. Somehow they preclude our forming a discourse connection. It is their contents—here determined by lexical meaning—that precludes our computing any discourse relation to hold between the two clauses and this lack of connection makes the discourse incoherent.

Thus, a syntactic operation like tree adjunction *cannot* get the right discourse structure by itself for examples like (10.2) or (10.3); it needs access to semantic information, and this now involves us in a different kind of computation for discourse structure. Nor can it explain judgments about well-formedness. Discourse structure and the kind of phenomena like discourse coherence, anaphora etc. it purports to explain have to do with how the information conveyed by one constituent contributes to its rhetorical function and interacts with the discourse context. So the structure that we are seeking to build is one that is sensitive to and exploits semantic information and as such is a semantic structure. But we still have to find out what sources of semantic information are needed to compute discourse structures. It turns out that they are more varied than one might think. Another question one might have is whether discourse structures are best represented as trees or graphs.

Let's tackle the second question first. If we model discourse structures as trees, the sort of examples like (10.5) that Moore and Pollack, 1992 and Moore and Paris, 1993 have used to argue that several discourse relations may obtain between two segments will not be representable within such a formalism. For instance in Asher and Lascarides, 1994, we analyzed (10.5) in terms of multiple discourse relations between segments.

(10.5) a. George Bush supports big business.

b. He's sure to veto House Bill 1711.

A plausible analysis of (10.5) is that (10.5a,b) are arguments in an *Evidence* relation, but they also support a causal or *Result* relation. One could, as do Thompson and Mann, argue that (10.5) is ambiguous, and the ambiguity would be resolved upon learning about the speaker's aims. However, this misses the point. The reason (10.5b) can act as evidence for (10.5a) is precisely because of the causal relationship between supporting big business and vetoing the bill. To recognize one relationship is to recognise the other. But one cannot permit *both* relations to hold between these clauses, because of the uniqueness constraint on relations that's imposed by the tree requirements.

Another difficulty for the view of discourse structures as trees is that one might require as in (10.2) that one constituent bear the relation of Narration to another while at the same time bearing the relation of Elaboration to a third. In that discourse, we need these relations to hold between (10.2d), (10.2c) and (10.2b) to get the right temporal structure between the constituents–namely that eating salmon is followed by eating cheese but both events are part of the fantastic meal. This cannot be expressed directly in the tree structure formalism. To get the right temporal effects we would need to compute temporal structure non-compositionally, not just from individual relations but from configurations of discourse relations in a tree. While this is possible, it greatly complicates any statement of the truth-conditional effects of discourse relations. In the absence of information to the contrary, we should go with a simpler compositional way of constructing temporal structure from discourse structure. This is possible, if we take discourse structures to be graphs rather than trees.

So let's suppose that discourse structures are graph-like. We can actually be quite agnostic here about the details. Since the same proposition or basic clause qua abstract object could occur as an inscription or utterance in many different places in a discourse and so could conceivably have many different even incompatible rhetorical relations, discourse structures must be constructed from occurrences of propositions in a discourse. To this end we introduce speech-act labels or discourse referents $(\pi, \pi_1, \ldots)$ that serve to indicate occurrences of propositional contents in a particular discourse structure. These propositional contents will include predications of discourse relations over labels as well as contents of basic clauses. A discourse structure is then a pair $(A, \mathcal{F})$, where:

- A is a set of labels
- $\mathcal{F} : A \longrightarrow \Phi$

Φ is a set of logical forms representing propositional contents

Every such discourse structure yields a strict partial ordering $<$ on the set of its labels such that $\pi < \pi'$ iff the formula assigned to π' contains π. We can then isolate among the labels in this partial order a particular subset of *open* nodes to which we can attach further information, refining Polanyi's right frontier constraint. Suppose now that such a discourse structure with its set of open labels is given as part of the context. One task is to compute a new discourse structure from this contextually given one and some new information (perhaps also in the form of a discourse structure); the task then of building a discourse structure for a discourse consists in incrementally updating a contextually given structure with new information from each clause, sentence or paragraph of the discourse. This incremental procedure is essential if we are to be able to construct discourse structures for arbitrary texts using only a finite lexicon and a finite set of construction rules. But to do anything else would place intolerable demands on storage for finite beings like ourselves.

What sources of semantic information do we use to infer such discourse structures? One might think that discourse coherence could be established lexically by the presence of certain cue words. Cue words indeed are a way of signalling discourse relations, but once again they aren't really sufficient for felicitous discourse–consider (10.6a,b)—nor are they necessary to establish discourse coherence–compare (10.6c,d).

(10.6) a. John will come home soon. So I'll be going now and you're going to be eating pea soup.

b. John is a student. Therefore, he is self-identical.

c. John went to jail, because he embezzled the pension funds.

d. John went to jail. He embezzled the pension funds.

Considerations of content needed to establish discourse structure thus go beyond the semantics of cue words; the presence of cue words alone doesn't make the discourse coherent or establish a well formed discourse structure.[5]

SDRT (Asher, 1993; Lascarides and Asher, 1993; Asher et al., 1995) and Hobbs's TACITUS (Hobbs et al., 1993) program are the only two approaches to discourse structure that have tackled the computation of logical forms task in any detail. And in both approaches, a wide variety of information sources combined with a nonmonotonic logic for making "best guesses" about the structure are exploited. The computation

[5]Similarly, one might try to find discourse coherence in the patterns of cue words—analyzing the covariation of various cue words or discourse particles. Here's an example that brings to mind a default pattern of the way various French words roughly synonymous with *then* interact.

(10.7) Voici comment Jean travaille. D'abord, il arrive au bureau vers 9h30. Puis il prend un petit café à la cafeteria et bavarde avec les serveuses. Ensuite il se met à lire son email pendant une heure. Enfin il range ses affaires et va déjeuner.

This might be a typical discourse pattern; we begin a narrative segment with *d'abord* (first); then we use *puis* (then), and then *ensuite* (then), finishing up the segment with *enfin* (finally). But in searching through occurrences of *puis* in a French corpus of the principal literary texts from the 17th to 20th century, researchers at the University of Toulouse found many more exceptions to this pattern than instantiations of it.

for building logical forms that include discourse structure is often quite complex; for both systems computation is understood as (nonmonotonic) deduction, where one tries to prove using defeasible rules a logical form for a discourse from premises representing various information sources. The paradigm of computation as deduction still in principle allows the derivation of a discourse structure for any discourse, unlike the script approach. But this sort of computation is inherently much more complex than say the operation of tree adjunction. SDRT, for instance, makes explicit use of semantic information given by compositional and lexical semantics, as well as a wide variety of other information sources, including pragmatics and world knowledge and then uses a nonmonotonic logic to infer a discourse structure defeasibly.

Why should computing a discourse structure be complex in this way? While computing logical forms in Montague Grammar for instance is, given an input syntactic structure, a relatively simple matter, once we look at the problem from the point of view of discourse interpretation, things become more complicated. Even at the clausal level, underspecification, coercion, metonymy and other phenomena that have recently become hot topics in lexical semantics make the logic of semantic composition less straighforward (cf. for instance, Pustejovsky, 1995). Discourse effects on logical form—e.g. lexical disambiguation and anaphora resolution—complicate further the process of constructing an appropriate LF.

4. Ways of computing logical forms

While SDRT and Hobbs's TACITUS have made certain decisions about how to compute logical forms for discourses, there are other options. To see what these are, I'll factor out those elements of logical form that discourse structure is involved in or has an effect on—leaving us thus with an *underspecified* logical form—what we get from lexical semantics and sentential syntax. Building a representation of the semantic content of a discourse then will be a matter of resolving where possible the underspecifications marked by the context sensitive elements of language.

There are many sources of ambiguity in language that can be resolved through the use of the (discourse) context.

- lexical ambiguity
- scopal ambiguity
- ambiguity of function or argument
- ambiguity of rhetorical function

- ambiguity of attachment point

The last two are plainly sources of ambiguity in the discourse structure itself, whereas the others are only sensitive to discourse structure effects. Here I'll focus on just the ambiguity of rhetorical function and attachment point in building a discourse structure (though for a study of the others in SDRT see Asher and Lascarides, 1995; Asher et al., 1997, Txurruka, 1997).

We'll begin by supposing an underspecified LF derived perhaps just from lexical and compositional semantics. We'll get, say, a representation for each clause, which we might take to be the basic informational unit. We'll then suppose that there are a variety of algorithms, logics or other mechanisms for resolving the underspecifications in the LF. As in Fernando (to appear), we take the various resolution mechanisms to define transitions

$$\leadsto_\alpha : e \longrightarrow \phi$$

from underspecified to more specified LFs. What interests us is the transition from a given structure and new input into another perhaps at least partially underspecified structure. So we rewrite the equation above to show the incremental effect of $\leadsto_\alpha$, on a sequence of input, possibly ambiguous (underspecified) expressions resulting in some partially specified logical structure, $(\phi_1, \cdots \phi_n, \phi)$.

$$\leadsto_\alpha : (e_1, e_2 \cdots, e_n, e) \longrightarrow (\phi_1, \cdots \phi_n, \phi)$$

As in Fernando (to appear), we may think of $\leadsto_\alpha$ as a consequence relation that has certain fixed points. At a fixed point, the inference procedure does not resolve any further underspecifications. So for instance, if the output of $\leadsto_\alpha$ is simply e for input e, then the resolution procedure $\leadsto_\alpha$ has no effect. When it doesn't, then the input can be resolved by $\leadsto_\alpha$. With this general framework in place, we now proceed to examine a variety of strategies.

4.1. Strategy 1: The lazy wait-and-see strategy

According to this strategy, we don't resolve underspecifications until forced to. If one isn't given any information for definite resolution, then one doesn't resolve. Interpretation thus remains monotonic but also typically highly underspecified. New information simply provides constraints on the final output LF. So this invites the equation where $\leadsto_\alpha$ is lazy and where C_e is the set of constraints derived from processing e:

$$(e_1, \cdots e_n), C_{e_1} \cup C_{(e_1,e_2)} \cup \cdots \cup C_{(e_1,\cdots e_n)} \vdash (\phi_1, \cdots, \phi_n)$$

As a simple example of this strategy, Asher and Wada, 1988 apply various syntactic and semantic and even pragmatic filters (in an attempt to define salience) so that given some ambiguous expression e and possibly ambiguous context C, they define a transition

$$(e_1, \cdots e_n) \rightsquigarrow_{aw} (\phi_1, \cdots, \phi_n)$$

where each ϕ_i is understood as a DRS (U, C) possibly with underspecified conditions of the form $z =?$ in C paired with a set of constraints CS and where

$$(\phi_1, \cdots, \phi_n) = ((U_{\phi_1} \cup \cdots \cup U_{\phi_n}), (C_{\phi_1} \cup \cdots \cup C_{\phi_n}), (CS_{\phi_1} \cup \cdots \cup CS_{\phi_n}))$$

A feature of that approach is that by adding resolved ambiguities to an ambiguous context, we might also help resolve those prior ambiguities. So for instance pragmatic constraints would suggest that *he* in the third sentence and *he* in the second sentence refer to different persons (because the pair is a question-answer response).

(10.8) a. John saw Fred.

b. He asked how the project was doing.

c. He gave him a very detailed and not very encouraging report.

So if *he* in the third sentence is resolved to *Fred*, then supposing the previous context was still ambiguous that would dictate that *John* be the antecedent of the pronoun in subject position in the second sentence. The Asher and Wada approach handles such examples via the system of constraints to which we monotonically add information that encodes the relations between possible disambiguations of successive utterances. But notice that resolution of ambiguity proceeds then *globally* and is delayed until monotonic constraints force it. In a similar vein, Reyle and Rossdeutscher, 2000 want to approach the construction of a discourse structure.

Is this a plausible model for ambiguity resolution in the construction of discourse structure? In dialogue we have examples to show that we can't wait forever to build a discourse structure and that in fact the inference of a particular rhetorical function or discourse relation happens locally, even in the absence of explicit cues.

(10.9) a. A: John went to jail. He was caught embezzling funds from the pension plan.

b. B: Yes, John went to jail, but he did so because he was convicted of tax evasion.

One couldn't understand B's correction without assuming that he had made the guess to fill in the underspecified discourse relation between A's two discourse constituents.

In this dialogue as in many, it appears that partners resolve or at least try to resolve underspecifications at least at each conversational turn; or else they ask for clarification. Turns constitute a natural break point for the accumulation of constraints on interpretation and a point at which to exploit these constraints to get the best preferred interpretation. This of course shouldn't be taken to mean that we resolve all underspecifications at each turn. Some resolutions may not be possible. But it appears that we do go beyond the purely semantically given information to resolve underspecifications at the end of turns.

What about in monologue? Couldn't we wait until the end? Here too, there does seem to be some resolution of the underspecification of discourse that we then later revise.

(10.10) John fell. Max pushed him. But that's not why John fell. He fell because he slipped on some ice.

We couldn't explain the use of the contrastive particle *but* in the third sentence in this discourse, unless there had been some computation of the rhetorical link between the constituents derived from the first two sentences. The contrastive particle *but* here functions to indicate not so much a contrast but a correction of what the listener might have jumped to as a conclusion. More evidence of correction is the natural focal stress put on *why* in the third sentence; this example of monologual correction is very similar to dialogue uses of Correction discussed in Asher (1995; Txurruka 1997). So once again the empirical evidence seems to be that a strategy of underspecification until monotonic information resolves the issue isn't either for dialogue or for monologue.

Besides apparent empirical difficulties, the wait-and-see approach has computational and conceptual problems. First, the problem of finding an appropriate attachment point, which doesn't seem to be specified by hard constraints, forces us to keep track of a burgeoning forest of discourse trees on the wait-and-see approach. The forest just for attachments reflecting the partial ordering of discourse-subordination possibilities grows at better than 2^n for n input sentences. This exponential growth makes tremendous demands on storage, and I've already presented linguistic evidence that *prima facie* such storage doesn't occur.

The wait-and-see approach keeps a very simple computation mechanism at the expense of high demands on storage. Sometimes, this strategy doesn't lead to combinatorial explosion; for instance, in Asher and Wada, 1988, we assembled constraints on a finite set of potential antecedents. There was no need to store explicitly all possible rankings of the objects in that set; the constraints generated (just one) partial ordering for the set at any given point in the processing. Also we're doing very limited inferencing on the information about the objects in this set. The demands of attachment and discourse interpretation aren't analogous, however. In order to resolve underspecifications, we need to reason about propositional contents given some sort of attachment. For example, to go back to our example (10.2), we need to reason about meals and eating cheese and salmon as well as the attachment points to infer the correct rhetorical relations between the constituents in that example and hence the right temporal structure for the text. In the standard semantics for underspecification (Reyle, 1993), the wait-and-see approach would have to consider every possible attachment and discourse relation and see what followed from all of these possible combinations. In this example, no temporal structure would be predicted, since the monotonic constraints don't force any temporal interpretation.

What the wait-and-see approach abandons is a locally incremental account of information in discourse. Locality is important computationally because local computations (with limited effects of revision) are less expensive than global ones. There are fewer premises in the deduction, fewer possibilities to deal with in the constraint satisfaction problem. Locality is also cognitively very plausible; it lies at the foundations, for instance, of dynamic semantics. Without a constraint to locality, one could in fact dispense with the dynamic semantic treatment of the quantifiers.[6] The wait-and-see strategy with monotonic computation of discourse structure is not an attractive option.

4.2. Strategy 2: Opportunistic, local resolution of ambiguity

Our second strategy resolves as much underspecification as possible *locally*. Supplementing the underspecified semantic LF derived from the lexicon and compositional semantics, pragmatic principles provide discourse content by completing the underspecified LF for the discourse and resolving the underspecified elements. In contrast to the earlier wait-and-see view of monotonic discourse interpretation, this view goes beyond what is given by lexical and compositional semantics to include defeasible implicatures and defeasible resolutions of underspecified ele-

[6] In effect the dynamic semantic view of indefinites and definites is that they do not have a predetermined rightward scope. But if the whole discourse were finished, we could fix their rightward scope—at the end of the discourse!

ments. To handle implicatures and preferred interpretations, we need a logic in which defeasible conclusions can be inferred. Such a logic for building logical forms is thus some species of nonmonotonic logic.

A nonmonotonic logic allows us in principle to have different resolutions of underspecifications or to acknowledge that these resolutions can be defeated by further information. Consider again (10.10):

(10.10) John fell. Max pushed him. But that's not why John fell. He fell because he slipped on some ice.

(10.10), like (10.9), is an example that shows that one cannot wait to compute a discourse relation between the first two clauses, because it is just this computation that is being revised by the Contrast in the third clause. If the computation of a discourse relation is not made locally, the Contrast can't make sense. Such examples show that local computation must occur. Nevertheless, (10.10) is not an inconsistent or contradictory discourse. So the discourse relation computed just from the information present in the first two clauses of (10.10) is not a monotonic entailment but rather an implicature, or from SDRT's point of view, a nonmonotonic entailment that can be revised or retracted in the light of further information.

Nonmonotonic logic is well suited to deal with local, revisable and uncertain computations. Other algorithms are possible—e.g., Hebbian learning on picking probabilistically preferred solutions, or optimality theory (De Hoop and De Swart, 1999). Nevertheless, the declarative nature of nonmonotonic logic and its truth-conditional semantics make it a convenient tool for investigating defeasible inference.

In SDRT, the rules of logical-form construction are axioms of a nonmonotonic logic; discourse parsing is deducing with these rules. We use such nonmonotonic axioms to compute discourse attachments and discourse relations between constituents. So for instance, we would compute Narration in (10.11a) and Explanation in (10.11b):

(10.11) a. John fell. Max helped him up.

b. John fell. Max pushed him.

The local and opportunistic strategy attempts to resolve ambiguities present in the input with guesswork in one go. A nonmontonic logic leads naturally to this resolution strategy. For in a nonmonotonic logic, whenever we can consistently reach a defeasible conclusion, we do. Thus, where consistent and applicable, we will exploit those rules to get a resolution of some underspecification. In a nonmonotonic logic such as that used in SDRT, if the result of the defeasible inference is consistent with the discourse context, it will be made; so in particular if a resolution of an underspecification is consistent it will be made. Such a theory makes as many underspecifications resolved as possible in a given local computation. Defaults for discourse-relation computation, attachment point, anaphor resolution all combine together non-deterministically to get a maximally resolved logical form locally.

In early versions of SDRT as presented in e.g. Asher (1993) or Lascarides and Asher, 1993, this integration is done incrementally and locally through the notion of SDRS update. With respect to the ambiguities of attachment and rhetorical function, early versions of SDRT made a simplifying assumption: SDRS update always attempts a resolution for these underspecifications. If it fails, SDRT predicts the discourse to be incoherent because it is unable to establish a rhetorical function for the new information to be attached. In so doing, these versions of SDRT went beyond what the logic gave them by adding a particular view of discourse coherence: a discourse coherent just in case every piece of information in it is related to some other bit by means of a discourse relation.

This early view of SDRT is the strongest type of localistic approach to building discourse structures. Before evaluating this approach, we should investigate in a bit more detail the nature of the computation being postulated here. We have already seen from earlier sections that the computation of logical forms needs access to semantic information. But how much access to the content of the clauses should the mechanisms for LF construction have? Too little and one won't be able to make the inferences needed to get discourse structures for many texts. Too much and the computation of LF becomes an open ended inference problem of the at least first-order logic that underlies the content of the information conveyed in discourse. Such open ended inference problems in first-order logic may not ever give us an answer even if we have in mind some logical form as a goal, since in first-order logic there is no decision procedure that tells us whether a given formula follows logically from a set of premises or not. When we widen the inference procedure from a monotonic one to a nonmonotonic one, the complexity of the computation goes up even further: the set of "theorems" of a nonmonotonic first-order logic are not even recursively enumerable; that is, there is no decision procedure to tell us that an arbitrary element φ of this set is in fact a "theorem" of the system. This certainly leads to an engineering difficulty; there is no program that will carry out such computations. But such proposals also pose a conceptual difficulty as well. Recall that we became interested in computation-intensive rather than storage-intensive methods for getting at discourse structure because of the need to come up with a method for generating reasonable interpretations for arbitrary discourses. But if the "computation" is so complex that it defines a non-recursively enumerable set, then there are good reasons like Church's thesis to doubt that humans could carry out such a computation as well. And at any rate, it is completely unreasonable to expect that such computations could be carried out in the real time it takes humans to interpret discourse.

Some people are not convinced by such abstract arguments. They point out correctly that complexity considerations of the sort adduced above pertain only to "worst case" computations. It may be that one can use one's nonmonotonic rules together with the rules of first-order logic to derive appropriate logical forms in many test cases. But given that one cannot *in principle* compute some cases, there is a real question as to what one is computing in these "easy cases". It's not clear that one is carrying out a procedure that really does correspond to nonmonotonic inference over first-order logic. All that one can show is that the procedure one is carrying out captures some nonmonotonic entailments. And lots of procedures might be compatible with that; in such a situation, we don't really know what we are doing.

Since I do take these abstract arguments seriously, I have tried to limit the complexity of the computation of logical forms. In order to make the nonmonotonic inference scheme in SDRT tractable (see Lascarides and Asher, 1993; Asher and Fernando, 1999), we assume a very limited access to content; the process of constructing a logical form only has access to information about contents that can be stated in a quantifier-free way. This reduces the complexity of the worst case for computing logical forms to that of calculating the satisfiability of a finite set of sentences in sentential logic. This is something then that we can program and a calculation that humans can carry out. We expect that for most cases the calculation is far more efficient. This strategy has had some success in constructing discourse structures for simple texts and in accounting for various linguistic phenomena of interpretation that are tied to discourse structure—e.g., temporal structure (Lascarides and Asher, 1993), VP ellipsis (Asher et al., 1997), lexical disambiguation (Asher and Lascarides, 1995), focus and intonation (Txurruka, 1997), and presupposition (Asher and Lascarides, 1998b). But we should not expect that this procedure will get us everything we need. Jokes like (10.12) are discourse where more extended reasoning is often required to understand the discourse structure.

(10.12) a. A: [A has entered a hotel and is looking at a dog next to B in the lobby; he asks] Does your dog bite?

b. B: No.

c. A: [A then goes to pet dog, and it bites him.] I thought you said your dog didn't bite!

d. B: That's not my dog.

Jokes like this one often play the cancellation of conversational implicatures and preferred disambiguations, which may require more extended reasoning.

4.3. A problem with the simple formulation of the local strategy

We've already seen evidence that decisions about discourse structure are made locally in arguing against the wait-and-see approach. However, there are at least two problems with the simple formulation of local computation that I set out in the previous section. The first concerns not so much the opportunistic, local computation of logical forms as much as what is to count as an acceptable logical form output. I'll turn to this problem first.

The formulation of a local strategy I presented in the previous section, which also appears in e.g. Lascarides and Asher, 1993, precludes an underspecification of discourse relations in any logical form. Discourse relations and rhetorical function are computed for some new information given some attachment site in the discourse context. When no discourse relation can be computed for a given attachment, then that attachment is understood as lacking in discourse coherence. Discourse incoherence is predicted if no discourse relation can be computed for any possible attachment. Now of course the logic itself simply fails to give us a discourse relation; the interpretation of this failure as a failure of discourse coherence is something over and above the logic, and one that we need not adopt. In terms of local opportunistic strategies, this one says that as regards rhetorical function you always have to guess and try to resolve the underspecification.

There were reasons for adopting this guess-always strategy. For instance, in Lascarides and Asher, 1993, we showed that this guess-always strategy gave a simple account of an example like (10.2), which I repeat below.

(10.2) a. Guy experienced a lovely evening last night.

b. He had a fantastic meal.

c. He ate salmon.

d. He devoured lots of cheese.

e. He won a dancing competition.

In this example—in particular, (10.2b), we have an elaboration of Guy's lovely evening last night in that he had a great meal. We then have an elaboration of the meal. So by the time we come to attach (10.2e), we have several possible attachment sites according to the analysis: (10.2a), (10.2b) and (10.2d) (see Lascarides and Asher, 1993 for details). Lascarides and Asher, 1993 postulated that attachment of a new constuent B to a subordinate constituent A requires that one be able to infer $R(C, B)$ from the information in C and B, if one has already inferred $R(C, A)$, where C was the superordinate constituent to A. We called this constraint Continuing Discourse Patterns. Now given Continuing Discourse Patterns, attachment to (10.2d) would require that one can infer Elaboration(10.2b, 10.2e), but since one cannot make that derivation, one cannot compute any discourse relation between (10.2d) and (10.2e). By the constraint on output logical forms in the guess-always strategy, this attachment is then blocked.

While there are good reasons to believe in Continuing Discourse Patterns (see for instance Asher 1996 as well as Lascarides and Asher, 1993), there are reasons to doubt the guess-always strategy. One reason we should not adopt the guess-always strategy is simply that it's unreasonable to expect that all ambiguities of attachment and rhetorical function can be resolved simply by information already given in the discourse context and in the new information to be integrated into the context. Many examples of other sorts of ambiguities are resolved by information that comes *after* the ambiguous expression or construction is introduced. Consider, for instance, scope ambiguities. (10.13) has two possible scopes:

(10.13) Every farmer admired a donkey at last week's market.

We can force a disambiguation of this construction by using a pronoun for the donkey in a subsequent sentence or by using other constructions. Clearly in the first sentence of (10.14a) the quantifiers have a different scope from that in (10.14b):

(10.14) a. Every farmer admired a donkey at last week's market. It is standing right over there.

b. Every farmer admired a donkey at last week's market. But it wasn't the same donkey that every farmer admired.

It seems as though ambiguities of rhetorical function should function in the way other ambiguities function. Maybe it doesn't matter exactly what the rhetorical function of the information is in some cases. Maybe there is no fact of the matter in some cases, and yet this doesn't affect discourse coherence. For example, consider a minimal temporal example like (10.15):

(10.15) John walked in to Max's office. Max greeted him.

As many have observed of this example (which we first gave in Lascarides and Asher, 1993), we could read (10.15) as John's walking in and Max's greeting as a result or we could read it as John's walking in because Max's greeted him. But there isn't any fact of the matter about which way the causal sequence here goes. Lascarides and Asher predict a simple narrative sequence here from their basic default on Narration, which says that in the absence of other information assume that two event sentences in the same tense form a narrative sequence. Asher's 1996 revision of defaults concerning Narration won't predict Narrative unless walking into someone's office typically generates the expectation of a greeting. The latter approach seems to be more on the right track. It's not that this example is incoherent; it just doesn't have much temporal structure. If that intuition about (10.15) is right, then a system that tries to predict a temporal structure for this sentence is wrongly predicting unambiguous temporal structure where there is in fact ambiguity.

There's also a complexity problem with this view of output logical forms. To be anywhere near accurate, a "guess-always" strategy will need an enormous number of axioms to handle special cases. We know that as the number of applicable default rules in SDRT's commonsense entailment, the computational complexity is directly affected (we have to do more consistency tests). How much this is true of other nonmonotonic formalisms is an open question. But even the consistency testing of sets of quantifier free sentences becomes prohibitively expensive. In light of our earlier discussion, we don't here have a trade-off between storage and computation; rather we have large demands on storage, along with a highly complex and (timewise) expensive computation. So at a certain point following the guess-always strategy will either lead to a majority of wrong guesses in the long run or be prohibitively expensive computationally. These observations lead us to conclude: an exclusively nonmonotonic strategy for disambiguation is not feasible.

4.4. Repairing the difficulty with the local strategy

To repair the local strategy, we have to get rid of the constraint on output logical forms that the guess-always approach requires. This means that we have to change the simple notion of discourse coherence, on which a coherent discourse is one in which every discourse constituent has at least one well-defined rhetorical function. For those interested in more formal details, this means that we must change the SDRT update rule of Lascarides and Asher, 1993 and other early work in SDRT. In words, an (early) SDRS update is defined (according to the guess-always strategy) iff there is a discourse relation that can be computed for a particular attachment point in the antecedent context. If such a relation can be computed, then it is incorporated into the discourse structure. To allow for ambiguities to persist after incorporation of new information into a discourse context, we must amend our notion of local update and change how we compute the rhetorical function or discourse relation R. In words the revised SDRS update definition allows for underspecified rhetorical functions when no rhetorical relation can be computed for the information given. Otherwise, like the old definition, it incorporates the rhetorical relation computed for the new information into the updated discourse structure. For those familiar with SDRT I give the technical definitions of both the original and revised update relations in the appendix.

An intuitive revision of the simple view of discourse coherence is that discourse coherence is not an all-or-nothing thing. The cohesiveness of discourse is rather a scalar phenomenon. Interpreters pick interpretations of discourse that maximize cohesiveness, but even relatively uncohesive discourses like (10.15) can be sometimes acceptable. One thing that we can say is that people prefer determinacy to indeterminacy: when we can, given a certain attachment, infer a particular discourse relation then we prefer that attachment over one where we can't infer a discourse connection. We have actually built this preference into a constraint in SDRT on interpretations that we call `Maximize Discourse Coherence` (Asher and Lascarides, 1998b). The output logical form according to this constraint must be one in which a maximal number of underspecified elements have been resolved and in which each discourse relation in the structure is as strong as it can be.[7]

It should be pretty clear how the new constraint on logical form outputs would allow for indeterminacy in (10.15). But the new view

[7] See Asher and Lascarides, 1998b for more discussion.

also explains why in (10.2) (10.2e) cannot attach to (10.2d). `Maximize Discourse Coherence` doesn't disallow this attachment in principle. But we still can't compute any discourse relation there. The high attachment, however, allows us to compute a discourse relation and so we choose that high attachment with its determinate discourse relation because of the constraint `Maximize Discourse Coherence`.

One problem that remains and that `Maximize Discourse Coherence` does not by itself solve is that some discourses where the rhetorical function cannot be specified really are bad. Recall

(10.4) My car broke down. Mary dyed her hair.

or

(10.16) John walked in. Mary's hair was black.

As it stands these examples are incoherent. But what is different about these examples from the example (10.15)? With (10.4) and (10.16), the reader can't coherently add any discourse relation that relates these two constituents together. With (10.15), the temporal relation may be underdetermined, but it's clear that one can see both constituents as elaborating a typical greeting situation. That is, there is a way of linking the two constituents via a discourse relation that doesn't violate any constraints on that relation. Technically, while a discourse may be more coherent if it is easy to infer the rhetorical functions of its constituents, we may still accept discourses where, although we cannot even defeasibly infer a discourse relation between constituents, adding a discourse relation would not lead to an inconsistency in the theory for computing logical forms.[8]

Notice that for (10.16) adding information does enable us to group Mary's hair being black together with other information which is what John sees upon walking in.

(10.17) John walked in. Mary's hair was black. Susan's hair was red. It was clear that the girls had been experimenting with hair color again.

Curiously, (10.4) is much less amenable to amelioration, even if one can imagine filling out a scenario where John's walking in is linked, say causally, to Mary's act of dyeing her hair black. But this is because a sequence of event sentences, one of which involves an experiencer verb,

[8]What I have in mind here is that we allow discourses as minimally coherent that meet the condition that there is a discourse relation between any two constituents that can be consistently added to the logical form.

impose much stronger constraints on what possible discourse relations may link these two constituents.

There are more complex examples of discourses, which like (10.15) are temporally indeterminate but not incoherent that seem to bear out this view.

(10.18e) John fell. Fred pushed him. John slid off the edge of the cliff.

Some speakers have the Explanation interpretation of the falling and the pushing in (10.18e), but some shift their interpretation to get a narrative sequence. How could we get different interpretations for these little discourses? One way this could happen is if we compute a local discourse structure between the constituents introduced by the second and third utterances, say, of (10.18d). This might suggest a particular temporal and causal structure that doesn't fit well with the structure given from the attachment of the first two constituents. In that case we would revise. What do I mean "not fit well"? Well consider if you take Fred's pushing John to result in John's sliding off the edge of the cliff. You might get a picture that Fred's pushing John was the immediate cause. When you put that together with the fall, if you take that to be a separate event from the sliding off the edge of the cliff you see that Fred's pushing can't occur before the falling; otherwise it wouldn't be the immediate cause. So you fall back on Narration as a default (Asher, 1996) and arrange them in a narrative (and causal) sequence. Of course, if you identify the sliding as part or an elaboration of the falling, you can still get a coherent picture where Fred's pushing explains and causes the falling, as well as the sliding. Given that we have alternative ways of satisfying the demand for coherence, we can live with this indeterminacy though not of (10.4).

So there does seem to be a way to correct the defects of the simple local approach and to get a workable theory about discourse structure. But I mentioned earlier that there is potentially a second problem with the local approach that I haven't addressed. That is the problem of revision. Given that our inferences to logical forms are defeasible, sometimes our guesses turn out to be wrong, and we are led to revision. Revision can be costly, especially if it's widespread. But we have already seen that there are revisions, in dialogue and in monologue; and so it would be foolish to rule them out of court as the wait-and-see approach is wont to do.

There is evidence that revisions do occur, but they are typically signalled by some sort of discourse particle. The examples below are indicative of this phenomenon. They exploit discourse particles and focus information to reduce the processing load of revision (see Asher, 1995; Txurruka, 1997 for details).

(10.18) a. John fell. Fred pushed him.

b. John and Fred arrived at the top of the cliff. Fred applied a sharp blow to John's neck. John fell. Fred pushed him. John slid off the edge of the cliff.

c. John and Fred arrived at the top of the cliff. Fred applied a sharp blow to John's neck. John fell, because Fred pushed him. John slid off the edge of the cliff.

d. John and Fred arrived at the top of the cliff. Fred applied a sharp blow to John's neck. But that's not why John fell. John fell, because Fred pushed him. John (then) slid off the edge of the cliff.

All speakers take *Fred pushed him* to be an Explanation in (10.18a) but in (10.18b) more contextual cues, in particular the previous inference to another cause of John's falling, block the inference to Explanation. The question is, can this inference be revised? Well, it looks as though you have to do some work. Simply forcing the interpreter to infer Explanation between Fred's pushing and John's falling makes the discourse (10.18c) sound pretty incoherent.[9] But if we use the particle *but* to signal as in the other examples above a revision of nonmonotonic inference made already in the context, then the example becomes acceptable again. So revision seems to need a trigger like *but*. If that's right, then there are constraints on what is amenable to revision, even if its inferred defeasibly. And given that revision is linguistically constrained in this way, allowing for revision doesn't complicate our computation of logical form in a way that we can't accept.

In conclusion, it appears as though a sophisticated but local approach to computation is our best bet for getting at discourse structure and interpretation. The sort of computation envisioned is complex but not beyond the bounds of what we might expect for complex reasoners like ourselves. I've argued that given that we have to be able in principle to compute a logical form for arbitrary discourses, we need an approach that is bottom up and incremental, unlike the script theories. In order to correct the fatal problems with script approaches, discourse theorists needed to come up with a different model for computing logical forms. Of the various candidates, I've argued that a modified, localist approach is the most promising.

---

[9]Thanks to Luuk Lagerwerf for this example.

5. Conclusions about storage and computation

This paper began with an examination of the trade-offs between storage and computation in discourse interpretation and the roles that they might play in a model of interpretation. Now that a reasonable model of computation for discourse structure has been proposed, we are in a position to determine a role for storage. Clearly an incremental theory like this requires detailed lexical entries, which must be explicitly stored. These are needed not only to get the semantics for clauses, but we need to know in detail from the lexicon what underspecifications are present that our computation may try to resolve. More than that, we need to store a great deal of knowledge about pragmatic interactions between speakers and typical ways situations unfurl, as this may be the key in seeing whether we could consistently add a rhetorical relation to hold between constituents if our theory doesn't allow us to infer it. The effort to develop the theory of computation of discourse structure with linguistic principles can be seen as a way of also trying to figure out the proper role of this store of information. Many have argued that all discourse interpretation is just a matter of world knowledge. The alternative view, which I have tried to motivate here, is one in which world knowledge has an important but not all encompassing role to play when coupled with a linguistic theory of discourse computation.

Acknowledgments

I would like to thank Tim Fernando, Isabel Txurruka, Cathy Berthouzoz, Luuk Lagerwerf and Alex Lascarides for helpful comments on previous drafts.

References

Asher, N. (1993). *Reference to abstract objects in discourse*. Dordrecht: Kluwer Academic Publishers.

Asher, N. (1995). From discourse micro-structure to macro-structure and back again: The interpretation of focus. In Kamp, H. and Partee, B., editors, *Conferences on semantics and context, Prague and Bad Teinach*, SFB Report, University of Stuttgart.

Asher, N. (1996). Mathematical treatments of discourse contexts. In Dekker, P. and Stokhof, M., editors, *Proceedings of the Tenth Amsterdam Colloquium on Formal Semantics*, ILLC publications, University of Amsterdam, pages 21–40.

Asher, N., Aurnague, M., Bras, M., Sablayrolles, P., and Vieu, L. (1995). De l'espace-temps dans l'analyse du discours. *Sémiotique*, 9: Numéro Spécial sur la sémantique et le langage naturel:11–62.

Asher, N. and Fernando, T. (1999). About anaphora: Inference and discourse structure. Talk given at the UT Discourse Workshop, January 1999. Paper available from the authors.

Asher, N., Hardt, D., and Busquets, J. (1997). Discourse parallelism, scope and ellipsis. In *Proceedings Semantics and Linguistic Theory*, 7:19-36.

Asher, N. and Lascarides, A. (1994). Intentions and information in discourse. In *Proceedings of the Annual Meeting of the Association for Computational Linguistics*, 31:35–41. Morristown NJ: ACL.

Asher, N. and Lascarides, A. (1995). Lexical disambiguation in a discourse context. *Journal of Semantics*, 12:69–108.

Asher, N. and Lascarides, A. (1998a). How questions in dialogue. *Linguistics and Philosophy*, 21:237–309.

Asher, N. and Lascarides, A. (1998b). The semantics and pragmatics of presupposition. *Journal of Semantics*, 15:239–299.

Asher, N. and Wada, H. (1988). A computational account of syntactic, semantic and discourse principles for anaphora resolution. *Journal of Semantics*, 6:309-344.

Beaver, D. (1997). Presupposition. In Van Benthem, J. and Ter Meulen, A., editors, *Handbook of Logic and Language*, pages 939–1008. Amsterdam: Elsevier Publications.

Bras, M. and Asher, N. (1994). Le raisonnement non monotone dans la construction de la structure temporelle de textes en Français. In *Actes 9ème Congrès RFIA*.

De Hoop, H. and De Swart, H. (1999). Optimal interpretations of discourse structure. Paper presented at the *Conférence de Syntaxe et Sémantique de Paris, Paris.*

Fernando, T. (1999). A modal logic for non-deterministic discourse processing. *Journal of Logic, Language and Information*, 9:445–468.

Fodor, J. and Lepore, E. (1998). The emptiness of the lexicon: Critical reflections on J. Pustejovsky's The Generative Lexicon. *Linguistic Inquiry* 29(2):269-288.

Gardent, C. (1991). *VP-Anaphora.* PhD thesis, University of Edinburgh, Scotland.

Hobbs, J., Stickel, M., Appelt, D., and Martin, P. (1993). Interpretation as abduction. *Artificial Intelligence*, 63:69–142.

Kamp, H. and Reyle, U. (1993). *From discourse to logic: Introduction to modeltheoretic semantics of natural language, formal logic and Dis-*

course Representation Theory. Dordrecht: Kluwer Academic Publishers.

Lascarides, A. and Asher, N. (1993). Temporal interpretation, discourse relations and commonsense entailment. *Linguistics and Philosophy*, 16:437–493.

Mann, W. and Thompson, S. (1987). Rhetorical structure theory: A theory of text organization. ISI Reprint Series: ISI-RS-87-190.

Minsky, M. (1975). A framework for representing knowledge. In Winston, P., editor, *The Psychology of Computer Vision*. New York: McGraw Hill, pages 211-277.

Moore, J. and Paris, C. (1993). Planning text for advisory dialogues: Capturing intentional and rhetorical information. *Computational Linguistics*, 19(4):651–694.

Moore, J. and Pollack, M. (1992). A problem for RST: The need for multi-level discourse analysis. *Computational Linguistics*, 18(4):537–544.

Polanyi, L. (1985). A theory of discourse structure and discourse coherence. In *Papers from the Regional Meetings Chicago Linguistics Society*, 21(1):306–322.

Prüst, H. and Scha, R. (1990). A discourse perspective on verb phrase anaphora. In Stokhof, M. and Torenvliet, L., editors, *Proceedings of the Seventh Amsterdam Colloquium*, pages 451–474. Amsterdam: ITLI Publications.

Pustejovsky, J. (1995). *The Generative Lexicon*. Cambridge, MA: MIT Press.

Reyle, U. (1993). Dealing with ambiguities by underspecification: Construction, representation and deduction. *Journal of Semantics*, 10(1): 123–179.

Reyle, U. and Rossdeutscher, A. (2000). Very short stories. Manuscript, University of Stuttgart.

Scha, R. and Polanyi, L. (1988). An augmented context free grammar for discourse. In Vargha, D., editor, *Proceedings of the 12th International Conference on Computational Linguistics (COLING88)*, Budapest, August 1988, pages 573–577, Budapest: John von Neumann Society for Computing Sciences.

Schank, R. and Abelson, R. (1977). *Scripts, plans, goals and understanding*. Hilldale, New Jersey: Lawrence Erlbaum Associates.

Thompson, S. and Mann, W. (1987). Rhetorical structure theory: A framework for the analysis of texts. *IPRA Papers in Pragmatics*, 1:79–105.

Txurruka, I. (1997). *Particion Informacional en el Discurso*. PhD thesis, University of the Basque Country, Donostia, Spain.

Van Eijck, J. and Kamp, H. (1997). Representing discourse in context. In Van Benthem, J. and Ter Meulen, A., editors, *Handbook of Logic and Language*, pages 179–238. Amsterdam: Elsevier Publications.

Webber, B., Knott, A., Stone, M., and Joshi, A. (1999). Discourse relations: A structural and presuppositional account using lexicalised tag. In *Proceedings of the 37th Annual Meeting of the Association for Computational Linguistics*, College Park MD, June 1999, pages 41-48.

Appendix

Here's the standard rule of SDRT update. It is a relation between a given discourse structure ($(\langle A, \mathcal{F}\rangle$ and some new bit of information e. The output is a new discourse structure $\langle A \cup \{\pi_e\}, \mathcal{F} * \cup\{\pi_e, \psi_e\}\rangle$ in which the logical form of e is now attached to some available node (π_1 below) via some discourse relation that we have deduced from the logical forms that are assigned to labels via $\mathcal{F}*$. π_e is a label for e; ψ_e is a logical form for e; R is a discourse relation and $\mid\!\sim$ is the nonmonotonic inference relation for SDRT.

`SDRT's Original Update Relation:`

$(\langle A, \mathcal{F}\rangle, e)\, \mathit{Update}_{\mathrm{SDRT}} \langle A \cup \{\pi_e\}, \mathcal{F} * \cup\{\pi_e, \psi_e\}\rangle$ iff

- if $A = 0$, then $\mathcal{F}* = \mathcal{F}$
- if $A \neq 0$, then $\exists \pi, \pi_1 \in A$ such that Available$(\pi_1, \langle A, \mathcal{F}\rangle)$ and

    1 $\mathrm{Th}(\mathrm{Rng}(\mathcal{F})), \psi_e) \mid\!\sim R(\pi_1, \pi_e)$ for some R, and

    2 $\mathcal{F}*$ is just like $\mathcal{F}$ except that $\mathcal{F} * (\pi) \rightarrow R(\pi_1, \pi_e)$

In the revised update relation below, I have allowed indeterminacies to remain in the output discourse structure, when no discourse relation can be calculated for the attachment.

`SDRT's Revised Update Relation:`

$(\langle A, \mathcal{F}\rangle, e)\, \mathit{Update}_{\mathrm{SDRT}} \langle A \cup \{\pi_e\}, \mathcal{F} * \cup\{\pi_e, \psi_e\}\rangle$ iff

- if $A = 0$, then $\mathcal{F}* = \mathcal{F}$
- if $A \neq 0$, then $\exists \pi, \pi_1 \in A$ such that Available$(\pi_1, \langle A, \mathcal{F}\rangle)$ and

    1 either:

    (a) $\mathrm{Th}(\mathrm{Rng}(\mathcal{F})), \psi_e) \mid\!\sim R(\pi_1, \pi_e)$ for some R, and

    (b) $\mathcal{F}*$ is just like $\mathcal{F}$ except that $\mathcal{F} * (\pi) \rightarrow R(\pi_1, \pi_e)$

    2 or:

    (a) For no R is it the case that $\mathrm{Th}(\mathrm{Rng}(\mathcal{F})), \psi_e) \mid\!\sim R(\pi_1, \pi_e)$, and

    (b) $\mathcal{F}*$ is just like $\mathcal{F}$ except that $\mathcal{F} * (\pi) \rightarrow ?(\pi_1, \pi_e)$:

Subject Index

Author Index

STUDIES IN THEORETICAL PSYCHOLINGUISTICS

18. J.L. Packard: *A Linguistic Investigation of Aphasic Chinese Speech.* 1993 ISBN 0-7923-2466-8
19. J. Archibald: *Language Learnability and L2 Phonology:* The Acquisition of Metrical Parameters. 1993 ISBN 0-7923-2486-2
20. M.W. Crocker: *Computational Psycholinguistics.* An Interdisciplinary Approach to the Study of Language. 1996 ISBN 0-7923-3802-2; Pb 0-7923-3806-5
21. J.D. Fodor and F. Ferreira (eds.): *Reanalysis in Sentence Processing.* 1998 ISBN 0-7923-5099-5
22. L. Frazier: *On Sentence Interpretation.* 1999 ISBN 0-7923-5508-3
23. S. Avrutin: *Development of the Syntax-Discourse Interface.* 1999 ISBN 0-7923-5936-4
24. B. Hemforth and L. Konieczny (eds.): *German Sentence Processing.* 2000 ISBN 0-7923-6104-0
25. M. De Vincenzi and V. Lombardo (eds.): *Cross-linguistic Perspectives on Language Processing.* 2000 ISBN 0-7923-6146-6
26. S.M. Powers and C. Hamann (eds.): *The Acquisition of Scrambling and Cliticization.* 2000 ISBN 0-7923-6249-7
27. M. Schönenberger: *Embedded V-to-C in child grammar: The acquisition of verb placement in Swiss German.* 2001 ISBN 0-7923-7086-4
28. M. Walsh Dickey: *The Processing of Tense.* Psycholinguistic Studies on the Interpretation of Tense and Temporal Relations. 2001 ISBN 1-4020-0184-3; Pb 1-4020-0185-1
29. C. Hamann: *From Syntax to Discourse.* Pronominal Clitics, Null Subjects and Infinitives in Child Language. 2002 ISBN 1-4020-0439-7; Pb 1-4020-0440-0
30. S. Nooteboom, F. Weerman and F. Wijnen (eds.): *Storage and Computation in the Language Faculty.* 2002 ISBN 1-4020-0526-1; Pb 1-4020-0527-X

KLUWER ACADEMIC PUBLISHERS – DORDRECHT / BOSTON / LONDON